PACEMAKER®

World History

GLOBE FEARON

Pearson Learning Group

Pacemaker® World History Fourth Edition

Reviewers

We thank the following educator, who provided valuable comments and suggestions during the development of this book:

Pacemaker Curriculum Advisor: Stephen C. Larsen, formerly of the University of Texas at Austin

Project Staff

Executive Editor: Jane Petlinski
Project Manager: Suzanne Keezer
Lead Designer: Janice Noto-Helmers
Manufacturing Buyer: Nathan Kinney

About the Cover

World History is the study of important people, places, and events of the world. The images on the cover represent the history and culture of the world's regions. The large image in the center is the statue of the Egyptian pharaoh, Rameses II. On the left, from top to bottom, are an Aztec calendar; a ceremonial mask from Africa; and a Japanese fan. On the right, from top to bottom, are a modern-day astronaut; a Portuguese astrolabe, which was used to find the altitude of stars; and a decorative box from Russia. If you were to make a time capsule of the present day, what objects from your culture or region would you include?

ISBN: 0-130-23828-7

Printed in the United States of America

6 7 8 9 10   06 05 04

Globe
Fearon

Pearson Learning Group

1-800-321-3106
www.pearsonlearning.com

Contents

TIMELINES

A Note to the Student

Do you think events of hundreds or thousands of years ago have anything to do with our lives today? How about 100 or even 50 years ago?

The study of world history shows the connections between past, present, and future events. It shows how all nations are related to one another. It also reminds us that history is still being written.

By the time you finish this book, you will have some idea of how the world came to be the way it is today. Chapter by chapter you will learn about the rise and fall of many nations, the ideas of the great thinkers, and the incredible richness of many cultures. You will be able to name important people in history and the times in which they lived. You will learn how geography has affected the history of nations and how scientific discovery has affected the history of the whole world.

As you read, look for the notes in the margins of the pages. These friendly notes are there to make you stop and think. Some notes comment on the material you are learning. Some notes extend your learning, while others remind you of something you already know.

You will also notice many maps and timelines as you read. The maps will help you to locate the part of the world you are learning about. Locators and other features on the maps will help you to understand where the area you are looking at is in relation to the rest of the world. Timelines in each chapter help you to understand the order of the events you read about.

You will also find several study aids in the book. At the beginning of every chapter, you will find **Learning Objectives.** These objectives will help you focus on the important points covered in the chapter. The **Words to Know** section at the beginning of each chapter will give you a review of the vocabulary you may find challenging. At the end of each chapter, a **Summary** will give you a quick review of what you have just learned.

As you read the chapters, pay special attention to the special features. The features will help you to gain new skills and introduce you to world history issues and important names from the past. You will also read about written or spoken words from the past that continue to affect the world today.

We hope you enjoy reading about the history of the world and its people. Everyone who put this book together worked hard to make it interesting as well as useful. The rest is up to you. We wish you well in your studies. Our success is in your accomplishment.

Unit 1 ▷ Looking at the World's History

Chapter 1
What Is History?

Chapter 2
Early Humans: The Story Begins

More than 6,000 life-sized clay soldiers were buried with an ancient Chinese emperor.

Learning Objectives

- Explain why life in ancient times was just as exciting as life today.

- Describe how historians learn about the past.

- Describe how archaeologists learn about the people of ancient times.

- Explain why people needed to make maps in the past, and why we still need maps today.

- Use a timeline to compare the dates of historical events and periods.

Words to Know

revolution	a complete change, especially in a way of life or a government
agriculture	the use of land for growing crops and raising animals; farming
imperialism	the practice of conquering other lands, forming colonies in other lands, or controlling the government and wealth of weaker lands
culture	the way of life—religion, ideas, arts, tools—of a certain people in a certain time
historian	someone who writes about the past; an expert in history
civilization	the society and culture of a particular people, place, or period
archaeologist	a scientist who studies cultures of the past by digging up and examining the remains of ancient towns and cities
artifact	a handmade object, such as a tool or weapon
B.C. **(Before Christ)**	dating from before the time Jesus Christ was born
A.D. **(Anno Domini)**	dating from the time Jesus Christ was born

History Is All About Change

World history is the story of how the people of different times and places lived. It is the record of discoveries such as better ways of farming and new machines. It is also the story of the building of cities and nations, and of the creation of beautiful art and music.

History is all about change—changing times and changing ideas. Long ago, for example, slavery was an accepted part of everyday life. The ancient Egyptians made slaves of their prisoners. So did the Greeks, the

Romans, the Aztecs, and many others. However, today, people in much of the world know that slavery is wrong.

About 500 years ago, there was a big change in the way people pictured their world. People came to understand the true shape of our planet. They realized that the Earth is round, not flat. Explorers set out from Europe on long ocean voyages. They discovered a huge body of land where they had thought there was only ocean. North and South America took their role in the story of the world.

Another word for change is **revolution.** Ideas of freedom, democracy, and independence swept across the world. This led people in many countries to revolt. In both the Eastern and Western hemispheres, people rose up and demanded freedom.

Revolutions in industry and in **agriculture** changed the way people lived. Discoveries and inventions often helped people lead better lives. Sometimes changes made life harder. For example, the development of industry in England made life better for many people.

You Decide

The invention of television in the twentieth century changed the way many people lived. If there were no TV, would your life be better or worse? Explain.

Christopher Columbus claimed land in the West Indies for Spain in October 1492.

However, life became harder for the people who had to work in the factories.

Out of the age of exploration grew an age of **imperialism.** Imperialism is the quest for more land and more power. Strong nations set out to rule weaker ones. Weaker lands were forced to accept foreign **cultures** and ideas. A strong Europe tried to set up colonies all over the globe.

Many countries tried to fight this. People wanted to control their own lands and lives. The spirit of nationalism led people to unite under their own flags.

As histories must, this book talks about wars. Down through the ages, there have always been wars. Tribe fought against tribe, city fought against city, and nation fought against nation. World Wars I and II in the twentieth century were the worst wars of all time. Sometimes history seems like nothing but a long list of wars. This book tells how wars happened and how they changed nations. Some nations became weaker; others found new power.

What is happening in today's world? We are still in the process of revolution. Day after day, there are changes in science, in technology, and in relations between countries. In addition, there are still many difficult problems that need to be solved.

To us, ancient times may seem very simple and uncomplicated. That is not really so. Five thousand years ago, the Sumerians in the city of Ur were very busy. They worried about feeding their people and making barren lands yield crops. They struggled to defend themselves against their enemies. They also had to face the dangers of nature, like floods. They invented new ways to get from one place to another faster. They set up governments and made laws. They tried to explain their own existence through religion. They also educated their children. They celebrated life through art and writing.

Remember
All human beings have the same basic needs for food, clothing, and shelter. In different times and places, people have met these needs in different ways.

Are we really so different today? People go into space. They use the great power of the tiny atom. However, the events of ancient days were just as exciting to the people who lived then. What about the day a human being first put ideas down in writing? Was the first wheel any less exciting than the first rocket engine? People in ancient times must have found discovery and changes to be just as exciting as we do today.

The cultures of the past are our best clues to history. By looking at yesterday's people, we can better understand the world as it is today—and as it might be tomorrow.

✓ **Check Your Understanding**

Write your answers in complete sentences.

1. What change has taken place over the years in the way people feel about slavery?

2. What did Europeans discover after they knew the Earth was round?

3. How was life in ancient times like life today?

How Historians Learn About the Past

We find out about the people of the past by looking at the things they left behind.

The easiest way we can look into the past is by reading papers and books of days gone by. **Historians** look at old maps that tell how the borders and names of countries have changed. They study all kinds of written records that have come down to us. Then they write books about what they have learned.

What about **civilizations** from long, long ago? There were times when no one wrote books or drew maps. How do we know so much about the ancient days? People called **archaeologists** dig in the ruins of ancient civilizations. They find **artifacts** that have long been underground. They study each artifact they find. They piece bits of information together. In this way, they come up with a picture of the past.

Scientists have many ways of deciding how old things are. A piece of cloth, an iron tool, and a painting on a wall may all be pieces of the puzzle. As the pieces come together, bit by bit the story is told!

These artifacts were used by ancient civilizations as weapons and for preparing food.

Learn More About It

THE TROJAN WAR

Thousands of years ago, the Greek poet Homer wrote about a mighty city called Troy. He wrote that Paris, son of the king of Troy, was visiting Sparta in Greece. There, Paris fell in love with Helen, the wife of King Menelaus. Paris took Helen home with him to Troy. The Greeks swore revenge. A huge army set sail for Troy. For ten years the Greeks fought the Trojans, but the Greeks were not able to capture the city. Then they built a gigantic wooden horse. The Greek soldiers hid inside it. The Trojans were curious about the horse and dragged it inside the city walls. The Greeks climbed out and killed most of the Trojans, including Paris. Then the Greeks looted and burned the city. Helen returned to Menelaus in Sparta.

Did all of this really happen? Was there ever a city called Troy? A German archaeologist named Heinrich Schliemann believed there was such a place. In 1870 he traveled to Turkey with a team of assistants. There they began digging in a mound that seemed to fit the location described in Homer's *Iliad*. Sure enough, they uncovered the ruins of several cities piled on top of each other. At least one of the cities had massive stone walls. Schliemann had discovered Troy!

Maps Show the Way

This book has many maps. These maps show how countries have changed and how groups of people have moved. They show that cities were built along rivers and on seacoasts. They show how waterways made it possible for different people to come together.

People have been making maps for a long time. They drew maps to try to understand their world. They also used maps to find their way from one place to another. Since ancient times, the art of mapmaking has come a long way. Now there are maps to show landforms, maps to show weather, and maps that picture continents, countries, and cities.

Mapmakers, however, have more work ahead. Think about the maps of the future. Will maps be needed to help people find their way among the stars?

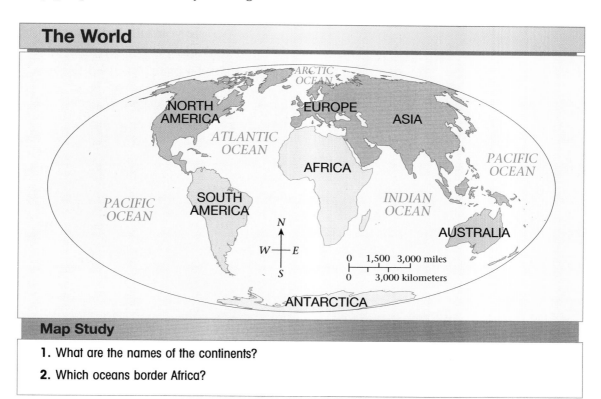

The World

Map Study

1. What are the names of the continents?

2. Which oceans border Africa?

✓ Check Your Understanding

Write your answers in complete sentences.

1. What are two ways that historians find out about the past?

2. How would you describe the work of an archaeologist?

3. What are two reasons why people first started making maps?

Timelines

The history of the people of the world is a long and exciting story. The timelines in each chapter will help you keep events clear and in order. Look at the timeline on page 11. It gives some idea of just how long the story is. The timeline shows some of the time periods and some of the people you will read about as the story unfolds. If you look closely at it, you should be able to find just where you fit on the timeline of history.

It may seem as if some of the civilizations in this book came and went very quickly. However, the timeline shows that the Roman civilization lasted for 1,250 years (from 750 B.C. to A.D. 500). The Sumerian civilization lasted 2,000 years (from about 4000 B.C. to 2000 B.C.). The timeline also shows that the "modern times" period is only about 500 years old so far. How does the period in history that we call ancient times compare in length with medieval times and with modern times?

You can use the same method to read most timelines.

1. Look at the whole timeline to figure out how much time it covers. Look for the earliest date. It is the first date on the left. Look for the latest date. It is the last date on the right. To read most timelines correctly, you will read the dates from left to right.

2. Remember that a timeline is like a ruler. It is divided into equal units. These equal units are called intervals. An interval may be one day, one month, one year, five years, or any other amount of time. To read any timeline correctly, you need to know how much time each unit or interval represents.

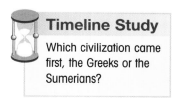

Timeline Study

Which civilization came first, the Greeks or the Sumerians?

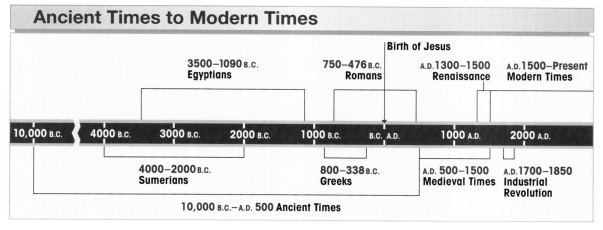

Ancient Times to Modern Times

3500–1090 B.C.
Egyptians

750–476 B.C.
Romans

Birth of Jesus

A.D.1300–1500
Renaissance

A.D.1500–Present
Modern Times

10,000 B.C. | 4000 B.C. | 3000 B.C. | 2000 B.C. | 1000 B.C. | B.C. A.D. | 1000 A.D. | 2000 A.D.

4000–2000 B.C.
Sumerians

800–338 B.C.
Greeks

A.D. 500–1500
Medieval Times

A.D.1700–1850
Industrial Revolution

10,000 B.C.–A.D. 500 Ancient Times

Chapter

1 ▶ Review

Summary

World history is the story of people, places, and events. What happened in the past helps to explain what is happening in the world today.
World history is about change. Discoveries and revolutions bring about change. The world is still changing today.
People in the past shared many of the same concerns as people today.
Historians study written records to learn about the past.
Archaeologists study artifacts to learn about the past.
Maps show many kinds of information about the world. People use maps to find their way from one place to the other.
Timelines list events in the order in which they happened.

archaeologist
artifact
culture
revolution
imperialism
A.D.
B.C.

Vocabulary Review

Complete each sentence with a term from the list.

1. A _____ brings about change, often in government.

2. A person who goes digging in ruins is probably an _____.

3. An _____ found underground can tell about life in the past.

4. Strong lands are practicing _____ when they try to conquer weak lands.

5. Religion and art are parts of the _____ of a people.

6. The letters _____ mean a year was after Jesus was born.

7. The letters _____ mean a year was before Jesus was born.

Chapter Quiz

Write your answers in complete sentences.

1. What is world history?

2. What made life exciting during ancient times?

3. How do historians learn from the past?

4. **Critical Thinking**   How can learning about the past help us understand what might happen in the future?

5. **Critical Thinking**   Why are today's maps more accurate than maps made during ancient times? Give at least two reasons.

Using the Timeline

Use the timeline on page 11 to answer the questions.

1. What four civilizations existed during ancient times?

2. How many years did the Industrial Revolution last?

Write About History

Complete the following activities.

1. Suppose you are an archaeologist who has uncovered the remains of an ancient city. What artifacts do you hope to find? Make a list of the top ten artifacts that you think will tell you the most about life in the ancient city.

2. Look at the timeline on page 11. You can see that ancient times were much longer than medieval or modern times. Why do we know so much more about medieval and modern times?

This cave painting in Lascaux, France, is thousands of years old. People of Stone Age cultures often painted pictures of animals they hunted.

Learning Objectives

- Describe what people learned when the Ice Age ended.
- Explain how the development of agriculture changed the world.
- Name the kinds of jobs people had in the new settlements.
- Locate the Fertile Crescent on a map.
- Explain how the people of ancient Jericho tried to protect their town.

Chapter 2 ▸ Early Humans: The Story Begins

Words to Know

glacier	a large, slow-moving mass of ice and snow
settlement	a small group of homes in an area that has not been populated
specialize	to work in, and know a lot about, one job or field
craft	a trade or art that takes special skill with the hands
fertile	able to produce large crops, as in rich soil
crescent	something shaped like a quarter moon

The Hunters

Our story of the world's history begins more than one million years ago. It was a time called the Ice Age. Most of the world was frozen then. It was covered with thick sheets of ice called **glaciers.** These glaciers had formed in the north.

In the northern parts of Europe, Asia, and North America, ice piled up about 10,000 feet thick. The weight of all that ice caused the glaciers to spread out. As they moved, the glaciers pushed soil and rocks out of their way. Many valleys and lakes were formed. Slowly, the glaciers moved farther and farther south.

Over time, in the southern parts of the three continents, the ice melted some during the short summers. Little groups of people lived there, scattered about. They were hunters. They had learned to make spears and other simple weapons and tools. They used wooden sticks, bones, and stones. They had not yet learned how to use metal. So historians call these people and their way of life a *Stone Age* culture.

Such was life on Earth for tens of thousands of years. The hunters left their caves in the summer to move around. They could not settle down for good. They had to follow the herds of wild animals. They also gathered some food from shrubs and trees, such as nuts, berries, and fruits. However, they mainly counted on animals for food and clothing. Hunting was the most important thing in their lives. Without a good hunt, they would die. Just staying alive was a constant struggle for people during the Ice Age.

Learn More About It

CAVE ARTWORK

During the Ice Age, some people were artists. They painted on cave walls or made sculptures from rock. Their art usually showed animals, especially the animals they hunted. Stone Age art has been discovered in caves in France, Spain, Italy, and other places. Most of the time, the caves were discovered by mistake. In 1940, for example, three teenage boys stumbled down a hole and discovered Lascaux Cave in France.

In 1994, three men discovered Chauvet Cave in France. The artwork in this cave was a surprise and some of the paintings were created more than 30,000 years ago! Another surprise was that the artwork included animals not usually pictured on cave walls. Horses and bison were there, but so were leopards, hyenas, rhinos, and bears. In addition, there were many pictures of cave lions. These pictures showed that the artists knew the habits of the cave lions very well.

It is possible that even older cave art has been discovered in Italy. In 2000, painted slabs of rock were found at Fumane Cave in Italy. The art, which includes a half-human, half-beast figure, may be 32,000 to 36,500 years old.

The Farmers

The Ice Age ended about 10,000 B.C. The glaciers began melting. The land was no longer frozen. People now learned how to grow food. They no longer had to chase wild animals across the lands. Once they learned to raise their own food, they could settle down. That change, from hunting to farming, made civilization possible.

The people of long ago watched the winds blow seeds across the ground. They noticed that new plants grew where the seeds landed. This is how the people learned. They tried planting seeds themselves. They broke up the ground to make it soft. They chose the best seeds, and they grew plants. Next, they made tools to use in farming. They used flint sickles to cut grain and wooden plows to help them dig up the ground.

Remember
The earliest farmers had no system of writing. We learn about them from the artifacts that archaeologists find.

Once the glaciers were gone, life became easier for people. Now they could count on a ready food supply. Often they grew more than they could eat in one winter. They could store food for the future. They would not have to move away from their homes to search for food. People began to live in **settlements.**

They also learned to tame animals. Some say the dog was the first animal tamed. Next came cows, goats, sheep, and pigs. With their own herds, people had a steady supply of meat, milk, and wool. They now had animals that could live side by side with them. The animals could carry loads and help people work.

✓ **Check Your Understanding**

Write your answers in complete sentences.

1. Where did people live during the Stone Age?

2. What did people learn to do after the Ice Age ended?

3. Why were people able to live in settlements?

For thousands of years, people have tamed animals to carry loads and help them with work.

The Agricultural Revolution

When people began to farm about 11,000 years ago, their lives changed. The change brought about by agriculture was very great. For this reason, the change is often called the Agricultural Revolution. Now people could settle in large groups, in one place. They chose areas with plenty of water and good soil. They built houses out of whatever materials were nearby. Often the houses were built of mud.

Now the people could plan on how much food to plant each year. They could decide on how many animals to raise in the herds. Now they had more control of their own lives.

Having a large enough food supply and staying in one place gave people spare time. Not everyone in the group was needed to raise food or care for the animals. People began to **specialize.** Some people farmed. Others took care of the animals.

Now there were also chances to do things they had never done before. People had time to work on their **crafts.** Weavers wove grass into fine baskets. Others made pottery from mud and clay and baked it in ovens. With wool from the sheep, some people learned to spin thread and to weave cloth.

As different jobs developed, so did trading. Weavers might trade their cloth for food from farmers. A goat might be traded for an ax from the toolmaker. First, trading was carried on within the village. Later people traded from one village to the next.

As people settled in large groups, they began to grow their own crops.

You Decide

There are still craftworkers today. Are craftworkers needed as much today as they were long ago? Why or why not?

With the Agricultural Revolution, people's most important needs—food, shelter, and clothing—were easier to meet. However, now people owned things. Potters had their jars and bowls. Herders had their animals. Now there were things to protect! New laws were needed. Most likely a group of the oldest, wisest people in the village would meet. They would decide on rules for the rest of the people.

People started to worry when their villages grew rich. Someone might attack them and try to steal some of their riches. Therefore, people formed armies to protect their villages.

As time went on, villages grew into cities. Later, cities joined together to form small kingdoms. Agriculture is what made this development possible.

The Fertile Crescent

The earliest known farming took place along the great rivers of the Middle East. These lands include what are now the countries of Jordan, Syria, Iraq, Iran, Kuwait, Lebanon, Israel, and Turkey. This area is called the **Fertile Crescent.** The Tigris and Euphrates rivers provided plenty of water for the land. The soil was rich. The land between the Tigris and Euphrates was called Mesopotamia. That name means *land between two rivers*.

Within the Fertile Crescent was the town of Jericho. It is one of the earliest known towns. By about 8000 B.C., Jericho was probably a farming village. Its people built rounded houses of mud and bricks. Archaeologists have found remains showing that the people of Jericho buried their dead right under their houses.

The land around Jericho was very fertile. The people grew many crops and became rich. The town grew. Jericho now had to protect itself. The people built a stone wall around their town.

The wall built to protect the town of Jericho was destroyed and the town was captured.

The wall was not enough protection. Around 7000 B.C., archaeologists say, Jericho was probably captured. The houses built after that time were no longer round but had square corners. This clue suggests that a new group of people must have taken over and settled there.

More is known about the early farming villages of the Fertile Crescent than anywhere else. However, farming was developing in other parts of the world, too. By 6000 B.C. farming had spread to Europe. By 4000 B.C. a culture of rice farmers had grown up in China. Between 5000 B.C. and 2000 B.C., agriculture spread across northern Africa.

People began to settle wherever there was good soil and plenty of water. Now they had food and clothing. They had time to learn. Certain cities began to grow into great civilizations.

Compare the maps on the next page. Notice how the Middle East changed over time.

Timeline Study

How many years passed between the beginning of agriculture and the first use of the wheel?

The Agricultural Revolution

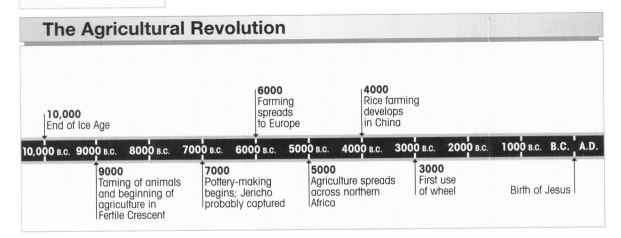

The Middle East: Then

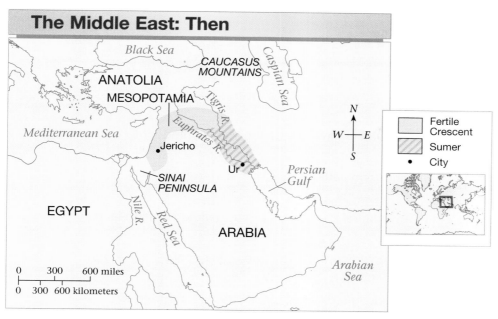

The Middle East: Now

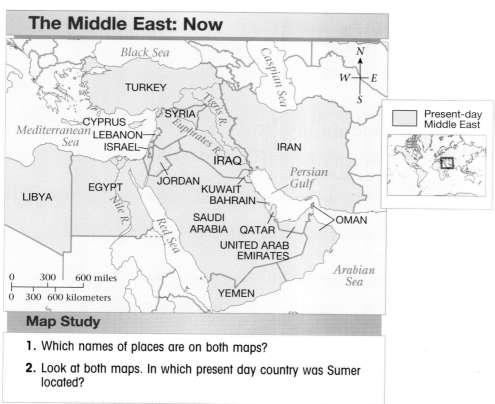

Map Study

1. Which names of places are on both maps?

2. Look at both maps. In which present day country was Sumer located?

Chapter

2 ▸ Review

Summary

During the Ice Age, people lived in caves all winter. They hunted for food during the short summers.

Hunters could not form long-term settlements. They had to follow the animals.

With the coming of the Agricultural Revolution, people learned to farm land and tame animals.

Farming meant that people could control their own food supply. They could build houses and settle in one place.

In the new settlements, people had different jobs. New crafts developed.

Thanks to agriculture, trading began and rich cities grew up.

One of the earliest areas of farming was in the Middle East, along two great rivers. This area is called the Fertile Crescent.

glacier
specialize
crescent
fertile
craft

Vocabulary Review

Write a term from the list that matches each definition below.

1. A thin, curved shape

2. Arts and skills such as weaving and making baskets

3. Rich soil that is suitable for farming

4. To work in a job that takes a certain kind of knowledge

5. A moving body of ice and snow

Chapter Quiz

Write your answers in complete sentences.

1. How did farming make life easier for people after the Ice Age ended?

2. Why did the people of Jericho build a wall around their town?

3. Where did the earliest known farming take place?

4. **Critical Thinking** Why did trading develop after people began to specialize?

5. **Critical Thinking** Why is the change from hunting to farming called the Agricultural Revolution?

Using the Timeline

Use the timeline on page 22 to answer the questions.

1. Which came first, pottery-making or the first use of the wheel?

2. Where and when did rice farming develop?

Write About History

Complete the following activity.

Form a group of three or four students. Discuss the ways life in early villages was like life in towns and cities today. Make a list of the ways they were alike. Share the list with the rest of the class.

Unit 1 **Review**

Comprehension Check

Write your answers in complete sentences.

1. What can archaeologists learn from artifacts?

2. What does a timeline show?

3. What was the Stone Age culture?

4. Why did people make pictures in caves thousands of years ago?

5. What did people begin to do after the Ice Age ended?

6. How did archaeologists know Jericho was captured?

7. Where did the earliest known farming begin?

Writing an Essay

Answer one of the following essay topics.

1. Explain why world history is the history of change.

2. Compare the work of a historian and an archaeologist.

3. Discuss the importance of the Agricultural Revolution.

Group Activity

Form a group of three or four. Prepare a TV program with the theme "Discovering World History." Have one student be the narrator. Other students can play the roles of an archaeologist, a historian, and a teenager who recently discovered some important cave art.

History in Your Life

During the Agricultural Revolution, people had to find new jobs. Fewer people were needed for farming, so some people began to specialize in other kinds of work. Do you think specialization is a good thing? How does specialization affect your life today?

Unit 2 ▷ Ancient Civilizations

This mosaic from ancient Sumer shows one of the greatest inventions of the ancient world, the wheel.

Learning Objectives

- Locate the land of Sumer on a map.
- Describe the Sumerian method of farming.
- Describe Sumerian trading.
- Discuss the growth of Sumerian city-states.
- Name the most important Sumerian inventions.
- Describe daily life in Sumer.
- Explain why Sumer grew weak.

Sumerians: The First Great Civilization

Chapter 3

Words to Know

swamp	an area of low, wet land
irrigate	to bring water to dry land by means of canals
canal	a waterway made by humans
dike	a wall built along a river or sea to hold back the water from low land
merchant	a person who buys and sells goods for profit; a trader
temple	a building for the worship of a god or gods
city-state	an independent city and the surrounding land it controls
ziggurat	a huge, towerlike temple
tablet	a small, flat piece of clay used for writing
cuneiform	a wedge-shaped form of writing used in ancient Sumer
scribe	a person whose job was to write out copies of contracts and other manuscripts
contract	a legal written agreement between two or more people
chariot	an open two-wheeled cart, pulled by horses

The Land Between Two Rivers

The land that would one day be called Mesopotamia lay between two rivers. The rivers were the Tigris and the Euphrates. Sometimes the rivers flooded and washed rich bottom-soil up on the land. This made the land good for farming. People settled on this rich land. They grew their crops and raised animals. In the south, in a land called Sumer, a great civilization grew.

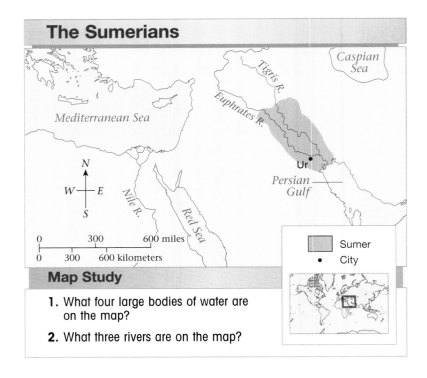

The Sumerians

Map Study

1. What four large bodies of water are on the map?

2. What three rivers are on the map?

The people of Sumer were called Sumerians. Although the land they settled was fertile, it was not a perfect place to live. The weather was very hot in the summer. In spring there was always the danger of the rivers flooding. Sometimes whole villages would be washed away. Many people would die.

Part of Sumer was **swamp** land. Other parts were very dry. Land that was flooded in the spring dried hard under the late summer sun. It was necessary to make the land ready for crops. The Sumerian farmers had to get water from the rivers to their fields.

Sumerian Farmers

The farmers found a way to **irrigate** their fields. They made cuts in the river banks and dug **canals**. The canals carried the river water out to the crops. The Sumerians also built **dikes** to hold back the flood waters.

A Sumerian farmer worked hard from early morning until late at night. Oxen were the farmer's treasure. They pulled the farmer's plow and carried the crops in from the field. Sumer was a wealthy land. Its wealth lay in farming.

Trading

The people of Sumer had different jobs. While some were farmers, others were **merchants**. Sumer had little metal, stone, or timber of its own. Sumerians depended on trading to get these things. They sent their fine crops to other lands. In return, they brought back the goods they needed at home.

Boats carried the goods to and from Sumer. The Sumerian boats were among the first ever used. There were two kinds of boats. River boats were small. They moved along under the power of long oars or poles. Trading ships were much longer, and they were narrow. They had big sails. The trading boats brought home treasures of gold, silver, pearls, and copper from other lands.

HISTORY FACT

Sumerians who had the same jobs often lived and worked on the same street. These shop-lined streets may have been the ancestor of today's shopping malls.

Villages Grow Into City-States

The earliest Sumerians lived in houses made from reeds. The reeds, or tall grasses, grew in the swamps. Later, the people learned to make bricks from mud. They dried the bricks in the sun and built houses from them. The brick houses stayed cool inside during the hot summers.

Each Sumerian village was built around a **temple**. The people believed a god or goddess lived in the temple and protected the village. The farmers took part of their crops to the temple to offer to the god or goddess. The priests of the temple became very wealthy and powerful.

Over the years, the villages grew. They became **city-states,** each one with its own government. A temple still stood at the center of each city-state. There was farmland all around the edge of the city. The city-states often fought among themselves. For protection, the Sumerians built walls around their cities.

One of the greatest city-states of Sumer was called Ur. A gigantic temple called a ziggurat was built in Ur. This tall temple-tower was built to honor the god who watched over the city. The people of Ur came in great numbers to bring gifts to the temple. They believed that if their god was happy, the city would be wealthy.

The ziggurat was built to honor the Sumerian god who watched over the city of Ur.

The Invention of Writing

The Sumerians' inventions were their gifts to the world. All the civilizations that followed used inventions of the Sumerians. There are still things in the world today that date back to Sumer.

The greatest gift the Sumerians gave to the world was the invention of writing. The Sumerians were a wealthy people. They needed some way to keep track of what they owned. They began by drawing pictures. They used a reed as a pen. They drew on soft pieces of clay. The soft clay was then dried in the sun. The **tablet** became a permanent record. Later, the Sumerian drawings changed into wedge-shaped symbols. This kind of writing is called **cuneiform**. By putting symbols together, the Sumerians could write whole sentences.

A clay tablet

Not all Sumerians knew how to write. Only wealthy parents could afford to send their children to school. Very few girls received an education, so students were often called school-sons. Their teachers were called school-fathers. Specially trained people called **scribes** learned how to write. The school-sons learned to write by copying texts over to tablets of clay.

The scribes were paid very well for their special skill. They were among the richest of the Sumerians. They drew up business **contracts** for the farmers and merchants. Some scribes learned to add, subtract, and multiply. They could become tax collectors.

We know a great deal about this earliest of civilizations. This is because Sumerian scribes wrote down their ideas and kept records.

Remember
Before the Agricultural Revolution, most people did not have other jobs besides farming.

WORDS FROM THE PAST
How Writing Changed

If you were trying to communicate with someone and you did not have a written language, how would you do it? You might use pictures to tell a story. That is how writing began in Sumer.

At first, pictographs, or drawings that represent actual things, were used. For example, a picture of a fish represented a fish. These early pictographs were drawn in vertical columns with a pen made from a sharpened reed.

In time, these pictographs began to look less like the real objects they represented. Instead, they became simple symbols that were easier to draw. These marks eventually became wedge-shaped strokes, or cuneiform. The Latin word for "wedge" is *cuneus*. People then began to write in horizontal rows. A new type of pen was used. It was pushed into the clay, forming the wedge-shaped symbols.

Writing eventually developed into something closer to an alphabet by other groups of people. However, it was the Sumerians who created the first efficient form of writing. There were symbols, or cuneiform writing, for thousands of words!

Word	Early Pictograph	Late Pictograph	Cuneiform
Bird			
Fish			
Ox			
Sun			

This chart shows how writing changed from simple pictures to symbols, called cuneiform.

Other Gifts from the Sumerians

The Sumerian farmers had to pay a tax on their property. To figure the taxes, they invented a way of measuring land. Fields were divided into even squares. Then the squares were counted to decide how much tax a farmer owed. Since the Sumerians used silver as money, payments were made in silver. The value of the silver was measured by its weight.

The Sumerians also learned to measure time. The 60-second minute and the 60-minute hour probably come from the Sumerian way of counting time.

Historians believe that the wheel was first used in Sumer. Sumerian armies rode in wheeled **chariots.** There were no horses in all of Sumer. Therefore, wild donkeys were taught to pull the chariots.

Irrigation canals came to us from the Sumerian farmer. Sailboats came from the traders.

Although there was little metal in Sumer itself, the Sumerians traded for metal. They became skilled metalworkers. They learned to make fine jewelry of copper, silver, and gold.

Sumerian ideas and Sumerian inventions brought about changes that would affect life for ages to come.

You Decide

What if the wheel had never been invented? What would the world be like today? How would people travel?

✓ **Check Your Understanding**

Write your answers in complete sentences.

1. Why did the Sumerians trade with other lands?

2. Why did the Sumerians have to invent a way to measure land?

3. What was the greatest gift the Sumerians gave to the world?

Life in Sumer

A Sumerian boy might awaken to a hot, dry summer day in the city of Ur. If his father were a farmer, the boy would go with him to work in the fields. The two of them would leave their small house with the earliest rays of the sun. Perhaps that day the father and son would clean the irrigation canals. Even if the day were very hot, the boy would work hard. Those canals were important to the farm. Without them, nothing would grow. The boy might work alongside other farmers. They would have help from the slaves from one of the larger farms.

Sumerian boys from wealthy families went to school, where they learned to write.

Boys from wealthy families could go to school. If a boy learned well, he might become a scribe. A scribe could work in the king's palace or perhaps in the great temple itself.

The king ran the city of Ur. He ruled in the name of the city's god. Priests, scribes, and nobles helped him rule. These people were very rich. They lived a fine life. They were members of the highest classes in the Sumerian culture.

The people of Ur believed that when they died, they went to another world. Archaeologists have discovered graves filled with fine gold jewelry. Some graves of the nobles hold many skeletons. It may be that other people killed themselves, or were killed, when the nobles died. This way they could follow the dead nobles to that other world.

Attack on Ur

The Sumerian city-states fought with each other. That is why, after a while, Sumer grew weak. Around 2000 B.C. Sumerian cities came under attack. The Sumerian armies, even with their wheeled chariots, were not strong enough to save Sumer. Ur was destroyed.

The city's wealth was stolen. Men and women were killed. Children were taken as slaves.

Soon other Sumerian cities fell, too. The invaders, called the Babylonians, built new cities. Later, some of those cities died away, too. Dust and dirt covered them over. Today archaeologists dig into great mounds that still stand in the Middle East. Under the mounds of dirt lay all that is left of these ancient civilizations.

Timeline Study

How many years passed from the rise of Sumerian city-states to conquest by Babylonians?

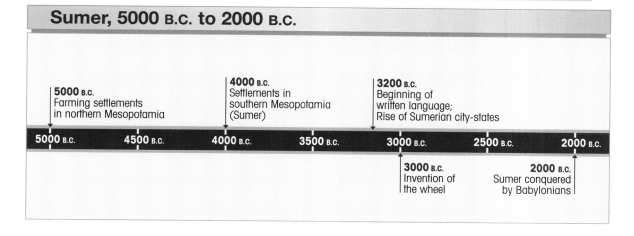

Sumer, 5000 B.C. to 2000 B.C.

5000 B.C.
Farming settlements in northern Mesopotamia

4000 B.C.
Settlements in southern Mesopotamia (Sumer)

3200 B.C.
Beginning of written language; Rise of Sumerian city-states

5000 B.C.   4500 B.C.   4000 B.C.   3500 B.C.   3000 B.C.   2500 B.C.   2000 B.C.

3000 B.C.
Invention of the wheel

2000 B.C.
Sumer conquered by Babylonians

Chapter

3 ▷ Review

Summary

The first great civilization grew up between the Tigris and Euphrates rivers in the land of Sumer.
The Sumerian civilization was based on farming. The Sumerians had to irrigate their land.
The Sumerians traded with other lands for the goods they needed.
The Sumerians lived in city-states. Each city-state had its own government.
The Sumerians invented writing. They also invented the wheel, the sailboat, irrigation, canals, and a way of measuring.
The Sumerians were conquered, but their ideas lived on.

irrigate
scribe
cuneiform
chariots
ziggurat

Vocabulary Review

Complete each sentence with a term from the list.

1. A large temple called a ＿＿ was built in Ur.

2. The Sumerian system of writing based on wedge-shaped symbols was called ＿＿.

3. A ＿＿ was a person who was trained to write.

4. Sumerian farmers found a way to ＿＿ their fields.

5. Sumerians used wild donkeys to pull their ＿＿.

Chapter Quiz

Write your answers in complete sentences.

1. How did the Sumerians invent writing?

2. What were five inventions of the Sumerians?

3. Why were scribes members of the richest and highest class of Sumerian culture?

4. **Critical Thinking** How do you think the Sumerians might have been able to prevent the destruction of their cities?

5. **Critical Thinking** How were Sumerian schools different from schools today?

Using the Timeline

Use the timeline on page 37 to answer the questions.

1. What two things were invented between 3200 B.C. and 3000 B.C.?

2. How many years passed between settlements in northern and southern Mesopotamia?

Write About History

Complete the following activity.

Choose five items found in your classroom and draw a symbol for each. Work in small groups to see if you can guess what one another's symbols represent. Once you have determined what each symbol means, create a sentence by putting certain symbols next to each other in a row. Present your group's sentence to the class to see if your classmates can guess what it says.

The Egyptians built these stone pyramids thousands of years ago. They are considered one of the wonders of the world.

Learning Objectives

- Explain why people settled along the Nile River.
- Describe what happened to the Nile River Valley every July.
- Explain why the pharaohs had their people build the pyramids.
- Tell what archaeologists found inside Egyptian tombs.
- Describe how the Egyptians lived and worshipped.
- Name some important Egyptian inventions.

Chapter 4 Ancient Egypt: Land of the Pharaohs

Words to Know

desert	dry, sandy land with little or no plant life
upstream	in the direction against the flow of the river; at the upper part of a river
pharaoh	a king of ancient Egypt
tax	money paid to support a government
tomb	a grave, usually one that is enclosed in stone or cement
pyramid	a huge stone structure with a square base and four triangular sides that meet in a point at the top. Egyptian rulers were buried in the pyramids.
mummy	a dead body kept from rotting by being treated with chemicals and wrapped in cloth
hieroglyphics	a system of writing using pictures or symbols to represent objects, ideas, or sounds
papyrus	a writing paper the Egyptians made from water plants of the same name

Along the Nile

At one time the area now called the Sahara was a green plain. People lived there. There was water and wildlife. Over time the weather changed. The plain dried up and became a **desert**. The people living there went looking for water. Some of them went to a land called Egypt.

A great river called the Nile ran through Egypt. The Nile River Valley was a swampland. It was a dark jungle filled with dangerous animals. The people needed water badly, so they cleared the land anyway.

They built their villages along the river where the jungle used to be.

Like the Sumerians, the people of Egypt built a civilization along a river. They were able to do this because the land along the Nile had what they needed. The Egyptians learned to farm, to tame animals, to make pottery, and to weave. They learned to make tools from metal.

The weather in Egypt was hot. Each year, in July, the Nile River spilled over its banks in a great flood. Land that stood dry all year was suddenly under water for several weeks. The floods left the land very fertile.

Farmers learned to use the floods to help them. They learned to save up some of the flood waters. Then they could water their crops during the rest of the year. Like the Sumerians, they learned to dig canals to irrigate their fields.

Each July the farmers moved to higher ground, taking their animals with them. They knew that the floods would be over in a few weeks. They waited until the Nile once again flowed peacefully within its banks. Then they planted their seeds in the rich, soft ground.

Lower Egypt and Upper Egypt Become One

The civilization along the Nile did well. Villages joined together to form larger settlements. There came a time, around 3200 B.C., when two kings ruled all of Egypt. One king ruled Lower Egypt, in the north. Another king ruled Upper Egypt, in the south. A look at the map on page 43 shows each of these areas. The Nile River flows northward. A person in Lower Egypt who followed the Nile River **upstream** would come to Upper Egypt.

Upper and Lower Egypt

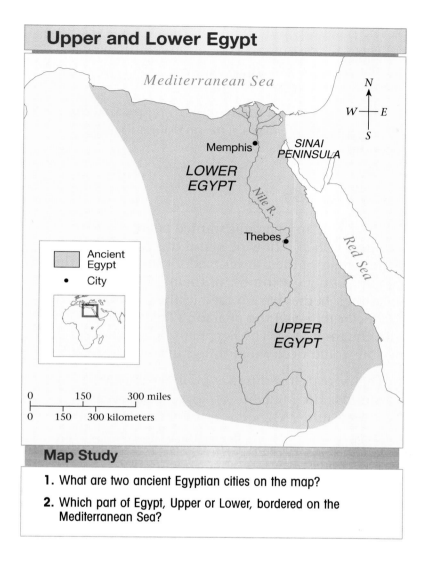

Map Study

1. What are two ancient Egyptian cities on the map?

2. Which part of Egypt, Upper or Lower, bordered on the Mediterranean Sea?

The king of Lower Egypt wore a red crown. The king of Upper Egypt wore a white crown. The two kings ended up fighting to control all of Egypt. Around 3100 B.C., King Menes of Upper Egypt conquered Lower Egypt. Now Menes wore a "double" crown. He ruled all of Egypt.

King Menes became the first great **pharaoh** of Egypt. The Egyptians called their ruler *pharaoh*, meaning "The Great House."

You Decide

People today still have to pay taxes. What do you think would happen if a government official used tax money to live a rich life?

The pharaohs were powerful rulers. Each year they collected **taxes**—huge taxes—from all the people. Farmers had to give the pharaoh a large part of their crops as a tax.

The pharaoh had many men to help carry out orders and collect taxes. The pharaohs lived rich, splendid lives.

The Pyramids

The Egyptian pharaohs wanted people to remember just how rich and how powerful they were. Some had huge statues of themselves made. They also had their people build great **tombs** for them. When the pharaohs died, their bodies were placed in the tombs. Jewelry, food, clothing—all the pharaoh's favorite things—went into the tomb, too. The Egyptians believed that a person would need those things in the next world.

These great, towering Egyptian tombs are called **pyramids.** The pharaohs of Egypt, from about 2650 B.C. until 1637 B.C., were buried within those huge pyramids. There are many pyramids still standing in Egypt today. They are considered one of the wonders of the world.

The most famous pyramid is the Great Pyramid near Cairo. It covers an area larger than ten football fields. It contains more than two million stone blocks, each weighing about 2 1/2 tons. Somehow, the stones had to be cut into shape and then transported to the building site. Then the stones were raised into place. They were laid so that they fit together exactly. From a distance, the pyramid looks as if it were cut out of a single stone. The Egyptians of 4,500 years ago had no machinery or iron tools. So how did they do it? We do not know for certain. In fact, we do not know if *we* would be able to build pyramids today, even with our modern building methods.

The ancient Egyptians did use copper chisels. They also probably hauled the stones on some sort of wooden sled. Most likely, they built a system of ramps and wooden planks to haul the stones into place. Mostly they had to rely on human muscle power. The ancient Greek historian Herodotus wrote about the pyramids. He said that 400,000 men worked each year for 20 years to build the Great Pyramid. Archaeologists doubt these numbers, but we will never know for sure.

Tombs within the pyramids have served as a wonderful record of the Egyptian civilization. However, robbers have broken into some tombs and stolen the artifacts. Fortunately, archaeologists have discovered some tombs still filled with goods from daily Egyptian life. The walls of the tombs are covered with picture-writing. The pictures tell the story of the ancient Egyptian world.

✓ Check Your Understanding

Write your answers in complete sentences.

1. Why did people settle along the Nile River?

2. Why did the Egyptian pharaohs have their people build the pyramids?

3. Why did the pharaohs want all of their favorite things to be buried with them?

This Egyptian tomb contains the mummy of Tutankhamen, an Egyptian pharaoh.

Egyptian Mummies

Archaeologists found more than bowls, pictures, jewelry, and pottery within the tombs. They found the pharaohs themselves! The Egyptians used certain chemicals to keep the dead body from rotting away. Of course, only the rich Egyptians could afford this special treatment.

Burying people this way was not a simple matter in ancient Egypt. First, the brain and organs had to be removed from the body. Then the body was treated with a special chemical. It was then wrapped around and around in cloth bandages. A body wrapped like this is called a **mummy**. Many mummies were found deep within the Egyptian tombs. Scientists have removed Egyptian mummies and artifacts from these tombs. They are on display today in museums around the world.

Egyptian Life and Religion

The Egyptian pharaohs and their nobles lived rich lives. However, all the rest of the people led very simple lives. The farmers worked hard in their fields. There was usually plenty of food. This meant that Egypt's craftworkers had more time to improve their skills.

The Egyptians were concerned about the way they looked. Drawings and statues show Egyptian women with long, dark hair worn in many braids and ringlets.

Both men and women wore makeup. They painted their lips red. They drew around their eyes with a dark green or gray paste called *kohl*. The Egyptians also liked perfume. Both men and women rubbed sweet-smelling oils into their skins.

Most ancient Egyptians believed in many gods. Just as in the land of Sumer, each city had its own special god. Osiris was the powerful god of death.

The river played an important part in Egyptians' lives. It also played a part in their belief about death. They believed that the dead were ferried across a great river to meet Osiris in the next world.

Remember
The earliest known farming took place along the great rivers of the Middle East. People settled where there was good soil and plenty of water.

Egyptian Inventions

The Egyptians learned to write. They invented a system of picture-writing called **hieroglyphics.** They learned to make paper from river reed called **papyrus.** Our word *paper* comes from the word *papyrus*.

The Egyptians learned to chart the stars. They also decided that there were 365 days in a year.

HISTORY FACT

The Egyptian calendar was based on the sun. There were three seasons of 120 days each. There was a five-day celebration at the end of the year.

The Egyptians made jewelry of gold and precious stones. They used metals for tools and weapons. The Egyptians made music, too. Archaeologists have found ancient Egyptian instruments and the words to songs. The Egyptians built ships. They traded with other people.

Most of all, the ancient Egyptians are remembered as the builders of the pyramids. The Egyptian builders have left us what may be the most amazing works of any civilization. Most likely, many of their secrets still lie buried within the pyramids.

Timeline Study

How many years did it take for a unified Egypt to become the world's greatest power?

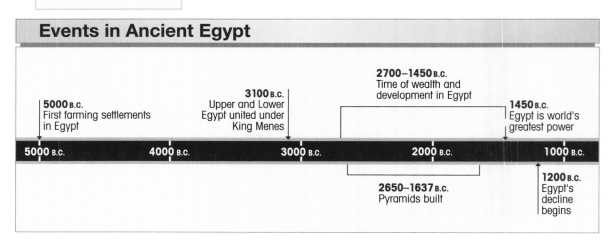

Events in Ancient Egypt

5000 B.C.
First farming settlements in Egypt

3100 B.C.
Upper and Lower Egypt united under King Menes

2700–1450 B.C.
Time of wealth and development in Egypt

1450 B.C.
Egypt is world's greatest power

5000 B.C.   4000 B.C.   3000 B.C.   2000 B.C.   1000 B.C.

2650–1637 B.C.
Pyramids built

1200 B.C.
Egypt's decline begins

WORDS FROM THE PAST
The Rosetta Stone

Hieroglyphics can still be seen in many places in Egypt. Yet for many hundreds of years, nobody could read them. The meaning of these ancient Egyptian symbols had been lost sometime in the distant past. Then in 1799, a French engineer in Egypt discovered a large stone. It was half buried near the mouth of the Nile River.

The Rosetta Stone has the same message written in three languages.

The Rosetta Stone, as it came to be called, was completely covered with writing. Carved into the stone were three languages: hieroglyphics, a second Egyptian language, and Greek. A French historian named Champollion translated the Greek portion first. Then he carefully compared this to the other languages. He realized that the same message was written in the three languages. He was finally able to learn the meaning of the hieroglyphics. In 1822 he published the results of his work.

Champollion had developed a system of sounds and meanings that could be applied to other hieroglyphics. For the first time, scholars could go into an Egyptian tomb or temple and read the name of a king and something about him. Suddenly, with hard work, a skilled translator could read a papyrus roll that had not been read for thousands of years.

Today, the Rosetta Stone is in the British Museum, in London, England. Many visitors come to see the black stone that provided the key to understanding ancient Egyptian hieroglyphics.

Chapter

4 ▷ Review

Summary

When the Sahara became a desert, people went to live along the Nile River.
The river flooded each year, leaving the land around it fertile.
Lower Egypt and Upper Egypt were united under King Menes.
Egyptian rulers, called pharaohs, were very powerful.
The pharaohs' tombs were in giant pyramids.
Ancient Egyptians believed in life after death. Many of the things they owned were buried with wealthy Egyptians.
We know a lot about the Egyptians from the mummies and artifacts found in their tombs.
The Egyptians made paper from a reed called papyrus.

upstream

pharaoh

hieroglyphics

desert

papyrus

pyramid

mummy

Vocabulary Review

Complete each sentence with a term from the list.

1. The area called the Sahara changed from a green plain to a ____.

2. An Egyptian ruler was buried in a ____.

3. The dead body of a rich Egyptian might be preserved as a ____.

4. The Egyptians made writing paper from a plant called ____.

5. A system of writing used by the Egyptians is called____.

6. Follow the Nile River ____, and you will reach Upper Egypt.

7. Long ago, an Egyptian ruler was called a ____.

Chapter Quiz

Write your answers in complete sentences.

1. What happened to the Nile River every year in July?
2. What did Egyptians believe about death?
3. What were some important Egyptian inventions?
4. **Critical Thinking** Why do you think so many people are fascinated by the Egyptian pyramids today?
5. **Critical Thinking** Why is it important to understand the written records of ancient civilizations?

Using the Timeline

Use the timeline on page 48 to answer the questions.

1. How many years passed between the first farming settlements in Egypt and the unification of Upper and Lower Egypt?
2. When the pyramids were built, was Egypt rich or poor?

Write About History

Complete the following activity.

With a small group, create a trivia game about the pyramids of Egypt. Use information from this chapter, encyclopedias and other books, and the Internet. New information about the pyramids is available from ongoing excavations. On the Internet, you may want to begin with http://www.Britannica.com and http://www.pbs.org.

Phoenician explorers were the first people who could sail beyond the sight of land. They spread their ideas and inventions throughout the ancient world.

Learning Objectives

- Locate Phoenician trading routes on a map.
- Name two important Phoenician inventions.
- Explain how the religion of the ancient Israelites was different from that of other Mediterranean people.
- Describe the Code of Hammurabi.
- Describe the secret knowledge of the Hittites.
- Tell what the Assyrians did when they captured a city.

Chapter 5 — Mediterranean Kingdoms

Words to Know

empire	a group of lands ruled by the same government or ruler
navigate	to plan the course of a ship; to sail or steer
colony	a group of people who settle in a far-off land but are still under the rule of the land they came from
nomad	a person who moves from place to place looking for food for his or her animal herds
conquer	to get control by using force, as in a war
capital	a city or town where the government of a nation or state is located
treaty	an agreement, usually having to do with peace or trade
siege	the surrounding of a city by soldiers who are trying to capture it so that food, water, and other supplies cannot get in or out
tribute	a payment or gift demanded by rulers of ancient kingdoms

Many groups of people settled along the eastern shore of the Mediterranean Sea. Others settled the lands farther east. They farmed the fertile valley between the Tigris and Euphrates rivers. New civilizations began to grow. These groups traded with each other. They also made war with each other. They fought for control over the Mediterranean lands. Strong kingdoms took over smaller city-states. Powerful kings ruled **empires.**

One of these civilizations was the Hittites. They learned how to make tools and weapons out of iron. Other Mediterranean civilizations left their mark on world history in different ways. The Hebrews gave us the Jewish religion. The Phoenicians invented an alphabet. It was very similar to our modern alphabet.

The Phoenicians: Traders on the Seas

The Phoenician civilization grew up along the eastern shores of the Mediterranean. It was unlike most of the other Mediterranean civilizations. The Phoenicians were not farmers. They built their cities on rocky shores. The Phoenicians were people of the sea. They were sailors and traders.

Few farm crops grew in Phoenicia. However, there were plenty of trees. The people cut down the trees to use as wood to build sailing ships.

The Phoenicians were the best sailors in the ancient world. They learned to use the stars to **navigate.** This made it possible for them to sail beyond the sight of land. The Phoenicians sailed where no other people dared to go. Their ships went to every corner of the Mediterranean. They reached the coast of Spain. They even sailed out into the Atlantic Ocean, beyond Gibraltar. They sailed along the west coast of Africa. Then they probably went all the way around the whole continent of Africa.

Wherever they traveled, the Phoenicians set up **colonies.** Their people settled in places all around the Mediterranean Sea. The Phoenician colonies became trading centers. One of the largest Phoenician colonies was Carthage. It was on the north coast of Africa. The people of Carthage traded their gold, ivory, and ebony for Phoenician pottery, glass, and beads.

The colonies paid taxes to the Phoenician homeland. Great Phoenician cities—like Tyre, Sidon, and Byblos—grew rich and strong.

The Phoenicians were traders and sailors, not warriors. They paid soldiers from other lands to protect their cities. They built high, stone walls to protect themselves from attack.

Phoenician Trading Routes

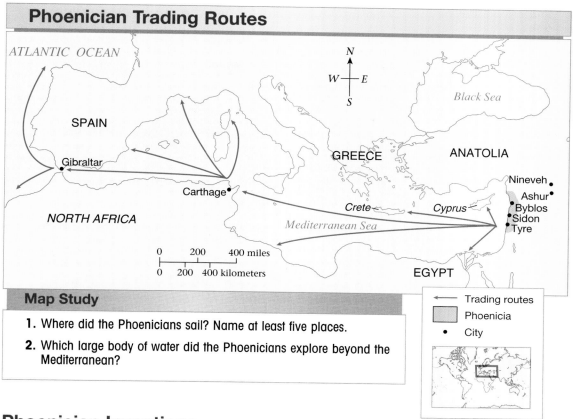

Map Study

1. Where did the Phoenicians sail? Name at least five places.

2. Which large body of water did the Phoenicians explore beyond the Mediterranean?

Phoenician Inventions

The Phoenician ships were powered by oars and sails. They sailed all about the ancient world. As the Phoenicians traded goods, they also traded ideas.

One of the most important ideas the Phoenicians spread was the alphabet. They turned pictures into letters. In fact, our own alphabet comes from the letters the Phoenicians invented.

The Phoenicians became famous for another invention, too. It was a secret dye used to color cloth. The dye was made from snails that lived along the coast. The Phoenicians boiled thousands of snails to make just a tiny bit of dye. The dye was very costly. Named after the city of Tyre, it was called Tyrian purple.

These are the Phoenician letters for A, B, C, D, and E.

The Phoenicians traded the purple cloth. Only very rich people could buy it. Royalty decorated their palaces with the purple cloth. They wore robes of Tyrian purple. The color purple came to stand for power and wealth. It became a royal color.

The Ancient Israelites: Under One God

The ancient Israelites lived along the east coast of the Mediterranean Sea. Their civilization grew up just south of Phoenicia.

The ancient Israelites wanted their own land where they could worship their god. In the Mediterranean world, most people believed in many gods. There were gods of death, sun, and rain. The ancient Israelites believed in one god, Yahweh.

The Bible says that a man named Abraham was the father of the Israelites. One day he left with his family to become a **nomad**. Abraham and his people followed their herds into a land called *Canaan*.

Abraham's people were eventually treated as slaves in Egypt. The Egyptian pharaoh was cruel. The man named Moses became the ancient Israelites' leader. He led them out of Egypt, into the desert, away from the cruel pharaoh. On Mt. Sinai, Moses received the Ten Commandments.

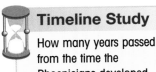

Timeline Study

How many years passed from the time the Phoenicians developed the alphabet until they rose to power?

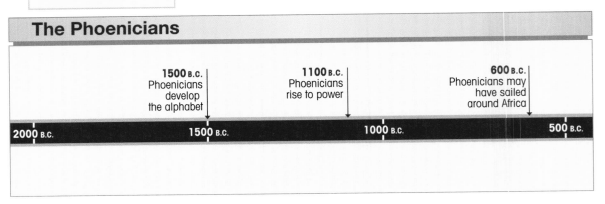

The Phoenicians

1500 B.C. Phoenicians develop the alphabet	**1100** B.C. Phoenicians rise to power	**600** B.C. Phoenicians may have sailed around Africa	
2000 B.C.	1500 B.C.	1000 B.C.	500 B.C.

WORDS FROM THE PAST
The Ten Commandments

The ancient Israelites did not find their land of freedom right away. They wandered, searching, for many years. The Bible says that during that time, Moses was given the Ten Commandments. It says that the commandments came directly from God.

The commandments are laws to live by. They became laws for the people of ancient Israel. The first commandment says that people must believe that their god is more important than any other gods. "The Lord is One," the Bible reads.

The Ten Commandments also tell people how they must act toward each other. For example, children must honor their parents. The commandments forbid unfaithfulness, killing, stealing, or wanting what belongs to someone else.

Over time, the Ten Commandments became an important part of Judaism and Christianity. Today, some people want to display the commandments in public schools to remind students of the things they should not do. Other people feel that displaying them in school would make it look like the United States is supporting a particular religion.

Moses holds the stone tablets which contain the Ten Commandments.

The Promised Land

The ancient Israelites finally reached Canaan again. They called it the "Promised Land." They believed it was the land that God had promised them. They settled there. They built towns. They followed their religion.

Holding onto the Promised Land was not always easy. The Philistines lived nearby. The Philistines fought the ancient Israelites for their land.

There were 12 tribes of ancient Israelites. At first, the Philistines were able to **conquer** some of the tribes. Divided, the ancient Israelites were weak. In time, the tribes joined together under one king to fight the Philistines.

There is a famous story of a shepherd boy named David. He fought a Philistine giant called Goliath. David killed Goliath with a rock from a slingshot. The ancient Israelites then won the war against the more powerful Philistines.

David later became king of the ancient Israelites. The town of Jerusalem became his **capital** city and was a religious center.

When David died, his son, Solomon, became king. Solomon built a beautiful temple in Jerusalem. He built a fleet of fine sailing ships. King Solomon was known to be good and very wise. Under his rule, Jerusalem became a mighty city.

Israel and Judah

When King Solomon died, his kingdom split. The tribes in the north made their own kingdom. They called it Israel. The tribes in the south formed the kingdom of Judah. Jerusalem was in Judah. The name of the Jewish religion came from the word *Judah*.

HISTORY FACT

The citizens of Israel are sometimes referred to as Israelites. The citizens of Judah were called Jews.

The two kingdoms were in danger! For the next 200 years they fought. They fought each other. They fought the powerful kingdoms that were all around them. These were the Egyptians, the Hittites, the Assyrians, the Babylonians, and the Persians. They all wanted control of the lands around Jerusalem.

At last the fierce neighbors were too strong. In 722 B.C. the Assyrians took over Israel. The Israelites were moved out or taken as slaves. In 587 B.C., Judah fell to a Babylonian people known as Chaldeans. The Babylonian king destroyed Solomon's fine temple in Jerusalem.

So it went. One power after another fought for the city that everyone wanted to control. Jerusalem was right in the middle of things. It came under many different rulers. Today it is more than 2,500 years since the Babylonians destroyed the temple. Very little has changed. Different groups of people have continued to argue over who should control Jerusalem.

Timeline Study

How many years passed before the ancient Israelites returned to Canaan?

The Ancient Israelites: Story of a People

1240 B.C. Ancient Israelites follow Moses out of Egypt	**1200 B.C.** Ancient Israelites return to Canaan		**722 B.C.** Assyrians conquer Israel

2000 B.C.   1500 B.C.   1000 B.C.   500 B.C.

920 B.C. Israel and Judah become separate kingdoms

587 B.C. Babylonians take Jerusalem

Elaborate gates such as this existed in ancient Babylon, which is now in Iraq.

The Babylonians: The Rule of Law

Babylon was the capital city of the Babylonians. It stood on the banks of the Euphrates River. Little remains of it today. There are a few ruins in the middle of some dirt mounds. Archaeologists have been digging through the ruins. They have learned that Babylon was one of the greatest cities of the ancient world. It contained some of the most beautiful temples and palaces to be found anywhere. They were decorated with blue glazed bricks and pictures of mythical beasts. People entered and left the city through huge bronze gates.

Near the center of the city stood the great Tower of Babel. This tower is mentioned in the Bible. Not far from the tower were the Hanging Gardens of Babylon. The gardens were one of the wonders of the ancient world. They were built by a Babylonian king for his

Remember
The Nile, another one of the seven wonders of the world, is in Egypt.

wife. She had been homesick for the beauty of her homeland in the mountains.

Babylon became an important city about 2000 B.C. This was nearly the same time that the Babylonians were destroying the Sumerian civilization. The Babylonians went on to build a large empire in what had been the land of the Sumerians.

✓ Check Your Understanding

Write your answers in complete sentences.

1. Name two important Phoenician inventions.

2. What happened to Solomon's temple in Jerusalem in 587 B.C.?

Great Names in History

HAMMURABI

Hammurabi was one of the greatest kings of Babylonia. He ruled from about 1792 B.C. to 1750 B.C. Hammurabi created a system of laws. It was called the Code of Hammurabi. These laws dealt with almost every aspect of life. There were nearly 300 laws. They applied to marriage and divorce, property and business, taxes, wages, loans, military service, and so forth. For anyone who broke a law, the Code listed harsh punishments in the form of an "eye for an eye" when seeking justice. The Code was created to protect the rights of the individual citizen.

You Decide

How do laws today protect the rights of individual citizens?

In time, the Babylonians were conquered by other civilizations. However, some of the Babylonians' ideas about laws and justice have lasted through the ages. Some are included in our own laws today. The Code of Hammurabi can be seen in the Louvre in Paris, France.

The Babylonian Empire

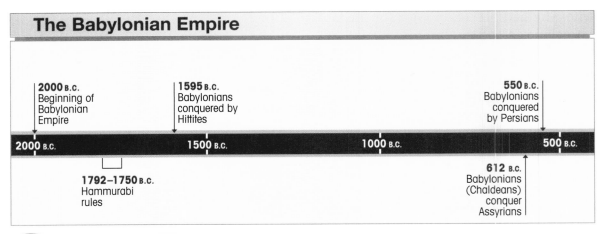

| 2000 B.C. Beginning of Babylonian Empire | 1595 B.C. Babylonians conquered by Hittites | | 550 B.C. Babylonians conquered by Persians |

2000 B.C.   1500 B.C.   1000 B.C.   500 B.C.

1792–1750 B.C. Hammurabi rules

612 B.C. Babylonians (Chaldeans) conquer Assyrians

Timeline Study

How long did the Babylonion Empire Last?

The Hittites

The Hittites were warriors who came to the eastern Mediterranean around 2000 B.C. No one knows for sure where they came from, but they quickly swept through the lands called Anatolia. They found city-states already there. They conquered one after another. By 1650 B.C. the Hittites ruled all of these lands. Today this area is called Turkey.

The Hittites were mighty fighters. They used their might to create an empire. After they conquered Anatolia, they began attacking neighboring lands.

The Secret

Remember
When the Egyptians built the pyramids, they had no machines or iron tools.

The Hittites had a secret that gave them their great power. For hundreds of years, they were the only people who knew how to make iron. Iron was strong. It made better weapons. No other people could beat the Hittite warriors and their iron spears.

The Egyptians looked upon the Hittites with great respect. They thought of the Hittites as the only other great power in the Mediterranean. In about 1258 B.C., after years of fighting with each other, the Hittites and the Egyptians made peace. To help keep the peace, a Hittite princess married an Egyptian pharaoh.

The Hittites and the Egyptians signed an agreement to keep the peace. It became the first recorded peace **treaty.**

In time other people learned the secret of making iron. The Hittites were no longer the strongest. Around 1200 B.C. new people came and attacked the Hittites. They were called the *Sea People*. They came from islands in the Mediterranean. They brought about the end of the Hittite empire.

The Assyrians

The Assyrians were another warrior civilization. At first Assyria was a small kingdom. When the Hittite civilization ended, the Assyrians began to want an empire of their own.

The Assyrians built up a great army. It was the best trained army of the ancient world. The Assyrians sent their army to attack the neighboring kingdoms. As more and more cities were captured, the Assyrian empire grew.

The Assyrians built their capital city on the banks of the Tigris River. The city was named Ashur, after one of the Assyrians' many fierce gods.

Assyrian kings were hard rulers. They made their people pay heavy taxes. Assyrians lived under strict laws. Anyone who broke a law could be cruelly punished. Many law breakers were beaten. Some even had their ears cut off!

A relief, or sculpture, from the Palace of Nineveh shows an Assyrian king.

The Assyrian Army

The Assyrian civilization was a military one. All Assyrian boys knew what their future held. All men had to go into the army. The Assyrians needed soldiers in order to keep their power. The Assyrians were builders as well as fighters. They built military equipment to help them conquer cities. They beat down city walls and gates with their huge machines called siege engines. A city under **siege** from fierce Assyrians stood little chance.

The Assyrians were not kind to the cities that they took. Sometimes they burned the city and killed the people who lived there. Often they took the people as slaves.

Sometimes, after they captured a city, the Assyrians acted as its new rulers. The people from the city had to pay **tribute** to the Assyrian king. If they did not pay the high price, they were punished.

Assyrian Developments

The Assyrian civilization did leave some things behind besides a successful military record. They built fine buildings and statues. They invented siege machines. They also built machines to help lift water from the river into canals.

The Assyrians were among the first people to have a library. The library stored clay tablets with writings from the ancient world.

Even the fierce Assyrians were defeated at last. By 670 B.C. the empire was so big that it was hard to control. It began to break up. In 612 B.C. the Assyrian city of Nineveh was under siege itself. The Assyrian empire came to an end. The Assyrians had been conquered by a new Babylonian people—the Chaldeans.

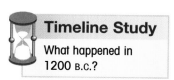

Timeline Study

What happened in 1200 B.C.?

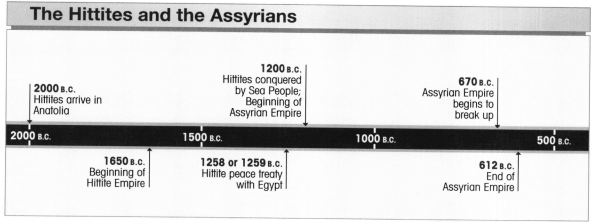

The Hittites and the Assyrians

2000 B.C.
Hittites arrive in Anatolia

1200 B.C.
Hittites conquered by Sea People; Beginning of Assyrian Empire

670 B.C.
Assyrian Empire begins to break up

2000 B.C.   1500 B.C.   1000 B.C.   500 B.C.

1650 B.C.
Beginning of Hittite Empire

1258 or 1259 B.C.
Hittite peace treaty with Egypt

612 B.C.
End of Assyrian Empire

Chapter

5 ▶ Review

Summary

There were many kingdoms around the eastern Mediterranean Sea.
The Phoenicians were sailors and traders. They developed an alphabet much like ours.
The ancient Israelites started the Jewish religion and were among the first to believe in one God.
The ancient Israelites left slavery in Egypt to follow Moses to the Promised Land. They lived by rules called the Ten Commandments.
A Babylonian king, Hammurabi, created one of the earliest systems of laws.
The Hittites and the Assyrians both had warlike civilizations.
The Hittites and the Assyrians were two groups who controlled the eastern Mediterranean world.

nomad

navigate

tribute

conquer

siege

empire

Vocabulary Review

Write a term from the list that matches each definition below.

1. To defeat an enemy in war

2. In war, surrounding a city to prevent necessary items from getting in or out

3. Something a ruler demands from the people

4. A large area of land controlled by a single ruler or government

5. A person who moves from place to place

6. To plan the route of a ship

Chapter Quiz

Write your answers in complete sentences.

1. How was the Phoenician civilization different from other civilizations on the shores of the Mediterranean?

2. How were ancient Israelite beliefs different from those of most other people in the Mediterranean world?

3. Who was King Hammurabi?

4. **Critical Thinking** Why did the Hittites keep a secret of their ability to make iron?

5. **Critical Thinking** Do you think anyone liked living under the harsh rule of the Assyrians? Why or why not?

Using the Timelines

Use the timelines on pages 56, 59, 62, and 65 to answer the questions.

1. What period of time is covered on the four timelines?

2. How many years after the Phoenicians rose to power did Moses lead the ancient Israelites out of Egypt?

Write About History

Complete the following activity.

With a partner, create a timeline that includes some events from all four timelines in this chapter. Give your timeline a title. Then write five questions based on your timeline. Exchange timelines and questions with other partners. Test each other on the questions.

The Great Wall of China is over 4,000 miles. It was built to protect China from invading armies.

Learning Objectives

- Name the social classes of the Indian caste system.
- Explain why Buddhism is called a gentle religion.
- Explain why the Chinese empire remained separated from the rest of the world.
- Tell why Chinese culture did not change for thousands of years.
- Name two early civilizations in the Americas.
- Name three new crops grown in the Americas.

Chapter 6 ▸ Early Civilizations of India, China, and the Americas

Words to Know

class	a group of people according to social rank
caste	a social class in India
reincarnation	a belief that living souls are reborn in a new body
enlightened	knowing the truth
ancestor	a person from whom one is descended
dynasty	a series of rulers who belong to the same family
isolate	to set apart from others
maize	Indian corn
shrine	a place of worship believed to be sacred or holy

Ancient India: The Indus River Valley

One of the world's earliest civilizations grew up around the Indus River. These lands are now known as India and Pakistan. The people, like so many others, settled near the river. They learned to irrigate their fields and to grow crops. They made pottery, jewelry, and statues. They traded goods and ideas with the civilizations of the Fertile Crescent.

One of the main cities in the Indus River Valley was Mohenjo-Daro. Mohenjo-Daro was a neat, well-planned city. It had long, straight main streets. Covered drainage systems ran under the streets. The people built brick houses. They even built apartment houses.

Life was good in Mohenjo-Daro. There were public swimming pools and bath houses. People could cool off on hot Indus Valley days. Brick courtyards circled shaded wells so that people and animals could drink in comfort. Many houses in Mohenjo-Daro had their own indoor wells and tile-lined baths. Wheat and date palms grew on farms outside the city.

Mohenjo-Daro stood peacefully for close to 1,000 years. Then, around 1500 B.C., the city was attacked. People from the north, the Aryans, swooped down on Mohenjo-Daro. The Aryans showed no mercy. They ran through the streets of Mohenjo-Daro killing most of the people.

The Indus River Valley

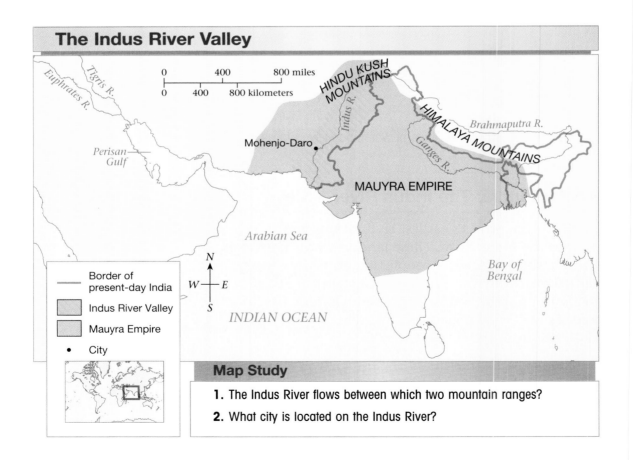

Border of present-day India

Indus River Valley

Mauyra Empire

• City

Map Study

1. The Indus River flows between which two mountain ranges?

2. What city is located on the Indus River?

The Aryans believed that they were born to conquer and control. The word *Aryan* meant *nobleman* or *owner of land*. The Aryans soon controlled all of the Indus River Valley.

The Aryans were fierce conquerors. However, they also brought new ideas. They became known for making beautiful cloth decorated with gold and silver. They also became known for their skilled doctors and mathematicians.

India's Caste System

The Aryans' religion was based on the idea that some people are born "better" than others. Their religion developed into the Hindu religion. People who believe in Hinduism worship many gods. These gods, or divinities, form one universal spirit called *Brahman*. The three most important divinities are *Brahma*, the creator of the universe, *Vishnu*, its preserver, and *Shiva*, its destroyer.

The Aryans divided all people into four social classes, or **castes**. The highest caste consisted of priests and scholars. Rulers and warriors were the next in rank, followed by craftworkers, merchants, and farmers. Unskilled workers made up the lowest caste.

The Aryans called the people they conquered *outcastes* or *untouchables*. The outcastes had no place in society. Any Aryan who married one of the conquered people would also become an outcaste.

Caste laws were strict. A person born into a certain caste would always stay there. No one could ever rise to a higher caste during his or her life. Hindus, however, believed in the rebirth of the soul, or **reincarnation.** When the body dies, the soul may be reborn in either an animal or a human being. If a person obeyed all the rules of Hinduism, that person would be born into a higher caste in his or her next life.

The Aryans conquered the Indus Valley first. Then some of their tribes moved on to the east and to the south. They conquered one kingdom after another. The people who had been living there were forced to flee farther south. The Aryan tribes settled down in the lands that they conquered. They formed a number of city-states. Each one was ruled by a *raja* or prince, who had highly trained armies to protect the lands.

Buddha

The man who would one day be called Buddha was born about 563 B.C., long before Jesus or Muhammad. He was the son of a wealthy Hindu in India. His father was a raja. Therefore, the boy, Siddhartha Gautama, also was considered a prince. His life should have been one of riches and plenty. Instead, Gautama chose a different path.

Buddha, the "enlightened one," had many followers.

He saw many of his people living in poverty and sorrow. He saw beggars in the streets. Gautama felt sorry for the unhappy people. Human life was full of suffering. The rich had so much; the poor had so little.

When he was a young man, Gautama gave up his own wealth. He left his father's palace and went to live in the forest. For about six years he lived simply, wandering around India. He spent his time thinking about how life could be better for humanity.

It is said that the truth came to Gautama one day as he sat under a fig tree. "The sorrows of the world are caused by selfishness," Gautama decided. If people could put aside their desire for riches, Gautama thought, the world would be a better place. So he developed a new religion, Buddhism, which is based on brotherly love. Gautama was called Buddha, which means the "**enlightened** one."

The Buddhist Religion

The Buddhist religion is known as a "gentle" religion. It teaches that the sacred life is found in unselfishness. People who get rid of all greed and selfishness will reach a state of mind known as *nirvana*. Like Hindus, Buddhists also believe in reincarnation. They believe that living beings, including animals, are reborn in another form after death. They see life as a continuing cycle of death and rebirth. A person can only break the cycle of death and suffering by reaching nirvana. Buddhists hope to reach nirvana someday. It is their idea of heaven.

In 321 B.C., a new empire was created in northern India. It was called the Maurya Empire. The third Maurya emperor was named Asoka. Asoka's rule began in about 268 B.C. He followed Buddha's teachings about brotherly love. Asoka made Buddhism the state religion. He taught that all people and animals were to be loved.

You Decide

Do you think that Asoka was a wise ruler? Why or why not?

Buddha's teachings were very different for the Indians. They were accustomed to Hindu ways. However, the Hindu caste system weakened during Asoka's rule. New laws treated all people more equally.

India's Maurya Empire came to an end in about 185 B.C. Then one foreign land after another invaded India. Most Indians went back to the Hindu religion. Buddhism, however, had spread. Followers of Buddha carried their ideas to China, Japan, and other parts of Asia. Beautiful Buddhist temples and pagodas are still standing today. They show that the gentle religion is still an important part of Asia's culture.

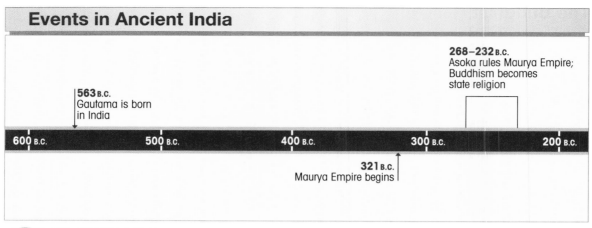

Events in Ancient India

563 B.C.
Gautama is born
in India

268–232 B.C.
Asoka rules Maurya Empire;
Buddhism becomes
state religion

600 B.C.   500 B.C.   400 B.C.   300 B.C.   200 B.C.

321 B.C.
Maurya Empire begins

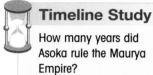

Timeline Study

How many years did
Asoka rule the Maurya
Empire?

China: The Huang He Valley

They called themselves the *Black-haired People*. They
lived in the valley of the Huang He, or Yellow River, in
China. Their civilization grew up apart from the rest of
the world. Steep mountains, wide deserts, and deep seas
circled their lands. Northern China and the people of the
Huang He Valley were cut off from other civilizations.

Most of the people in the Huang He Valley were
farmers. They fought floods that were so terrible that
the Huang He became known as "China's Sorrow."

They dug pitlike houses in the ground and wove
roofs of grass. Their kings lived in palaces made of
wood and mud.

In 1700 B.C. these early Chinese learned to write.
They cut letters, or characters, into animal bones. They
kept a record of their own history. It is one of the
world's oldest written histories.

The people of the Huang He Valley made fine cloth.
They raised silkworms. They carefully unwound the
long, thin threads that the silkworms spun. They wove
the threads into silk cloth.

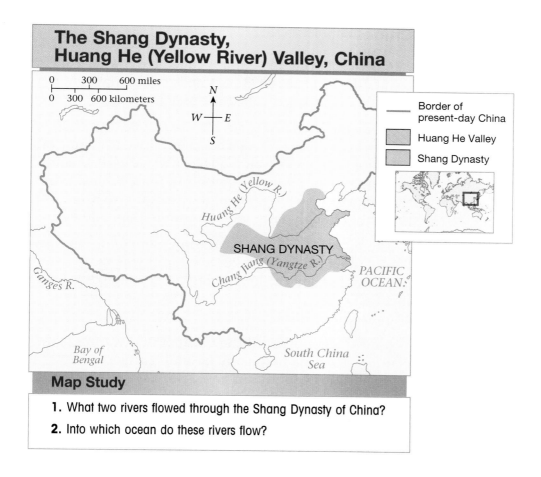

The Shang Dynasty, Huang He (Yellow River) Valley, China

0   300   600 miles

0   300   600 kilometers

N
W — E
S

Border of present-day China

Huang He Valley

Shang Dynasty

Huang He (*Yellow R.*)

SHANG DYNASTY

Chang Jiang (*Yangtze R.*)

PACIFIC OCEAN

Ganges R.

Bay of Bengal

South China Sea

Map Study

1. What two rivers flowed through the Shang Dynasty of China?

2. Into which ocean do these rivers flow?

The Chinese had a special feeling for their **ancestors.** They also showed honor toward their homes, their families, and their land. There were many rules of courtesy in the Chinese culture. Those rules made it possible for large families to live together happily.

The Chinese culture did not change for many thousands of years. This is because people honored the ways of their ancestors. Also, the land was cut off from the rest of the world.

Chinese Dynasties

A period of rule in China is called a **dynasty**. For about 500 years Shang kings ruled the Huang He Valley. This period is called the Shang dynasty.

Around 1028 B.C. a more warlike people, the Zhou came to power. The Zhou leaders developed systems of irrigation and flood control. They also extended their rule southward. Chinese civilization now reached from the Huang He to the Chang Jiang, or Yangtze River. The powerful Zhou dynasty lasted for more than 750 years.

The name *China* may have come from Qin. The Qin family ruled China from 221 B.C. until 206 B.C. This period was called the Qin dynasty. Shi Huangdi was the first Qin emperor. His empire was the first Chinese empire with a strong central government.

Shi Huangdi planned the Great Wall of China. The country of China had many natural barriers to keep foreigners out. Mountains and deserts lay all around. The only border that could be easily crossed was to the north. Enemies crossed this northern border to raid Chinese farms. The Chinese of an earlier period had also tried to protect the border. Short walls had been built by the Zhou dynasty. Shi Huangdi decided to connect these walls. He wanted to build one great stone wall. Work on the wall continued on and off until around A.D. 1600.

The Great Wall of China is over 4,000 miles long, the longest structure ever built! The Great Wall is 25 feet high and about 15 feet wide at the top. The wall once had 2,500 watchtowers. It helped to protect the northern borders from invaders, especially those on horseback. It also further **isolated** China from the rest of the world.

HISTORY FACT

The Great Wall of China was built to prevent people from entering China. Another famous wall—the Berlin Wall— was built by East Germany in 1961 to prevent people from *leaving* the country. The Berlin Wall was torn down in 1989.

Great names in History

CONFUCIUS

Confucius was born in 551 B.C. For more than 2,000 years his ideas were the single strongest influence on Chinese life. Confucius gave people rules to live by. He was most interested in how people treated each other.

"Never do to others what you would not like them to do to you," Confucius taught. He taught that family life was most important. In China large family groups lived together. Grandparents, parents, and children usually shared the same house. Therefore, if family members loved and honored each other, the family would enjoy good fortune. Old people were honored. Ancestors were respected. Respect for the ways of the ancestors kept Chinese culture from changing.

Confucius prized scholarship. Only well-educated people could be government officials. The greatest honor came to a family if a son became a scholar. Then he could study to take the government exams. A young man who passed the exams could become an official.

For centuries in China, people had to take tests to hold government jobs. China had the world's first civil service system.

Shi Huangdi had planned a wall that would last for thousands of years. Unfortunately, the Qin dynasty only lasted a few years. It was expensive to build the wall. So Shi Huangdi forced people to pay very high taxes. Many people began to hate the Qin dynasty. Soon after the emperor died in 210 B.C., a civil war broke out. The Qin dynasty quickly collapsed. By 206 B.C. the Han dynasty had gained control of China.

Write your answers in complete sentences.

1. What are the classes of the Indian caste system?

2. Why did India's young prince Gautama give up his wealth and go to live in India's forests?

3. Name the three most important things that Confucius taught the Chinese people.

The Americas

There were faraway lands that the people of the Middle East and Asia knew nothing about. For the most part, these lands were wild, thick woods and deep rain forests. They were lands that would one day be known as North and South America.

Native Americans lived in the Americas. Many Native Americans believe that their people have always lived there. Many scientists believe that Native Americans first came from Asia. They say that Native Americans traveled across a bridge of land and ice at the Bering Strait. Such a land bridge would have stretched 56 miles between Asia and Alaska. No trace of a land bridge exists now.

Why would these people have crossed the land bridge? Perhaps they were following animal herds. Then, over thousands of years, they kept on traveling south. Some stayed in North America. Others continued on to Central and South America.

For a long time, the people hunted and fished for their food. Then farming settlements began to spring up. This took place about 5,000 years after the people of

You Decide

Nobody knows for sure that Native Americans migrated to North America over a land bridge. What do you think? Why?

Possible Route to the Americas

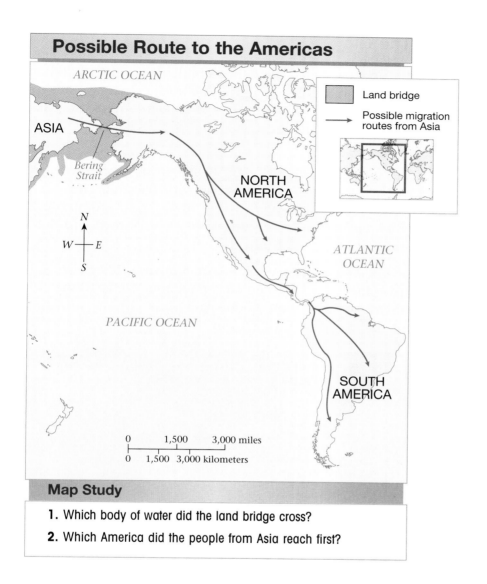

Land bridge

Possible migration routes from Asia

ARCTIC OCEAN

ASIA

Bering Strait

NORTH AMERICA

ATLANTIC OCEAN

N
W—E
S

PACIFIC OCEAN

SOUTH AMERICA

0   1,500   3,000 miles

0   1,500   3,000 kilometers

Map Study

1. Which body of water did the land bridge cross?
2. Which America did the people from Asia reach first?

the Middle East and Asia began farming. The new lands produced new crops. Farmers grew **maize**, or Indian corn. They grew squash and tomatoes and beans.

South American farmers grew cotton as early as 3000 B.C. They raised herds of tall, woolly animals called llamas. They wove the llama wool into beautiful cloth.

The Olmecs

A people called the Olmecs built what might have been the first real city in the Americas. Their city was in Mexico, just west of the Gulf of Mexico. Archaeologists have discovered Olmec jade and pottery dating back to 1200 B.C.

The Olmecs carved giant heads out of stone. Some of their carvings are more than nine feet tall. The Olmecs also built **shrines** atop high mounds of earth. The Olmecs did an amazing job. They worked without metal tools and without the wheel.

The Olmecs had a system of counting. They also invented a simple calendar. The Olmec civilization lasted for more than 1,000 years.

Remember
Historians believe the Sumerians first used the wheel in 3000 B.C. on their chariots.

The Maya temple is in Chichén Itzá, Mexico.

The Maya

Just as the Olmec civilization ended, the Maya arose. The Maya civilization began in southern Mexico and Central America. The Maya cleared rain forests and built towns. They built temples to the gods of rain and of earth.

The Maya used what the Olmecs had learned. They studied the Olmec calendar. Then they watched the sun, the moon, and the stars. They made their own calendar. It showed many feast days set aside to honor their gods. The Maya civilization was strongest from about 250 B.C. until A.D. 800.

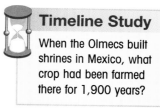

Timeline Study

When the Olmecs built shrines in Mexico, what crop had been farmed there for 1,900 years?

Events in Ancient China and the Americas

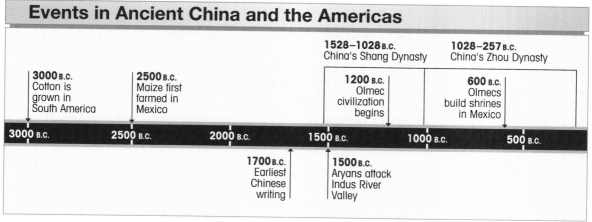

1528–1028 B.C.
China's Shang Dynasty

1028–257 B.C.
China's Zhou Dynasty

3000 B.C.
Cotton is grown in South America

2500 B.C.
Maize first farmed in Mexico

1200 B.C.
Olmec civilization begins

600 B.C.
Olmecs build shrines in Mexico

3000 B.C. 2500 B.C. 2000 B.C. 1500 B.C. 1000 B.C. 500 B.C.

1700 B.C.
Earliest Chinese writing

1500 B.C.
Aryans attack Indus River Valley

Chapter
6 ▷ Review

Summary

An early civilization developed along the Indus River Valley in what is now India and Pakistan.
The Aryans brought a caste system to India. The Aryans' religion developed into the Hindu religion.
An early Chinese civilization grew up along the Huang He, or Yellow River.
Native Americans possibly crossed a land bridge from Asia to the North American continent.
The Olmecs of Mexico were one of the earliest civilizations in the Americas.
The Maya built cities in southern Mexico and Central America.

Vocabulary Review

Write *true* or *false*. If a statement is false, change the underlined term to make it true.

1. All people are descended from their <u>ancestors</u>.

2. An <u>enlightened</u> person knows the truth.

3. A social class in India is called a <u>dynasty</u>.

4. A <u>shrine</u> is a place of worship.

5. According to the belief of <u>reincarnation</u>, a person who dies is reborn.

6. The Shang kings were a <u>caste</u>.

Chapter Quiz

Write your answers in complete sentences.

1. What did the Aryans believe about the people they conquered?

2. Why is Buddhism known as a gentle religion?

3. What helped family members live together happily in China?

4. **Critical Thinking** Was is good or bad for China to be isolated for a long time?

5. **Critical Thinking** How were the Olmecs and the Maya civilizations like ancient civilizations in India and China?

Using the Timelines

Use the timelines on pages 74 and 81 to answer the questions.

1. Which was grown first in the Americas, cotton or maize?

2. How many years passed between the time the Olmecs built their shrines in the Americas and Gautama was born in India?

Write About History

Complete the following activity.

Form groups of three or four. Create a guidebook to the most interesting structures around the world. You might begin with the Great Wall of China or the Great Pyramid of Egypt. Ask classmates to name places they have been to or know about. Do some further research. Arrange your guidebook in some kind of order, such as alphabetical or geographical.

Unit 2 **Review**

Comprehension Check
Write your answers in complete sentences.

1. How did Sumerians farm the land?

2. What did the Sumerians use for money?

3. How did the Egyptian pharaohs pay for their rich way of life?

4. What did archaeologists find in tombs of the pharaohs?

5. How did purple become a royal color?

6. What was the "Promised Land"?

7. Why was the Huang He, or Yellow River, known as "China's sorrow"?

8. What is the longest structure ever built?

9. How might Asians have first traveled to North America?

10. What were four Native American crops?

Writing an Essay
Choose one of the essay topics below. Write your answer on a separate sheet of paper.

1. Describe daily life in Sumer.

2. Explain why archaeologists have been able to learn so much about ancient Egypt.

3. Describe Babylon, the capital of Babylonia.

4. Discuss the beliefs about ancestors in China.

Group Activity
Form a group of three or four students. Discuss the inventions of ancient civilizations. Then make a giant timeline of these inventions.

History in Your Life
The people of ancient times had many inventions and ideas. For example, writing was invented. The idea of one God was formed. The belief in the rule of law began. What idea or invention from ancient times affects your life the most?

Unit 3 ▷ The Origins of Western Civilization: Greece and Rome

The ancient Greeks built the Parthenon on a hill high above the city of Athens.

Learning Objectives

- Contrast two ways that Greek city-states were governed.
- Compare life in Sparta and in Athens.
- Name two Greek gods or goddesses.
- Explain the reason for the name "Golden Age."
- Name three Greek thinkers.
- Explain how democracy developed in Athens.

Chapter 7 · Greek City-States and the Golden Age

Words to Know	
tyrant	a ruler who has complete power
democracy	a government that gives the people the ruling power
myth	a story, often about gods or goddesses, that is handed down through the years and is sometimes used to explain natural events
citizen	a person who has certain rights and duties because he or she lives in a particular city or town
revolt	to rise up against a government; to refuse to obey the people in charge
constitution	the basic laws and rules of a government
jury	a group of people who listen to the facts and decide if a person on trial is guilty or not guilty
plague	a deadly disease that spreads quickly
athlete	a person trained to take part in competitive sports. The ancient Greek word *athlete* means "one who tries to win a prize in a contest."

The Greeks were people with ideas. Greek thinkers asked questions about everything. They wanted to learn as much about their world as they could.

Most early civilizations were mainly farming societies. The Greek civilization, however, was different. Greece is a very rocky land with many mountains. Much of Greece made poor farmland. The Greeks could not grow much wheat or other grains. Instead, they raised grapevines and olive trees. Greece is surrounded by the sea on almost every side. The Greeks took to the sea and became traders.

Ancient Greece

MACEDONIA

Mt. Olympus ▲

Aegean Sea

LYDIA

Marathon

Athens

Olympia

Sparta

N
W — E
S

Crete

Mediterranean Sea

Ancient Greece
• City
▲ Mountain peak

0   100   200 miles
0   100   200 kilometers

EGYPT

Map Study

1. What are three Greek cities on the map?

2. Greece is surrounded by which two bodies of water?

Remember

Like the Phoenicians, the Greeks were also sailors and traders.

The Aegean and the Mediterranean seas made perfect travel lanes. The Greeks traded with most of the Mediterranean world. Greek traders set up colonies in the lands they visited. Greek culture spread across the seas.

Greek harbors were always busy. The air was filled with sounds. There was the clink of Greek coins and foreign coins. There was the chatter of many different languages as people of the world met. Merchants traded olive oil for wheat. Ships from Egypt unloaded papyrus. Ebony and ivory came in from Africa.

Greek City-States

The earliest people who settled in Greece began to build villages about 1500 B.C. As time passed, the small villages grew into city-states. Through trading, the city-states became wealthy. By about 750 B.C. the Greeks had begun to build colonies in other areas of the Mediterranean. Some Greeks settled on the Greek islands. Many others, however, traveled as far as southern Italy, France, Spain, and Portugal. They built cities there. Naples, Syracuse, and Marseilles began as Greek cities. Cities were also built in western Turkey and on the shores of the Black Sea.

On the Greek mainland, the city-states were becoming more powerful. The city-states were separated from each other by rugged mountain ranges. For this reason there was limited contact between the city-states. Each one developed in its own way.

Each city-state had its own government. Each had its own ideas about the way people should live. Some of the city-states were ruled by a **tyrant**, a single powerful person. Some of the tyrants were cruel and unjust, while others ruled fairly. The first **democracy** developed in the city-state. There, citizens could vote and have a say in government.

Because the city-states were so different from each other, they often fought among themselves. Tyrants with big ideas would decide that the time had come to expand their rule. They would make plans to attack a nearby city-state. They might convince other city-states to join them. There was a constantly shifting pattern of friendship and hostility between the different city-states. This was a very unstable political situation. It would later lead to a major war between two of the largest city-states, Athens and Sparta.

The Acropolis

Each city-state was made up of a city circled by villages and farms. The farms provided food for the citizens. The city offered protection from invaders.

The Greeks usually built their city-states near a high hill. The hill was called the Acropolis. On that hill, they built special buildings, such as temples and theaters.

The people who lived in Athens built a beautiful temple atop their Acropolis. It was built to honor the goddess Athena. The temple was called the Parthenon.

Athens and Sparta

Athens and Sparta were the most powerful Greek city-states. Their citizens spoke the same language. They believed in the same gods. They told **myths** or stories about their gods and goddesses. However, life in Athens was very different from life in Sparta.

The Spartans lived in a military society. Sparta's government was led by a small group of men. They were most interested in keeping Sparta a great military power. Spartan children belonged to the state. A healthy boy was turned over to the government at the age of seven. He was raised to be a soldier. He was taught to fight and to stand up under pain. He had to obey orders without question. Soldiers defeated in battle were not allowed to return home.

If a baby boy were born with something wrong, he might be left on a hillside to die. The Spartans only wanted boys who could grow up to be soldiers. Spartans had little use for girls. Girls and women were seldom seen in public. They kept to their houses. The Spartans were great warriors. However, they left the world little in the way of ideas or art or music.

HISTORY FACT

Today we use the word "spartan" to mean "harsh" or "strict." The word comes from the Spartans of ancient Greece.

The Greeks carved outdoor theaters into hillsides.

The Spartans, like most of the Mediterranean peoples, kept slaves. Most of the work in the city was done by slave labor. The Spartan army was often kept busy fighting other city-states. At other times it had the job of keeping rebel slaves in line.

Although life was harsh in Sparta, things were very different in Athens. The Athenians gave less thought to warfare. They were more interested in enjoying life.

Athens was a wealthy city. The Athenians decided that their wealth gave them more time to enjoy the beauties of life. They wanted their city to be glorious. They built the Parthenon. Their marble statues show the human body in its ideal form. The Athenians put on plays in huge outdoor theaters. For the first time, plays were written about how people thought and acted. Some of these plays are still performed today.

The Athenians took time to ask questions about their world. Great teachers, like Socrates, led the Greeks to ask, "What makes people good? What makes people evil?" "Always ask questions," Socrates taught. So the Greeks questioned, and they learned.

You Decide

It is wrong for one person to own another. Why do you think slavery has existed, even though it is wrong?

Some Greeks even questioned slavery. That slavery might be wrong was a brand new idea. Most of the ancient world used slaves as laborers. In Athens, too, work was done by slaves. A few Athenian thinkers, however, were possibly the first to ask, "Is it right for people to own other people? Is it right to force a person to labor for another?"

Learn More About It

GREEK RELIGION

The Greeks believed that people were very important. They celebrated the human mind and the human body. Therefore, their gods were much like humans. The Greeks worshipped many gods and goddesses. They gave each one a name and a humanlike form and personality. The gods and goddesses, according to the Greek storytellers, lived on top of Mount Olympus. This is the highest mountain in Greece. There, they enjoyed life. They laughed and they argued just as humans do. They played tricks on each other and on the humans they ruled.

Zeus was the king of the Greek gods. His wife was Hera, queen of the gods. The Parthenon on the Athenian Acropolis was built to honor Athena. She was the goddess of wisdom and learning.

The Greeks told myths, which explained things in nature. They told of the doings of the gods and goddesses.

Myths were told about jealous and angry gods and goddesses. Some fell in love with humans and others helped humans. Greek myths made exciting stories.

Democracy

In Athens's early years, government was in the hands of landowners. If a man owned land, he was a **citizen.** He had a voice in running the city-state. As the city grew, many merchants and businesspeople, shippers and traders became wealthy. They did not own land, but they wanted a say in city government. They wanted to be citizens. A **revolt** led to a new government. In 508 B.C. this government drew up an Athenian **constitution.** Under the new laws, all free men were citizens. Women and slaves, however, did not have the rights of citizenship.

A citizen had the right to vote. He was also expected to hold office if called upon, sit on a **jury,** and serve in the army. The Athenian democracy was a government "by the people." The problem was that so many of "the people" (women and slaves) were not allowed to be citizens.

✓ **Check Your Understanding**

Write your answers in complete sentences.

1. What are two ways that Greek city-states were governed?

2. Why did Greek city-states often fight with each other?

3. What type of buildings did the Greeks build on the Acropolis?

The Persian Wars

As Greek city-states grew strong and wealthy, another land began to look toward Greece. The Persian Empire under Cyrus the Great had become the strongest military power in the world. In 546 B.C. Persia attacked and conquered the Greek colonies in Lydia. This was along the coast of what is now called Turkey. About 50 years later, the Greeks in Lydia revolted. King Darius I of Persia crushed their uprising. Then he sent his huge army to invade Greece.

In 490 B.C. the Persian armies headed for Athens. On the plain of Marathon, the Athenians beat the mighty Persians! An excited Greek citizen ran 25 miles (about 40 kilometers) to Athens to spread the good news. An Olympic event of today is named after that run from Marathon to Athens.

But the Persians were not ready to give up. Darius's son, Xerxes, continued the war. About ten years later, Xerxes led an even stronger force into Greece. The Greek city-states put aside their quarrels to fight the common enemy. Xerxes's navy attacked. The Greeks fought the Persian invaders long and hard. Yet the Persians were too strong. Xerxes's men attacked the city of Athens next. In 480 B.C. they destroyed the Parthenon and burned much of the beautiful city.

Xerxes left Athens thinking that he had won the war. He was in for a surprise, however. His men met the Athenian navy off the harbor of Salamis. There was a great sea battle. The Persians were defeated. The Greeks sent the Persians back across the Aegean Sea. Greece was then left to enjoy a time of peace.

You Decide

If the Persians had conquered Greece, our lives today might be very different. Why do you think this is so?

The Golden Age

The peace following the Persian Wars lasted for about 50 years. During that time, Athens grew in power and strength. It became the greatest city-state in Greece.

Athens collected money from the other city-states. The Athenians insisted that their navy must be kept strong in order to protect all of Greece.

A great Athenian leader named Pericles rose to power in 461 B.C. Pericles helped the Athenians continue their democratic government. He used some of the money collected from other city-states to rebuild the Parthenon.

Athens flowered with Pericles as its leader. It was a time known as the *Age of Pericles,* or the *Golden Age of Athens.* The Athenians, at peace now, had time to study science and geography. They wrote their greatest plays and created their finest statues.

Athens of the Golden Age was one of the most beautiful cities in the world. Many other Greek city-states followed the Athenians' way of life and their ideas of democracy.

Sparta, however, continued as a military state. The Spartans did not like the way Athens was building and growing. They were also angry that Athens had been collecting money from the rest of Greece.

The Peloponnesian War

Peace ended in 431 B.C., when Sparta led some of the other city-states against Athens. Sparta was a land power with a strong army. Athens was a sea power. Most of its strength was in its navy. Both cities fought for control of Greece. The war between Athens and Sparta was called the Peloponnesian War. It was named after the Peloponnesus, the part of Greece in which Sparta was located. This war went on for 27 years!

The Spartans tried to cut off supplies to Athens to starve the people. The Athenians held on even though the Spartans were among the world's best fighters.

Then a terrible **plague** broke out in the city of Athens. One-fourth of the Athenian people died during the plague. Their leader, Pericles, was among those who died.

Athens could no longer hold out against Sparta. In 404 B.C., Athens surrendered to Sparta.

Gifts from the Greeks

The Doric, Ionic, and Corinthian columns are examples of classical Greek architecture.

Greek thought and Greek works are very much a part of life today. Greek ideas in building can be seen in modern buildings. Greek statues still influence today's artists. The style of art and architecture the Greeks developed is called the "classical" style.

Today's students still read the works of Greek thinkers like Socrates, Plato, and Aristotle. "Know yourself," the great teachers said. "Ask questions. Search for the truth."

The Greeks were the first people to ask, "What is the world made of? Why is it the way it is?" They developed ideas about the sun, the Earth, and the stars.

"The Earth is round," Eratosthenes said. "The Earth moves around the sun," Aristarchus said. Euclid and Pythagoras helped invent geometry.

We can also thank the Greeks for a model of a democracy. "Our government is called a democracy because power is in the hands of the whole people," said the Athenian leader Pericles.

Greek words and ideas show up in our own language. *Astronomy, biology, geography,* and *geology* are all taken from the Greek language. So are the words *music, theater, drama, comedy,* and *tragedy*.

The word **athlete** comes from the Greeks, too. Our Olympic Games are athletic contests. They are modeled after those played by Greek athletes so long ago.

The first known Olympic games took place in 776 B.C. Early Olympic games were held to honor the gods and goddesses. They were held every four years at the temple of Zeus in Olympia. All wars in Greece had to stop when it was time for the games. The athletes came from Athens and Sparta and all the other city-states.

The earliest Olympic games were just foot races. Later the Greeks added events such as boxing, wrestling, jumping, discus throwing, and chariot racing.

Today, just as in early Greece, it is a great honor to win an Olympic event. Winners get medals of gold, silver, and bronze. In ancient Greece the winners were crowned with a circle of laurel leaves. The athletes brought glory to their city-state and themselves.

The Greek leader Pericles saw the greatness of Greece in the Golden Age.

"Mighty indeed are the marks and monuments of our empire . . . ," Pericles said. "Future ages will wonder at us."

In the 2000 Olympics, Cathy Freeman of Australia held the Olympic torch.

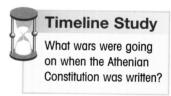

Timeline Study

What wars were going on when the Athenian Constitution was written?

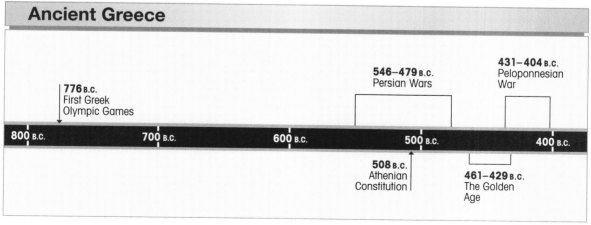

Ancient Greece

776 B.C.
First Greek
Olympic Games

546–479 B.C.
Persian Wars

431–404 B.C.
Peloponnesian War

800 B.C.   **700** B.C.   **600** B.C.   **500** B.C.   **400** B.C.

508 B.C.
Athenian Constitution

461–429 B.C.
The Golden Age

Summary

Most of Greece's wealth came from trading rather than from farming.
Greece was divided into city-states, each one with its own government.
Athens and Sparta were two powerful city-states. Athens was a democracy. Sparta had a military government.
The Greeks worshipped many humanlike gods and goddesses.
The Greeks fought the Persians, and they drove the Persian army away.
Quarrels between Athens and Sparta turned into the Peloponnesian War. Sparta won.
The Greeks were great thinkers. Because they questioned their world, they learned.

tyrant
democracy
myth
citizen
constitution
jury

Vocabulary Review

Complete each sentence with a term from the list.

1. Some Greek city-states were ruled by a powerful ruler called a ____.

2. The Greeks told ____ about their gods and goddesses.

3. Athens developed a form of ____, or rule of the people.

4. In Athens, a woman was not a ____.

5. A basic set of rules and laws is a ____.

6. A ____ is a group of people who decide whether a person has disobeyed the law.

Chapter Quiz

Write your answers in complete sentences.

1. Why did Greek culture spread?

2. How were the Greek gods and goddesses like human beings?

3. How did democracy develop in Athens?

4. **Critical Thinking** Would you rather have lived in Sparta or in Athens? Give at least two reasons why.

5. **Critical Thinking** Why is the period after the Persian Wars called the Golden Age of Athens?

Using the Timeline

Use the timeline on page 97 to answer the questions.

1. When were the first Olympic Games?

2. What came after the Golden Age?

Write About History

Complete one of the following activities.

1. Form a group of three or four. Make a poster about the Olympics. Feature your group's favorite Olympic stars.

2. Work with a partner to create an illustrated timeline of the history of the Olympics.

Alexander was king of Macedonia at age 20. By the time he died at age 33, he expanded his empire and the whole world had heard of him.

Learning Objectives

- Explain how King Philip II of Macedonia became ruler of Greece.
- Tell why Alexander was called the Great Conqueror.
- Locate Alexander's empire on a map.
- Tell why Alexander made Babylon the capital of his empire.
- Describe what happened to Alexander's empire after his death.

Chapter 8 ▸ Alexander the Great

Words to Know

assassinate	to murder a leader or other important person
campaign	a series of battles all aimed at one military end
ambition	the drive to become powerful, successful, or famous
conqueror	a person who gains control by winning a war
general	a high-ranking military officer

King Philip of Macedonia

The Peloponnesian War was over. The Greek city-states were now under Sparta's rule. They still argued with each other, however.

To the north was a land called Macedonia. It was ruled by a king named Philip II. Macedonia had always been poor. Things changed, however, when Philip became king. Philip saw to it that Macedonians farmed their good soil. He sent out Macedonian traders. He built new roads. King Philip II had ideas.

Philip built up the Macedonian army. He built war machinery. He taught his men new ways of fighting. Philip soon had a strong army of foot soldiers and soldiers on horseback.

King Philip's plan was to conquer the great Persian Empire. To do that, Philip needed military strength. He needed more strength than he had with only Macedonia behind him. Philip wanted the power of all the Greek armies.

King Philip told some of the nearby city-states about his plan. They agreed to join him. Philip, however, needed more power. He needed the largest city-states, Athens and Thebes, behind him. For that reason he used all his military know-how along with his well-trained men and their fine machinery. With this support Philip conquered Athens and Thebes.

Soon all of Greece fell under Macedonian control—all except Sparta, that is. Philip never conquered Sparta.

Now Philip was ready for war with the Persians. Yet King Philip II would never lead his men into Persia. By now he had made enemies. There was a plot to **assassinate** him. Before he could begin his **campaign** against Persia, he was killed.

You Decide

Philip never conquered Sparta. What do you think stopped him?

Philip's Son

Philip had a son, Alexander. Alexander was not an ordinary boy. From his father, Alexander inherited **ambition** and a love of power. Philip taught his son all about warfare and leadership. Alexander's mother, Olympias, was very smart and hot-tempered. Alexander, too, was bright and very easily angered.

As a boy, Alexander seemed almost fearless. Stories tell of the young Prince Alexander taming a certain horse. No other person in the kingdom could ride it. Alexander named that horse Bucephalus. Bucephalus would carry Alexander across an empire!

King Philip always thought highly of the Greek way of life and of Greek ideas. His son, Alexander, was to have the best of teachers—the Greek thinker, Aristotle. At age 14, Alexander began his lessons.

Aristotle taught Alexander to love Greek stories of heroes and adventure. He taught the boy about far-off lands and about other cultures. Aristotle saw to it that Alexander took part in sports, too.

By the time Alexander was 18, he was able to take a command in his father's army. Alexander was 20 when

Aristotle was a great thinker and teacher.

his father was killed. Now he was ready to take over as king of Macedonia and to become a **conqueror.**

Alexander, the Great Conqueror

Philip II had planned to conquer an empire. Greece would be the center of that empire. Now that job fell to his son Alexander.

Since birth, Alexander had been raised to be a ruler and a warrior. He was ready for the job. Alexander and the Macedonian army headed for Persia.

The next two years saw Alexander and his men crossing the Middle East. They conquered one land after another. Then in 334 B.C. Alexander began his campaign against Persia. In 333 B.C. Alexander did battle with the king of the Persian Empire, Darius III. Alexander won the battle, but King Darius escaped.

On through the Persian Empire, on to Syria, swept the conquering Macedonians. They attacked the great Phoenician city of Tyre. Alexander ordered his men to build a raised road over the sea to reach the city. The battle at Tyre was one of his greatest military victories.

Alexander in Egypt

After taking over Phoenicia, Alexander moved south, toward Egypt. Alexander's army easily took Egypt.

The Egyptians had been under harsh Persian rule. They were glad to have Alexander as their new ruler. Some Egyptians even hailed Alexander as the son of an Egyptian god.

Alexander built a city on the Mediterranean coast of Egypt. He named it after himself, like many other cities he had built. Egypt's *Alexandria* became the most famous of the Alexandrias.

One of Alexander's **generals** was named Ptolemy. Alexander chose him to rule Egypt. Ptolemy's family would rule Egypt for 300 years.

✓Check Your Understanding

Write your answers in complete sentences.

1. What did King Philip II of Macedonia need in order to conquer the Persian Empire?

2. How did Philip become ruler of Greece?

3. Why did Philip choose a Greek teacher for young Alexander?

Learn More About It

ALEXANDRIA

Alexander drew up plans for building the city of Alexandria in Egypt in 332 B.C. The Ptolemies continued to carry out Alexander's plan after his death. The city grew rapidly. It became one of the largest and most important cities of the ancient world. Within 200 years after it was founded, more than a million people were living in Alexandria.

It was a beautiful city. Many of its buildings were Greek in style. A giant lighthouse rose 370 feet high. It was built of white marble and was known as one of the wonders of the world. The huge fire at the top of the lighthouse could be seen by sailors 30 miles away.

Alexandria was also famous for its fine schools and its library. The library contained more than 700,000 scrolls. A scroll is a roll of paper or parchment with writing on it. Scrolls were used instead of books. The library of Alexandria was the largest in the world. It became a famous center of learning and culture. The glory of Greece had come to Egypt.

The End of the Persian Empire

Alexander was more interested in conquering than in ruling. Just as with Ptolemy in Egypt, he would set up many more rulers in other lands. When Alexander felt his work in Egypt was done, he moved on. He still wanted the whole world.

In 331 B.C. Alexander met King Darius III of Persia again. Alexander defeated Darius. Once again, however, Darius escaped. Yet Alexander had no more trouble with his old enemy. King Darius was to die that same year, killed by his own men. With Darius gone, Alexander was the ruler of all of the Persian Empire.

The city of Persepolis, in southwestern Persia, was the greatest city of the Persian Empire. Much of the wealth of the empire was stored in the palaces of Persepolis. Alexander and his army easily captured the city. They killed most of the people who lived there. They took the rest as slaves. The Macedonians took all the treasures and then burned the Persian palaces. In 480 B.C. the Persians had burned Athens. Now Alexander had gotten even.

Then Alexander looked east. What was left for him in the world? India would be next.

Alexander in the Valley of the Indus

In 326 B.C. Alexander the Great arrived in India. The Aryan rajas along the Indus River battled the Macedonian soldiers. The Aryans rode great, lumbering war elephants. Yet Alexander's men, riding horseback, were faster. Alexander conquered the Indus River Valley. He wanted to go deeper into India, but his men were tired. Heavy rains had come, and marching was hard. They wanted to go home.

"Back to Greece," the soldiers cried.

"On through India," Alexander demanded.

> **HISTORY FACT**
>
> From the age of 14 to 16, Alexander the Great was taught by Aristotle. He inspired him to be interested in philosophy, medicine, and science.

Alexander's Empire

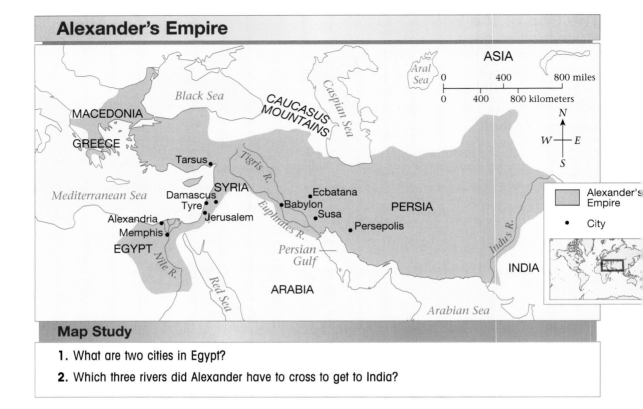

Map Study

1. What are two cities in Egypt?

2. Which three rivers did Alexander have to cross to get to India?

Alexander's armies insisted on turning back. They would go no farther. For that reason, Alexander had to give up his campaign.

The Death of Alexander

Alexander was 30 years old when he conquered the Aryan kingdoms in India. He had been fighting and building his empire for 12 years. In all that time he had never lost a single battle!

Alexander made his father's dreams real. He spread Greek culture and ideas over a large part of the world. Alexander's empire was the largest the ancient world had ever known.

Alexander imagined Europe and Asia as one big country, united under his rule. He wanted to blend the two into one. He chose Babylon as his capital city because it was in the center of his empire. He had plants brought in from one continent and planted on the other. Alexander married an Asian woman. He also rewarded his soldiers if they did the same.

Alexander ruled a giant empire from his palace in Babylon. He had big plans for his empire. Then in 323 B.C. he fell sick. He had a high fever. No medicines of the day could help him. Within a few days, 33-year-old Alexander the Great was dead. His soldiers placed his body in a gold coffin. It was taken to Alexandria in Egypt to be buried.

After his death, Alexander's lands were divided among some of his generals. The great empire was gone forever, split into separate smaller empires.

Yet the man who set out to conquer the world had left his mark. The lands Alexander touched would always show something of Greek style and Greek customs.

Remember
At a much earlier date Hammurabi, a great ruler of Babylon, drew up a code of laws.

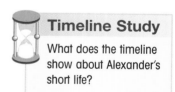

Timeline Study

What does the timeline show about Alexander's short life?

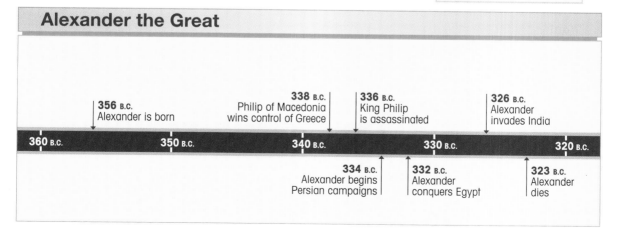

Alexander the Great

356 B.C.
Alexander is born

338 B.C.
Philip of Macedonia wins control of Greece

336 B.C.
King Philip is assassinated

326 B.C.
Alexander invades India

360 B.C.　　350 B.C.　　340 B.C.　　330 B.C.　　320 B.C.

334 B.C.
Alexander begins Persian campaigns

332 B.C.
Alexander conquers Egypt

323 B.C.
Alexander dies

Chapter

8 ▷ Review

Summary

King Philip of Macedonia planned to conquer the Persian Empire.
Because Philip needed all of Greece behind him, he first conquered the Greek city-states (except Sparta).
King Philip was assassinated, and his son Alexander led the Macedonian armies into Persia.
Alexander set out to conquer the world.
Alexander conquered Persia and then went on to Egypt and India.
Alexander brought Greek ideas and culture to the lands he conquered.
Alexander died at the age of 33.
Alexander's empire split up after his death.

conqueror
assassinate
campaign
general
ambition

Vocabulary Review

Complete each sentence with a term from the list.

  1. Alexander the Great had the _____ to take over the world.

  2. A _____ takes over people and land by winning a war.

  3. A _____ has a top position in the military.

  4. To win a war, a military leader must plan a _____ of a number of battles.

  5. The people who _____ a leader are murderers.

Chapter Quiz

Write your answers in complete sentences.

1. Why was Alexander called the Great Conqueror?

2. Why did Alexander choose Babylon as the capital of his empire?

3. What happened to Alexander's empire after he died?

4. **Critical Thinking** Why was Aristotle a good teacher for Alexander?

5. **Critical Thinking** What was Alexander's greatest accomplishment? Explain why.

Using the Timeline

Use the timeline on page 107 to answer the questions.

1. How old was Alexander when he began the Persian campaigns?

2. What is the order of the following: the conquest of Egypt, the invasion of India, the Persian campaigns?

Write About History

Complete the following activity.

Write a mini-biography of Alexander the Great. Include basic information, such as birth, accomplishments, death. Include information from this chapter and from other books. In the last paragraph of your biography, express your opinion of Alexander. Tell why you think he was able to do so much during his short life.

This Roman aqueduct was built more than 2,000 years ago to bring water to dry lands.

Learning Objectives

- Describe how the Roman Republic was governed.
- Name some things Julius Caesar did for Rome.
- Name the first Roman emperor and tell what he did.
- Explain why Jesus' teachings appealed to the poor. Tell how the Romans persecuted the Christians.
- Describe how the Emperor Constantine helped the Christian religion grow in Rome.
- Explain why the Roman Empire began to fall.

Chapter 9 | The Rise of Rome

Words to Know

peninsula	a long piece of land almost completely surrounded by water (from the Latin word meaning "almost an island")
republic	a government in which the citizens have the right to elect their representatives to make laws
elect	to choose someone for an office by voting
representative	a person who is chosen to act or speak for others
senate	a governing or lawmaking body
province	a part of a country, with its own local government, much like a state in the United States
governor	a person chosen to run a province or territory
civil war	a war between people who live in the same country
forum	a public square in an ancient Roman city; lawmakers met there
emperor	a person who rules a group of different countries, lands, or peoples
aqueduct	a channel made by humans that carries flowing water over a long distance
crucifixion	the putting to death of someone by nailing or tying that person to a cross
persecute	to treat in a cruel way, to hurt or injure
convert	to change from one religion to another
bishop	a high-ranking church official; from the Latin word that means "overseer"
pope	the head of the Roman Catholic Church

Early Rome

Seven hills rose up along the Tiber River in the center of Italy. Small villages dotted the seven hills. One of those villages was called Rome. It had been built by the Latins in 753 B.C. The Latins, or Romans, were one of several groups of people that had moved down from central Europe. They settled in the Italian **peninsula** around 1000 B.C. Rome was not very important then. However, it would one day grow into a great city. That city would become the center of an empire.

From 750 B.C. to 600 B.C., the little Italian villages were ruled by a series of Roman kings. During those years, the Romans lived in peace. They were mainly farmers and herders. Things changed in about 600 B.C. North of the Tiber River lived a people called the Etruscans. They decided to conquer Rome and the other villages. The Romans did not stand a chance against them.

For about the next 100 years, Rome was ruled by Etruscan kings. The Etruscans had many skills. They built a wall around the city. They drained nearby swamps and laid the first sewer. The Romans even adopted the Etruscan alphabet. Slowly Rome changed from a little farming village into a city-state.

Then, in 509 B.C., the people of Rome rebelled against a very harsh Etruscan king. They took the government of Rome into their own hands and set up a **republic.**

The Roman Republic

In a republic, government is controlled by the people. In a republic, there is no king. Roman citizens **elected** men to make their laws and run their government. Three hundred elected **representatives** met in a **senate.** The Republic was democratic because citizens voted for the people who would represent them. The Roman Republic was a model for our own democratic system of representative government.

The members of the Roman Senate were usually wealthy landowners. Once elected, they held office for life. Some of the Senate members were very old. The people thought them very wise. The word *senate* comes from the Latin word that means *old.*

The early years of the Republic were not peaceful. At first Rome was attacked by armies from other lands. However, Rome grew more and more powerful. After a time, Rome wanted to gain more land.

Roman Warriors

The Romans became skilled soldiers. Every Roman male spent some time in the army. Rome's military power grew. The Romans began battling for more land. By about 270 B.C., Rome had taken over the whole Italian peninsula.

One of Rome's greatest enemies was Carthage. Carthage was on the north coast of Africa. It was a city settled by the Phoenicians. Carthage and Rome quarreled over Mediterranean trade routes.

Rome fought three wars with Carthage. These were called the Punic Wars. The first clash between the two states came in Sicily. They battled for the city of Messina. Rome finally won this war in 241 B.C., after 23 years of fighting!

Over the next 50 years, Carthage grew strong again. Once more, Rome felt threatened. So Rome declared war and sent its army back to Africa. This time, in the final Punic War, the city of Carthage was totally destroyed.

Great Names in History

HANNIBAL

In 218 B.C. a fierce Carthaginian general named Hannibal arrived in Spain. He brought a huge army with him. He led his soldiers over the Pyrenees and the Alps. Many of Hannibal's soldiers rode elephants. The mountains were hard on the huge animals. Many elephants lost their footing on the narrow mountain paths and fell to their deaths. Most of them, however, made it to the Po Valley of Italy. Hannibal was a clever general. He caught the Romans by surprise and beat the Roman army. Thus began the second of the Punic Wars.

For the next 13 years, Hannibal led his army up and down Italy. He won more battles against Roman forces. Nevertheless, little by little the Romans grew stronger. Finally Hannibal was driven out of Italy. Then the Romans invaded Africa and defeated Hannibal's army in 202 B.C.

Hannibal crossed the Alps to invade Rome because he knew the Romans would be surprised.

During the second war between Carthage and Rome, Macedonia had sided with the Carthaginians. Macedonia was still the most powerful state in Greece. After taking Carthage, Rome sent armies into Greece. Roman armies conquered the Greek city-states. They brought Greek treasures back to Rome, introducing Roman citizens to Greek art and style.

Remember
Philip II and Alexander the Great were Macedonians.

The Romans made slaves of the conquered Greeks. Many of the slaves were used as laborers. Some of the Greek captives, however, were very well educated. They became teachers and doctors in Rome. Many Greek slaves found themselves with kind Roman masters, masters who respected them. Some Greeks were able to earn their freedom. Therefore, in many ways, Roman culture was influenced by the Greeks.

By 140 B.C. Rome controlled all of the Mediterranean lands. Citizens of the Republic thought of the Mediterranean Sea as a Roman sea.

The Provinces

Rome conquered many lands. Some of them were very far from the city itself. To make the lands easier to govern, they were divided into sections called **provinces.** Each province was ruled by its own **governor.** Some people in the provinces accepted the Roman rule. Others were not happy with their new rulers. Furthermore they did not like Roman customs.

To keep the people in order, Rome sent large armies to each province. A general was at the head of each of these armies. The soldiers in the provinces were a long way from Rome. They often felt more loyalty to their generals than they did to Rome. The generals became very powerful men.

Sometimes the generals and their armies fought among themselves. The most powerful of the generals was a man named Julius Caesar.

Julius Caesar

Caesar is one of the most famous names in history. Who was Julius Caesar, and why is he so famous?

Julius Caesar was the Roman general in the province of Gaul. Gaul was a land to the northwest of Rome. It would one day be called France. People liked Julius Caesar. His soldiers were very loyal to him. The people of Rome admired his success. He won many battles in Gaul and expanded Roman control. After awhile senators in Rome began to worry about Caesar's popularity. Was Julius Caesar becoming too powerful?

The senate called Caesar back to Rome. "Leave your army in Gaul," the senators ordered. Caesar returned to Rome, but he brought his army with him. It was 49 B.C. The common people welcomed Caesar as a hero. Soon Caesar and his army took control of the Roman government.

Some of the other generals were not happy about this. They challenged Caesar's power. This led to **civil wars**, with one Roman army fighting another.

Julius Caesar

Julius Caesar was always the winner. He won battles in Greece, in Spain, and in North Africa. While fighting in Egypt, Caesar met the beautiful Egyptian princess, Cleopatra. He found time to fall in love with her. He helped her win the throne of Egypt.

By 45 B.C. Caesar controlled the Roman world. The people hailed him as their ruler. For the most part he used his power wisely. He made citizens of many of the people in the provinces. He even allowed some to sit in the Senate. He made sure the governors ruled the provinces fairly. Caesar made more jobs for the people of Rome. He set up colonies where poor Romans could start their own farms.

Caesar even improved the Roman calendar. Borrowing from the Egyptians, he changed it to a system of 365 days in a year. He added an extra day every fourth year, creating "leap year." The new calendar was much better than the old one.

The people of Rome cheered Caesar. They stamped his picture on Roman coins and built a temple in his name. At the Roman **Forum**, Mark Antony offered Caesar the crown of king. Mark Antony was a senator and Caesar's friend. Caesar refused the crown.

You Decide

Julius Caesar named a month after himself. What do you think it was?

Death to Caesar

Many of Rome's leading citizens were worried. It did not help that Caesar had not accepted the crown. They were still afraid he planned to make himself a king and put an end to the Republic.

Some of the Roman senators, led by Brutus and Cassius, plotted to kill Caesar. Many of these men had been Caesar's friends. They did not want to lose the Republic, however. Their first loyalty was to Rome. On March 15, 44 B.C., Julius Caesar was stabbed to death as he entered the Roman Senate.

✓ Check Your Understanding

Write your answers in complete sentences.

1. Why did the Romans think of the Mediterranean Sea as a Roman sea?

2. What are three things that Julius Caesar did for Rome?

3. Who was the Egyptian princess with whom Caesar fell in love?

The Emperor Augustus

Even though Julius Caesar was dead, the days of the Roman Republic were numbered. Most of the people had been happy under Caesar. They wanted a ruler who would continue with Caesar's policies and plans.

Once again there was a struggle for power, and civil wars shook Rome. First Brutus and Cassius fought against Mark Antony and Octavian. Mark Antony and Octavian had remained loyal to Caesar. When Octavian and Mark Antony won, they turned against each other.

Mark Antony fell in love with none other than Egypt's Cleopatra. They were determined to rule Rome together. Yet they were defeated by Octavian. The defeat led Antony and Cleopatra to kill themselves.

Now Octavian ruled all of the Roman world. It was the beginning of a new age for Rome. It was the start of the Roman Empire. Octavian became Rome's first **emperor.**

You Decide

Do you think it is a good idea to allow one person to have complete power? What would happen if that person were not a wise ruler?

An emperor had even more power than a king. To his people, he was only one step below a god. In 27 B.C. the Roman Senate gave Octavian the title of "Augustus." The title meant that he was above all others. He was to be worshipped.

The Roman Senate continued to meet, but the Republic was as dead as Caesar. Augustus chose new senators to make his laws. Augustus, indeed, held complete power.

Under Emperor Augustus the Roman Empire flourished as never before. Augustus ended the civil wars. The time of peace that he brought about was called the *Pax Romana* (Roman Peace).

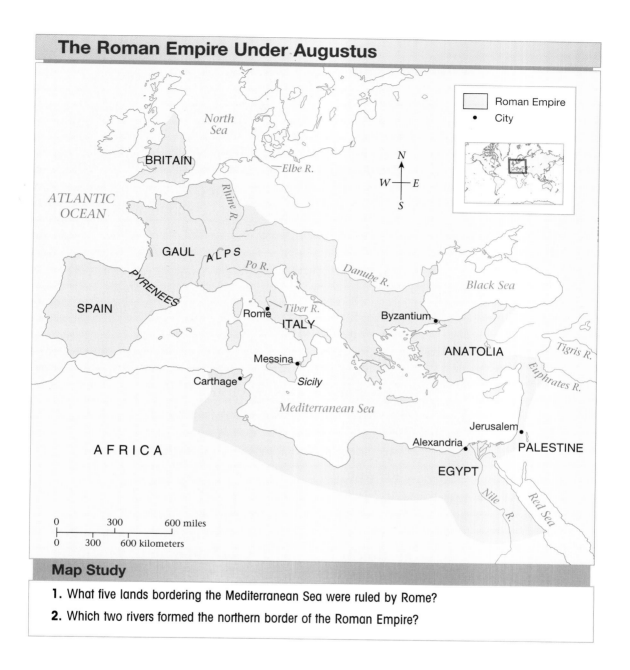

The Roman Empire Under Augustus

North Sea

BRITAIN

Elbe R.

ATLANTIC OCEAN

Rhine R.

GAUL ALPS

Po R.

Danube R.

PYRENEES

SPAIN

Black Sea

Rome   Tiber R.

ITALY

Byzantium

ANATOLIA

Tigris R.

Messina

Euphrates R.

Carthage

Sicily

Mediterranean Sea

AFRICA

Jerusalem

Alexandria

PALESTINE

EGYPT

Nile R.

Red Sea

N
W — E
S

Roman Empire

• City

| 0 | 300 | 600 miles |
| 0 | 300 | 600 kilometers |

Map Study

1. What five lands bordering the Mediterranean Sea were ruled by Rome?

2. Which two rivers formed the northern border of the Roman Empire?

Augustus chose good, honest men as government leaders. He built roads connecting all the provinces with Rome. He improved harbors and made trade easier. Life became better for most people.

Life in Rome

Rome was a busy place. A million people lived in or near the city. Rome had come a long way from that tiny village on a hill. It was a fine and beautiful place. The wide main streets were paved with stone. Fresh water came to the city through overhead **aqueducts.** The water was piped into houses and public fountains.

The Romans built beautiful temples to their many gods and goddesses. There were 300 temples in Rome alone. One of the most famous of these was the Pantheon.

The Roman Forum was a gathering place. It was there that the Senate met in the Senate House. Columned temples lined the edges of the Forum. Merchants built shops there.

The Romans also built huge public baths. They were more than a place to bathe in hot and cold pools. The baths were also a center of social life. The baths held libraries, gymnasiums, and even small theaters. The public baths were free of charge.

Wealthy Romans lived in big houses. These houses had swimming pools and large dining halls for parties. Many rich people also had country homes. They hired workers to live there and look after the land.

The average Roman family lived in a small house or apartment. The poorer people lived in tiny rooms in big apartment buildings. They often had to struggle for enough to eat.

Rich and poor people alike enjoyed the free entertainment provided by the emperors. The Romans celebrated many holidays—to honor their gods and goddesses or to honor military heroes. On these days they often held chariot races. These exciting races took place at a sports stadium called the Circus Maximus. The Romans loved to watch these events. They also enjoyed more violent forms of entertainment.

Roman Builders

The Romans admired the Greeks. They put up statues taken from Greek city-states. They copied Greek style in statues of their own. Many of the great buildings in Rome were also based on Greek style and form.

Roman builders liked to use arches. Arches spanned streets, supported bridges, and held up great aqueducts. Visitors often passed under a great arch to enter a Roman city.

The Romans wanted their art and architecture to be useful. The 14 aqueducts that carried water into Rome were certainly beautiful. They were also useful—and they were built to last. Some aqueducts built more than 2,000 years ago still stand today.

Some roads of ancient Rome are in use today, too. "All roads lead to Rome," a famous saying goes. That means that Roman highways, paved layer upon layer, linked all the provinces to Rome. The Romans were fine builders. They built a sewer system to serve ancient Rome. Parts of it are still being used in the modern city.

Roman Language and Law

Italian, French, Spanish, Portuguese, and Romanian are all called Romance languages. They all come from Latin, the language of the Romans.

There are many words that we have taken from the Romans. We have *colosseums* today. Our government has a *senate*. The Russians changed the word *Caesar* to *Czar*, the Germans to *Kaiser*.

"Justice for all!" was an idea that came from the Roman Senate. Many of our ideas about laws and courts of law came from the Romans. Roman laws and lawmaking served as a model for many other nations.

✓ Check Your Understanding
Write your answer in complete sentences.

1. Why did Mark Antony and Cleopatra kill themselves?

2. What was the significance of the title "Augustus"?

3. What was the *Pax Romana*?

WORDS FROM THE PAST
Borrowed Words

English-speakers use many words and phrases borrowed from Latin, the Romance languages, and other languages. In fact, about half of the words in present-day English come from languages other than English.

The Romance languages developed from Vulgar Latin. This was the spoken Latin of ordinary Romans. Soldiers and settlers brought Latin to areas throughout the Roman Empire. In each area, the language became a dialect of Latin. Over time, the dialect became a separate language. Italian, French, Spanish, Portuguese, and Romanian are national languages that developed from Latin.

England was a part of the Roman Empire, too. However, the English language developed from the language of Germanic tribes that invaded England in the fifth century A.D. Ever since that time, English has borrowed words from other languages.

Many words about the church came from Latin, such as *priest* and *bishop*. Many English words for technology also come from Latin. Even the word *computer* has Latin beginnings.

Many words about law and society come from French. A few words are *judge, jury, parliament, duke,* and *baron*. During one period of English history, the French-speaking Normans ruled England. English people cooked for the Normans. English names for animals, such as *cow, sheep,* and *swine,* are real English words. However, the names of meats from those animals—*beef, mutton, pork,* and *bacon*— are from French.

Modern day words, judge *and* jury, *come from French.*

The Birth of a New Religion

Look at any of the timelines in this book. Each one shows how important a man named Jesus was to history and to the calendar we use today. All the dates before the birth of Jesus Christ are labeled B.C., or "Before Christ." All the dates after the birth of Christ are labeled A.D. The letters A.D. stand for the Latin words *Anno Domini,* or "in the year of our Lord."

The Christian religion began with Jesus. Jesus was a Jew. He lived during the time of the Roman Emperor Augustus. He was born in Bethlehem, a little town south of Jerusalem. This was in a far-off province of the Roman Empire. Much of what we know about Jesus comes from the Bible. The first four books of the New Testament are about his life. These books are called the Gospels. The Gospels contain stories passed down over the years.

The Gospels say that Jesus taught people to love one another, to do good deeds, and to love God. If people were good, Jesus taught, they would be rewarded in an afterlife.

The teachings of Jesus were most popular with poor people and enslaved people. His teachings offered some hope for happiness, if not in this life, then in the next. Other religions also spoke of an afterlife.

However, those religions said that princes would remain princes. Commoners would keep their lowly station—even after death. In contrast, Jesus spoke of a happy afterlife for all who were good on Earth.

Jesus' followers called him "Christ," or messiah. Jesus was 33 years old when he was sentenced to death. His **crucifixion** did not end his teachings. In the next years, the Christian religion spread to many lands.

The Bible explains how Jesus preached and performed good deeds as he traveled.

One man who carried word of the Christian religion was named Paul. Paul spent almost 30 years of his life traveling the Mediterranean world. He told people about Jesus' teachings. Paul could speak Greek. Therefore, he could take Christian beliefs to Athens and to other Greek cities. Paul started churches wherever he traveled. Even in Rome, Paul found people willing to listen. People were ready to accept a new religion that spoke of equality and hope.

Christianity in the Roman Empire

The Roman Empire had many religions. At first, one more religion did not seem too important. Therefore, the emperors allowed the Christians to worship as they pleased.

However, the Christians would not bow down to the Roman emperor. They would not call the emperor a god. Therefore, the Roman government decided that the Christians were a threat. The Roman emperors began to **persecute** the followers of Christ. They blamed the Christians for everything that went wrong.

You Decide

Can you do anything to help when the wrong people are being blamed for something? Explain.

A terrible fire burned in Rome in A.D. 64. This was the time when Nero was emperor. "The Christians started the fire!" Nero shouted. As a result many Christians were executed. Paul, one of the men who had spread Jesus' teachings, was one of those killed.

The Romans persecuted the Christians for 300 years. Christian men and women were forced into Roman arenas to fight wild animals. Some of the emperors worried more about Christianity than others. Sometimes Christians were safe; other times they were in danger.

You Decide

Why do you think people risk their lives sometimes to follow their religion?

Christians often held secret church meetings. They met in tunnels, called catacombs, deep under the city of Rome. It was dangerous to follow the Christian religion. Yet even though it could mean death, people continued to join the Christian religion. At first only the poor Romans and slaves turned to Christianity. After a time, however, some of the Roman leaders became interested, too.

The Emperor Constantine

Constantine became emperor of Rome in A.D. 306. In A.D. 312 a Roman general named Maxentius threatened to seize the throne. One night, Constantine dreamed that he saw a cross in the sky. He thought it was the Cross of Christ. He dreamed that if he carried that cross into battle, he would win a great victory. In response, Constantine rode into battle against Maxentius. He carried a flag that pictured the cross. And he won that battle. Maxentius was defeated.

At the time Constantine became emperor, he had to share power with others. The Roman Empire had been divided into an eastern and a western part. In A.D. 286 the Emperor Diocletian decided the empire had grown too big to be ruled by just one man. Thus he set up a system of shared rule.

Constantine was not happy with this arrangement. In A.D. 324 he clashed with Licinius, the ruler of the eastern part of the empire. That same year, Constantine became the sole ruler of the Roman Empire. In A.D. 330 he set up a new capital at Byzantium in the east. He renamed the city Constantinople. Today this city is known as Istanbul.

In A.D. 313 Constantine had made Christianity legal. Christians were no longer persecuted. More and more Romans now turned to the religion. Constantine himself **converted** to Christianity in A.D. 337 and became the first Christian emperor of Rome. He built the first great Christian cathedral in Rome. He then built churches in Constantinople and in other cities.

Roman Emperor Constantine

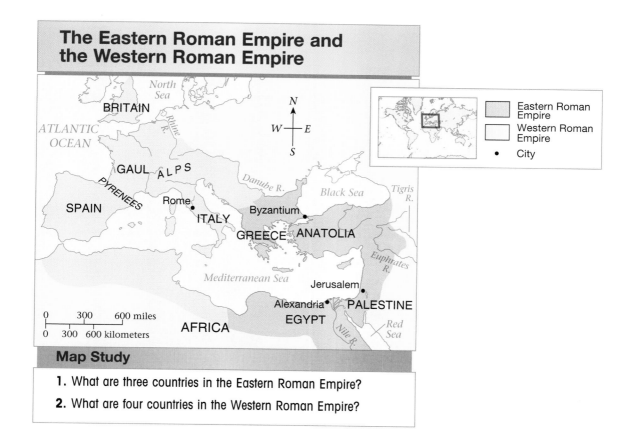

The Eastern Roman Empire and the Western Roman Empire

Legend:
- Eastern Roman Empire
- Western Roman Empire
- • City

Map Study

1. What are three countries in the Eastern Roman Empire?

2. What are four countries in the Western Roman Empire?

The Roman government and the Christian church became very much a part of one another. Officials of the church were powerful men. The largest churches chose **bishops** as their leaders. The bishop of the Church of Rome became the **pope**. While the government of the Roman Empire was weakening, the Christian church was gaining power.

✓ **Check Your Understanding**

Write your answers in complete sentences.

1. Why did Jesus' teachings appeal to poor people and enslaved people?

2. How did the Romans persecute the Christians?

3. Why did the Emperor Diocletian divide the Roman Empire into an Eastern and Western Empire?

⧗ **Timeline Study**

When did Christianity become legal in Rome?

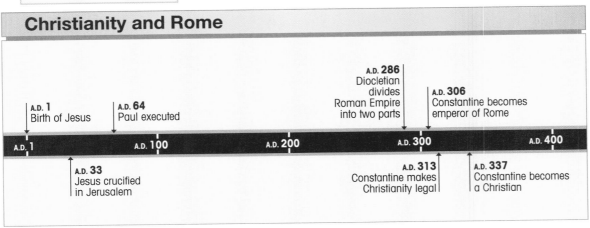

Christianity and Rome

| A.D. 286 Diocletian divides Roman Empire into two parts | A.D. 306 Constantine becomes emperor of Rome |

A.D. 1 Birth of Jesus

A.D. 64 Paul executed

A.D. 1 A.D. 100 A.D. 200 A.D. 300 A.D. 400

A.D. 33 Jesus crucified in Jerusalem

A.D. 313 Constantine makes Christianity legal

A.D. 337 Constantine becomes a Christian

The End of the Empire

Not all of the emperors that followed Augustus were wise and good. Indeed, some were mad with power. Some were greedy. Royal families often fought among themselves over who would get the throne. Yet there were always skilled men to do the actual work of running the empire. The *Pax Romana* lasted for two centuries. During that time there were no serious threats to Rome's power.

Around A.D. 180, however, things began to go wrong. The Roman world faced invaders from northern and eastern Europe. Rome had to double the size of its army to protect the empire. A bigger army meant higher taxes—taxes that people could not pay! Prices of goods rose. Trading fell off. People were out of work. Life in the city was no longer good. More and more wealthy people left Rome to live in the country.

The Roman Empire did not fall in a day, or in a month, or even in a year. Yet the empire grew weaker with each passing year. Its fall was coming.

Timeline Study

How many years passed between the foundings of Rome? (Remember to account for the change from B.C. to A.D.)

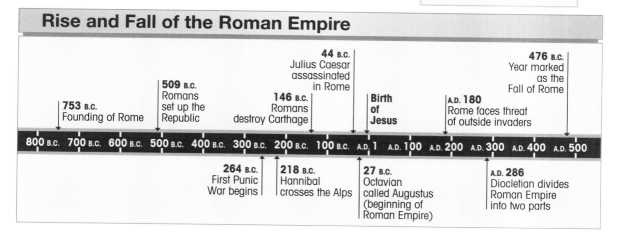

Rise and Fall of the Roman Empire

753 B.C.
Founding of Rome

509 B.C.
Romans set up the Republic

264 B.C.
First Punic War begins

218 B.C.
Hannibal crosses the Alps

146 B.C.
Romans destroy Carthage

44 B.C.
Julius Caesar assassinated in Rome

27 B.C.
Octavian called Augustus (beginning of Roman Empire)

Birth of Jesus

A.D. 180
Rome faces threat of outside invaders

A.D. 286
Diocletian divides Roman Empire into two parts

476 B.C.
Year marked as the Fall of Rome

800 B.C. 700 B.C. 600 B.C. 500 B.C. 400 B.C. 300 B.C. 200 B.C. 100 B.C. A.D. 1 A.D. 100 A.D. 200 A.D. 300 A.D. 400 A.D. 500

Summary

In the Roman Republic, laws were made by elected representatives. There was no king.
Roman armies conquered many peoples, including the Carthaginians and the Greeks. Conquered lands became Roman provinces.
Julius Caesar was a powerful general in the province of Gaul. Caesar became the leader of the Roman Republic. Some senators killed Caesar because they feared he had too much power.
Civil wars ended with Octavian as head of the Roman Empire. The people called Octavian the Emperor Augustus. His reign began 200 years of peace and growth.
The ancient Romans were great builders and lawmakers.
The Christian religion is based on the teachings of Jesus. Some Roman emperors persecuted the Christians. Constantine became the first Christian emperor of Rome.

Vocabulary Review

Write *true* or *false*. If the statement is false, change the underlined term to make it true.

1. The Romans settled on a piece of land called a <u>forum</u> around 1000 B.C.

2. The Romans built huge <u>republics</u> to transport water.

3. Constantine chose to <u>convert</u>, or change his religion, to Christianity.

4. The <u>pope</u> is the head of the Roman Catholic Church.

5. A <u>governor</u> is a high-ranking official of a church.

6. In a <u>republic</u>, citizens have the right to elect their own representatives.

Chapter Quiz

Write your answers in complete sentences.

1. Who controlled the government in the Roman Republic?

2. What were some of Julius Caesar's accomplishments as ruler of the Roman world?

3. What kind of leader was Augustus?

4. **Critical Thinking** What was Nero trying to do after the fire in Rome?

5. **Critical Thinking** Why was Constantine's conversion to Christianity important to the future of the Roman Empire?

Using the Timelines

Use the timelines on pages 128 and 129 to answer the questions.

1. What happened about 280 years after Jesus was crucified?

2. How many years passed between the founding of Rome and the setting up of the Republic?

Write About History

Complete the following activity.

Form a group of five or six. You are some of Rome's leading citizens in the Roman Republic. Caesar has been doing some good things in Rome, and he has just refused the crown. Still, you are worried that the end of the Republic is in sight. What will you say to your friends about your concerns? Write and perform a skit for the rest of the class.

Unit 3 **Review**

Comprehension Check

Write your answers in complete sentences.

1. What was the Acropolis in Greek city-states?

2. What was the result of the Peloponnesian War and the plague in Athens?

3. Who participated in the Olympic Games in ancient Greece?

4. Why did the Egyptians welcome Alexander the Great?

5. How did Alexander the Great leave his mark on the world he conquered?

6. What happened to the language of Rome as the Roman Empire grew?

7. Why did Jesus' teachings appeal to poor people and enslaved people?

8. What were two reasons for the fall of the Roman Empire?

Writing an Essay

Answer one of the following essay topics.

1. Discuss the ideas of three Greek thinkers.

2. Explain how Alexander the Great affected Egypt for centuries.

3. Describe daily life in Rome under the Emperor Augustus.

Group Activity

Form a group of three or four to make a poster. Your poster should teach younger students about Greece, Rome, or Alexander the Great. Feature the most interesting people, events, and ideas in your poster.

History in Your Life
Alexander the Great did many important things at a young age. What lessons from his life can you apply to your own?

Unit 4 ▷ The Middle Ages

Many Vikings sailed from their homeland in the north in search of food and treasure.

Learning Objectives

- Describe the lifestyle of the German tribes.
- Explain why the barbarians invaded the Roman Empire.
- Describe what happened to the city of Rome.
- Describe the Byzantine Empire.
- Tell why Charlemagne proved to be a fine ruler.
- Name the places that Vikings explored, settled, or conquered.
- Tell who William the Conqueror was and what he did.

Chapter 10 — The Barbarians and the Vikings

Words to Know

Middle Ages	the period of European history extending from the Fall of Rome in A.D. 476 to about A.D. 1450
frontier	land just beyond the border of a country
uncivilized	primitive; without training in arts, science, government
barbarians	uncivilized primitive people; people living outside Greece or Rome in the days of the Roman Empire
Vandal	a member of a Germanic tribe that invaded the Roman Empire
exiled	forced to live away from home in a foreign land
saga	a long story of brave deeds

The Roman Empire was growing weaker. The tribes that lived beyond the northern borders were growing stronger. The day was coming when these tribes would sweep across the borders. The empire would be destroyed. New people would come into power. These people had cultures very different from the Roman culture. A new period in history was being born—the **Middle Ages**. This period would last about 1,000 years.

The Germanic Tribes

Tribes of nomads lived along the northern **frontiers** of the Roman Empire. These people were known as Germans. The Romans called the Germanic tribes **uncivilized**. The Germans wore clothing of rough cloth and animal skins. They carried spears, swords, and battle-axes.

You Decide

Under which system of laws would there be more justice— the German or the Roman? Why?

The Germans' tribal laws were different from the well-ordered Roman system of law. An assembly of men ruled each German village. When villagers broke the law, the assembly would ask, "Guilty or not guilty?" If the villager said he or she was not guilty, a test was used to prove innocence or guilt. For example, the villager's hand might be thrust into boiling water. If the burn healed easily, innocence was proven. If not, he or she was guilty. The gods had spoken! This was not at all like the Roman courts of justice.

Germanic tribes often fought each other. The men took pride in their bravery in battle. They had fierce loyalty to the tribal chief. "I am a man now!" a German boy would shout when he received his first spear and shield. To lose his shield in battle would be his greatest dishonor.

The Romans called these German outsiders **barbarians.** Today this word is used to describe any uncivilized person. The Roman frontiers were protected from the barbarians by natural boundaries such as rivers and mountains. Where there were no natural boundaries, the Romans built forts and stone walls. The Roman Emperor Hadrian, who ruled between A.D. 117 and A.D. 138, built a huge wall. Hadrian's wall stretched across northern England.

The Germanic tribes lived just on the edge of the frontier. They were bound to cross over the borders. Therefore, the cultures mingled. The Germans learned to use Greek and Roman letters to write their own language. The Romans began to wear furs, as the Germans did. Many Roman women wore blond wigs made from German hair.

The Romans recognized the Germans' war skills. Some Germans joined the Roman armies. German soldiers sometimes married Roman women. It was all very neighborly at first. However, the Germans would not be friendly neighbors for long.

Barbarian Invasions

The tribes from the north grew restless. They wanted adventure. They wanted power of their own. They saw that they could take power, and riches too, from the weakening Roman Empire. Barbarian armies begun pouring across the frontier.

Besides being driven by greed, the Germans were fleeing an enemy of their own. A tribe of wild horsemen, called Huns, had swept out of Asia. Later, they were led by their fierce leader, Attila. They took more and more German lands. They forced the German tribes into the Roman Empire.

Barbarian invaders from the north attacked Rome in hopes of defeating the powerful empire.

A barbarian tribe called the Goths marched into Italy. Germans who had become Roman soldiers left their armies to join the Goths. In A.D. 410 the Goths, led by Alaric, entered Rome. The city was weak. The Goths took Rome with little trouble. They destroyed much of the city and stole what they could. Then they went on, leaving the ruins of Rome behind them.

Now other tribes of Germans swept through the Roman Empire. In A.D. 455 the city of Rome was attacked—this time by the **Vandals.** Like the Goths, they looted and destroyed everything in their path. Then they moved on into Spain and northern Africa.

Another army of Goths settled in Italy and Spain. Then the Angles, Saxons, and Jutes invaded the island of Britain. The Angles gave England its name. Their language would be called English. A tribe known as the Franks were on the move, too. The Franks settled in Flanders, just north of the province of Gaul.

The Roman Empire fell. Many Romans buried their treasures—including art and religious objects. They tried to save things from the barbarians. Long after that, people were still finding remains of the great empire. The treasures of Rome were buried in the fields and pastures of Europe.

HISTORY FACT

By A.D. 476, the Roman Empire was over. Barbarians had conquered all the Roman cities and states and set up their own states.

The days of the Western Roman Empire were over. In A.D. 476 the German chief Odoacer overthrew the last of the Roman emperors. The fine cities were gone. There were no new schools. Few people studied art or literature or science. Barbarians set up new states. Their kings ruled, blending Roman law with tribal law. The Latin language changed. It became different in each of the different states. Only the Christian church kept its power and its organization.

✓ Check Your Understanding
Write your answers in complete sentences.

1. How did the Romans describe the people living beyond the northern frontiers of the Roman Empire?

2. Why did the Emperor Hadrian build a wall across northern England?

3. What were two barbarian tribes that attacked Rome?

The Byzantine Empire

The Western Roman Empire fell to the barbarians. The Eastern Empire, with Constantinople as its capital, resisted attack. The Eastern Empire was known as the Byzantine Empire. It would last for almost 1,000 years after German tribes took the Western Roman Empire. Life in the Western Empire was grim. The Byzantine Empire, however, put up fine buildings trimmed in gold. A new university was built there. The people grew wealthy from trading.

The language of the Byzantine Empire was Greek. This became the official language of the Eastern church. In A.D. 1054 the Christian church split into two sections. The church in the west was called Roman Catholic. The church in the east was called Eastern Orthodox.

Remember
The language of the Roman Catholic Church was Latin.

The Franks and Charlemagne

"A giant of a man! About seven feet tall! He had blond hair and a merry face." That is the way a writer of the time described Charles the Great, or Charlemagne. Charlemagne was king of the Franks, the German tribe that took Flanders. The Franks had continued their conquests. They ended up ruling all the lands that would one day be France.

You Decide

Do you think
Charlemagne was
a fine ruler? Why
or why not?

Charlemagne's father was called Pepin the Short. He had died in A.D. 768. Charlemagne proved to be a fine ruler when he became king of the Franks. He conquered more land—much of Germany and part of Italy. He showed an interest in education and in the Christian religion, and won favor with the pope.

On Christmas Day, A.D. 800, the pope crowned Charlemagne "Emperor of the Holy Roman Empire." Although the empire was called "Roman," Charlemagne was still a barbarian. He dressed in the Frankish style and spoke the language of the Franks. His was a Germanic land rather than a Roman one.

Charlemagne's empire was a good one. Charlemagne built schools and encouraged artists. He learned to read Latin and worked closely with the church.

When Charlemagne died, his empire went to his son, Louis I. The empire began to crumble. It was finally divided among Charlemagne's three grandsons—Charles the Bald, Lothair, and Louis the German. The divided lands would one day become France, Germany, and part of Italy.

Charlemagne was crowned emperor of the Holy Roman Empire by the pope.

Raiders from the North

People called the attackers Northmen because they sailed down from the north. They came from lands that are today Norway, Sweden, and Denmark. The Northmen were adventurers. They loved sailing and fighting. Their ships, powered by oars and sails, were swift. The sailors set their course by the stars and by the sun. They called themselves Vikings.

The Viking raids began in A.D. 793. The Vikings attacked an island off the east coast of England. This was followed by a wave of raids against England, Scotland, and Ireland. During the mid-800s the Vikings burned and looted towns on the coasts of France, Spain, and Italy.

Viking Settlers and Explorers

For many years the Vikings kept on the move. They plundered, then sailed back home. Later, they settled in the lands that their ships reached.

Swedish Vikings settled in Russia. Other Vikings found homes in England and along the coast of France. The Vikings in France became known as the Normans. Their new land was called Normandy.

Some Vikings sailed the Atlantic Ocean and set up colonies in Iceland. In about A.D. 982, a red-bearded Viking, Eric the Red, was **exiled** from his home in Iceland. In response, Eric decided to sail to Greenland to set up a colony.

Eric had a son named Leif Ericson. In A.D. 1000 Ericson sailed as far as the east coast of North America. The Vikings stayed there for several years. Ericson called the land Vinland (or Wineland), possibly for the grapes he found.

We do not know why the Vikings left Vinland. For centuries afterward, they made trips to North America, but they did not stay. They had to give up their colony in Greenland during the 1400s. By that time, the climate had become much colder.

Songs and stories of Leif Ericson, Eric the Red, and other Viking heroes are called **sagas**. Much of what we know about the Vikings comes from these sagas. Some sagas tell of Norse gods like Odin and Thor. They tell of Valhalla, the hall of the gods, where dead Viking warriors live forever.

WORDS FROM THE PAST
Thor, Viking God of Thunder

Thor was the popular Viking god of thunder. The Vikings believed that thunder was the sound of Thor's chariot wheels as he flew across the heavens.

Thor was a son of Odin, king of the Norse gods. Thor was a great red-bearded fellow with a huge appetite. Thor wielded a magical axe-hammer called Mjolnir. Many Vikings and other Scandinavians carried small copies of this axe-hammer for their own protection. Thor could help sea voyagers and farmers because he controlled the sea, the wind, and the rain.

Thor had many adventures. Some of them were funny, and he did not always come out on top. Usually Thor used his hammer to smash his enemies' skulls. Sometimes he threw hot metal at them.

The hammer of Thor, Viking god of thunder.

Stories about Thor and other Norse gods were part of the Vikings' oral tradition. In the Middle Ages, these stories were written down in the Icelandic literature. Some famous stories featured Thor's battle with the serpent of the world. This serpent, or dragon, was said to wrap itself around the whole world under the sea.

When Christianity came to Scandinavia, the Vikings and other Norse people stopped worshipping Thor and carrying small axe-hammers. However, Thor's popularity continued in poems and stories. Today, our Thursday is Thor's Day. In literature and even in comic books, the adventures of Thor continue.

The Normans

The Normans were adventurous, like their Viking ancestors. In 1066 William, the Duke of Normandy, decided to make himself King of England. He waited for fair breezes to blow his ships across the English Channel. At last the moment came.

There was a savage fight known as the Battle of Hastings. William killed the English king, Harold. William became king of England. He became known as William the Conqueror.

Gifts of the Vikings

With new settlements and new languages, the Vikings turned to a new religion. They became Christians, leaving behind the Norse gods of the sagas. The Viking days of raiding ended.

The Vikings kept sea trade alive and booming. They used their fine ships and sailing skills to travel oceans and rivers. Their art is found throughout Europe. They decorated buildings, as well as ships, with carved dragon heads and carved animals. The adventurous Vikings settled in many lands. Therefore, they left their mark on many cultures.

Timeline Study

How many years after Eric the Red settled in Greenland did Leif Ericson reach North America?

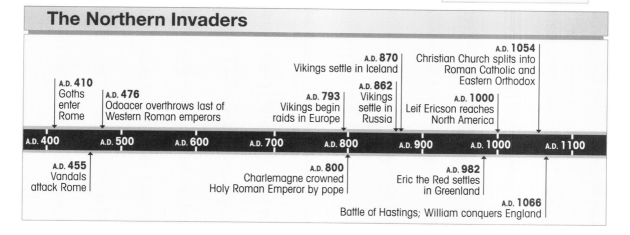

The Northern Invaders

- A.D. 410 Goths enter Rome
- A.D. 476 Odoacer overthrows last of Western Roman emperors
- A.D. 793 Vikings begin raids in Europe
- A.D. 870 Vikings settle in Iceland
- A.D. 862 Vikings settle in Russia
- A.D. 1000 Leif Ericson reaches North America
- A.D. 1054 Christian Church splits into Roman Catholic and Eastern Orthodox

A.D. 400   A.D. 500   A.D. 600   A.D. 700   A.D. 800   A.D. 900   A.D. 1000   A.D. 1100

- A.D. 455 Vandals attack Rome
- A.D. 800 Charlemagne crowned Holy Roman Emperor by pope
- A.D. 982 Eric the Red settles in Greenland
- A.D. 1066 Battle of Hastings; William conquers England

Summary

Tribes of Germans lived along the northern frontier of the Roman Empire. The Romans called those people barbarians. Barbarians attacked and conquered the Western Roman Empire.

The Eastern Roman Empire, or Byzantine Empire, did not fall for another 1,000 years.

The pope crowned Charlemagne, a Frank, emperor of the Holy Roman Empire.

Vikings sailed to other parts of Europe from Norway, Denmark, and Sweden. The Vikings settled many of the places they raided. The Viking Leif Ericson started a colony in North America.

William the Conqueror was a Duke of Normandy who conquered England.

The Vikings influenced cultures in many parts of the world.

barbarian
exiled
frontier
sagas
uncivilized

Vocabulary Review

Complete each sentence with a term from the list.

1. A person living outside Greece or Rome was called a ____.

2. The Vikings told ____ about their heroes, gods, and goddesses.

3. Eric the Red went to Greenland because he was ____, or forced from his homeland.

4. The Romans thought the Germans were ____ because they were more primitive.

5. Explorers go beyond their country's borders to the next ____.

Chapter Quiz

Write your answers in complete sentences.

1. How did the Germanic tribes live before they invaded Rome?

2. What are two reasons that Germanic tribes attacked the Western Roman Empire?

3. What was the Byzantine Empire like after the fall of Rome?

4. **Critical Thinking** Could a barbarian become an excellent ruler in the Roman Empire? Give an example to support your answer.

5. **Critical Thinking** Are the sagas reliable sources of information about the Vikings? Explain why or why not.

Using the Timeline

Use the timeline on page 143 to answer the questions.

1. When was Charlemagne crowned Holy Roman Emperor?

2. How many years passed between the time the Vikings began their raids in Europe until they reached North America?

Write About History

Complete the following activity.

Create a fact sheet about one person or event in this chapter. Use facts from the chapter as well as information from other books. Be sure to write the source where you found each fact. Form a group of students who have completed fact sheets about the same person or event. Share and compare your facts.

A country estate such as this included a feudal manor house where a noble family could feel safe from enemies. Many estates included small villages and fields for growing crops.

Learning Objectives

- Describe the life of the lord of a manor.
- Describe the life of a serf.
- Name the three classes in feudal society.
- Explain the role of religion in feudal life.
- Describe the life of a knight.

Chapter 11 ▷ The Lords and the Serfs

Words to Know

feudalism	the political and military system of much of Western Europe during the Middle Ages
vassal	a noble who received land from a king in return for loyalty and service
homage	a pledge of loyalty; a promise to serve, made to kings and lords during the Middle Ages
manor	the lands belonging to a medieval lord, including farmland, a village, and the home of the owner
estate	a large piece of land with a large home on it
serf	a person legally tied to the land
medieval	belonging to the Middle Ages
fortress	a building with strong walls for defense against an enemy
clergy	people trained or ordained for religious work
knight	a high-ranking soldier of the Middle Ages who received his title from a noble

The Feudal System

When the Roman Empire fell, the period of European history known as the *Middle Ages* began. Many people in Europe moved from the cities to the country. The splendor of the great cities faded. After a time, some towns no longer existed. Trade all but disappeared. People no longer used money. Education and learning became less and less important. Only in the church was there an effort to continue the reading and writing of Latin. The church also saved many writings from ancient times.

Life was now organized under a new system called **feudalism.** A king ruled a whole country. He divided the land among important men, or nobles. These nobles were called **vassals** of the king. In exchange for land, the nobles paid **homage** to the king. This meant that they promised to serve the king. They swore to fight for him and protect him.

A noble, or lord, lived in a **manor** house on a country **estate.** The estate included a small village and fields for growing crops. Freemen and **serfs** lived on the feudal estate. They depended on the ruling noble and his land for their living.

The manor fields were divided into strips of land. Freemen were allowed to buy and farm their own strips. In return they had to pay the lord of the manor a part of their crops. Also, they had to promise to fight for the lord. A noble always had to worry about attacks by neighboring estates.

The serfs did not own their own land. They worked for the lord of the manor, farming his land. Serfs were tied to the land on which they were born. They could not leave the estate, even if they wanted to.

The serfs provided every service for the lord of the manor and his family. The serfs grew crops and gathered wood. They took care of the lord's lands and his house. In the feudal system, each class owed loyalty and service to the class just above it.

Remember
Nobles were people of high social rank. The king gave them land, and they promised to serve him.

Life on a Feudal Estate

Very little trade went on under the feudal system. Each feudal estate had its own village and met its own needs. Each village had a blacksmith who made tools and weapons. Each village had a miller who ground grain into flour. The serfs had to use the services of the manor. They also had to pay whatever price was asked for these services.

Many nobles and their families lived in great houses made of stone. Some **medieval** manor houses were real castles. They were still very cold, however, and often gloomy. They had no glass in the windows or running water. They were dimly lit by burning torches made of twigs. The damp, shadowy castles were cold **fortresses** in which noble families could feel safe from enemies.

Many of the manor lords had several manors. They lived part of the year at one and part of the year at another. The lords chose managers to oversee the land when they were away.

While the noble family lived in the manor house, the villagers lived in small, smoky huts. They ate from wooden bowls and sat on backless, three-legged stools. They could not read or write. Their only contacts from outside the manor came when the village held a fair. Then merchants from around the countryside might bring their wares.

A manor lord could treat his serfs much as he pleased. "Between you and your serf there is no judge but God" was a medieval saying. Serfs had little protection from the lord's treatment.

You Decide

Even rich people lived under harsh conditions during the Middle Ages. Do you think you would have liked living in a castle? Why or why not?

✓ **Check Your Understanding**

Write your answers in complete sentences.

1. What jobs did the serfs have to do for the lord of the manor?

2. Describe the castles that some nobles and their families lived in.

3. Where was the main place that education and learning were carried on during the Middle Ages?

Men and Women of the Church

Medieval society was a Christian society. Higher officials in the church were nobles. Large pieces of land were often given to the **clergy**. The highest-ranking clergy were as wealthy and powerful as the most important lords.

Some men and women wished to devote their entire lives to serving God. These men became monks and lived in monasteries. These women became nuns and lived in convents. In monasteries and convents, they spent their days studying, praying, working, and taking part in religious services.

Knights

Except for the church leaders, every important man in feudal society was a fighter. Even the kings were warriors. The estates fought each other. There were bands of

Knights were noble warriors. They tested their skills in tournaments called jousts.

robbers to be controlled. Tribes of people from other parts of the country often came looking for new lands.

Warriors of the noble class were known as **knights**. Knights fought to defend their own manors. They fought for their king as they had promised. They also fought to protect Christianity from being threatened.

Learn More About It

KNIGHTS IN ARMOR

Being a knight was a costly business. Armor and weapons were elaborate and expensive. The serfs had to work very hard to pay for their lord's fancy armor, many horses, and fine weapons. If a boy wanted to grow up to be a knight, he began training at age 7. He started out as a page. He learned to fight and to have the proper knightly manners.

The next step in becoming a knight was acting as a squire. A squire served a knight. He helped the knight with his armor and weapons. The squire also rode with his knight into battle. When he was 21, a worthy squire was "knighted" by a noble. The young squire became a knight when a sword was tapped on his shoulder.

Knighthood was both a military and a religious honor. A young man spent the night before he was knighted in a church. There he kept watch over his armor, as he knelt and prayed. He thought about the honor he was about to receive.

Knights kept their fighting skills ready by entering tournaments, or jousts. Two knights on horseback would fight each other with long lances. The goal of each knight was to knock the other one off his horse. The winner's honor was not only for himself. It was also for his favorite "lady," whose ribbon he wore into battle.

A Hard Life!

The feudal way of life was most widespread during the 1100s and 1200s. Life on a feudal manor was hard. There were floods and years of bad crops. There were always battles to fight. There were plagues, too.

In A.D. 1348 a ship from the East docked at an Italian port. Some sick sailors came ashore. They brought with them a terrible plague. This disease became known as the Black Death. It got its name because it caused spots of blood to turn black under the skin.

Little was known about medicine during the Middle Ages. There were few doctors, and those doctors that were around did not understand the causes of diseases or how diseases were spread. The villages were not very clean. A large population of rats lived off the garbage. Doctors today think that bites from infected rat fleas caused the plague. Doctors in the 1300s, however, did not know much about the prevention or treatment of disease. They had little help to offer. As a result, nobles and serfs alike fell sick and died.

The Black Death quickly spread across Europe killing thousands of nobles and serfs alike.

Feudal society lasted for almost 700 years. By A.D. 1400, however, the great manors had almost disappeared. Trade had picked up. Money had come back into use. Nobles no longer received land for services. People moved back to the towns.

New methods of warfare were being developed. Gunpowder and new weapons, such as cannons, were now available. In addition foot soldiers were being used more effectively. Because of these changes, knights were no longer needed.

For hundreds of years, the picture of life in Europe had been the feudal manor. It was a world where most people fit into one of three classes: nobles, clergy, or serfs. "Some fight," a medieval bishop wrote. "Others pray. And others work."

Timeline Study

How long did the Middle Ages last?

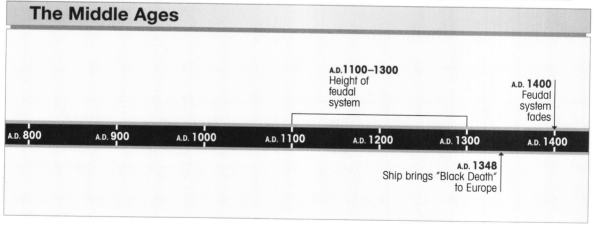

The Middle Ages

A.D.**1100–1300**
Height of feudal system

A.D. **1400**
Feudal system fades

A.D. **800**   A.D. **900**   A.D. **1000**   A.D. **1100**   A.D. **1200**   A.D. **1300**   A.D. **1400**

A.D. **1348**
Ship brings "Black Death" to Europe

Chapter

11 Review

Summary

During the Middle Ages many people lived under the feudal system.

In return for land, nobles paid homage to their king.

Medieval estates, or manors, included a manor house, a village, and fields. The lord of the manor was the absolute ruler of the feudal estate. Serfs worked the land for the lord of the manor.

Knights were warriors of the noble class.

Most medieval society was divided into three classes: the nobles, the clergy, and the serfs.

A plague called the Black Death killed one-fourth to one-third of Europe's people in the Middle Ages.

clergy

knight

manor

feudalism

serf

Vocabulary Review

Write a term from the list that matches each definition below.

1. A peasant who was almost a slave during the Middle Ages

2. A warrior trained to defend the manor, the king, and Christianity

3. A way of life during the Middle Ages

4. People who do religious work as their job

5. The house where a noble, or lord, lived

Chapter Quiz

Write your answers in complete sentences.

1. What happened in Western Europe after the Roman Empire fell?

2. What were the main social classes in the feudal system?

3. What did men and women do if they wanted to give their lives to serving God?

4. **Critical Thinking** Why were knights so important in feudal society?

5. **Critical Thinking** Do you think the serfs were more slave than free? Tell why or why not.

Using the Timeline

Use the timeline on page 153 to answer the questions.

1. When was the feudal system at its height?

2. When the feudal system faded, how long had it been since the Black Death arrived in Europe?

Write About History

Complete the following activity.

During the Middle Ages, each noble family had a coat of arms. The coat of arms used shapes, colors, and symbols to represent the family. Design your own coat of arms. Use a favorite background color, or field. Draw a band of another color across the field. Draw a symbol for each family member.

Christians joined the Crusades to recapture the Holy Land from the Muslims.

Learning Objectives

- Discuss the importance of Muhammad.
- Give four reasons people went on the Crusades.
- Explain how the Crusades affected European trade.
- Name three new developments in farming in the Middle Ages.
- Describe what life was like in a medieval town.
- Tell why the Magna Carta was important.
- Describe the spread of Islam.

Chapter 12 / Islam and the Crusades

Words to Know

pilgrimage	a visit to a holy place
prophet	a religious leader who claims to speak for God; one who tells what will happen in the future
paradise	a place or condition of perfect happiness; heaven
truce	a time when enemies agree to stop fighting
surplus	more than what is needed
fallow	land not used for farming during a season
population	people living in a place, or the total number of those people
migrate	to move away from one country or region to settle in another
guild	an organization formed to protect the interests of workers
apprentice	a person who learns a trade under a master
journeyman	a worker who has finished an apprenticeship and receives wages, but who is not yet a master
justice	fairness according to the principles of right and wrong

The Middle Ages is sometimes thought of as a time of darkness, of little advancement. There were changes going on in medieval Europe, however. The Crusades, or Holy Wars, brought new ideas and new interests to Europeans. There were changes happening on medieval farms and in towns. Some people began to recognize that kings had too much power. People could see that their rights were being denied. Europe changed slowly during the Middle Ages, but it did change.

Christian Pilgrims

During the Middle Ages, the Christian religion was the strongest force in Europe. People made **pilgrimages** to show their faith. From Germany, France, England, and Italy they traveled to holy shrines. Thousands of pilgrims went on foot and on horseback.

Pilgrims traveled east to the holy city of Jerusalem. Jerusalem had been a holy city for the Jews since the days of Solomon's splendid temple. Now it was a holy city for the Christians as well. Christian pilgrims flocked to Jerusalem. They went to see the place where Jesus had lived and taught.

Muhammad and the Birth of Islam

Another group of people called Jerusalem a holy city, too. They were the Muslims, followers of a religion born in the desert land of Arabia. Today this land is called Saudi Arabia.

In A.D. 570 Arabia was a vast desert southeast of the Mediterranean Sea. The people who lived there, the Arabs, believed in many gods. They worshipped idols made of gold and silver. Tribes of nomads lived on the edges of the desert in tent camps. They drove caravans of camels across the sands. Wealthy people lived in fine homes in the cities. They dressed in rich silks and wore bright jewels.

It was not a peaceful land. Bands of thieves rode into the cities, waving swords. They looted and killed, taking riches off into the desert. The nomadic tribes also fought among themselves. More and more trouble spread throughout Arabia. Trade became harder and the people became poorer. Fewer people lived in fine palaces; more people struggled for even enough to eat.

Arabian people riding camels traveled great distances across empty deserts.

Around the year A.D. 570, in the Arabian city of Mecca, a man named Muhammad was born. Not much is known about Muhammad's early life. Yet Muhammad was to become a religious figure who would change the shape of the world.

When Muhammad was 40 years old, it is said, he had a vision. Muhammad believed he saw an angel on a hillside outside of Mecca. The angel spoke to him, saying that Muhammad was a **prophet** of God. "Teach your people," the angel said, "that there is one God, and that God is Allah."

Like Jesus, Muhammad became a teacher. He tried to teach people that Allah was the one true god. Most Arabs would not listen. They still worshipped their many gods.

Muhammad did have some followers. They heard his words about Allah. Muhammad promised that Allah would reward people for good deeds with a wonderful life after death. Poor people listened. Slaves listened. People whose lives were hard or sad listened to Muhammad.

The powerful leaders of Mecca began to worry. They had laughed at him at first, this man called Muhammad. Now he was growing popular. What if he stirred the commoners into a rebellion? The leaders began to persecute Muhammad and his followers. The Muslims were forced to flee the city of Mecca. In A.D. 622 Muhammad took his people to the Arabian city of Medina. Still, the number of Muslims grew. New converts became soldiers for Islam. With an army of followers, Muhammad returned to Mecca. They took the city in A.D. 630.

In A.D. 632 Muhammad died. By the time of his death, the prophet Muhammad had done his job. Most of Arabia was united under one religion. The religion of the Muslims was called Islam. The Islamic religion promised that any followers who died battling for Allah would go to **paradise.** This idea alone created huge armies of enthusiastic soldiers. The Muslim soldiers were ready to carry the word of Allah throughout the world.

The Spread of Islam

Then came one of the greatest series of conquests the world had ever seen. Between A.D. 640 and A.D. 660, Arab armies swept through Syria, Persia, and Egypt. They conquered Palestine, or the Holy Land. It included the holy City of Jerusalem. The Arab conquests continued for hundreds of years. Arab lands would stretch from North Africa and Spain to the Indus River and Central Asia.

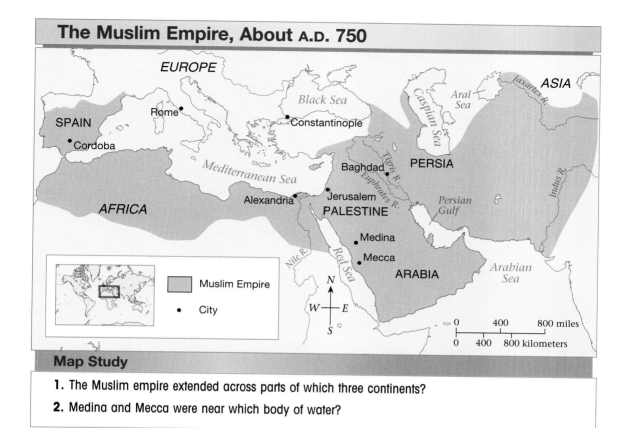

The Muslim Empire, About A.D. 750

EUROPE

ASIA

Black Sea

Rome

Constantinople

SPAIN

Cordoba

Caspian Sea

Aral Sea

Jaxartes R.

PERSIA

Baghdad

Tigris R.

Euphrates R.

Indus R.

Mediterranean Sea

Alexandria

Jerusalem

PALESTINE

Persian Gulf

AFRICA

Nile R.

Red Sea

Medina

Mecca

ARABIA

Arabian Sea

Muslim Empire

City

N
W — E
S

0   400   800 miles
0   400   800 kilometers

Map Study

1. The Muslim empire extended across parts of which three continents?

2. Medina and Mecca were near which body of water?

Some of the conquered people welcomed the new religion with its hope of paradise. The Arabs, however, gave them little choice—the people must become Muslims or die. Only Jews and Christians were allowed to keep their own religion. The Muslims respected those who also worshipped one God and followed the words of a holy book.

Indeed, Muhammad was influenced early in his life by the Jews and Christians he knew. His God, Allah, was the one God of the Jews and Christians. According to Muhammad, God revealed himself to humanity through his chosen prophets. The major prophets were Adam, Noah, Abraham, Moses, Jesus, and, finally,

Muhammad. God gave the Ten Commandments to Moses, the Gospels to Jesus, and the Koran to Muhammad. Even so, the Christians and Jews were forced to pay tribute to the new Arab rulers.

The conquering Arabs brought their culture as well as their religion. They built fine cities, new schools, and beautiful places of worship called mosques. Their language and writing became part of world culture. The Arabs made their mark on the world in many ways. The numerals that we use now in the United States, for example, are Arabic numerals.

Today Islam is one of the world's great religions. Most Muslims live in the Middle East, Pakistan, India, North Africa, and parts of Asia. They live in lands that the Arabs conquered during the seventh and eighth centuries. About $5\frac{3}{4}$ million people of Islamic faith are estimated to live in the United States.

These are early Arabic numerals representing the numbers 1 through 5.

✓ **Check Your Understanding**
Write your answers in complete sentences.

1. Where was Muhammad born?

2. How does Allah reward good deeds?

3. Why did the Muslims respect Christians and Jews?

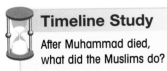

Timeline Study
After Muhammad died, what did the Muslims do?

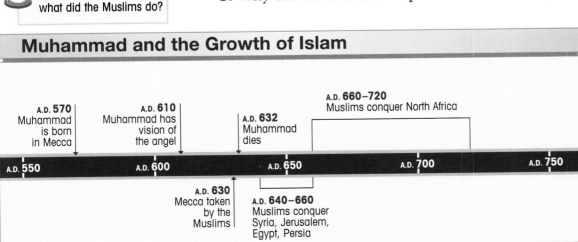

Muhammad and the Growth of Islam

A.D. **570**
Muhammad is born in Mecca

A.D. **610**
Muhammad has vision of the angel

A.D. **632**
Muhammad dies

A.D. **660–720**
Muslims conquer North Africa

A.D. 550   A.D. 600   A.D. 650   A.D. 700   A.D. 750

A.D. **630**
Mecca taken by the Muslims

A.D. **640–660**
Muslims conquer Syria, Jerusalem, Egypt, Persia

WORDS FROM THE PAST
The Koran

The Koran is the sacred book of Islam. The verses in the Koran are a collection of verses said to be revealed to Muhammad by the angel Gabriel. His followers memorized his words or wrote them down. Later they were collected to form the Koran. Muslims believe the Koran is the word of God and cannot be changed in any way although translations are permitted.

The holy book of Islam is the Koran.

The Koran emphasizes that Allah is the one and only God. Muslims must submit, or yield, to Allah and his word. Allah will judge each person by his or her deeds and submission to him.

There are several things a good Muslim must do, according to the Koran. A Muslim must pray five times a day, facing toward Mecca. A Muslim must give to the poor. A Muslim must not eat or drink during daylight hours of one special month called Ramadan. A Muslim should, if at all possible, make at least one visit to Mecca. Today Muslim pilgrims from many lands still journey to the holy city of Mecca.

"There is no God but Allah," a Muslim declares, "and Muhammad is His prophet!"

The Soldiers of Christ

When the Christian pilgrims of the Middle Ages journeyed to Jerusalem, that city was under Muslim control. The Arab Muslims respected the Christian religion. They allowed Christian pilgrims to visit Jerusalem.

In 1071, the Seljuk Turks, who dominated Syria, took power in Jerusalem. The Turks were Muslims, too. The Turks were not as friendly to the Christians. The Turks would not allow Christians to visit their city. They would not let them worship at the holy shrines.

An angry pope, named Urban II, stirred Europeans to action in 1095. He spoke before a gathering of important people. He reminded them that the Turks held Jerusalem. He told them that Christians there were in danger. It was their Christian duty, he said, to free the Holy Land.

People listened. Feudal lords, knights, and commoners were all moved to action. Word spread across Europe. Soon armies of Christians were ready to travel to the Holy Land. They wore crosses on their clothing as a symbol of their mission. Then the Christian armies set forth on the Crusades. The Holy Wars they started were to last for 200 years.

Many crusaders marched because of strong religious feelings. Some went on the Crusades for other reasons. Some were looking for adventure. Others were looking for wealth in new lands. Soldiers wanted military glory. Merchants wanted new markets for their goods. Criminals wanted a safe place to hide.

Crusaders came from every social class—kings and nobles, knights and lords. The serfs saw a chance to escape feudal manors. They joined the march, too. They all set out to take Jerusalem from the Muslims.

The earliest Crusade, in 1096, was led by a man called Peter the Hermit. This Crusade was made up of

You Decide

If you were a Christian during those days, would you have wanted to go on the Crusades? Why or why not?

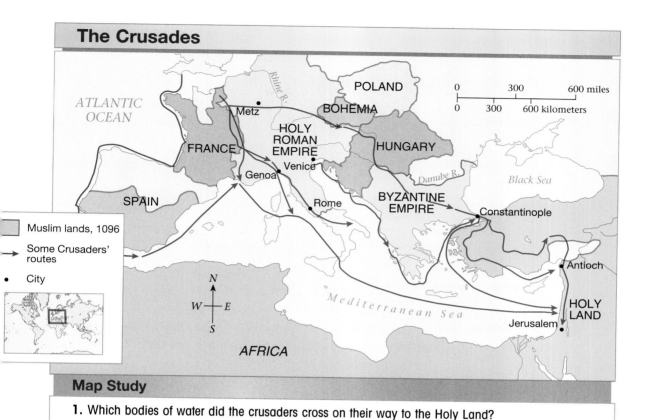

The Crusades

Muslim lands, 1096

Some Crusaders' routes

City

Map Study

1. Which bodies of water did the crusaders cross on their way to the Holy Land?

2. According to the map, who did the Holy Land belong to in 1096?

French and German peasants. They started out for the Holy Land before the huge armies of knights did. The peasants were not well organized. They had to steal food along the way to keep from starving. The Turks had little trouble defeating them. Most of the peasants were killed before they reached Jerusalem.

In the autumn of 1096, several armies of knights set out from Europe. Nobles from France led the march. It was a hard trip. Over the next two years, many died from hunger and from disease. The knights had to fight many battles along the way. Those who made it to Jerusalem, however, were ready for another fight. They started a bloody battle. It lasted six weeks. When it was over, the crusaders had taken Jerusalem and much of the Holy Land from the Muslims. The crusaders had killed many of the people who lived there—Jews as well as Muslims. The year was 1099.

The nobles from Europe set up several small states in the Holy Land. Christians back home were pleased. The Holy Land was under Christian control. Most of the crusaders returned to Europe.

Then European leaders in the Holy Land began to quarrel among themselves. The Turks launched new attacks. In response, more crusaders went off to help protect the Holy Land.

A Truce

The Muslims' leader was Saladin, who was said to be strong and wise. Saladin's troops won back the city of Jerusalem in 1187.

Then European rulers joined together to fight for the Holy City. The German emperor Frederick I, King Philip II of France, and King Richard I of England set off on a Crusade. Together they went to fight to regain Jerusalem.

The German emperor Frederick, accidentally drowned on the trip to the Middle East. King Philip of France returned home before the Crusade was over. He claimed he was too sick to fight. It was up to Richard the Lion-Hearted to face Saladin.

Richard and Saladin were both great leaders and brave warriors. They had much respect for each other's skills. When they met in battle, Saladin's forces gained the upper hand. Then word came that Richard was needed back in England. Saladin agreed to a five-year **truce**. Under the terms of the truce, Christians would be allowed to visit Jerusalem. They could also keep control of a few cities on the coast.

PLATE A

Saladin, a Muslim leader, seized Jerusalem from the Christian crusaders in 1187.

The Holy Land Falls to the Ottomans

When Saladin died, the truce weakened. By 1291 the Muslims again held all of the Holy Land. In 1453 the Ottoman Turks took power in Constantinople and much of Anatolia. Like the Seljuk Turks, the Ottomans were Muslims. The Holy Land fell under their rule. The Ottomans also put an end to the Byzantine Empire. They changed the name of their capital city, Constantinople, to Istanbul. By 1500 the Ottomans would rule over a huge empire. The Middle East, North Africa, and much of eastern Europe fell to the Ottomans. The Ottoman Empire would last for hundreds of years.

Costs of the Crusades

Europeans found the Crusades costly in many ways. It took a lot of money to equip the warriors and send them such great distances. The Crusades were also costly in terms of lives. Many people—Christians, Muslims, and Jews—died bloody deaths fighting for the Holy Land. In the name of God, people looted, burned, and killed.

In the beginning, people thought the Crusades would lead them to glory. The Holy Wars, however, caused much suffering and misery. And this was all in the name of religions based on brotherhood and love.

Learn More About It

THE CHILDREN'S CRUSADE

One of the saddest of the Crusades became known as the Children's Crusade. In 1212 an army of 30,000 French boys and girls set out to fight. Most of them were 12 years old or younger. They were gathered together and led by a shepherd boy named Stephen.

At first it must have seemed like an adventure for the children. Sadly, however, few of them ever returned home. Nearly all of the 30,000 children died. Most fell sick along the way, or they starved to death.

Another army of German youths headed for Jerusalem. Led by a boy named Nicholas, these 20,000 children never saw the Holy Land either. When seven ships offered to take them to Jerusalem, they accepted. How lucky, they thought, to get a ride!

Unfortunately, the free ride was bad luck indeed. Two of the ships were wrecked in storms. All of the children aboard drowned. The rest of the ships were not headed for Jerusalem at all. The children had been tricked. The ships took them to Egypt, where they were sold as slaves.

Learn More About It

THE OTTOMAN EMPIRE

The Ottoman Turks first appeared in Asia Minor in the late 1200s. They were named Osmanli or Ottoman after their leader, Osman. It was under Osman that the Ottomans began to conquer the Byzantine Empire. The ruler of the Ottoman Empire was called a *sultan*. The sultan was a powerful man who ruled through a group of high officers.

The Ottoman Empire continued to grow after Osman's death. By the early 1400s, Constantinople was a Christian city surrounded by Muslim lands. Then the Ottomans, under the rule of their sultan, Mehmed II, captured Constantinople. Mehmed's troops also captured Bulgaria and parts of Hungary, and Mehmed II became known as "the Conqueror." In the 1400s and 1500s the Ottoman Empire extended into Asia and Africa. The Ottoman sultans took the title of *caliph,* or spiritual leader of Islam. Under the caliph known as "Suleiman the Magnificent" the Ottoman Empire grew to include Palestine, Egypt, and parts of Arabia, North Africa, Europe, and Persia.

The Ottomans continued to rule their vast empire for hundreds of years. During the 1800s, however, they began to lose territory. The government grew harsher. Minority groups in all parts of the empire suffered persecution. Many people wanted independence from Ottoman rule.

The Ottoman Turks joined Germany and Austria in World War I (1914–1918). With defeat came the loss of all non-Turkish lands. A free republic of Turkey was declared in 1923.

The Crusades Bring Change to Europe

By 1291 the Christians had lost all of the lands they once held in the Middle East. The crusaders, however, brought back Middle Eastern ideas. In addition, crusading merchants brought home new products. The Crusades created a new Europe.

The merchants introduced Europeans to foods like lemons, rice, apricots, and melons. New spices, such as ginger and pepper, cloves and cinnamon, now seasoned European food. The merchants brought fine cloth. Europeans began wearing brightly dyed silks. With the new trading, Europe's whole economy became stronger.

When the crusaders left Europe, their journeys gave them fresh ideas. There was a new interest in travel and exploration. People learned to make better maps. All the fighting that went on encouraged even more interest in warfare. Crusaders returned with new weapons and better battle skills.

The feudal society had kept medieval people tied down to the manors. The Crusades sent them out into the world. The Crusades were sad and costly. However, they increased trade and brought a sharing of cultures.

✓Check Your Understanding
Write your answers in complete sentences.

1. What are four reasons people went on the Crusades?

2. Who was the Muslim leader who agreed to a truce with Richard the Lion-Hearted?

3. What effect did the Crusades have on European trade?

Changes in Agriculture

The world's first agricultural revolution had taken place long ago. It occurred along the Mediterranean Sea when people began planting seeds and raising animals. During the Middle Ages another farming revolution was going on. Now people were learning about new and better methods of growing food. These changes in agriculture also changed society as a whole.

Emperor Charlemagne had opened new iron mines. With more iron available, farm tools improved. Now there were new metal axes and hoes.

Remember

An angry pope, Urban II, encouraged Europeans to "free" the Holy Land in 1095. Some Christian armies set off in the Crusades.

During the Middle Ages, new tools changed the way people farmed.

The new tool that most changed farming in the Middle Ages was the plowshare. Early plows had been little more than large sticks. These sticks were dragged across the ground by one or two oxen. They only scratched the earth. It took hours and hours of work to break up even a small field.

The new plowshare was made of sharp, curved iron. The plow itself was fastened to a heavy, wheeled frame. Eight oxen were needed to pull the plowshare. With the new, heavier equipment, farmers could till even the heaviest soil. Working in long, narrow strips, they could plow the land more quickly.

The plowshare meant that more land could be farmed and more food could be grown. People did not have to eat all that they grew. They had a **surplus** of food now. They could use this surplus to trade for other goods.

Medieval farmers discovered that horses were better workers than oxen. Horses could work longer without rest. They moved faster. With more iron around, it was easy to make enough horseshoes.

The farmers invented a new kind of harness for their horses. It fit over the horse's shoulders instead of across its chest. Now the horse could breathe easier and could pull heavier weights. It took fewer horses than oxen to pull the new plowshare.

Farmers learned to get more out of their fields. They maintained three fields now. They planted one field in the autumn and one in the spring. A third field lay **fallow** each season. Each field was given a season to be fallow. This let the soil rest and grow rich again.

The three-field method of crop rotation worked well. If one crop failed, there was always a second crop to rely on. More food was produced.

The Population Grows

During the 1000s Europe's **population** began to grow. However, more people meant a need for even more farmland. Farmers cleared forests and drained swamplands in England and in France. People began to **migrate** eastward. Germans colonized new lands in eastern Europe. Changes in agriculture caused people to live in new places.

As farm production increased, workers had more food to trade for goods. Beginning in the 1000s, craftworkers and traders began to settle in medieval villages to sell their goods. In addition to the blacksmith and the miller, there were now new shops in the villages. The villages grew into towns.

Medieval towns were usually surrounded by stone walls. Their narrow streets were often just mud. Sometimes the streets were paved with cobblestones. The towns were often dirty and dark.

With walls closing them in, the towns were small and crowded. People threw their garbage into the streets. There were no fire departments, no police departments, and no health services. Most of the houses were just huts made of wood. With these conditions, there was always a danger of fire and of disease. The town of Rouen in France burned to the ground six times between 1200 and 1225! It is easy to see how the plague spread so quickly in such crowded, dirty towns.

In spite of their problems, the medieval towns grew. As they did, the workers, merchants, and craftworkers became more specialized.

People used money more often now. On the manors, services had been exchanged for goods. Now people paid money for new leather shoes, a pottery bowl, or a tasty cake.

Serfs saw the town as a place to win freedom from manor lords. Sometimes serfs ran away and hid within the walls of a town. "Live free for a year and a day," the rule went, "and go free." A serf who could manage to escape his lord for that long became a free person.

The Feudal System Weakens

During the late Middle Ages, business and trade increased. As the towns became stronger, and the merchants became richer, the feudal system weakened. The towns wanted to govern themselves—to be free of the manor.

Some feudal lords sold charters of freedom to the towns. No longer were so many people "tied" to the land. Most towns were dirty and crowded. People, however, were freer than they had been on the feudal estates. It was not so surprising that they wanted to live in the towns.

Guilds

The towns offered opportunity. Peasants could work their way up in the world. They could learn a trade or a craft.

Each trade and craft had its own group, or **guild.** The guild helped set prices. It also set standards for workmanship. The guilds decided how long shops should stay open each day.

The guilds also offered a chance to learn. Boys and girls could become **apprentices** and go to work for a guild member. The apprentice lived in the master's house and worked in the master's shop. An apprentice received no pay.

An apprentice served for seven years. Then the apprentice could become a **journeyman** and earn wages. When the apprentice became skilled enough, the journeyman made one special piece of work for the master. It was called a "masterpiece." If the masterpiece was good enough, the journeyman might became a master and join the guild.

Streets in medieval towns often were named after different guilds. *Tailors Row* and *Boot Street,* for example, were typical street names.

Big Cities

Most Europeans lived in small, walled towns during the late Middle Ages. However, there were a few fine, wealthy cities. Trade flourished in those cities. There were theaters and hospitals, schools and libraries.

There were cities like Constantinople, capital of the Byzantine Empire. One million people lived there. As many as one thousand ships might dock at Constantinople's harbor at the same time.

There were cities like Baghdad, center of the Islamic world. There, scientists studied mathematics and astronomy. Doctors made new discoveries in medicine. Geographers mapped the world.

There were cities like Córdoba, Spain. It was called the *Lighthouse of Learning.* Spanish Muslims and Spanish Jews studied there.

There were cities like Venice and Antwerp. Trade and manufacturing made these places wealthy.

All these cities grew during the Middle Ages. Trade kept them powerful and rich. They were centers for art, science, and education.

Progress in Human Rights:
The Magna Carta

There was little concern with human rights during the early Middle Ages. A lord had a great deal of power over the lives of serfs.

When King John ruled England, he showed no interest at all in anyone's rights. He did not even treat the nobles very well! Suppose that King John did not like a certain noble. Suppose he thought that noble was becoming too powerful. He might very well have the noble put to death.

Nobles were angry. In 1213 a group of powerful men met in England. They drew up a list of rights that they wanted the king to grant them. The final document would make sure that **justice** would not be denied to freemen.

King John did not want to give up any power. He refused to sign the list. In 1215 the nobles sent an army after him. King John saw that he could not defeat the army, so he finally gave in. At Runnymede, near the Thames River, King John signed the list of rights. It became known as the *Great Charter,* or the *Magna Carta.*

Timeline Study

How many years passed from the time of Pope Urban's sermon to the end of the Crusades?

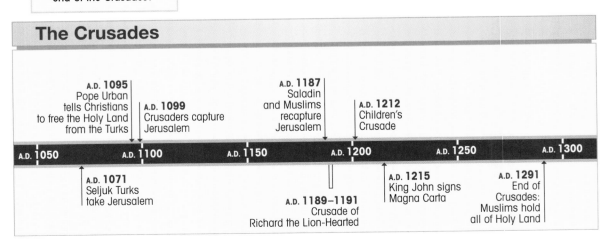

The Crusades

A.D. **1095**
Pope Urban tells Christians to free the Holy Land from the Turks

A.D. **1099**
Crusaders capture Jerusalem

A.D. **1187**
Saladin and Muslims recapture Jerusalem

A.D. **1212**
Children's Crusade

A.D. 1050 | A.D. 1100 | A.D. 1150 | A.D. 1200 | A.D. 1250 | A.D. 1300

A.D. **1071**
Seljuk Turks take Jerusalem

A.D. **1189–1191**
Crusade of Richard the Lion-Hearted

A.D. **1215**
King John signs Magna Carta

A.D. **1291**
End of Crusades: Muslims hold all of Holy Land

WORDS FROM THE PAST
The Magna Carta

When King John signed the Magna Carta in 1215, he gave some rights and liberties to the nobles, or barons. He also reformed the legal system and gave a few rights to freemen. Most people in England, however, were not free—they were serfs. None of the liberties in the charter applied to them.

King John signed the Magna Carta.

How could a charter giving most rights to barons become such an important document? One reason was that when King John signed the charter, he was admitting that even the king had to obey the law. For another reason, over time many people came to believe that the rights in the charter belonged to all English people. In England, later laws granting liberties to all English people were based on the Magna Carta.

The Magna Carta said that:
- A freeman must be tried by a jury of his equals before being sent to prison.
- Taxes would be collected by legal means, not by force.
- Punishment should fit the crime.

The Magna Carta was important to the development of a new nation, the United States of America. The Magna Carta inspired colonists to fight for their rights against King George and Great Britain. The Declaration of Independence, the U.S. Constitution, and many state constitutions were based partly on the ideas of the Magna Carta.

Chapter
12 Review

Summary

Christian crusaders fought to win Jerusalem from the Muslims.
Muslims were followers of Muhammad. Their religion was Islam. Muslims conquered many lands, spreading Islam and the Arabic culture.
The Christians won the Holy Land for a time, but the Muslims got it back.
The Crusaders brought back new ideas, new products, and new plans for trade in Europe.
A medieval revolution in agriculture meant new tools and better methods of farming. Many people migrated eastward.
Medieval towns saw an increase in craftworkers and merchants. The craftworkers formed guilds.
In 1215 King John signed the Magna Carta, giving new rights to the English.

Vocabulary Review

Write *true* or *false*. If the statement is false, change the underlined term to make it true.

1. A religious person might make a <u>pilgrimage</u> to visit the Holy Land.

2. An <u>apprentice</u> receives wages but is not a master.

3. Master craftworkers could belong to a <u>guild</u>.

4. The Magna Carta said that freemen should have <u>paradise</u>.

5. Muhammad was a <u>prophet</u>.

Chapter Quiz

Write your answers in complete sentences.

1. Who went on the Crusades to the Holy Land?

2. How did farming change during the Middle Ages?

3. Why did towns begin to grow in the 1000s?

4. **Critical Thinking** How did Muhammad affect the world beyond his own followers?

5. **Critical Thinking** What was the most important right in the Magna Carta? Explain why.

Using the Timelines

Use the timelines on pages 162 and 176 to answer the questions.

1. How old was Muhammad when he died?

2. When was the Children's Crusade?

Write About History

Complete the following activity.

Form a group of five or six. Assign each person a role such as merchant, soldier, king, noble, knight, serf, or child. Have each person write a speech about the reasons he or she wants to go on a Crusade. When the speeches are ready, perform them for the class.

Unit 4 **Review**

Comprehension Check

Write your answers in complete sentences.

1. Who were the Angles, Saxons, and Jutes?

2. What are three places the Vikings explored or settled?

3. Why was feudal life hard for the serfs?

4. Why did the Black Death strike all classes of feudal society?

5. Where did the Islamic religion begin?

6. After the Crusades, who controlled the Holy Land?

7. Why did the feudal system weaken?

8. What did the Magna Carta say about the relationship of the king to the laws of the land?

Writing an Essay

Answer one of the following essay topics

1. Describe the invasion and conquest of the city of Rome.

2. Compare and contrast the training for knighthood and the training for a medieval trade.

3. Describe a typical medieval town.

Group Activity

Work with a partner to make a storyboard of events in the Middle Ages. Your storyboard might highlight Viking explorations, preparing to become a knight, the Children's Crusade, or another topic.

History in Your Life
In the Middle Ages, guilds developed. How do you think a guild, with its system of apprenticeship, might help you today?

Unit 5 ▷ The Renaissance

Galileo first used the telescope to search the night sky. His discoveries changed the way people thought about the universe.

Learning Objectives

- Explain what the word *Renaissance* means.
- Tell how the invention of movable type helped in the spread of knowledge.
- Name four important people of the Renaissance.
- Explain what the Reformation was.
- Name two leaders of the Reformation.

Words to Know

Renaissance	the revival of art, literature, and learning in Europe in the fourteenth through sixteenth centuries
scholar	a person who has learned much through study
humanism	a concern with the needs and interests of human beings rather than religious ideas
patron	a wealthy person who supports artists
sculptor	a person who makes statues out of wood, stone, marble, or other material
astronomy	the study of stars, planets, and other heavenly bodies
pendulum	a weight hung so that it swings freely back and forth; often used to control a clock's movement
theory	an explanation of how and why something happens, usually based on scientific study
reform	to change for the better
protest	to speak out against or act against something
heretic	a person who is against the teachings of a church

During the Middle Ages the culture and learning of the Greeks and Romans were all but forgotten. For most people it was as if Greece and Rome had never existed. For this reason the Middle Ages, especially the early part, is sometimes called the Dark Ages.

During the Middle Ages, Christianity united the people of Western Europe. This was not, however, a Dark Age. Great universities were founded. Immense cathedrals were built. Toward the end of the Middle Ages, around A.D. 1300, trade and travel increased. New ideas exploded throughout Europe. The period after the Middle Ages became known as the **Renaissance.** *Renaissance* means "rebirth" or "awakening."

The Renaissance was a time of new ideas. During the Middle Ages the Catholic Church was all-powerful. Thinking centered on God. Most **scholars** were also people of the church. During the Renaissance, people began to think about themselves as well as about God. People used to worry about whether or not they would go to heaven after they died. Now they thought more about making a good life on earth. This new belief in the importance of human beings became known as **humanism.** The spirit of humanism sparked new ideas in art, in science, in literature, and in philosophy.

Learn More About It

THE HUMANISTS

Humanists were scholars whose main interest was in human beings. They began to question the church and its leaders. A Dutch scholar, Erasmus, eyed the church critically.

"It seems," Erasmus decided, "that the church is more concerned with wealth and power than with helping men find God."

Erasmus wrote books that questioned the church's practices. He believed that simple ways were best. There was too much ritual and ceremony in the church, he said. Erasmus was a humanist. He believed that if people were just shown what was right, they would live that way. Erasmus was among the first Renaissance scholars to criticize the church. However, he certainly was not the last.

Renaissance Art

The Renaissance began in Italy. Then it spread northwest across Europe. More and more people began to appreciate beautiful things. The work of Italian craftworkers became very fine. People thought of it as art. Europeans showed a new interest in the civilizations of ancient Greece and Rome.

"Perhaps," people said, "that is when civilization was as its best!"

"Look at the art that came out of Greece," they said. "Look at the beautiful statues and the paintings. Look at the fine architecture of the Romans." At first Italian artists tried to copy the work of the ancient Greeks and Romans. Then they began to improve on it.

During the Middle Ages most paintings were of religious scenes. The people in these pictures were not very lifelike. Renaissance artists studied the human form. They tried to make the people in their pictures look more like real people. For the first time, artists used live models.

Craftworkers could make a good living from their work. It was harder for artists to earn a steady wage. Wealthy Italians served as **patrons** for promising young artists. A patron provided food, housing, and enough money for the artist to live on. Because of their patrons, artists were able to work and study to improve. Some of the world's finest artists lived during the Renaissance.

Michelangelo Buonarroti

One of the most famous artists of the Italian Renaissance was Michelangelo Buonarroti. During the Renaissance, people were encouraged to be good at many things. Michelangelo, in true Renaissance spirit, was more than just a fine painter. He was also a **sculptor,** a poet, and an architect.

Michelangelo earned his greatest fame for his sculptures. He studied the human body. He studied the human form at work and at rest. Michelangelo even studied dead bodies. This helped him understand the lines of bone and muscle. His sculptures seem alive and real. Each muscle is perfect. Each position is totally lifelike.

Michelangelo was born in A.D. 1475 in a mountain town in Italy. He began showing artistic talent as a young boy. A wealthy Italian, Lorenzo de' Medici, noticed Michelangelo's brilliance. He became Michelangelo's patron.

One of Michelangelo's most famous works is the sculpture, Pietà.

At age 24 Michelangelo created his first masterpiece, a huge statue called the *Pietà*. Michelangelo sculpted it for St. Peter's Church in Rome. In the *Pietà*, the body of Christ is shown held in his mother's arms. The word *Pietà* came from the Italian word for pity.

Michelangelo's statue *David* is another of his most famous works. Completed in 1504, it is a perfect example of the Renaissance interest in the human form. "David" is strong and looks alive. The statue is 18 feet high and made of solid marble. Michelangelo's *David* is very heavy. It took 40 men to move it from the workshop to a central square in Florence, Italy.

Pope Julius II hired Michelangelo to paint the ceiling of the Sistine Chapel in Rome. Michelangelo painted a series of pictures showing events in the Bible. Over 300 figures from the Bible appear on the 60-foot-high chapel ceiling. Michelangelo had to paint the scenes lying on his back. He lay on a platform held by ropes. He worked on that ceiling for four years.

Later in his life, Michelangelo turned to architecture. He worked on the rebuilding of St. Peter's Church. He took no pay then. He believed it was a task that would please God.

Michelangelo died when he was 90. He had had a long life in which to sculpt, to paint, and to build. His art brought light and beauty to all of Europe.

Education and Learning

All writing was done by hand during the Middle Ages. Books were copied on parchment made of animal skin. Therefore, books were beautiful, but they were also expensive and few in number. Only wealthy people could own books of their own. Most books were written in Latin, the language of the church. The only scholars were clergy. The church was the main place where studying went on. The church dominated all learning.

Remember
Latin, the language of ancient Rome, became the language of the church. Rome was the first place that made Christianity its official religion.

Then, about A.D. 1450, things started to change. Secrets of making paper were brought to Europe from China. They were introduced by the Moors, or Spanish Muslims. Then a new invention eventually made books available to everyone! A German printer named Johannes Gutenberg discovered how to use movable type for printing.

With movable type, letters were molded onto small metal blocks. The letters could be moved around to spell different words. When inked and pressed onto paper, the movable type printed a whole page at one time.

Now books could be made quickly at low cost. Now many people could read the stories of the Greeks and Romans and tales of travel. The ideas of the past and the present were widely available. Books were translated into the languages of the common people, not just that of Latin scholars.

Johannes Gutenberg's printing press made written information available to people.

With the *Gutenberg Bible* Europeans could read the Bible for themselves. People did not have to rely on the church to tell them what the Bible said. The Bible was translated into English, Italian, French, and German.

It became important to be able to read. More schools opened. Schools that taught Greek and Latin grammar were called "grammar" schools. There were new universities. Studies went beyond religious thought. People studied the world. They also studied about their own place in the world.

Science and Invention

The Renaissance was a time for progress. There were some important changes during the Middle Ages. However, change had come slowly. Now new books—and new ideas—were available for anyone who could read. Universities were growing. With the spirit of the Renaissance, change came rapidly.

People explored new ideas. Gutenberg's printing press was just one of the new inventions. Inventors discovered how to make springs. Then they made watches that were small enough to be carried in a pocket. Before, the only clocks had been huge ones on public buildings. Now people could keep time at home.

New instruments helped sailors find their way on the open seas. New maps improved travel. People experimented with metals. Soon they came up with cast iron to replace expensive bronze.

In medicine, the English doctor William Harvey discovered that the heart pumps blood throughout the body. In 1600 the microscope was invented. It led to a new look at the world. Suddenly people learned that there were tiny creatures—smaller than the eye could see!

The Center of the Universe

Some of the greatest scientific discoveries of the Renaissance came in the field of **astronomy**. These new ideas changed people's thinking in many ways. Not only were there new ideas about the way the Earth and stars moved. Now there was also a new way of seeing humanity's place in the whole system. These ideas shook up the scientific world and shook up the church.

For hundreds of years people had believed that the Earth was the center of the universe. They believed that the sun, moon, and stars all moved around the Earth. Then in 1543 the Polish astronomer Nicolaus Copernicus wrote a book. He said that the planets, including the Earth, revolve around the sun.

Most people would not believe him!

You Decide

Why do you think people were not willing to believe Copernicus?

Galileo Galilei

The invention of the telescope challenged more old ideas. Now scientists could get a better look at the sky. An Italian scientist, Galileo Galilei, took up where Copernicus had left off. Galileo was born in Pisa in 1564. He made his first important scientific discovery at the age of 20. Galileo watched a great lamp swing from the ceiling of the cathedral in Pisa. Then he came up with the idea of the **pendulum.**

Later, he discovered the "law of falling bodies." Galileo found that gravity pulls all bodies to the Earth at the same speed, no matter what their weight. Galileo climbed to the top of the Leaning Tower of Pisa to prove his **theory.** Then he dropped a ten-pound weight and a one-pound weight. He showed that they both hit the ground at the same time.

Some people were angry. They were shocked that Galileo would dare to challenge the ideas of the wise Greek, Aristotle. Galileo's discoveries would bring him a lot of angry words.

The invention of the telescope brought another breakthrough. Galileo was not its inventor, but he was the first to use the telescope to study the heavens. With his telescope, Galileo discovered that the moon did not have its own light. It reflected light. He discovered moons around Jupiter and the mass of stars in the Milky Way. All of Galileo's discoveries led him to support Copernicus's theory. The Earth was not the center of the universe. The Earth was just another planet revolving around the sun!

No matter how well Galileo proved his theory, the church would not hear of it. Church members were ordered not to read Galileo's books. The church sent Galileo warnings. He was not to teach his theories. In 1632 Galileo was called to a church hearing. There was a long trial. Galileo had to promise that he would give up his belief in Copernicus's theory. The church forced him to say that the Earth was the center of the universe. Church officials watched Galileo closely for the rest of his life. He became a prisoner in his own home.

✓ Check Your Understanding

Write your answers in complete sentences.

1. What is the meaning of the word *Renaissance?*

2. Why were Michelangelo's sculptures so lifelike?

3. What is the name of the famous ceiling that Michelangelo painted?

The Renaissance Man

The great artists, writers, and scientists of the Renaissance had many kinds of knowledge, talents, and skills. Michelangelo could paint, sculpt, write poetry, and build. Galileo studied medicine, physics, and astronomy.

Today we think of a Renaissance man as one who was expected to enjoy art, to write poetry, and to play a musical instrument. Renaissance education taught people to read and write Latin and to speak several other languages. People were expected to understand the politics of the day. They were supposed to ride well on horseback and to be good at sports.

A Renaissance man should be able to put up a good fight if necessary. A Renaissance man also had to learn proper manners of courtesy and grace. Great importance was placed on being well educated and very well rounded. One of the best examples of the perfect Renaissance man was Leonardo da Vinci.

Leonardo da Vinci

A list of what Leonardo da Vinci could *not* do would very likely be shorter than a list of what he could do! Italian-born da Vinci was a Renaissance genius in not one field, but many. He was one of the world's greatest artists and scientists. Da Vinci was a painter, a sculptor, an architect, and a musician. He was an inventor, an astronomer, and a geologist. He was one of the first to show an interest in "flying machines."

Da Vinci's sketchbooks show drawings of many different machines. His ideas for flying machines were based on the flight of birds. These sketches also show great understanding of the human body and of engineering.

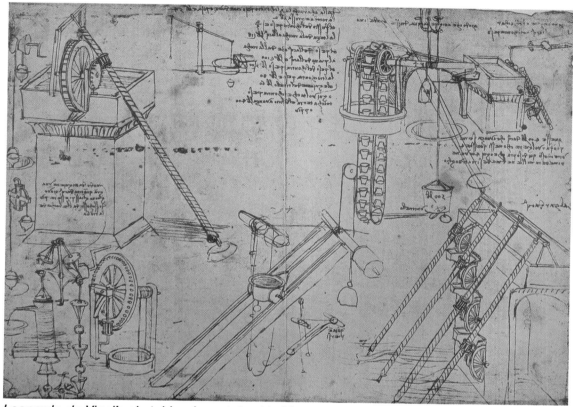
Leonardo da Vinci's sketchbook contains his ideas for machines. Da Vinci was one of the greatest inventors of all time.

Da Vinci had a sure sense of the way things worked. He understood the way parts joined together to form a whole. This great knowledge helped make Da Vinci such a good artist.

Da Vinci's *Mona Lisa* is a painting of a woman with a mysterious smile. It is one of the world's most famous masterpieces. Today it hangs in the Louvre Museum in Paris, France.

For 17 years Da Vinci served the Duke of Milan. He worked as a painter, a sculptor, and an engineer. He was then hired as a painter by the government of Florence. For the last two years of his life, Da Vinci lived in France at the invitation of King Francis I.

The Mona Lisa by Leonardo da Vinci

Da Vinci, the Renaissance man, used one talent to benefit another. His scientific studies helped him understand people and the world. This understanding made his paintings seem all the more real. He had a desire to know more about everything. It was curiosity like Da Vinci's that made the Renaissance a time of new ideas and new inventions.

The Reformation

During the Middle Ages most of the people in Western Europe were Roman Catholics. The Catholic Church held great power. It owned lands and collected taxes. Popes, bishops, and priests were wealthy men.

During the Renaissance, more people went to school and learned to read. They began to question many things, including the ways of the church.

Was it right for the clergy to be so interested in wealth? Was it right that church officials should have so much power? Some people also questioned the ceremonies and rituals that filled church services. They wondered what had become of the simple ways taught by Jesus.

The movement that questioned the practices of the Catholic Church was called the *Reformation.* Some Europeans set out to **reform**, or change, the church.

Martin Luther

A German monk named Martin Luther became a leader among the reformers. Luther was born a German peasant. He grew up as a Roman Catholic. He studied at a university and became a monk. The more Luther studied religion, however, the more he worried. His concern was that the Catholic Church was headed in the wrong direction.

A person did not need fancy rituals or pilgrimages to find God, Luther said. He began to criticize the Catholic Church in public sermons. In 1517 Martin Luther wrote a list of 95 complaints about the church. He nailed it to the door of the Castle Church in Wittenberg, Germany.

Luther continued to question church practices. In 1521 he spoke out against the power and authority granted the pope. This did not please the pope. Luther was told to recant, or take back, what he had said. Luther refused. He said that unless the Bible itself proved him wrong, he would not recant.

Luther was thrown out of the Catholic Church. Emperor Charles V declared Luther an outlaw. He said that anyone could kill Luther without punishment.

Several German princes supported Luther and his feelings about the church. One prince hid him in a castle. The church could not take him prisoner. Soon Luther had so many supporters that before long he was able to set up a whole new church.

The new church, based on Luther's ideas, simplified religion. Religious practices would be based on what was found in the Bible. In 1529 the Catholic Church declared that no one should practice Lutheranism. Lutheran princes decided to **protest.** Because of this, they were called *Protestants*.

Other leaders across Europe also protested against Catholic practice. Other Protestant churches were started. The Reformation was under way.

Other Protestants

A man named John Calvin developed his own version of Protestantism in Switzerland. He set up strict rules for Christians to live by. Calvin's teachings were followed in many parts of Europe.

French Calvinists were called Huguenots. However, most French people were Catholic. They began to resent the Huguenots. On St. Bartholomew's Day, in August of 1572, the Catholics carried out a plot. They murdered all the Protestants they could find in the city of Paris. The killing then spread throughout France. Thousands died during the next few days.

In Spain the Inquisition was at work. The Inquisition was a special court. It had been set up by the Roman Catholic Church to punish **heretics.** Besides Spain, the Inquisition was also going on in France, Germany, and Italy. The Inquisition hunted down anyone who was not a practicing Catholic. It forced people to confess their beliefs, often by torturing them. Some of those who would not accept the Catholic faith were burned to death.

HISTORY FACT

The Inquisition held secret trials, and people on trial were not told who their accusers were.

The Counter Reformation

Many people who wanted change had turned away from the Catholic Church. Others hoped to make changes within the church itself. The movement for reform within the Catholic Church was called the Counter Reformation.

In 1545 the pope called a meeting of clergy at Trent in Italy. The Council of Trent looked for ways to keep the Catholic Church from losing followers. The Council clearly spelled out the beliefs of the church and insisted that people obey them. To reawaken faith among the people, church leaders approved of some new religious orders. One of these was the Society of Jesus.

St. Ignatius Loyola

St. Ignatius Loyola was one of the most powerful leaders of the Counter Reformation. Once a Spanish soldier, Loyola was crippled when a cannonball hit his leg. While recovering, he read a book about the life of Jesus. He decided to begin a spiritual life. He studied to become a priest at the University of Paris.

In 1534 Loyola gathered six followers and formed the Society of Jesus. Its members were called Jesuits. The society quickly gained many more members. Their mission was to win Protestants back to the Catholic Church. The Jesuit order, with ex-soldier Loyola at its head, was run much like an army.

The Jesuits stopped the spread of Protestantism in Europe. However, they carried Catholic ideas to far-off lands. When Loyola died in 1556, the Jesuit order was well established.

Throughout the Reformation, Catholics and Protestants competed for religious control of Europe. The kings and queens of Spain, England, and France became caught up in the struggles of the Reformation. Religion played an important part in shaping Europe's history.

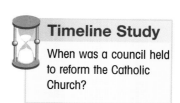

Timeline Study

When was a council held to reform the Catholic Church?

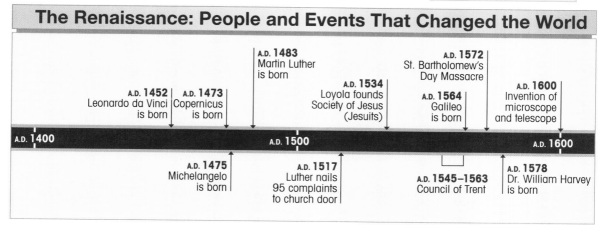

The Renaissance: People and Events That Changed the World

A.D. **1483** Martin Luther is born

A.D. **1572** St. Bartholomew's Day Massacre

A.D. **1452** Leonardo da Vinci is born

A.D. **1473** Copernicus is born

A.D. **1534** Loyola founds Society of Jesus (Jesuits)

A.D. **1564** Galileo is born

A.D. **1600** Invention of microscope and telescope

A.D. **1400**

A.D. **1500**

A.D. **1600**

A.D. **1475** Michelangelo is born

A.D. **1517** Luther nails 95 complaints to church door

A.D. **1545–1563** Council of Trent

A.D. **1578** Dr. William Harvey is born

Summary

Renaissance means "rebirth" or "awakening."
Renaissance Europeans were interested in the art and ideas of the ancient Greeks and Romans.
During the Renaissance, great work was done in art and in science. More books became available to more people.
Human beings were considered important, and the human form in pictures and statues became realistic.
During the Renaissance, some people began to question the practices of the Catholic Church. Martin Luther led the Reformation.
People who protested against the Catholic Church were called Protestants.
Protestants and Roman Catholics competed to control Europe.

heretic

reform

patron

theory

protest

humanism

Vocabulary Review

Complete each sentence with a term from the list.

1. A wealthy person who helps an artist is a ____.

2. Martin Luther wanted to make the church better, or ____ it.

3. A scientific explanation of why something happens is a ____.

4. A person who is against certain church teachings is often called a ____.

5. The belief in the importance of human beings is called ____.

6. A ____ against the Roman Catholic Church led to new forms of Christianity.

Chapter Quiz

Write your answers in complete sentences.

1. How was the art of the Renaissance different from the art of the Middle Ages?

2. What changes did the invention of movable type bring about?

3. Why did Galileo get in trouble with the church?

4. **Critical Thinking** How were the Reformation and the Counter Reformation similar and yet different?

5. **Critical Thinking** During the Renaissance, a well-rounded person was admired. Do you think the same thing is true today? Why or why not?

Using the Timeline

Use the timeline on page 197 to answer the questions.

1. Who was born first, Leonardo Da Vinci or Michelangelo?

2. What event shows that some Protestants died for their faith?

Write About History

Complete the following activity.

Work in a small group to create a biographical dictionary of important people of the Renaissance. If possible, include copies of their works or pictures of their inventions. Be sure to tell why each person was important during the Renaissance and after.

London's Globe Theater was built in 1599. A reconstructed Globe Theater, shown here, stands near the site of the original theater.

Learning Objectives

- Describe the goal of King Philip II of Spain.
- Describe the Spanish Armada and tell what happened to it.
- Name the good things that King Henry IV did for France.
- Explain why King Henry VIII set up a Church of England.
- Explain why the English people called Queen Elizabeth "Good Queen Bess."

Chapter 14 Kings and Queens

Words to Know

monarch	a ruler, like a king, queen, or emperor
loyal	faithful and true to one's country or to a person
nationalism	love of one's nation; patriotism
decline	a period of increasing weakness
reign	the rule of a monarch; or to rule as a king, queen, or emperor
fleet	a group of warships under one command
galleon	a large Spanish sailing ship of long ago, having many decks
annul	to cancel; to make something no longer binding under law
Parliament	England's body of lawmakers

The Age of Monarchs

Spain, France, and England had each become unified into nation-states. Now a separate government ruled each of these three lands. The rulers were **monarchs**—kings and queens who held power over a whole nation.

The people of each nation were **loyal** to their rulers. They felt a bond with their country and with each other. Within a country everyone spoke similar languages and followed similar customs. This feeling of pride and loyalty toward one's nation is called **nationalism**. Nationalism and religious beliefs became very important. Both were powerful forces that shaped sixteenth-century European history.

The monarchs of Spain, France, and England followed different religious teachings. Some were

Roman Catholics. Some were Protestants. One ruler even started his own church. Because of their separate beliefs, the monarchs led their people into wars. They led them through times of peace, through cultural growth, and into national **declines.**

The history of each nation affected each of the others. The religions and the personalities of the monarchs changed the lives of the people of Western Europe.

Spain

In the late 1400s King Ferdinand and Queen Isabella ruled Spain. They were Roman Catholics. They wanted no one but Roman Catholics living in their nation.

You Decide

Do you think that Ferdinand and Isabella were wise rulers? Why or why not?

There were not many Protestants in Spain, but there were Jews and Muslims. Spanish Muslims were called Moors. Ferdinand and Isabella called upon the Inquisition to hunt down anyone who was not Catholic. Many Jews and Moors were tortured and killed. Those who were lucky enough to escape the Inquisition had to flee the country. The Jews left for other European countries and the Middle East. Many of the Moors fled to North Africa.

King Philip II

King Philip II ruled Spain from 1556 until 1598. He began his rule as the most powerful monarch in all of Europe. At that time, Spain was the strongest European nation. It held many other provinces. Spain controlled rich colonies in the Americas. However, Philip's **reign** marked the beginning of Spain's decline.

Like Ferdinand and Isabella, Philip II was a Catholic. He also supported the Inquisition and its methods. King Philip saw himself as a man with a job to do. He wanted to see not only Spain, but all of Europe, under the Catholic Church. King Philip's goal was to crush Protestantism.

King Philip and the Netherlands

Spain ruled the Netherlands. Many Protestants lived there. Philip II would not stand for Protestants living under his rule. He issued a royal command: "People of the Netherlands will accept the Catholic religion!"

Philip did not count on the spirit of the Dutch people. They wanted to worship as they chose. Even the Dutch who were Catholics did not like King Philip. He was a Spaniard, not Dutch. He expected them to send too much tax money to Spain.

The proud people of the Netherlands rebelled. A Dutch prince, William of Orange, led the rebellion in 1568. Things looked grim. However, the Dutch would not give in to Spain. In 1581 the Dutch declared independence. The Netherlands was on its way to freedom from Philip and from Spain.

King Philip and England

King Philip was not alone in his dream of a Catholic Europe. Before he became king, Philip had married Queen Mary I of England. Mary was a loyal Catholic, too. She hoped to see all Protestants converted to Catholicism.

That was not to be. Queen Mary only reigned for five years. When she died, the English throne went to her Protestant half-sister, Elizabeth. Although Philip had been her brother-in-law, Elizabeth saw him as England's enemy. She sent aid to the Netherlands in its fight for freedom from Spain. She gave English ships permission to attack Spanish ships on the world's seas. Queen Elizabeth I was definitely getting in the way of Philip's plans to unite Europe under Catholicism.

Learn More About It

THE SPANISH ARMADA

King Philip II decided to go to war with England. Philip built up a mighty **fleet.** It was called the Armada. The Armada was the largest fleet of ships that Europe had ever seen. In 1588, 130 Spanish ships set out against England. They were giant ships. There were crosses on their billowing sails. King Philip thought that his Armada could not be beaten.

The Armada reached the English Channel. English ships sailed out to meet it. The English ships were much smaller than the Spanish ships. At first it looked as if they would not stand a chance. However, the English crafts were fast. They could dart among the heavy Spanish **galleons,** firing from all sides. The English had skilled captains like Sir Francis Drake. They kept King Philip's Armada busy. The Spanish giants could not stop the quick, little English ships.

The fighting lasted for more than a week. Most of the Spanish ships were damaged. The crippled Armada fled to the North Sea. It escaped the English by sailing north around the British Isles. Heavy winds wrecked many ships off the coast of Ireland. What was left of Philip's once-glorious Armada headed back to Spain. Only 67 ships returned home.

Philip's dream of a Catholic Europe ended with the destruction of his Armada. He had lost many soldiers. The Armada had cost Spain much money. Instead of conquering Europe, King Philip had sent Spain into a decline.

By defeating the Spanish Armada, England's navy ruled the seas.

✓Check Your Understanding

Write your answers in complete sentences.

1. What did the Spanish Inquisition do to the Moors and Jews in Spain?

2. What was the goal of King Philip II of Spain?

3. What happened to the Spanish Armada when it reached the English Channel?

France

France had problems of its own. There, too, wars broke out because of religion. Civil wars had torn the country apart for more than 30 years. The Protestant Reformation had started all the trouble. French Protestants, the Huguenots, fought the Catholics. King Philip of Spain and the pope supported the Catholics. England's Queen Elizabeth sent aid to the Huguenots.

In 1572, thousands of Protestants died in the massacre on St. Bartholomew's Day.

France's Catholic king was assassinated in 1589. Before he died, he named Henry of Navarre as the next king. Henry of Navarre became King Henry IV. Henry IV was a Huguenot!

"Good King Henry"

The French Catholics were in an uproar. A Huguenot was king! Henry IV had to fight to keep his throne. He won several battles, but he could not bring peace. The French, especially those in Paris, would not accept a Protestant as king.

To keep the peace, Henry IV declared himself a Catholic. Most French people welcomed this move. Henry IV was then officially crowned king of France. At last he was able to restore peace to the country.

Yet King Henry IV did not turn his back on the Huguenots. In 1598 he issued the Edict of Nantes. This gave religious freedom to the French Protestants. It was better, Henry said, than seeing France torn apart by civil war.

King Henry turned out to be a good king. Once there was religious peace, Henry worked hard to make France rich and strong. He passed laws to help the farmers. He built new roads. He also encouraged trade and manufacturing.

King Henry sent French explorers out on the seas. Under Henry's reign the first French colony was founded in North America. It was called Quebec. Feelings of nationalism grew. The French called their king "Good King Henry."

Their "good king" was assassinated in 1610. However, the religious freedoms that he had brought to France lasted long after his death.

England

In England in 1485, a man named Henry Tudor became King Henry VII. His reign ended years of civil war. He was the first of several monarchs from the Tudor family.

Henry VII was not a very colorful character, but he was well-liked. He kept England out of wars. He was a good businessperson and built up the country's economy. King Henry VII saw to it that everyone, especially the nobles, paid their taxes.

King Henry VIII

When Henry VII died in 1509, his son became king of England. King Henry VIII was the second Tudor monarch. He had a more colorful personality than his father. He is well remembered for having six wives.

The story of Henry VIII and his wives involves religion. To begin with, Henry VIII was a Catholic. The people liked him. His father had been a good king. The new King Henry seemed good humored and kind.

Problems began when Henry no longer wanted to be married to his wife, Catherine of Aragon. Catherine had only been able to have one child. That child was a girl, the princess Mary, who later married King Philip of Spain. Henry wanted a son to follow him on the throne.

Henry showed an interest in Anne Boleyn. She had been one of his wife's maids of honor. Anne, he thought, was beautiful. She would make him a fine wife. She also might give him a son.

King Henry asked the pope to **annul** his marriage to Catherine. The pope refused, so Henry VIII took matters into his own hands. In secret he married Anne Boleyn in 1533. His marriage to Catherine was annulled by the man who would become the

King Henry VIII separated England from the Catholic Church.

Henry VIII's second wife was Anne Boleyn.

Archbishop of Canterbury. Henry then broke with the Roman Catholic Church. In 1534 England's **Parliament** passed a law making Henry the head of the Church of England.

The new Church of England was still Catholic in its practices and beliefs. However, it was not subject to any control by Rome. Henry's break with the church increased his own power and wealth. He seized all the lands, all the gold, and all the silver that had belonged to the Roman Catholic Church in England.

Things did not go so well for King Henry VIII and his new wife, Anne Boleyn. Like Catherine, Anne gave him a daughter, the princess Elizabeth. However, Henry still wanted a son. He wanted a new wife, too. He accused Anne of being unfaithful. He had her imprisoned in the Tower of London. She was sentenced to death and beheaded in 1536.

Henry married a third wife, Jane Seymour. At last Henry fathered a son, Prince Edward. Henry married again after Jane Seymour died. In fact, he married three more times. One wife, he divorced. Another, he ordered killed. The sixth and last wife outlived Henry.

"The Boy King"

Prince Edward was Henry's only son. When Henry died, Edward took the throne of England. He became the monarch Edward VI at the age of 9.

Under Edward's rule, the number of Protestants increased in England. Protestantism, in fact, became the state religion. Edward was very young. Therefore, the affairs of his country were handled by his uncle, Duke Edward Seymour.

Edward was called "The Boy King." He died after reigning for only six years. Now two women were next in line for the throne of England. They were Henry VIII's two daughters, Princess Mary and Princess Elizabeth.

"Bloody Mary"

Henry's older daughter, Mary, reigned after Edward's death. Queen Mary I was a strong Roman Catholic. She was determined to make England Roman Catholic again. First she struck down all the religious laws passed under Edward VI. She made new laws enforcing Catholicism. Mary married Philip II of Spain. Together they planned to reduce the strength of Protestantism in Europe.

History calls Queen Mary "Bloody Mary." She persecuted Protestants. She had more than 300 Protestants burned to death.

The English Parliament did not like it when Mary married Spain's King Philip. They were afraid of Spanish power. They refused Queen Mary's request to make Catholicism the state religion. Queen Mary I died after reigning for five years. Her spirit was broken because she never saw Protestantism crushed.

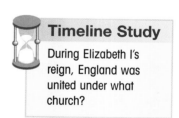

Timeline Study

During Elizabeth I's reign, England was united under what church?

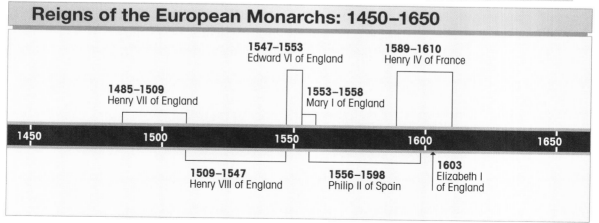

Reigns of the European Monarchs: 1450–1650

1547–1553
Edward VI of England

1589–1610
Henry IV of France

1485–1509
Henry VII of England

1553–1558
Mary I of England

1450   1500   1550   1600   1650

1509–1547
Henry VIII of England

1556–1598
Philip II of Spain

1603
Elizabeth I
of England

"Good Queen Bess"

Queen Elizabeth I was known as "Good Queen Bess."

The next Tudor on the throne of England was Mary's half-sister, Elizabeth. Elizabeth declared that the Church of England was Protestant. The country became firmly united under the one church.

Elizabeth reigned for 45 years, until her death in 1603. Her reign became one of the most glorious periods in English history.

Nationalism grew during Elizabeth's reign. Trouble with Spain only served to strengthen that spirit. England's defeat of the Spanish Armada caused England to cheer.

Queen Elizabeth I did have her faults. She was said to be hot-tempered. She was also called vain. However, the English people loved Elizabeth. Most important, Queen Elizabeth, despite any other faults, loved her England!

Queen Elizabeth never married. Her reign ended the Tudor line. But the English remember her as "Good Queen Bess." She had brought a bright age to England.

HISTORY FACT

Romeo and Juliet, Hamlet, and *Macbeth* are some of Shakespeare's most famous plays.

Elizabeth's England

The reign of Queen Elizabeth became known as the Elizabethan Age. Great writers like William Shakespeare, Edmund Spenser, and Francis Bacon lived in England then. London's Globe Theater was built in 1599. Many of Shakespeare's plays were first performed at the Globe.

Elizabeth helped make her people wealthier and England's cities safer. Except for fighting the Spanish Armada, she kept the country out of expensive wars. This meant there was more money to spend on other things. Elizabeth made new laws. The laws gave work to poor people and shelter for those who could not work.

During the Elizabethan Age, ship captains, like Sir Walter Raleigh, brought new products back to England. They brought tobacco and potatoes from America. Daring sailors like Sir Francis Drake captured treasures from Spanish ships. In Elizabeth's name, English sailors went out to explore the world.

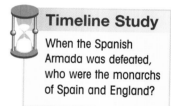

Timeline Study

When the Spanish Armada was defeated, who were the monarchs of Spain and England?

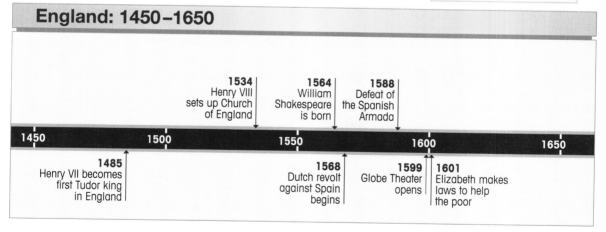

England: 1450–1650

1534 Henry VIII sets up Church of England

1564 William Shakespeare is born

1588 Defeat of the Spanish Armada

1450   1500   1550   1600   1650

1485 Henry VII becomes first Tudor king in England

1568 Dutch revolt against Spain begins

1599 Globe Theater opens

1601 Elizabeth makes laws to help the poor

Summary

King Philip II of Spain wanted to make all Europeans Catholic.

Philip II sent his Armada out to conquer England. However, quicker, smaller English ships sent the Armada home in defeat.

King Philip's reign sent Spain into a decline.

The French King Henry IV converted to Catholicism to keep peace in France. Henry IV passed laws giving religious freedom to the Protestants in France.

The Tudors ruled England from 1485 until 1603.

King Henry VIII of England broke from the Roman Catholic Church and set up a Church of England.

The last Tudor monarch was Queen Elizabeth I. Elizabeth made the Church of England Protestant, and she encouraged English nationalism.

During the Elizabethan Age there were many famous writers in England.

monarch
nationalism
decline
reign
galleon
annul
Parliament

Vocabulary Review

Write a term from the list that matches each definition below.

1. The feeling of pride and loyalty to one's nation

2. A king or queen who holds power over a nation or empire

3. A ship in the Spanish Armada

4. English body of lawmakers

5. A period in which a nation loses strength

6. To cancel something as if it had never been

7. The period of time that a monarch rules

Chapter Quiz

Write your answers in complete sentences.

1. In what ways was Henry IV a good king of France?

2. Why did Henry VIII break with the Roman Catholic Church?

3. In what age did Shakespeare live and write his plays?

4. **Critical Thinking** Which Tudor monarch is the most interesting? Give a reason for your answer.

5. **Critical Thinking** Why did some monarchs want everyone in the nation to belong to one religion?

Using the Timelines

Use the timelines on pages 209 and 211 to answer the questions.

1. For how many years did Henry VIII rule England?

2. Did Elizabeth I make laws to help the poor early or late in her reign?

Write About History

Complete one of the following activities.

1. With your group, practice a scene from one of Shakespeare's plays. Perform it for the rest of the class.

2. Shakespeare's plays were performed at London's Globe Theater. Find out about the new Globe Theater today. Use the Internet for your research.

Unit 5 Review

Comprehension Check

Write your answers in complete sentences.

1. Where did the Renaissance begin?

2. Who were two famous artists of the Renaissance?

3. Who were Martin Luther and John Calvin?

4. What did Henry VII, Henry VIII, Edward VI, Mary I, and Elizabeth I have in common?

5. What happened to Henry VIII's wife Anne Boleyn?

6. What was Queen Mary's dream for England?

7. Why was Queen Elizabeth I called "Good Queen Bess"?

8. How did the defeat of the Spanish Armada affect England?

Writing an Essay

Choose one of the essay topics below. Write your answer on a separate sheet of paper.

1. Describe the major changes in science and invention during the Renaissance.

2. Describe the ideal person during the Renaissance.

3. Explain how religion affected the governments of Europe during the sixteenth century.

Group Activity

Form a group of three or four. Skim through the unit to find times that people disagreed. Make a list of the things they disagreed about. Discuss which side won the argument, and how life might be different today if the other side had won.

History in Your Life

During the Renaissance, many people struggled for freedom to have and express new ideas. Do you ever feel that you are not free to form new ideas? Explain.

Unit **6** ▷ # The Age of Exploration and Conquest

Chapter 15
To the East; To the West

Chapter 16
Explorers, Traders, and Settlers

The Taj Mahal in India was built as a tomb for the emperor Shah Jahan's wife.

Learning Objectives

- Name three Chinese inventions.
- Name the lands conquered by Genghis Khan.
- Describe the role of samurai and shoguns in Japan.
- Tell what religion the Moguls brought to India.
- Name and describe the early Native American civilizations.

Chapter 15

To the East; To the West

Words to Know

forge	to work into shape by heating and hammering
acupuncture	treating pain or illness by putting needles into certain parts of the body
samurai	a class of warriors in the Japanese feudal system
shogun	a great general governing Japan
missionary	a person sent by a church to other countries to spread a religion
barter	to trade goods or services without using money
mosaic	a design made by putting together small pieces of colored stone, glass, or other material

In China ...

European nations battled each other. Empires rose and fell. Nevertheless, Chinese culture continued over the centuries with little change.

The Chinese invented many things. However, China was isolated. The rest of the world would not learn about Chinese discoveries for hundreds of years to come. The Chinese kept their secrets.

Papermaking first began during the Han dynasty. The Chinese made paper from wood ash and cloth pulp. The Chinese also knew how to melt iron and how to **forge** it. They knew how to mine salt. They learned to use **acupuncture** to cure pain and disease. Later, the Chinese used woodblocks with carved characters to print books. Chinese sailors developed compasses. Gunpowder also was invented in China. It was used first for fireworks. Not until A.D. 1161 were the first explosives used in actual battle.

The Silk Road

A route known as the *Silk Road* was China's main link to the Western world. A few traders traveled this road. They made their way across deserts and over mountains. They brought Chinese goods to the West. Many Europeans were fascinated with Chinese art and style. They especially liked the fine silk cloth. It was made from threads spun by silkworms.

The Silk Road was not a one-way road. Chinese products came out of China. New ideas filtered into China along this road. Buddhism came to China from India in the second century A.D. In the next centuries it spread across China.

Mongol Invasion

To the north of China are the vast plains of central Asia. In the second century, the people who lived there were called Mongols. They were nomads, who were loosely organized into groups. They wandered over their lands with their horses, sheep, camels, oxen, and goats. The Mongols were expert horsemen. They were also skilled at using the bow and arrow. In their camps they lived in felt tents called *yurts*.

In A.D. 1206 a great chief took power over all the Mongols. His name was Genghis Khan. *Khan* was a title given to rulers. Genghis Khan believed that he was destined to rule a great empire. He built up a huge army of Mongol soldiers. They conquered many lands including parts of China, Russia, Persia, and India.

Genghis Khan had little education. Yet, he was clever and ruthless. With his soldiers on horseback, he swept across the countryside. The thunder of hooves of Mongol horses was a terrifying sound. The Mongols were among the most fierce conquerors in history. If any city in their path tried to fight, the Mongols showed no mercy. Every single person in the city would be killed.

Great Names in History

KUBLAI KHAN

Perhaps the greatest of the Khans was Kublai Khan. He was a grandson of Genghis Khan. Kublai Khan completed the conquest of China. Chinese farmers were no match for the Mongol armies. The Mongols ruled China from A.D. 1260 until A.D. 1368.

Kublai Khan ran his empire well. He was a Buddhist, but he allowed religious freedom. He saw to it that roads were good and travel was pleasant. There were stones to mark the way. Trees were also planted to give shade to travelers.

Kublai Khan developed a postal service. He wanted to make it easy for people throughout his empire to communicate. Horsemen carried messages along China's Great Wall. A post house stood every 25 miles along the wall. At each post house messengers could change horses, and travelers could rest. The Grand Canal was built to transport goods from north to south. Chinese boats called junks carried goods along the 850 miles of waterway.

Marco Polo

Marco Polo was a trader and a traveler. He lived in Venice, Italy. Marco Polo traveled to China with his father and his uncle. In about 1275 they went to see Kublai Khan. Khan's palace was in the city of Beijing, then called Cambaluc by Marco Polo.

Kublai Khan welcomed the traders. He allowed Marco Polo to travel about his empire. The young Italian stayed in China for 17 years. Marco Polo saw sights that no other European had ever seen.

HISTORY FACT

Kublai Khan's kingdom was huge. It extended as far as Russia.

Then Marco Polo returned to Italy. He got caught up in a war. The fight was between Venice and another Italian city, Genoa. He was taken as a prisoner of war. He was thrown into jail in Genoa. There he told some amazing tales to a fellow prisoner. The tales eventually became a part of his book, *Description of the World*. The book contained many stories of the great Chinese civilization and of the empire of Kublai Khan.

Many people did not believe Marco Polo's tales. Later, however, the stories proved to be true. Marco Polo had written a good description of his adventures in China.

Marco Polo had found China a rich land. He found that travel in China was quite easy.

Marco Polo was impressed with all he saw in China. The Chinese were using gunpowder and compasses. They used coal for heat. Marco Polo wrote that coal

Marco Polo was the first European trader to visit China.

was "a sort of black stone, which they dig out of the mountainside... ." He was interested in their use of paper, especially for money. Europeans were still using heavy, metal coins.

Marco Polo's stories gave Europeans their first glimpse of life inside China.

The End of Mongol Rule

In the 1300s the Chinese revolted against Mongol rule. Mongol rule ended in China. The Mongols were driven away. The Ming dynasty reigned.

Ming emperors lived in Beijing in a great palace known as the *Forbidden City*. The Mings ruled there for nearly 300 years. Chinese art and literature thrived during this period. Europeans found Ming art beautiful. They wanted to trade their European goods for the Ming art. China said no. The Chinese would only accept payments of gold and silver.

You Decide
Blue and white Ming porcelain is still much admired. Why do you think antiques, or very old things, are often popular with people today?

In Japan ...

Japan is a group of islands off the coast of China. Very little is known about the early history of Japan. The reason is that the ancient Japanese had no system of writing. Writing first came to Japan from China during the fifth century A.D. Customs, crafts, arts, and ideas of government and taxes also came to Japan from China. The Japanese adapted the Chinese calendar system and the ideas of Confucius. About A.D. 552 Buddhism came to Japan from China and Korea.

The Japanese visited China. The Chinese came to Japan. The Japanese began to model their way of life after Chinese ways. In the seventh century one Japanese emperor was especially drawn to Chinese ways. He *ordered* changes in Japanese life to make it more like Chinese life.

Japan's Feudal System

Remember
The European feudal warriors were called knights. Like the samurai, they defended their lords.

Europeans of the Middle Ages lived under a system of feudalism. At the same time so did the Japanese. Japanese feudal society was divided into classes. Nobles were at the top. A class of warriors fought for the nobles. Japanese feudal warriors were called **samurai.** Samurai were given many privileges. The nobles gave them wealth and land. The samurai were respected as an upper class. In return, samurai warriors pledged loyalty and protection to their nobles.

Samurai warriors protected people. They fought with large, two-handed swords.

The samurai were highly trained soldiers. They were expected to die, if necessary, for their noble. Samurai fought with huge, two-handed swords. Before attacking, a samurai would first shout his own name. Then he would shout of the bravery of his ancestors. This was meant to scare his enemy.

The nobles and samurai made up the upper classes of Japanese feudal society. However, most of the people in Japan were peasants. They raised the food for the nobles and warriors.

Japanese society also included craftworkers and a few traders. Traders were looked down upon. Buying and selling goods was not considered honorable.

Over time feudal clans, or families, later united into larger groups. Eventually Japan became a nation-state under one emperor. The emperor was called the mikado. Japanese people honored their mikado. However, the mikado had no real power. The country was actually ruled by a warlord, a military leader.

One of those warlords was a man called Yoritomo. In A.D. 1192 he began to use the title of **shogun**. For almost 700 years one powerful shogun after another ruled Japan. Highly trained samurai enforced the shogun's rule. Shogun rule lasted until 1867.

Kublai Khan, the Mongol emperor of China, tried twice to conquer Japan. He launched attacks in 1274 and in 1281. Both times, his fleet was defeated because of fierce storms. The Japanese called these raging storms *Kamikaze*, which means "Divine Wind."

HISTORY FACT

The shoguns were so powerful that they actually took over leadership from the emperors.

Kublai Khan, the Mongol emperor of China, was twice defeated in attacks on Japan.

The Hermit Nation

A hermit is someone who lives alone, away from others. Japan under the shoguns could be called a hermit nation. Japan showed little interest in the rest of the world. For years it remained isolated, like China.

The Italian traveler Marco Polo first told Europeans about Japan. He called the country *Cipango,* land of gold and riches. Europeans liked the sound of "gold and riches"! Traders began to travel to Japan.

At first the Japanese allowed the trade. They even welcomed Christian **missionaries.** Soon, however, the shogun began to worry. He thought that Christianity and European ways might upset the Japanese culture. Therefore, the ruling shogun of the Tokugawa family closed the doors to Japan. Only the Dutch were allowed to continue a little trade. Just one Dutch ship a year could come to the port of Nagasaki.

The Japanese were strict about their rules. Stories tell of foreign sailors shipwrecked on Japanese shores being put to death. Their crime was that they had dared to set foot on Japanese soil.

The shogun also forbade the Japanese to travel outside of their country. Beginning in about 1600, Japan was totally separated from the rest of the world. For about the next 250 years, Japan remained alone.

✓Check Your Understanding

Write your answers in complete sentences.

1. What were three Chinese inventions?

2. What lands were conquered by Genghis Khan?

3. What was the role of the shogun in Japanese society?

In India ...

For a long time India was divided into different kingdoms. Wealthy princes ruled each one. The people followed the Hindu religion. But in about 268 B.C., Asoka became emperor. He converted to Buddhism. Most of India's people turned away from the Hindu religion with its strict caste laws. Many turned to the teachings of Buddha.

Later, however, the Hindu religion became popular in India again. Hindu believers flocked to the Ganges River to wash away their sins. The Hindus believed that all rivers came from the gods. They thought that the Ganges was especially holy.

The Moguls Invade India

In the eighth century A.D., Muslim warriors began a series of invasions into India.

The first Muslims came from Arabia. Three hundred years later, the invaders came from Persia and Afghanistan. The city of Delhi was captured several times. In 1206 Muslims set up a government in Delhi. In 1398 the conqueror Tamerlane and his army from central Asia raided India and captured Delhi once again.

In 1526 a Muslim prince of Afghanistan named Babar invaded India. He was a direct descendant of Genghis Khan. Babar conquered most of northern India. He established the Mogul empire and made himself emperor.

The greatest Mogul emperor was Babar's grandson, Akbar. He extended Mogul rule to most of India. He was a wise ruler. He was a Muslim, but he let others worship as they pleased. He tried to bring people of all religions together to live in harmony. Most of the empire remained Hindu.

The Mogul Empire lasted for about 200 years. These were good years. The strong central government provided a time of peace. The arts thrived. A special blend of Middle Eastern and Indian culture developed. The Moguls left fine buildings. One of these is the famous Taj Mahal. It was built in Agra by Shah Jahan as a tomb for his wife, Mumtaz Mahal. Shah Jahan was the grandson of Akbar.

Shah Jahan had a son called Aurangzeb. In 1658 Aurangzeb took the throne. Aurangzeb was a harsh ruler. He threw his father in prison. He made Hindus pay a special tax. He destroyed many Hindu temples. Aurangzeb tried to force people to convert to Islam. In central India the Hindus revolted. The empire was weakened. Aurangzeb died in 1707. Shortly after, the Mogul Empire began to break up.

History Fact

It took 20,000 workers 20 years, from 1630 to 1650, to complete the building of the Taj Mahal.

In the Americas ...

Until the end of the fifteenth century, most Europeans did not know about the Americas. Only the Vikings knew that land existed across the western sea. One day the Europeans would call these lands the New World. To the Native Americans, however, the Americas were home.

Mound Builders and Cliff Dwellers

Groups of Native Americans, or Indians, lived in different parts of the Americas. From about 100 B.C. to A.D. 500, the Hopewell Indians lived in the Ohio River Valley. They built huge burial mounds. As many as 1,000 people were sometimes buried in a single mound. Other Native Americans lived along the Mississippi River. They too built giant mounds of earth around A.D. 1000. They built their temples on top of the mounds. These Indians were called Mississippians. They lived mainly by farming.

To the west, in what is now New Mexico, Arizona, and Colorado, lived the cliff dwellers. These Indians were called Anasazi. Some descendants of the Anasazi are called Pueblo Indians, from the Spanish word for *town.* Around A.D. 1000, the Anasazi began building villages on the sides of cliffs. All building was done with sandstone blocks and mud. Some homes were on protected ledges. Others were in hollow spaces in the cliff walls. Most homes were two or three stories high. As many as 1,500 people lived in one of these villages. No one knows why the Anasazi moved away by about A.D. 1300. They left behind their empty villages, which can still be seen today. Perhaps the climate had become too dry to allow farming.

These early Native Americans did not have a system of writing. What we know about them comes from the findings of archaeologists.

Early Civilizations of North America

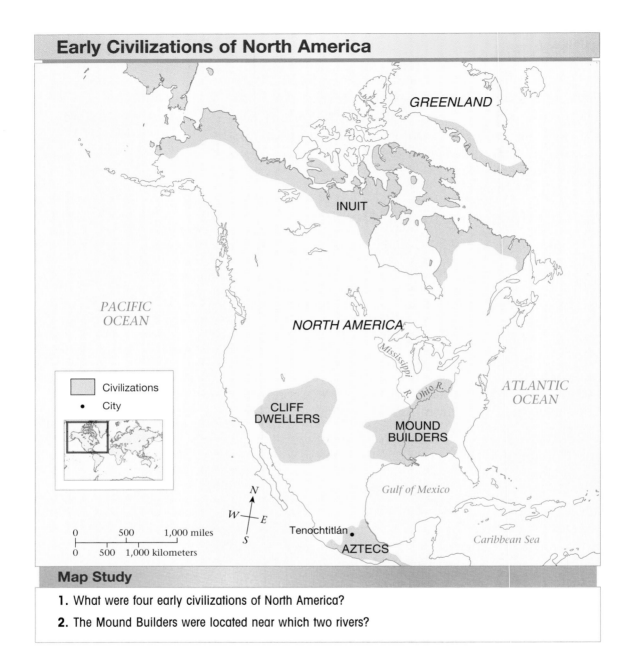

GREENLAND

INUIT

NORTH AMERICA

PACIFIC
OCEAN

Mississippi R.

Ohio R.

ATLANTIC
OCEAN

CLIFF
DWELLERS

MOUND
BUILDERS

Gulf of Mexico

Caribbean Sea

Tenochtitlán •

AZTECS

Civilizations

• City

N
W — E
S

0   500   1,000 miles
0   500   1,000 kilometers

Map Study

1. What were four early civilizations of North America?

2. The Mound Builders were located near which two rivers?

The Inuit

The Inuit, or Eskimos, lived in the far north of North America. The Inuit ate the meat of caribou, seals, whales, and birds. They also ate fish from icy northern waters. They had no greens to eat. They got their vitamins by eating every part of an animal. They often ate the meat raw. The word *eskimo* is an American Indian word. It means "eater of raw meat." The Eskimos call themselves *Inuit,* which means "people."

The Inuit lived in one of the coldest places in the world. They made tools and weapons to fit their cold land. They traveled in sleds made of driftwood and leather. The sleds were pulled by teams of dogs. In the summer the Inuit lived in tents made of animal skins. In winter they lived in houses made of blocks of snow. These houses were called *igloos.*

The Inuit loved feasts and celebrations. Their medicine men danced and sang to the spirits of the earth and the air.

The first Europeans to meet the Inuit were the Vikings. The Inuit arrived in Greenland about A.D. 1100. They found Vikings already living there.

The Aztecs

The Aztecs were an important civilization. In the 1200s they settled in a large valley in Mexico. The Aztecs built one of the most advanced civilizations in the Americas. Over time they conquered and ruled five to six million people.

"Find a place where a great eagle sits on a cactus," Aztec priests declared. "The eagle holds a snake in its beak. At that place, you shall build your temple."

The Aztecs followed the words of their priests. They believed that these words came from the gods. So that

Remember
The Olmecs and the Maya were some of the earliest civilizations in the Americas. They built their cities in Mexico and Central America.

is how they decided on a site for the capital. Where they found the eagle, they built the city of Tenochtitlán. Modern-day Mexico City is on the same site as Tenochtitlán, the ancient Aztec capital.

The Aztecs were feared by other Native Americans. During the 1400s, Aztec warriors conquered all the lands around Tenochtitlán. When Montezuma II came to the throne in 1502, he ruled the Aztec empire.

The Aztecs collected tributes from those they conquered. The tributes came in the form of gold and silver, craftwork, food, and human prisoners. Some prisoners were offered as sacrifices to Aztec gods. The Aztec religion called for sacrifices to keep the gods happy. The Aztecs developed advanced methods of farming. In mountainous areas, they used terracing to stop the soil from eroding. In dry areas, they used irrigation canals. The Aztecs' greatest achievement, though, was the system of farming called *chinampa*. In this system, the Aztecs farmed in swamps and lakes. They dug drainage ditches and created islands of mud where they grew crops.

The Aztecs had a well-ordered society. They invented a form of picture writing. They also developed a system of numbers to help them keep track of what they owned. They had a calendar stone that recorded time. They built temples and buildings in a pyramid style.

The Aztecs had no need for money since they **bartered** for goods. Chocolate was a favorite drink. So cocoa beans were often traded. Our word *chocolate*, in fact, comes from the Aztec language.

The Aztecs made some beautiful craftwork. Archaeologists have found **mosaic** masks made of turquoise and jade. The Aztecs also used colorful feathers to make headdresses and cloaks.

The Aztecs liked games and contests of athletic strength and skill. One of their favorite games was called *tlachiti*. It was a combination of handball and basketball. The players had to put a very bouncy rubber ball through rings at either end of a court.

The Aztec empire ended in 1521. Cortéz and his army arrived in Tenochtitlán in 1519. They were amazed at what they found. Tenochtitlán was a beautiful city, with floating gardens, drawbridges, and markets. It was larger than any Spanish city of that time.

The Spaniards were welcomed in friendship. The Aztecs may have believed that Cortéz was a long lost Aztec god. The god sailed away across the sea and was expected to return someday. Yet Cortéz captured the emperor, Montezuma, and made him a prisoner. In 1520, Aztecs drove the Spaniards away. Montezuma died during the fighting. The next year Cortéz returned and destroyed Tenochtitlán.

The Incas

The earliest history of the Incas is only legend. What we know for sure is that the Incas lived in the mountains of what is now Peru in South America. Around A.D. 1200 they began to build their empire. In time, the Incas conquered much of western South America. They took over the rest of Peru and parts of what are now Colombia, Bolivia, Ecuador, and Chile.

One man ruled the entire Inca Empire. He was called the *Inca*. His people worshiped him as a direct descendant of the sun. The sun was the Inca's most powerful god. The Inca's word was law. He had many officials to see that his laws were obeyed.

The Inca ruled over a giant empire from his capital at Cuzco. More than six million people lived under his rule. Communicating with all these subjects was a problem. Therefore, the Incas built a fine network of roads. These roads improved communication. They connected all corners of the empire.

These are the ruins of the Inca city of Machu Picchu in Peru.

The Incas also built bridges of twisted vines to stretch across steep rain forest ravines. They had no horses or wheeled vehicles. All traveling was done on foot. Llamas carried the Inca's goods.

Swift runners raced along the Inca roads to deliver messages. The Incas had no system of writing. Messages were passed by word of mouth. Runners also carried *quipus*. These were different colored ropes with knots to stand for numbers. They used the quipus to keep track of things.

The Incas built rest stops along their roads. At each stop a tired runner could tell his message to a fresh runner. Then that messenger would hurry to the next stop. This relay system kept communication moving across the empire.

The Incas were fine builders. They used huge stone blocks. They fit the blocks together very carefully. They needed no mortar or cement of any kind. Some of the stones fit together so tightly that the blade of a knife could not slide between them! Inca buildings still stand at Cuzco today, even after earthquakes have destroyed modern structures.

The Incas had plenty of gold and plenty of silver. Their temples were decorated with both of the valuable metals. Inca artists made beautiful objects of solid gold. These were often inlaid with precious jewels.

It is no wonder that the Spanish explorers were drawn to the Incas. In 1532 tales of great wealth brought Francisco Pizarro to South America. His visit was the beginning of the end of the Inca civilization.

Two Worlds Meet

For centuries the rest of the world did not know about the Americas or the people living there. Then the Vikings landed in North America. They met Native Americans, but the Vikings did not stay long in North America. Much later, European explorers found the continent by accident. What they were really looking for was a quicker route to India and the Far East. The place they found instead seemed like a land of wealth and plenty. It seemed well worth exploring and conquering.

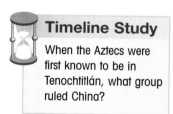

Timeline Study

When the Aztecs were first known to be in Tenochtitlán, what group ruled China?

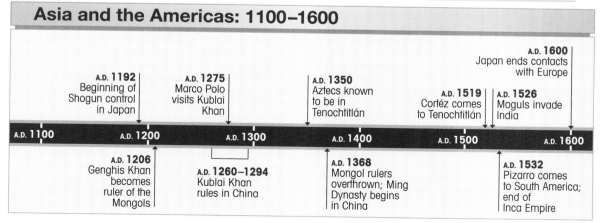

Asia and the Americas: 1100–1600

A.D. 1192 Beginning of Shogun control in Japan

A.D. 1275 Marco Polo visits Kublai Khan

A.D. 1350 Aztecs known to be in Tenochtitlán

A.D. 1519 Cortéz comes to Tenochtitlán

A.D. 1526 Moguls invade India

A.D. 1600 Japan ends contacts with Europe

A.D. 1100 — A.D. 1200 — A.D. 1300 — A.D. 1400 — A.D. 1500 — A.D. 1600

A.D. 1206 Genghis Khan becomes ruler of the Mongols

A.D. 1260–1294 Kublai Khan rules in China

A.D. 1368 Mongol rulers overthrown; Ming Dynasty begins in China

A.D. 1532 Pizarro comes to South America; end of Inca Empire

Summary

China was isolated for centuries, and Chinese culture changed very little. The Chinese, however, were ahead of the Europeans in making paper, using gunpowder, and in printing. After the Mongols from the north invaded China, Marco Polo visited a Mongol ruler, Kublai Khan.

Japan was a feudal society in the Middle Ages and shoguns and their samurai, or warriors, ruled the country. About 1600, the ruling shogun forbade the Japanese to leave their country. Japan was isolated for the next 250 years.

The people of India turned from Hinduism to Buddhism and back to Hinduism. The Moguls brought Islam to India in the eighth century A.D.

Most Europeans did not know about the Americas until the late 1400s. However, Native Americans built civilizations in the Americas long before that time. The mound builders, cliff dwellers, and the Inuit lived in North America. The Aztecs built a great empire in Mexico, in southern North America. The Incas lived in Peru, in South America.

Vocabulary Review

Write *true* or *false*. If the statement is false, change the underlined term to make it true.

1. A <u>samurai</u> was a great general governing Japan.

2. The Aztecs would <u>forge</u> for goods, exchanging them without the use of money.

3. Small pieces of stone or glass can be used to create a <u>mosaic</u>.

4. The Chinese invented <u>acupuncture</u>, which uses needles to treat pain and illness.

Chapter Quiz

Write your answers in complete sentences.

1. How did Marco Polo feel about what he had seen in China?

2. What was the role of the samurai in Japan?

3. What religion did the Moguls bring to India?

4. **Critical Thinking** Why was the Silk Road important?

5. **Critical Thinking** Why did the early civilizations of the Americas develop in such different ways?

Using the Timeline

Use the timeline on page 233 to answer the questions.

1. How long did Kublai Khan rule in China?

2. What happened in India in A.D. 1526?

Write About History

Complete the following activity.

Work with a partner to make a poster that compares the civilizations in the Americas before the European explorers arrived. Include categories such as the following: Location, Climate, Building Styles, Religion, Food, and Economy. Try to include one picture for each civilization.

Pilgrims celebrated their first year in Plymouth, Massachusetts, by holding a harvest festival with Native Americans.

Learning Objectives

- Tell how Columbus came to land in the Americas.
- Identify the Spanish conquistadors and the lands they claimed.
- Describe the relationship between Spanish settlers and the Native Americans.
- Explain how the slave trade developed.
- Name the groups of Europeans who settled the east coast of North America.

Chapter 16 Explorers, Traders, and Settlers

Words to Know

conquistador	a Spanish conqueror
piracy	the robbing of ships on the ocean
Puritan	a member of a sixteenth- or seventeenth-century English group of Protestants who wanted to make the Church of England stricter
trapper	a person who traps wild animals for their furs
stock	shares in a business
shareholder	a person who owns one or more parts (shares) of a business
investment	money lent to businesses in order to get even more money back
interest	money paid for the use of other people's money
insurance	a guarantee that a person or company will be paid money to cover losses

Christopher Columbus

Christopher Columbus set sail from Spain in August of 1492. He was not out to prove that the world was round, as stories often tell. He was not out to conquer new lands. Columbus was looking for a water route to Asia. He believed that by sailing west he might find a shorter route to the treasures of Asia. He had convinced Queen Isabella of Spain to support his voyage. Queen Isabella and King Ferdinand gave Columbus three ships for the voyage. They were the *Niña,* the *Pinta,* and the *Santa Maria.*

Columbus sailed westward. Instead of reaching Asia, Columbus landed on an island in the Bahamas. There it was—a new world where no land should have been!

Early Voyages of Exploration

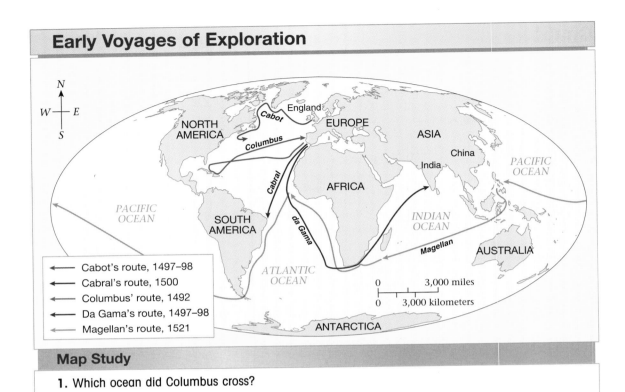

Map legend:
- ← Cabot's route, 1497–98
- ← Cabral's route, 1500
- ← Columbus' route, 1492
- ← Da Gama's route, 1497–98
- ← Magellan's route, 1521

Map Study

1. Which ocean did Columbus cross?

2. How would you describe da Gama's route to India?

Columbus claimed the land in the name of Spain. He named the land San Salvador.

Columbus thought he had reached an island off the coast of India. That is why he called the people living there "Indians." It was not too many years before people realized Columbus was wrong about the land's location. However, one term for Native Americans is still "Indians." Those islands that Columbus explored are called the "West Indies."

Many places in the Americas have been named after Columbus. The word *America*, however, comes from the name of another explorer, Amerigo Vespucci. He was a European explorer who reached the mainland of South America in 1500. A cartographer honored his accomplishment by naming the Americas after him.

Portuguese Explorers

Other explorers searched for that water route to Asia. The Spaniards and the Portuguese led the way in voyages of discovery.

In 1497 Vasco da Gama sailed around Africa's Cape of Good Hope. Vasco da Gama was a Portuguese noble and sailor. He became the first explorer to reach India by a sea route.

Another Portuguese explorer, Pedro Cabral, set out for India in 1500. He sailed wide of Africa and found Brazil. Thanks to Cabral, Brazil was claimed in the name of Portugal.

In 1519 the Portuguese navigator Ferdinand Magellan began a voyage around the whole world. His own king had refused to back his trip. However, the Spanish king agreed to supply five ships and 241 men.

Magellan sailed around South America and across the Pacific. However, Magellan himself did not make it all the way. In 1521 he was killed by people in the Philippine Islands. However, one of the ships, the *Victoria,* completed the trip around the world. With only 18 survivors, it returned to Spain in 1522. This was the first ship to have sailed completely around the world. The *Victoria's* voyage was the first proof that Earth is round.

Remember
Marco Polo had introduced Europeans to the treasures of Asia.

The Conquerors

Europeans quickly realized what a prize they had found in the new lands. They thought it did not matter that people already lived there. Europeans did not recognize that the natives had civilizations and cultures of their own. Europeans wanted the new lands for themselves.

Hernando Cortéz met the Aztec ruler, Montezuma. Cortéz went on to conquer the Aztec Empire.

When the Spanish **conquistadors** arrived in Mexico and South America, they found great civilizations. The conquistadors brought guns and horses to help them claim gold. The Native Americans had neither one.

Hernando Cortéz attacked the Aztec capital of Tenochtitlán in 1521. The Spaniards soon conquered all of Mexico. They called it New Spain.

In South America, Francisco Pizarro attacked the Inca Empire in 1532. Again, the Native Americans were no match for the new enemy they did not understand. The Spaniards tried to make the Indians accept the Christian religion. Many Indians who refused were burned to death.

The Spaniards treated the Indians cruelly in other ways, too. They used the Indians as slaves, working them harder than animals. Many Europeans thought these people were only savages.

The Europeans caused the Indians to suffer in yet another way. The Europeans brought their diseases with them to the Americas. Thousands of Native Americans died from the new diseases.

You Decide

Many people think the Native Americans would have been better off if the Europeans had never set foot in the Americas. What do you think?

Learn More About It

THE SLAVE TRADE

In Africa, too, some Europeans were treating people like work animals. The Europeans discovered that there was money to be made in the slave trade. The Spanish and Portuguese brought ships full of Africans to the Americas, where the Africans were sold into slavery.

For a time the Spanish and Portuguese controlled the slave markets. Soon England and France joined the slave trade, too.

An English naval commander, Sir John Hawkins, was the first English slave trader. In the 1560s Hawkins made three voyages. On each one, he stopped in Africa to find the strongest, healthiest men. Then Hawkins carried these Africans to Spanish colonies in the Americas. There he sold them into slavery. Slave-trading led the way in setting up trade between England and the Americas.

✓**Check Your Understanding**

Write your answers in complete sentences.

1. How did Columbus happen to land on the Americas?

2. Where does the name *America* come from?

3. How did the Spaniards treat the Native Americans?

Pirates

When the English and French set sail for the Americas, they were a little late. South American land had already been claimed. Therefore, they often resorted to **piracy** to claim their share of South American treasures.

You Decide

Do you think Drake was an explorer or a pirate?

Sir Francis Drake was English. He was the first English person to sail around the world. The English called him an explorer. The Spanish called him a pirate! Drake made daring attacks on Spanish ships and towns in the West Indies. He brought his treasures home to England. The English loved Drake, but the Spaniards feared his piracy. They called him "The Dragon."

Settlers

By A.D. 1600, Spain had created an empire in present-day New Mexico, Florida, Central America, the Caribbean islands, and South America. The English, French, and Dutch explored and settled in North America.

The first Europeans landed on the east coast of North America. There they found Native Americans living in villages. Each nation had its own customs and culture. Most of the Native Americans farmed, hunted, and fished. They grew corn and other vegetables. Although the Native Americans were friendly at first, they did not fit in with the newcomers. The Europeans brought new ways, new religions, and new diseases. The Native Americans became wary of the settlers.

In 1607 a group of English colonists settled in Jamestown in Virginia. Another group of English, the Pilgrims, arrived on the sailing ship *Mayflower* in 1620. The Pilgrims landed at Plymouth, Massachusetts. They were seeking religious freedom. The **Puritans** were another religious group from England. They built several settlements on Massachusetts Bay in the 1630s.

The 13 Original Colonies

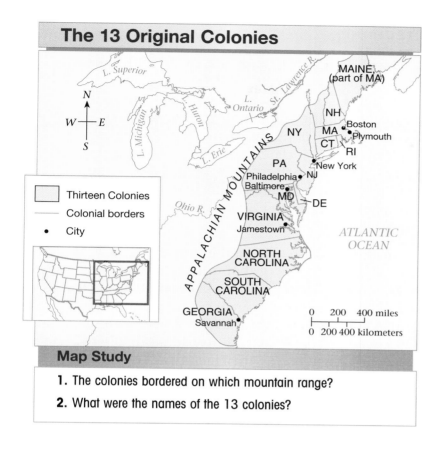

Map Study

1. The colonies bordered on which mountain range?
2. What were the names of the 13 colonies?

In 1626, the Dutch started a village at the mouth of the Hudson River, in present-day New York state. This village is New York City today. More Europeans came seeking religious freedom, a better life, and adventure. Most of the colonists became farmers. In the south, tobacco became a money-making crop. Slave traders brought Africans to help on the tobacco plantations.

The settlers on North America's east coast formed 13 colonies. The colonies were under the control of the English government. Trade with Europe helped the colonies grow. Port towns like Boston sprang up.

The Native Americans and the Europeans did not continue to live peacefully. Slowly, the Native Americans were driven westward. Over time they lost their lands to the newcomers.

Traders

Not all of the people who came to North America were interested in settling and farming. Some newcomers were **trappers.** These people made their living by hunting animals and selling the furs. Many French trapped along the Mississippi River. They explored the area, claiming lands in the name of France. Other French trappers went north to Canada. Hunting was good there, and fishing too. The French created outposts from Canada to south of the mouth of the Mississippi River.

The English also held land in Canada. This land had been claimed by John Cabot in 1497. Sometimes fights over Canadian land broke out between the French and the English. In 1608 the French founded the Canadian settlement of Quebec. In 1759 the English captured that settlement. By 1763 the English had taken all of Canada from the French during the French and Indian War.

Trading Companies

Trade between Europe and the Americas became big business. Merchants set up trading companies. The trading companies offered shares of their **stock** for sale. Sea voyages were expensive, so the **shareholders' investments** helped pay for the trips. Profits from successful trips were divided among the shareholders. In 1613 the Amsterdam Stock Exchange was built. This was the first building meant just for the buying and selling of stocks.

Three European countries became leaders in trade: the Netherlands, England, and France. These were the trading powers of the 1600s. Banks were set up to help pay for trading trips. They lent money to the merchants and charged a fee called **interest.** London and Amsterdam became important banking cities.

HISTORY FACT

Today many countries have stock exchanges in which people can buy and sell stocks.

Shipping could be a risky business. There were storms and shipwrecks and lost cargoes. Although merchants could make a lot of money, they could also lose everything. The merchants paid companies a fee for **insurance** to protect their businesses. Then if their ships were lost at sea or attacked by pirates, the insurance companies covered the losses.

Three trading companies became powerful forces in the growing trade between Europe and the East Indies. These were the English East India Company, the Dutch East India Company, and the French East India Company. They brought home ships loaded with spices and rice, diamonds and ivory.

The New Middle Class

Successful trade ventures created a new, rising middle class in Europe. European merchants became wealthy. They often lived in the style of nobility. They built grand houses in the cities or settled on country estates. With their new-found wealth, some merchants became interested only in money, fashion, and fine living. Other merchants used their own good fortune to help others. They paid to set up hospitals, orphanages, and schools.

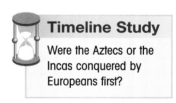

Timeline Study

Were the Aztecs or the Incas conquered by Europeans first?

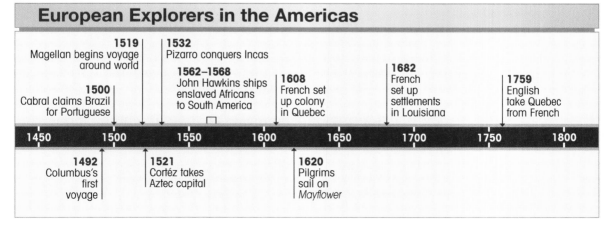

European Explorers in the Americas

1519
Magellan begins voyage around world

1500
Cabral claims Brazil for Portuguese

1532
Pizarro conquers Incas

1562–1568
John Hawkins ships enslaved Africans to South America

1608
French set up colony in Quebec

1682
French set up settlements in Louisiana

1759
English take Quebec from French

1450   1500   1550   1600   1650   1700   1750   1800

1492
Columbus's first voyage

1521
Cortéz takes Aztec capital

1620
Pilgrims sail on *Mayflower*

Summary

Columbus was looking for a sea route to Asia when he landed in the Americas.
The Spanish and Portuguese led the way in early explorations. Spanish conquistadors like Cortéz and Pizarro claimed lands and gold for Spain.
Africans were brought to the Americas to be sold into slavery.
The Spanish and Portuguese set up colonies in South America. The Spanish also settled in present-day New Mexico and Florida. The English, French, and Dutch settled in North America.
French trappers explored the Mississippi River and lands in Canada. England and France fought over lands in Canada.
The Netherlands, England, and France set up big trading companies. Successful trade created a new, wealthy middle class in Europe.

trapper
stock
investment
insurance
Puritans
conquistador

Vocabulary Review

Complete each sentence with a term from the list.

1. Hernando Cortéz, a Spaniard who conquered the Aztecs, was a _____ .

2. The _____ wanted to make the Church of England simpler.

3. A person who buys shares of a company will own _____ in the company.

4. A person who makes an _____ is lending money in the hopes of earning more.

5. French _____ hunted animals for their fur.

6. When a business loses money, an _____ company may pay for the losses.

Chapter Quiz

Write your answers in complete sentences.

 1. What city in Mexico did Hernando Cortéz attack?

 2. Why did the Europeans begin the slave trade?

 3. Why did the first English colonists come to the eastern coast of North America?

 4. Critical Thinking Columbus was mistaken when he named the first people in the Americas. Do you think *Indian* or *Native American* is a better name? Explain why.

 5. Critical Thinking Do you think trade with the Americas was important to Europe? Give at least one reason.

Using the Timeline

Use the timeline on page 245 to answer the questions.

 1. Who conquered the Incas?

 2. Did the French settle in Quebec or Louisiana first?

Write About History

Complete the following activity.

Discuss this question with a partner: What if the European explorers had traded with the Native Americans but not conquered them? Write a description of what life might be like in the Americas today. Share your ideas with the rest of the class.

Unit 6 Review

Comprehension Check

Write your answers in complete sentences.

1. Where did the Ming emperors of China live?

2. What were the classes in Japan during the Middle Ages?

3. How did the Mogul emperor Akbar treat Indians who were not Muslims?

4. Why did some Native Americans build mounds?

5. What did the Aztecs have to do to please their gods?

6. Why were the Spaniards interested in the Incas?

7. Where did the first settlers in Virginia and Massachusetts come from?

8. What European countries were the trading powers of the 1600s?

Writing an Essay

Answer one of the following essay topics.

1. Discuss the importance of Marco Polo's visit to China.

2. Compare and contrast two Native American cultures.

3. Describe trade between Europe and the Americas during the 1600s.

Group Activity

Create a trivia game about the information in Unit 6. Have each person in your group write three index cards. Write the question on one side and the answer on the other side. Get rid of duplicates. Decide how much each question is worth. Trade cards with another group. Play a game by drawing cards and answering the questions.

History in Your Life

In the 1600s, traders needed insurance. What kind of insurance do people need today? How does insurance affect you and your family?

7 **The Birth of Democracy**

Americans signed the Declaration of Independence on July 4, 1776.

Learning Objectives

- List three main ideas from the Age of Reason.
- Tell why a civil war began in England in 1642.
- Explain how the Glorious Revolution gained more power for Parliament.
- List the main complaints that colonists in America had against King George III and Britain.
- Name five freedoms and rights that Americans won.

The Struggle for Democracy

Chapter 17

Words to Know

divine right	the idea that a monarch's right to rule comes directly from God
petition	a written request, often with many signatures, to a person or group in authority
commonwealth	a nation in which the people hold the ruling power
representation	sending one or more people to speak for the rights of others before a body of the government
patriot	a person who is loyal to his or her own country
independence	freedom from control by others
declaration	a public statement

"People have certain natural rights! They are entitled to life, liberty, and property!"

"Man is born free! A monarch's right to rule is given to him not by God but by the people!"

"If a monarch rules badly, throw him out!"

Whoever heard of such wild ideas! These were shocking things to say in seventeenth-century Europe. Yet in the 1600s and 1700s, such ideas were being written and spoken in Europe. It was a time called the *Enlightenment* or the *Age of Reason.*

Philosophers at that time believed that every person is born with the ability to reason. Everyone had the power to decide what was true or false, or good or bad. They also said that people should use their abilities to question things. Why were things the way they were?

How might they be better? Why should one person have so much power over others?

Questions like those were asked by the Englishman John Locke and the Frenchmen Voltaire and Jean Jacques Rousseau. These men were thinkers. They believed in freedom of thought, of action, and of speech. Their writings spread ideas of democracy and equality throughout the world. Their questions sparked flames of revolution in Europe and in America.

The Road to Revolution in England

In 1215 King John of England was forced to sign the Magna Carta. This document limited certain powers of monarchs, and it granted certain rights. Mainly, it served to ensure the rights of nobles. It did little for the common people. Yet the ideas in the Magna Carta marked the beginning of democracy in England.

Now a king or queen could not simply go ahead and order new taxes. He or she first had to bring the matter before a council of nobles. That council was called the Great Council.

In 1272 King Edward I became king of England. In 1295, when Edward needed more money to fight a war, he called the Great Council into session. Edward, however, made some changes. He invited not only nobles to the Council, but also merchants, knights, and rich landowners. Now more people had a voice in the king's decisions.

HISTORY FACT

The words *Magna Carta* mean "great charter."

Parliament

The Great Council became known as Parliament. The word *parliament* comes from a French word, *parler*. It means "to speak." Members of Parliament could speak out, advise monarchs, and affect their decisions.

After 1295 Parliament was divided into two parts. One group, called the House of Lords, was made up of nobles. Another group was called the House of Commons. Members of the middle class, such as merchants and rich farmers, served in the House of Commons. For those first few hundred years, the House of Lords held the most power. The day would come when the House of Commons became the real lawmaking body.

King Charles I Does Away with Parliament

The power of Parliament grew. Some kings did not like that! King Charles I ruled England from 1625 until 1649. He did not want Parliament limiting his power.

In 1603 the line of Stuart kings had begun with the reign of James I. King Charles I was the son of James. He believed in the **divine right** of kings. He believed that God gave him the right to rule. He also thought he should rule with absolute power.

King Charles decided to ask people to pay higher taxes. When people did not pay the high taxes he demanded, he had them thrown in jail.

Parliament did not like that. "What about the Magna Carta?" Parliament asked. "Rulers must have our approval on new taxes!"

In 1628 Parliament presented King Charles with a **Petition** of Right. The petition said that a king could not demand new taxes without Parliament's consent. It also said the king could not throw people in jail without a jury trial.

You Decide

Should any ruler ever be allowed to claim that he or she rules by "divine right"? Why or why not?

King Charles agreed to the petition, but he did not keep his word. He kept raising taxes. When Parliament disagreed with King Charles about money, religion, and relations with other countries, Charles I decided to disband the whole group. King Charles ruled without a Parliament from 1629 until 1640.

Then trouble developed with Scotland. Charles I had been forcing the Scottish people to follow the English religion. Scotland rebelled. In response, Charles called Parliament back into session in 1640. He wanted money to go to war with Scotland.

Remember
Parliament was created to limit a monarch's power.

Again Parliament tried to put reins on the king's power. Charles I reacted by arresting five of the leading members of Parliament. His troops marched right into a session of Parliament and made the arrest! That was too much. The people rebelled.

Civil War in England

In 1642 a civil war began in England. It lasted until 1649. The nobles who supported the king were called *Royalists*. The greatest supporters of Parliament were the Puritans. They were called *Roundheads* because they cut their hair short. They disagreed with King Charles about the church and other matters.

A man named Oliver Cromwell became a leading figure in the civil war. Cromwell was a member of Parliament. He led the Puritan army against the king.

Cromwell's military victories meant the end of King Charles's reign. In 1649 Charles I was captured and tried by Parliament. He was found to be a "public enemy of the nation." Charles I was beheaded.

✔ **Check Your Understanding**

Write your answers in complete sentences.

1. What are the two houses of Parliament?

2. Why did a civil war begin in England in 1642?

3. Who were the Roundheads?

The Commonwealth and Oliver Cromwell

Parliament set up a republic. The republic, known as the **Commonwealth** of England, lasted from 1649 until 1660. Under the Commonwealth, England had no monarch. The country was governed by a committee of Parliament and its leader, Oliver Cromwell.

Cromwell, however, fought with Parliament. To solve the arguments, he put an end to Parliament in 1653. For the rest of the Commonwealth period, Cromwell ruled England alone.

Cromwell had believed in freedom. He had refused the title of king when Parliament once offered it to him. He had been against the total power of kings. Yet, now he had sole power in England. Cromwell's official title was Lord Protector of the Commonwealth. During his rule, he brought Ireland and Scotland under English control. His actions in Ireland were especially brutal.

Oliver Cromwell governed the Commonwealth of England. Yet, in 1653 he put an end to Parliament.

Oliver Cromwell died in 1658. His son Richard tried to carry on his father's policies. Richard, however, was not as strong as his father. The people of England were also ready to return to the royal Stuart line.

William and Mary understood the importance of democracy and involved the Parliament in their decisions.

The Glorious Revolution

In 1660 Charles II became king. He restored Parliament, and things were quiet for a while. Unfortunately, new problems came up when James II came to the throne.

King James II became a Catholic. He asked for too much power. In response, Parliament sent word to James II's daughter Mary and her husband William of Orange. Parliament asked them to come from the Netherlands and take over James II's throne.

Did this anger King James? Yes. Did it cause another war? No. James II left the throne quietly. It was a bloodless takeover. Parliament persuaded William and Mary to sign over many of their royal rights and powers. The change came to be called the *Glorious Revolution*.

In 1689 William and Mary signed a Bill of Rights. This bill stated that the ruling monarch could act only after consulting Parliament. With that, England took another big step toward democracy. Now Parliament was truly a strong force in government.

One day the Americans would write their own Bill of Rights. The English Bill of Rights would serve as their model.

Over time, Parliament itself became more democratic. By the late 1600s, the House of Lords held less power. The House of Commons held more. Members of the House of Lords still inherited their positions. House of Commons members, however, were elected.

Revolution in America

George III became king of England in 1760. When he came to the throne, England had colonies in North America. George asked for the loyalty of his subjects in America. They seemed happy to give that loyalty.

George III had wars to pay for. Great Britain had fought a major war, the Seven Years War. In North America this war was sometimes called the French and Indian War. In 1763 the French and Indian War ended in America. The Americans and British had defeated the French and some Native American nations. Now someone had to pay the bills for war costs. King George decided to demand high taxes from his subjects in the colonies.

"High taxes, but no rights!" the American colonists complained. They had seen that people had won new rights in England. They read the words of Locke,

HISTORY FACT

The American Revolution gave hope to people in other lands. It made them confident that one day they would also have freedom. They watched the United States become a nation that promised individual freedoms and a voice in government.

Rousseau, and Voltaire. The Americans wanted rights and freedom, too.

"No taxation without **representation**!" was their cry. If they paid taxes to King George, they wanted a say in the government.

Some colonists wanted more than representation. People like Samuel Adams, did not want representation at all. They wanted freedom!

Many colonists were willing to fight for that freedom. **Patriots** like Thomas Jefferson spoke out for liberty. Jefferson used his pen to fight for **independence.** He wrote that Parliament had no right to control the colonies. He also said that unfair acts by the king meant the colonists owed him no loyalty. The colonies asked Jefferson to write a **declaration** of independence.

On July 4, 1776, the Declaration of Independence was approved. King George sent troops to the colonies. The colonists had to fight the British for their independence. General George Washington led the fight. Washington would later become the first President of the new United States of America.

Timeline Study

Who ruled England after the Commonwealth?

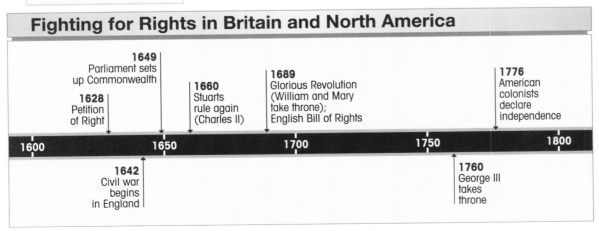

Fighting for Rights in Britain and North America

1628 Petition of Right

1642 Civil war begins in England

1649 Parliament sets up Commonwealth

1660 Stuarts rule again (Charles II)

1689 Glorious Revolution (William and Mary take throne); English Bill of Rights

1760 George III takes throne

1776 American colonists declare independence

1600 — 1650 — 1700 — 1750 — 1800

WORDS FROM THE PAST
The Declaration of Independence

In the Declaration that Thomas Jefferson wrote, he tried to speak for all colonists.

The Declaration was the colonists' announcement that the colonies were becoming a separate nation—the United States of America.

The following passages are from Thomas Jefferson's Declaration of Independence.

We hold these truths to be self-evident, that all men are created equal, that they are endowed by their Creator with certain unalienable Rights, that among these are Life, Liberty and the pursuit of Happiness.

Thomas Jefferson is famous for his beliefs, writings, and support of American independence.

That to secure these rights, Governments are instituted among Men, deriving their just powers from the consent of the governed.

That whenever any form of Government becomes destructive of these ends, it is the Right of the People to alter or to abolish it, and to institute new Government ...

We, therefore, the Representatives of the United States of America ... do ... declare, That these United Colonies are, and of Right ought to be Free and Independent States... .

Summary

Ideas of freedom, equality, and fairness came out of the Age of Reason.

The English Parliament helped limit the powers of the monarch. Parliament has a House of Lords and a House of Commons. Some rulers did not like asking Parliament to allow them to raise taxes.

During England's civil war, Oliver Cromwell led Parliament in overthrowing the king. After the war, Cromwell headed the Commonwealth from 1653 to 1658. The Stuart monarchy returned in 1660.

The Glorious Revolution was a bloodless takeover of the throne by William and Mary. The Glorious Revolution brought still more power for Parliament and a Bill of Rights for the English people.

English colonists in North America had thoughts of freedom, too. In 1776 the American colonists declared their independence. They fought a war and won their freedom.

---

petition

representation

declaration

divine right

independence

Vocabulary Review

Write a term from the list that matches each definition below.

1. Freedom from outside control

2. The idea that a monarch's right to govern comes from God

3. A statement for the public to hear or read

4. When one or more persons are chosen to speak for the rights of others

5. A signed written request to an authority, especially to a government

Chapter Quiz

Write your answers in complete sentences.

1. What was the Glorious Revolution in England?

2. Why did the American colonists want to revolt against British rule?

3. Who wrote the Declaration of Independence?

4. **Critical Thinking** How were the new ideas of the Age of Reason different from the old idea of divine right?

5. **Critical Thinking** Why were the American colonists affected by the British fight for freedom and rights?

Using the Timeline

Use the timeline on page 258 to answer the questions.

1. Which came first, the Petition of Right or the English Bill of Rights?

2. When the American colonists declared their independence, how long had George III been king of England?

Write About History

Complete the following activity.

Work with a partner. Read the passages from the Declaration of Independence on page 259. Discuss with your partner what each paragraph means. Look up words in a dictionary if you need to. Then rewrite the paragraphs in your own words.

An angry French mob stormed the Bastille, the royal prison, on July 14, 1789. This marked the start of the French Revolution.

Learning Objectives

- Name two French writers in the 1700s who had new ideas.
- Explain how the Age of Reason and the American Revolution led to revolution in France.
- Identify the Three Estates.
- Explain how the storming of the Bastille led to a bloody rebellion.
- Describe how the rest of Europe reacted to the French Revolution.
- List Napolean's accomplishments in government and in war.

Chapter 18 — Revolution in France

Words to Know

oath	a serious promise, often pledged in the name of God
symbol	an object that stands for an idea
dungeon	a dark, underground room used as prison
riot	a violent disturbance created by a crowd of people
arsenal	a place where guns and ammunition are stored
betray	to give help to the enemy; to be unfaithful to
motto	a word or phrase that expresses goals, ideas, or ideals
fraternity	brotherhood
guillotine	an instrument used for cutting off a person's head; it has two posts crossed by a heavy blade
turmoil	a condition of great confusion
dictator	a ruler who has total power
colonial	having settlements in far-off lands

The Age of Reason in France

France, in the early 1700s, had a government that was still locked into the Middle Ages. French kings believed they ruled by divine right. No matter how unfair the rule, French people had to accept it. King Louis XIV is said to have declared, "I am the State."

Nobles led lives of luxury. They lived in fine palaces paid for by taxes collected from the lower and middle classes. While the nobles lived splendidly, the peasants often went without enough to eat.

Remember
The British and the American colonists had also read Rousseau and Voltaire.

By the 1780s, however, the French were listening to new ideas. They read the works of Rousseau and Voltaire. "Look at Britain," the writers said. "The people there are free. Look at the Americans, at their successful fight for freedom. We, too, deserve some rights!" Political conditions did not yet show it, but the Age of Reason had come to France.

The French had helped the Americans in their war for independence from British rule. French nobles were happy to see the British defeated by anyone. French peasants liked the idea of a fight against tyranny. The French noble, Lafayette, went to America and joined the colonists' battle. George Washington gave Lafayette command of a division, and the two fought side by side.

When the Americans won the war, the French began thinking about freedom for themselves.

The Estates-General

By 1788, trouble was brewing in France. The peasants and the middle class were unhappy. The government was in trouble, too. It was out of money. Fancy living and too many wars had resulted in an empty treasury.

In 1789, King Louis XVI called a meeting of the Estates-General. This was a government body that was something like Britain's Parliament. The Estates-General had not met for 175 years. Now there was to be a meeting at Versailles. This was the name of the fine palace just outside of Paris where King Louis lived with his queen, Marie Antoinette. King Louis wanted the Estates-General to grant him more money in new taxes.

Marie Antoinette

Three groups of people made up the Estates-General. Each group was called an *estate*. The First Estate included wealthy clergy. They arrived at King Louis's meeting dressed in fine clothing and riding in beautiful carriages.

Members of the Second Estate were the nobles. Many were wealthy and came from large country manors. Some of the nobles, however, had lost most of their wealth. They had only their titles left.

The First and Second Estates represented only a tiny part of the French population. The Third Estate represented most of the people of France. The Third Estate represented a middle class of merchants and city workers as well as all the peasants of France.

Each of the three estates had one vote in meetings. This was hardly fair since the Third Estate represented 98 percent of the population. The First and Second Estates could band together. They could then outvote the Third Estate every time they wanted to. Members of the Third Estate were ready for change.

At the 1789 meeting in Versailles, the Third Estate asked for more votes. King Louis XVI refused.

King Louis XVI and Marie Antoinette lived in luxury in the royal palace of Versailles.

The Tennis Court Meeting

The Third Estate rebelled. The members called their own meeting. They declared themselves the National Assembly of France. The king refused to give them a government meeting hall. So the Third Estate held its own meeting at a nearby tennis court.

At the meeting, members of the Third Estate took the Tennis Court **Oath**. They swore that they would give France a constitution. The people of Paris celebrated. They supported the National Assembly. They wanted a constitution.

In the meantime, the king was organizing his troops. When he gathered an army near an assembly meeting, people began to worry. Was the king planning to stop the National Assembly by force? The people grew angry. Force, they said, would be met by force! France was now approaching the boiling point.

The Storming of the Bastille

To the people of Paris, the Bastille was a terrible **symbol**. It stood for the tyranny of their king and for the injustices they faced. The Bastille was a gloomy fortress built in 1370. It was used as a prison. All that was needed to throw a French person into prison was the say-so of the king.

The Bastille was a dark, mysterious place. People were locked away there for disagreeing with the king or for failing to pay taxes. There were stories of men rotting away in the Bastille's dark **dungeons** and of terrible tortures. Actually, under earlier kings the prison had done away with dungeons and tortures. However, the horror stories remained. Most French people hated and feared the Bastille.

On July 14, 1789, a **riot** broke out in Paris. The people had become alarmed by the king's gathering of his troops. The people decided it was time to make a stand for freedom. They would attack that symbol of the king's unjust powers—the hated Bastille.

Early in the day, rioters broke into an **arsenal**. They took muskets and cannons. Then they attacked. "Down with the Bastille!" the excited rebels shouted. There was no stopping the mob. They murdered the governor of the prison. They carried his head on a stick through the streets.

The rebels then freed the prisoners. They opened the cells to find only seven prisoners inside! However, the Bastille had fallen, and the Revolution had begun.

On this same day, the king returned to his palace at Versailles after a day of hunting. Communication was slow in the eighteenth century. Therefore, he knew nothing of the riots and murders. It had been poor hunting that day. No deer had been killed. To describe his day, King Louis wrote only one word in his diary on July 14, 1789. He wrote *Rien,* a French word meaning *nothing.*

The day that King Louis wrote *nothing* was a day that France would always remember!

You Decide

Would a leader of a country today ever be out of contact with the world? Why or why not?

✔ Check Your Understanding

Write your answers in complete sentences.

1. What did King Louis XIV mean when he declared, "I am the State"?

2. What effect did the Age of Reason and the American Revolution have on the French people?

3. What groups made up each of the Three Estates that met in Versailles in 1789?

The French Revolution

Revolutionaries throughout France were excited by the storming of the Bastille. They began their own protests for freedom. In October, a group of women set out from Paris. They wanted the king to give the people more grain. To keep order, the king marched with them from Versailles to Paris.

Peasants rose up against feudal lords. Many nobles did not feel safe in France. They fled the country.

During the next three years, 1789–1791, the National Assembly wrote the new constitution it had promised. New laws were made that did away with the feudal system. The nobles lost most of their rights and privileges. The king lost much of his power. The old system of taxes was also ended.

On August 26, 1789, the National Assembly wrote the Declaration of the Rights of Man. It was based on the English Bill of Rights and the American Declaration of Independence.

"Liberty, Equality, and Fraternity!"

Rulers throughout Europe saw what was happening in France. They were frightened. They worried that ideas of revolution could spread to their lands. The rulers of Austria and Prussia sent armies into France to try to crush the Revolution.

The leaders of the French Revolution were outraged. They thought that their own king had called for the outside armies. They accused Louis XVI of **betraying** France. They forced him off the throne. Then they held elections for a new lawmaking body called the *National Convention*.

In 1792, the National Convention declared France a republic. The **motto** of the new republic was "Liberty, Equality, and **Fraternity**!"

The Reign of Terror

Leaders of the new republic became fearful of their enemies. Their main goal was to seek out those enemies and to do away with them. The Revolution became bloodier.

Revolutionaries found King Louis XVI guilty of betraying his country. In 1793, Louis XVI and Marie

Those considered to be enemies of the new French Republic were executed by guillotine.

Antoinette were executed. Throughout 1793 and 1794, the new leaders of France arrested and executed many people. Anyone suspected of being against the Republic was attacked. It was a time known as the *Reign of Terror*. "Off with their heads!" became the cry of that stage of the French Revolution.

A Frenchman had invented the **guillotine**, a machine for quickly cutting off heads! Hundreds of suspected enemies of the revolution were beheaded. Carts rolled through the streets of Paris, carrying victims to the guillotine.

A man named Robespierre was one of the most violent leaders of the Revolution. Robespierre believed the Republic would never be safe as long as one enemy lived. Later, the people turned on Robespierre himself. They blamed him for the bloodshed. After sentencing so many others to death, Robespierre lost his own head to the French guillotine.

The country was in a **turmoil**. The leaders of the Revolution could not control the people or organize the government. The fighting and bloodshed went on and on.

You Decide

Do you think Robespierre got what he deserved? Why or why not?

Napoleon Bonaparte

The Revolution had created a strong, new army. That army drove Austrian and Prussian forces out of France. One of the officers in the French army was a young man named Napoleon Bonaparte.

Meanwhile, the National Convention of France had been growing steadily weaker. In October 1795 it came under attack by an army of 30,000 national guardsmen. The guardsmen wanted to get rid of the National Convention and bring back the monarchy. The Convention called on General Napoleon Bonaparte to put down the uprising. Napoleon, a general at age 26, proved his military worth. On October 5, 1795, he brought in a battery of cannons. The uprising was ended "with a whiff of grapeshot," he said.

The Directory soon replaced the National Convention in the leadership of France. The Directory eventually became corrupt. As Napoleon won battles and gained power, the Directory began to worry. Was Napoleon trying to become the sole ruler of France?

That is exactly what Napoleon did. He pushed out the Directory. Then in 1799, he made himself **dictator** of France. One of the first things Napoleon did as ruler was to set up the Napoleonic Code. This was a new constitution that contained a single set of laws for all of France and its territories. The Napoleonic Code remains the basis of French law to this day.

Dictator and later Emperor of France, Napoleon Bonaparte was very powerful.

France soon discovered that Napoleon was a good politician as well as a good soldier. Napoleon put himself directly in charge of the army. He brought a quick end to the fighting within France. He set up a police force responsible only to him. He invited back the nobles who had fled France during the Revolution "You will be safe," Napoleon told them, "if you are loyal to me."

France Under Napoleon

Napoleon put an end to the French Republic that the Revolution had won. In 1804 Napoleon had himself crowned emperor. He then crowned his wife, Josephine, empress. He let his ambition and desire for power spread war across Europe. Yet he also made some good changes in the French government.

Napoleon's Empire, 1812

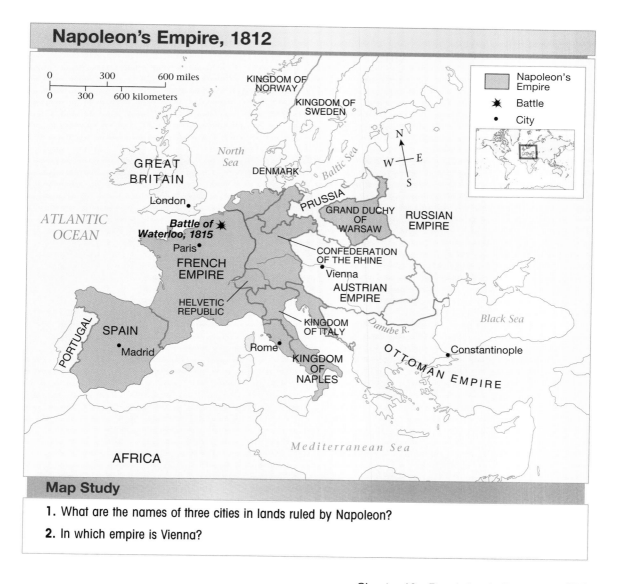

Map Study

1. What are the names of three cities in lands ruled by Napoleon?

2. In which empire is Vienna?

Napoleon changed unfair tax laws. He required all people, rich and poor, to pay taxes under the same laws. The rich received no favors. Napoleon also strengthened and reorganized the French schools.

Napoleon made most things, including education and the press, subject to strict government control. In fact, the French government *was* Napoleon!

Napoleon had a strong, wealthy France behind him now. He had the loyalty of the people. He now set out to conquer a European empire. He led France into war with Great Britain and most of the rest of Europe. Napoleon was a clever general. He won battle after battle. By 1812 Napoleon controlled most of Europe. However, he had been unable to invade and conquer Great Britain.

Napoleon's retreat from Moscow was one of the greatest military disasters of all time.

Learn More About It

NAPOLEON'S MISTAKE

In 1812, Napoleon declared war on Russia. He attacked with an army of nearly 600,000 men. He won a major victory over the Russians at the battle of Borodino. However, the Russian armies were clever. They fled eastward, leading Napoleon's army on a chase deep into the heart of Russia. As the Russians retreated, they destroyed everything of value in Napoleon's path.

When Napoleon and his army reached Moscow, they found a deserted city. Most of the people had fled. Those who stayed behind set fire to the city. The French soon found themselves occupying a city of ruins.

Then winter came. It was an icy Russian winter. Napoleon's army had almost run out of food. His army was starving. They were freezing. There was only one thing to do. Napoleon gave the orders to head for home. The Russians attacked again and again as Napoleon's weakened forces struggled toward France. The French suffered terrible losses during the retreat from Russia. Over 500,000 men were killed or died of illness or starvation. Others deserted or were captured. Many simply froze to death. The attack on Russia was Napoleon's big mistake.

The End for Napoleon

Other countries took heart when they heard of France's defeat in Russia. Napoleon could be beaten! These countries joined together. Prussia, Sweden, and Austria joined with Great Britain and Russia to march as allies against Napoleon.

The French saw that their emperor was beaten. The French Senate turned against Napoleon. It called for a new king to rule France. On April 11, 1814, Napoleon gave up his throne. Louis XVIII was crowned King of France. Napoleon was exiled and sent to live on the island of Elba off the coast of Italy.

Napoleon was not a man who gave up easily. In less than a year, he had escaped from Elba and returned to France. There, he found supporters and actually ruled France again for 100 days. However, Napoleon's dream of ruling Europe was about to come to an end.

The Battle of Waterloo

The allies against Napoleon joined forces as soon as they heard of his return. With about 75,000 troops, Napoleon marched into Belgium to meet the allied forces. The Duke of Wellington had about 67,000 troops from Britain, Belgium, Hanover, and the Netherlands.

The fighting began on June 18, 1815. The battle between the French and the allies was just about even for a few hours. Then Prussian troops arrived to back up the allies. That tipped the scale. After one last, fierce attack by France's famous *Old Guard*, the French had to retreat.

Again, Napoleon was sent away as a prisoner. The British sent him to far-off Saint Helena. This was a tiny island off the west coast of Africa. It was there on May 5, 1821, that Napoleon died.

France After Napoleon

A royal line of kings ruled France once more. Then again, there was a revolution. For the next 55 years, France saw change after change—three revolutions in all. There was a Second Republic, a Second Empire, and then, in 1870, a Third Republic.

Under the Third Republic, France built a **colonial** empire. French colonies around the world strengthened French trade and industry. France's Third Republic lasted until World War II when Germany took over France.

After World War II, a Fourth Republic was set up— and then a Fifth. Social revolution continued. Women struggled to take their place in society, to hold property, and to take jobs. Minority groups looked for work, for fair pay, and for good housing. The French still worked toward "Liberty, Equality, and Fraternity."

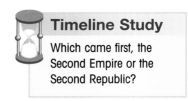

Timeline Study

Which came first, the Second Empire or the Second Republic?

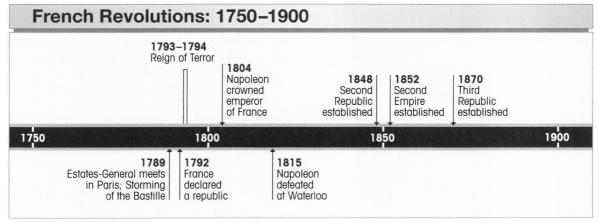

French Revolutions: 1750–1900

1793–1794 Reign of Terror

1804 Napoleon crowned emperor of France

1848 Second Republic established

1852 Second Empire established

1870 Third Republic established

1750 — 1800 — 1850 — 1900

1789 Estates-General meets in Paris; Storming of the Bastille

1792 France declared a republic

1815 Napoleon defeated at Waterloo

Summary

The Age of Reason and the American War of Independence gave the French people ideas of fighting for their own freedom.
French kings, like Louis XVI, believed that they ruled by divine right.
The Third Estate of the French Estates-General represented all the common people.
The French Revolution officially began on July 14, 1789, with the storming of the Bastille.
The Reign of Terror from 1793 to 1794 led to increased turmoil and bloodshed.
Napoleon Bonaparte stepped in to restored order in France. He conquered much of Europe and brought about many changes in French government.
France underwent several social and political revolutions in the late 1700s and in the 1800s.

Vocabulary Review

Write *true* or *false*. If the statement is false, change the underlined term to make it true.

1. A <u>symbol</u> is something that stands for something else, such as an idea.

2. A <u>guillotine</u> is an underground prison.

3. Napoleon took total power and became a <u>dictator</u>.

4. A <u>motto</u> is a serious promise, often given in the name of God.

5. Weapons are sometimes stored in an <u>arsenal</u>.

6. During periods of <u>turmoil</u>, there is confusion and a lack of control.

Chapter Quiz

Write your answers in complete sentences.

1. What ideas did Rousseau and Voltaire give the French people?

2. Why did members of the Third Estate think the Estates-General was unfair?

3. Why did so many people hate the Bastille?

4. **Critical Thinking** Why were European countries afraid the revolution would spread to them?

5. **Critical Thinking** Overall, was Napoleon a success or a failure? Give reasons for your answer.

Using the Timeline

Use the timeline on page 275 to answer the questions.

1. What happened almost immediately after France became a republic?

2. When Napoleon was defeated at Waterloo, how long had he been emperor of France?

Write About History

Complete the following activity.

Form a group of three or four. Choose an event in the chapter. Write a skit about it. Practice performing the skit. Then present it to the rest of the class.

Unit 7 **Review**

Comprehension Check

Write your answers in complete sentences.

1. How did Voltaire, Rousseau, and Locke influence Britain and America?

2. What was the problem between Parliament and King Charles I of England?

3. Who was Oliver Cromwell?

4. Why did King George II try to get more money out of the American colonists?

5. In France, who did the Three Estates in the Estates-General represent?

6. What was the motto of the French Revolution?

7. What was Napoleon's big mistake?

8. What did France do under the Third Republic, established in 1870?

Writing an Essay

Answer one of the following essay topics.

1. Compare Oliver Cromwell and Napoleon. List ways they were alike and ways they were different.

2. Discuss the effect of the American Revolution on France.

3. Describe the Reign of Terror.

Group Activity

With your group, make a chart that compares the English Civil War, the American Revolution, and the French Revolution. Include dates, events, leaders, documents, slogans, and other information.

History in Your Life

If the American Revolution had not taken place, how do you think your life would be different today?

Unit 8 ▷ The Age of Imperialism

The Industrial Revolution changed the way people worked. However, new technology did not always make life better for workers.

Learning Objectives

- Tell why the Industrial Revolution began in Great Britain.

- List five inventions of the 1700s.

- Explain how the Industrial Revolution encouraged imperialism.

- Describe how the Industrial Revolution both improved and worsened people's lives.

- Explain how the Industrial Revolution made countries more dependent on each other.

Chapter 19 / The Industrial Revolution

Words to Know

natural resource	material that is provided by nature, such as forests, minerals, and water
industry	business and manufacturing
transportation	the act of carrying from one place to another
investor	a person who expects to make a profit by lending money to a business
raw material	matter in its natural condition, not changed by some human process
factory	a building where goods are made by machinery
textile	cloth or fabric made by weaving
import	to bring into one country from another
labor union	a group of workers who join together to protect their wages, working conditions, and job benefits

The name *Industrial Revolution* is used to describe one of the biggest changes in history. It describes the time when people went from making goods by hand to making them with machines.

Before the 1700s most goods were made by hand. Individual workers crafted tools and jewelry, cloth and housewares. Any machines that were used were small, simple, and privately owned. Work was done in homes or in small workshops.

Before 1750 any changes in production methods came slowly. After 1750, however, those changes were rapid. The changes in the ways goods were produced happened fast enough to be called a "revolution."

Great Britain Leads the Industrial Revolution

HISTORY FACT

In 1707, Scotland joined England and Wales to become Great Britain, or Britain.

The most dramatic changes in industry began in Great Britain by about 1750. It is true that people had been inventing things during earlier years. However, most of their work centered around scientific theories and ideas. Now inventors took a more practical turn. They developed machines especially designed to increase the production of goods and to help people make a profit.

The Industrial Revolution began in Great Britain for a number of reasons. For one thing, Britain had a large supply of workers. Women, as well as men, were ready to leave their homes and join the industrial workforce.

Great Britain also had the **natural resources** needed for **industry**. Britain had a good supply of coal and iron. Coal could produce the energy to keep the new steam engines running. Coal was also needed to produce iron. Iron could be used to improve machines and tools. It could also be used to build railroad tracks, bridges, and ships.

Britain developed the **transportation** that industry needed. Products had to be marketed and moved. Steam locomotives and steam-only ocean-going ships were developed in Britain in the 1700s and 1800s.

Britain had **investors.** These were people with money to back the new businesses.

Remember
The Southern colonies of North America had supplied cotton to Britain.

Britain had colonies to serve as ready markets for the goods. British colonies also supplied **raw materials**, like cotton, to the **factories** in London and other cities. Finally the British government was eager to support growing industry. For all these reasons, Great Britain saw a burst of industrial development. In the late 1700s and early 1800s, Britain became known as the "Workshop of the World."

The Textile Industry

Britain's **textile** industry produced cloth. This industry is a good example of what the early Industrial Revolution was all about.

In the earliest days, British merchants **imported** cloth from other lands. Because of the costs of shipping finished goods, cloth was very expensive.

Later, in the 1600s, Britain began to import raw cotton. The British spun their own threads and then wove their own cloth.

Farm families did the work. They set up spinning wheels and looms in their cottages. Both spinning wheels and looms were operated by hand. The families who worked this way were called *cottage weavers*.

Merchants would buy the finished cloth from the cottage weavers. The amounts of cloth produced were never very large. In order to meet their own needs, the weavers had to farm the land, too. They could only make cloth in their spare time. There was never enough finished cloth for all the people who wanted to buy it. Therefore, British business leaders looked for ways to improve and increase the production of textiles.

New Inventions Move Textile-Making Out of Cottages

In the 1700s some new machines were invented that changed the textile industry. Spinners and weavers left their cottages and went to work in new factories.

The first important invention in the textile-making revolution was the *flying shuttle*. In 1733 a British man named John Kay invented a shuttle, a device on a loom. The shuttle made it possible to weave wider pieces of cloth. Now one worker could do the work of two.

The spinning jenny made spinning yarn faster and easier.

Soon more cotton yarn was needed than could be produced. Business leaders offered prizes to the inventor of a machine to spin yarn. In 1764 James Hargreaves came up with just such a machine. He named it after his wife. The *spinning jenny* used the same ideas as the spinning wheel. However, the spinning jenny could spin as many as 80 threads at one time.

The biggest change came in 1769. In that year, Richard Arkwright invented a machine called the *water frame*. Now even more cotton thread could be spun at once. The water frame ran by water power. It was so big that it could not fit into a cottage. It was also an expensive piece of machinery. The water frame required a special building of its own.

New machines forced the textile business out of the English cottages. Mills and factories were built. Workers were no longer their own bosses. Workers became factory hands. They worked in large mills that often employed up to 600 people.

In 1779 Samuel Crompton combined the spinning jenny and the water frame into one machine. He called it the *mule*. The mule could spin much finer threads very rapidly.

Now the weavers had to keep step with the spinners. With so much thread being produced, the textile industry needed a better loom. In about 1785 Edmund Cartwright invented a steam-powered loom.

Workers sometimes feared the new machines. Would the machines completely replace the workers? Would they lose their jobs? At one point, antimachine riots broke out. Workers smashed machines, shouting, "Men, not machines!" Sometimes progress was a frightening thing. The Industrial Revolution, however, could not be stopped.

Within 50 years' time the textile industry had entirely changed. What had been a cottage industry had turned into a big business. As a result, a way of life had changed, too, for thousands of textile workers.

HISTORY FACT

Workers who destroyed machines in the early 1800s were called *Luddites.* The name came from Neal Ludd, who reportedly led a mob which smashed some weaving machinery in the 1770s.

✔ **Check Your Understanding**

Write your answers in complete sentences.

1. What are four reasons why the Industrial Revolution began in Great Britain?

2. What was the first important invention in the textile-making revolution?

3. What machine did Richard Arkwright invent in 1769?

The Steam Engine

The new machines needed power. Water power was not strong enough to run heavy machines. During the 1600s, inventors had begun experimenting with "fire engines," or steam engines. In 1698 Thomas Savery built the first commercial steam engine. Around 1712 Thomas Newcomen improved on Savery's engine. It was, however, far from perfect. It used too much coal.

The power unit called the *watt* was named in honor of the man who made steam power practical.

In 1769 a Scottish engineer named James Watt invented an improved steam engine. For several years only the textile industry made use of Watt's engine. By 1850, however, it was being used throughout Britain. Then it spread throughout the rest of Europe.

The invention of the steam engine completely changed transportation. In 1804 a British engineer, Richard Trevithick, built the first steam locomotive. Steam locomotives came into general use in Britain in the late 1830s. By 1850, Great Britain had 6,600 miles of railroad track. The United States, France, and Germany built their own rail systems during the next ten years.

An American, Robert Fulton, built the first successful river steamboat in 1807. Within a few years, steamboats were being used on British rivers. By the mid-1800s, steam-powered ships were carrying raw materials and finished goods across the ocean.

Early steam locomotives were simple but powerful.

Electricity and Petroleum

In 1831 an Englishman named Michael Faraday invented a machine called the *dynamo.* It generated an electric current by using magnets. Faraday's discovery led to the building of more powerful electric generators and electric motors. In time the use of electricity as a source of power would become widespread.

In the 1850s Americans discovered that petroleum, or unrefined oil, could be used for many things. It could be used to make kerosene, and kerosene could be used for heat and light. Oil could make machinery run more smoothly. Fortunately, there was a good supply of crude oil available in the United States.

Oil was to become one of the most valuable resources in the world. This would come about with the invention of the internal combustion engine and the diesel engine. Petroleum could be turned into gasoline and diesel fuel to run those engines. Oil would give some nations new wealth and power.

Imperialism

The Industrial Revolution meant new inventions and new products. It also meant new needs. As the ability to produce goods increased, so did the need for more raw materials. Britain needed even more coal to fire its steam engines. It needed more cotton to spin into thread. It also needed more iron to make railroad tracks and machinery.

Imperialism seemed to be a solution to the problems of getting raw materials. Britain took over territories in Africa and Asia and formed colonies. The colonies were sources of raw materials. In addition, the colonies became markets for finished products from Britain.

The Industrial Revolution Changes Life: The Workers

Did the Industrial Revolution improve the lives of the British people? Or did it make life harder? A look at life in Great Britain in the late 1700s and early 1800s gives a mixed picture.

In many ways life was better. Average incomes tripled between 1700 and 1815. Between 1815 and 1836, incomes increased 30 times over! People had better food to eat. They had more meat, sugar, tea, and coffee. Coal not only fueled the industrial machines, it also heated homes and cooked food.

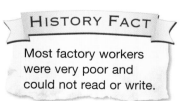

HISTORY FACT

Most factory workers were very poor and could not read or write.

For the merchants, bankers, shipowners, and factory owners, the Industrial Revolution meant wealth. The middle class now had a greater voice in the British government.

New inventions in communication let people learn what was going on in their world. In 1837 Samuel F. B. Morse developed the telegraph. He also developed a code to send telegrams—the Morse code. By 1866 a telegraph cable reached across the Atlantic.

Life, however, did not improve for everyone. As the Industrial Revolution went on, life got harder for many city workers. People spent long days in dirty, dangerous factories, working for poor wages.

At first factory work had paid well. Soon the owners found they could hire women and children for lower wages than men. Soon most of the factory workers were women and children. Many children were very young. Factory wages dropped.

Young children often worked at machines under dangerous conditions.

Learn More About It

CHILD LABOR

Many of the children working in factories came from orphanages or very poor families. They were treated much like slaves. They often had to work from five in the morning until eight at night. Some factory owners treated the children quite well. Others beat the young workers for such crimes as falling asleep at their work or working too slowly.

In the 1800s there were new laws called Factory Acts. These laws took the very youngest children out of the factories. The laws also put limits on the number of hours children and women could work.

Despite the new laws, work could be dangerous. There were no safety measures or protection against industrial accidents. It is sad to imagine what happened to many little children working on dangerous machines with no safety devices.

The Industrial Revolution Changes Life: The Cities

Britain's cities were becoming dark with ash from the new coal-burning factories. As the skies blackened, the factories drew people to the cities. As a result, British cities went through a population explosion. In 1801 about 78 percent of the people in Britain lived on farms. By 1901 about 75 percent lived in cities.

Where were all these people going to make their homes? Housing had to be built quickly and cheaply. The results were poorly built slum buildings. Inside were small apartments where whole families often shared one room. Sewage and garbage could not be disposed of properly. These conditions led to the outbreak and spread of disease.

You Decide

If factory work and living conditions in the cities were so awful, why do you think so many people moved to the cities?

Earning a living became difficult as more people moved to cities.

It would not be long before people began to protest against this kind of life. They protested against factories that employed young children and paid terrible wages. They protested against having to work with dangerous machines that had no safety devices.

The Industrial Revolution taught workers that they had to band together. They formed **labor unions** to demand better, fairer conditions. Of course factory owners were not in favor of the workers' unions. Until 1825 unions in Great Britain were against the law.

The Industrial Revolution Spreads

Industrialization began in Great Britain. However, during the 1800s, it spread to France, Germany, the United States, Russia, and finally Japan.

Over time industrialization forced nations of the world to depend on each other. Countries had to work out trade agreements. The more industrialized countries built the factories and produced the goods. They often depended on other nations for raw materials. Less developed countries needed finished products. Many of these countries profited from their natural resources.

The United States, Germany, Japan, and Great Britain depend on Saudi Arabia, Mexico, Indonesia, Nigeria, and other nations for crude oil. They get uranium from nations in Africa. Chile and Peru export copper.

The results of the Industrial Revolution can be seen in British coal mines, in Japanese electronics factories, in cities, and on farms. The Industrial Revolution has changed the way people live and where they live. It has changed the way they depend on each other.

At one time, some people thought that the Industrial Revolution would come to an end. They thought that all the great changes and developments had already happened. In the late 1800s, it was actually suggested that the United States Patent Office be closed. Surely, some people thought, everything possible had already been invented. We know now that the revolution is far from over. New developments continue every day. In fact, in recent years, large international companies have their finished products made in developing countries. There, labor is cheap. Developed countries may produce many services and fewer finished products.

Timeline Study

When was the machine invented that was a combination of the spinning jenny and the water frame?

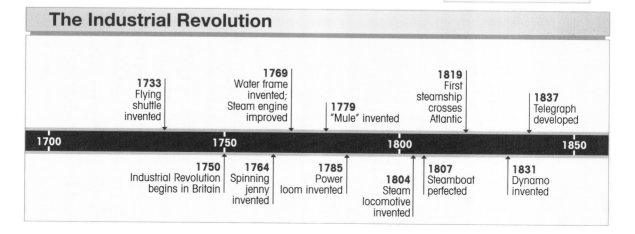

The Industrial Revolution

1733 Flying shuttle invented	
1769 Water frame invented; Steam engine improved	
1779 "Mule" invented	
1819 First steamship crosses Atlantic	
1837 Telegraph developed	

1700 — 1750 — 1800 — 1850

1750 Industrial Revolution begins in Britain	
1764 Spinning jenny invented	
1785 Power loom invented	
1804 Steam locomotive invented	
1807 Steamboat perfected	
1831 Dynamo invented	

Chapter

19 Review

Summary

During the Industrial Revolution, people went from making goods by hand to making goods by machine.

Great Britain led the Industrial Revolution with rapid changes beginning around 1750. Machines forced Britain's textile industry from country cottages to city factories.

The invention of steam power revolutionized manufacturing and transportation.

To gain raw materials, Europeans formed new colonies.

Industrialization caused a rapid growth in city populations. Life for many improved. A strong, wealthy middle class grew. Life for many became harder. Working conditions in the factories were often unsafe and unhealthy.

More countries industrialized over the years. Nations became dependent on each other for needed goods and services.

factory

natural resource

raw materials

textile

labor union

import

Vocabulary Review

Complete each sentence with a term from the list.

1. A place where goods are made is a ____.

2. A ____ is an organization of workers.

3. Water, cotton, and wool are ____ that may be needed to make cloth.

4. Business and manufacturing are two areas of ____.

5. Great Britain was a leader in the cloth, or ____ industry.

6. Many countries ____ , or bring in, cloth from other countries.

Chapter Quiz

Write your answers in complete sentences.

1. What natural resources did Britain have that were important for industry?

2. How did new inventions in the textile industry change workers' lives?

3. How did industrialization encourage imperialism?

4. Critical Thinking Why did factory owners like to hire women and children?

5. Critical Thinking The Industrial Revolution made countries more dependent on each other. Do you think this was good or bad? Give at least one reason.

Using the Timeline

Use the timeline on page 291 to answer the questions.

1. When did the Industrial Revolution begin in Britain?

2. When did the first steamship cross the Atlantic Ocean?

Write About History

Complete the following activity.

With a partner, debate this question: Should labor unions be allowed in Great Britain? One should take the part of a factory owner in 1810. The other should take the part of a factory worker. Before the debate, prepare a few notes to help you remember the points you hope to make.

Although Spain colonized Latin America, native cultures are still strong. The Peru Indians, shown above, are an example of people who have kept their own traditions.

Learning Objectives

- Explain how Central and South America came to be called "Latin America."
- Tell why the Creoles and mestizos were ready to fight for independence.
- Name six Latin American revolutionaries.
- Describe the governments of the new, independent Latin American nations.

Chapter 20 Independence in Latin America

Words to Know

hacienda	a large Spanish-style ranch or country home
descendant	a person who comes from certain ancestors
discrimination	treating a person or people unfairly because of his or her race or religion
liberator	one who frees a group of people
viceroy	the governor of a country or province, who rules as the representative of the monarch
burro	a small donkey, usually used as a pack animal
mural	a large picture painted on a wall
dominate	to be most important, most powerful, strongest
influence	the power to affect other people or things

Colonization

For 300 years Spaniards built colonies in the Americas. From about 1500 until about 1800, they controlled areas of Mexico, Central America, and South America. Some Portuguese settled in the eastern part of South America. The French also founded a few settlements. Most of the lands, however, fell to the Spaniards. All the lands in this area are called *Latin America*. That is because the Spanish, Portuguese, and French languages came from Latin.

Wherever Spaniards settled, they took power. Many Spanish settlers came from wealthy families. They felt they should not do certain kinds of work. Therefore, they made the Indians work for them. The Spaniards also brought Africans to the Americas to work as enslaved persons on farms and in mines.

Many wealthy Spaniards lived on **haciendas.** These were large cattle ranches with rich farmlands. Much of the work on the haciendas was done by Indian field hands or by enslaved Africans.

Latin America Is Late to Industrialize

Spain and Portugal controlled all trade in their colonies. The colonies were not allowed to trade among themselves or with other nations. They were kept dependent on the mother country. In addition, any effort to develop industry in the colonies was crushed. Latin America had to sell all its raw materials to Spain and Portugal. It had to buy all its finished products from them, too.

This kind of control kept industry from developing in Latin America. Eventually the people of Latin America rose up against their foreign rulers. The 1800s saw waves of revolution sweep through Latin America.

Social Classes in the Colonies

Most people who had been born in Spain felt superior to the other Latin Americans. The Spaniards did not adopt any native customs. Instead, they tried to make the new land as much like Spain as possible.

The Creoles were people of Spanish blood who were born and raised in Latin America. Many Creoles resented the haughty attitude of the Spanish-born people. The Creoles would play a large part in the soon-to-come struggles for independence.

Most of the Spaniards and Portuguese who settled in Latin America did not bring their families. Many were soldiers and fortune-seekers. They did not plan to stay any longer than it took to get rich. Some Spaniards fathered the children of native women. These children and their **descendants** became part of a large class of people of mixed race, called *mestizos*.

Many of the mestizos were angered by their lack of social standing. They hated the **discrimination** they felt from their Spanish rulers. The mestizos were ready for freedom from European rule.

The Indians and the enslaved Africans were certainly ready for a change of government. Year after year, they worked hard yet remained poor. They had nothing for themselves under European rule—no land, no wealth, no power, little hope.

The poor people of Latin America were now ready to fight for freedom. They saw Britain's colonies in North America win their freedom. They saw the people of France rise up against tyranny. Now they needed leaders to call them together and organize revolts.

You Decide

Is there discrimination against any groups of people in the United States today? If so, what kind of discrimination do they face?

Toussaint L'Ouverture

Haiti covers the western third of the island of Hispaniola in the Caribbean Sea. Haiti was the first Latin American colony to fight for freedom. Haiti was a French colony. When news of revolution in France reached Haiti, the people of the colony got excited. They began to think about freedom, too.

In 1791 the enslaved people rebelled against their French masters. A black revolutionary named Toussaint L'Ouverture became a leader in Haiti's fight for freedom. Toussaint was an enslaved person himself until he was 50. He led the slave revolt until 1793, when France freed all enslaved people. In 1801

Toussaint L'Ouverture led slaves in a rebellion.

Toussaint became governor of Haiti. The very next year, however, Napoleon sent a French army to Haiti. He planned to reestablish slavery in the country. War broke out again. The French threw Toussaint into prison, where he died in 1803. However, by 1804, the French army was defeated, and French rule in Haiti ended. Haiti declared its independence.

Wars of revolution continued. Other Latin American countries demanded freedom.

Hidalgo and Morelos

Miguel Hidalgo and José Morelos led Mexico's revolt against Spain. Both men were Catholic priests. They organized the Indians in a revolution.

On September 16, 1810, in the town of Dolores, Miguel Hidalgo rang church bells. He shouted the *grito de Dolores,* or "cry of Dolores": "Long live independence! Down with bad government!"

Both Hidalgo and Morelos lost their lives fighting for Mexico's independence. By 1821, the fight was won. Now Mexico celebrates September 16th as its independence day. Furthermore, the town of Dolores is now called Dolores Hidalgo.

Simón Bolívar

Perhaps the best-known Latin American **liberator** was Simón Bolívar. Today he is called "The Liberator" and the "George Washington of South America."

Bolívar spent much of his life fighting for the independence of South American nations. He was a Creole, born in Venezuela. His parents were wealthy Spaniards. To keep his wealth and social position, Bolívar might have sided with Spain. Instead, he spent all his money backing revolutions because he believed in freedom from European rule.

Starting in 1810, Simón Bolívar helped to organize an army. He then led the army in a series of victories against the Spanish. He liberated one country after another. At one time he ruled the newly formed Republic of Gran Colombia. This was made up of Colombia, Venezuela, Ecuador, and Peru. Then, one by one, each country withdrew from the union. By 1828 Bolívar ruled only Colombia. His own people did not appreciate him. After a failed attempt on his life, he resigned as president in 1830.

Bernardo O'Higgins

Chile owes its liberation to the son of an Irishman. Bernardo O'Higgins's father had been a **viceroy** of Peru. Bernardo O'Higgins led a revolution that began in 1810. After winning Chile's independence from Spain in 1818, O'Higgins acted as the country's dictator. He planned to bring about reform in Chile. He taxed the wealthy landowners to pay for new schools and roads. He also tried to break up their big estates. A revolt by the landowners in 1823, however, sent O'Higgins into exile.

✓ **Check Your Understanding**

Write your answers in complete sentences.

1. Why did Central and South America come to be called Latin America?

2. Who were the Creoles and the mestizos?

3. Why were the Creoles and the mestizos ready to fight for independence?

Great Names in History

JOSÉ DE SAN MARTÍN

Bernardo O'Higgins was helped in his struggle against Spain by another great leader, José de San Martín. San Martín was born in Argentina, but was educated in Spain. While in Spain, he fought with the Spanish army against Napoleon. When he returned to Argentina, the fight for independence had already begun in South America.

In 1812 San Martín took command of a rebel army. For the next several years he fought to free Argentina from Spain's rule. In 1816 Argentina declared its independence. Then San Martín decided to help the rest of South America become free. He planned a daring surprise attack against the Spanish army in Chile. In 1817 he joined forces with Bernardo O'Higgins. Together, they led their army across the Andes Mountains. It was a difficult and dangerous march. Blizzards struck without warning. The men had to plow through deep snowdrifts. Slowly they made their way across the icy mountain passes. Many men died along the way. Finally the brave leaders and their army came down from the mountains in Chile. There they attacked the Spanish army. The Spaniards were completely taken by surprise, and they were easily defeated.

San Martín then went on to help win independence for Peru in 1821. When he finally returned to Argentina, a fierce struggle for political power was going on. San Martín felt bad about this and would have nothing to do with it. He went back to Europe and lived in France for the rest of his life.

Dom Pedro

Dom Pedro led Brazil to independence without bloodshed. He was a Portuguese prince. He inherited the Brazilian kingdom when it was still under Portuguese rule. The Brazilian people wanted independence. They also wanted Dom Pedro to go home to Portugal.

"I remain!" he stated. Then on September 7, 1822, he declared Brazil an independent country. He took the throne of the newly independent nation as Pedro I.

Governments of the New Nations

The Latin American countries' struggles for independence did not necessarily mean freedom for the people. Most of the countries did not become democracies. Life did not change much for many Native Americans and mestizos in those lands.

Dictators ruled most of the new nations. These dictators were powerful men with strong armies behind them. Any changes in government usually came only by military takeovers.

Latin American Cultures

Latin American culture is really more than one culture. It is a mixture of several different peoples: Indian, Spanish, Portuguese, African, and French.

Some Native Americans who live in rural areas still live much like their ancestors. They wear woven shawls and take their goods to market along mountain roads on **burros** and llamas. They play music on handmade wooden instruments and weave baskets of cane and reed. Indian women still spin and weave colorful cloth. There is often a note of sadness to the Indians' art. A **mural** in Mexico City shows the Indians suffering at the hands of Spanish conquistadors.

Latin American Nations Become Independent

UNITED STATES

ATLANTIC OCEAN

BAHAMAS 1973

Gulf of Mexico

MEXICO 1821

BELIZE 1981

HAITI 1804

DOMINICAN REPUBLIC 1844

CUBA 1902

JAMAICA 1962

ANTIGUA AND BARBUDA 1981

ST. KITTS-NEVIS 1983

ST. LUCIA 1979

DOMINICA 1978

HONDURAS 1821

Caribbean Sea

GUATEMALA 1821

NICARAGUA 1838

GRENADA 1974

BARBADOS 1966

ST. VINCENT 1979

TRINIDAD AND TOBAGO 1962

EL SALVADOR 1841

VENEZUELA 1821

GUYANA 1966

SURINAME 1975

COSTA RICA 1821

PANAMA 1903

COLOMBIA 1819

FRENCH GUIANA

ECUADOR 1822

BRAZIL 1822

PACIFIC OCEAN

PERU 1824

BOLIVIA 1825

CHILE 1810

PARAGUAY 1811

ARGENTINA 1816

URUGUAY 1828

Present-day boundaries

N
W — E
S

| 0 | 500 | 1,000 miles |
| 0 | 500 | 1,000 kilometers |

Map Study

1. In what year did Brazil become independent?

2. Which Latin American country shares a border with the United States?

The Spanish and Portuguese brought their languages and religion to Latin America. Most of the people of Latin America speak Spanish. Portuguese is the main language of Brazil. The different Native American groups speak their own native languages. Roman Catholicism is the main religion.

Spanish architecture is common in Latin America. Many homes, churches, and public buildings have a Spanish flavor. However, much Latin American music reflects the music of Africa. The Africans brought their songs and dances with them when they came to Latin America as enslaved people.

Different races and cultures **dominate** different areas of Latin America. In some countries, most of the people are Indians. The art, music, dress, and customs in Guatemala, Bolivia, and Peru are strongly influenced by Native American cultures. In some countries, like Haiti, the people are mostly descendants of Africans.

Latin America gets its name from the colonization and **influence** of Latin peoples—the Spanish, the Portuguese, and the French. However, the Indians and the Africans have played a large part in making Latin America what it is today.

Spanish colonial architecture

 Timeline Study

During what time period did many Latin American countries win their independence?

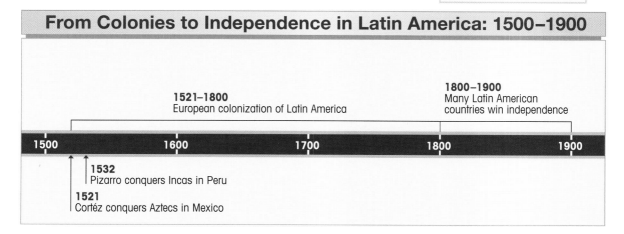

From Colonies to Independence in Latin America: 1500–1900

1521–1800
European colonization of Latin America

1800–1900
Many Latin American countries win independence

1500   1600   1700   1800   1900

1532
Pizarro conquers Incas in Peru

1521
Cortéz conquers Aztecs in Mexico

Summary

Most areas of Latin America were settled by the Spaniards and the Portuguese.
The European settlers made workers of the Indians and enslaved Africans.
Colonial powers did not allow industry to develop in Latin America.
Between 1500 and 1900, Europeans, Creoles, mestizos, Indians, and enslaved Africans lived in Latin America.
During the 1800s, revolutions gained independence for many Latin American countries. The new countries were often ruled by dictators.
Latin American culture is a blend of Spanish, Portuguese, French, Indian, and African cultures.

descendant

liberator

mural

discrimination

hacienda

influence

Vocabulary Review

Write a term from the list that matches each definition below.

1. A large cattle ranch or country home

2. Unfair treatment of a person, often based on race or religion

3. The power to affect the way that people or nations act

4. A person from a particular ancestor

5. A leader who frees a group of people

6. A large painting on a wall

Chapter Quiz

Write your answers in complete sentences.

1. Why was Latin America late to industrialize?

2. Why does Mexico celebrate September 16 as independence day?

3. Where does Latin American culture come from?

4. **Critical Thinking** How did the American and French revolutions affect Latin America?

5. **Critical Thinking** Why do you think O'Higgins wanted to break up the big estates in Chile?

Using the Timeline

Use the timeline on page 303 to answer the questions.

1. How long did European colonization of Latin America last?

2. What happened in 1532?

Write About History

Complete the following activity.

Work with a group to make a large wall chart of Latin American revolutionaries. Include their personal background, nicknames, famous words, countries they liberated, and other information.

The Panama Canal was completed in 1914. Ships can now sail from the Atlantic to the Pacific Ocean without going around South America.

Learning Objectives

- Tell how the United States gained the Louisiana Territory.
- List the problems the United States faced in establishing its northern and southern borders.
- Identify the causes and main events of the Civil War.
- Tell how the United States acquired Alaska and Hawaii.
- Explain the effects of the Spanish-American War.

Chapter 21 / The United States Gains Power

Words to Know

territory	the land ruled by a nation or state
reaper	a machine for cutting down and gathering grain crops
victor	the winner of a battle, war, struggle, or contest
international	having to do with many nations

Imperialism and the Monroe Doctrine

Smaller nations are often threatened by larger and stronger nations. The new, independent countries in Latin America struggled to survive. The United States wanted these countries to remain independent.

In 1823 James Monroe, President of the United States, spoke before Congress. He said that the United States would not allow Europe to set up new colonies in North or South America. The United States would also forbid any existing colonies from taking over more land. The President's statement against European imperialism was later called the Monroe Doctrine.

A Growing United States: The Louisiana Purchase

The United States grew rapidly during the early 1800s. Settlers moved west, taking lands from the Native Americans.

In 1803 Thomas Jefferson was President of the United States. He arranged for the United States to buy the Louisiana **Territory**, a large piece of land, from

The Louisiana Purchase

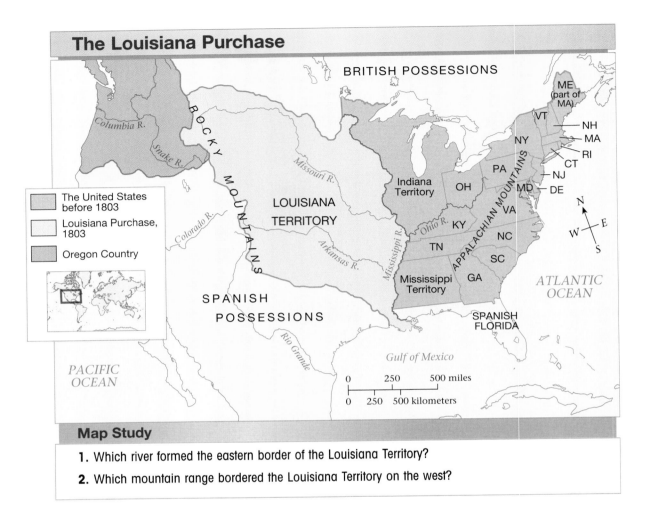

Legend:
- The United States before 1803
- Louisiana Purchase, 1803
- Oregon Country

Map Study

1. Which river formed the eastern border of the Louisiana Territory?

2. Which mountain range bordered the Louisiana Territory on the west?

France. The United States paid about $15 million for 828,000 square miles of land. The Louisiana Purchase almost doubled the size of the United States.

American pioneers streamed into the new land. They settled first in what would become the states of Louisiana, Arkansas, and Missouri.

United States Borders

The United States needed to set up clear northern and southern borders. Britain still controlled Canada to the north. War broke out between Britain and the United States in 1812. However, the United States-Canadian border was not the cause. Other problems had led to the war. Britain had been interfering with United States trade. A peace treaty was signed in December of 1814. The border remained the same.

In the southern United States, however, border disagreements *were* the cause of war. What is now the state of Texas once belonged to the Republic of Mexico. Many settlers from the United States moved into Texas.

The Mexicans worried about the large numbers of settlers from the North. They said that no more settlers could come in from the United States. In response, the settlers rebelled. In November 1835 they declared themselves free from Mexico. Then the battles began.

> **HISTORY FACT**
>
> General Santa Anna made himself dictator of Mexico in 1834. Americans in Texas did not want to live under his rule.

"Remember the Alamo!"

The Battle of the Alamo was one of the most famous battles in the Texas war of independence. The Alamo was an old Spanish mission in San Antonio that the Texans were using as their fort.

It was February 23, 1836. Five thousand Mexican soldiers stormed the fort. Inside the Alamo were 187 Texans, among them Davy Crockett and James Bowie. They managed to hold the fort for 12 days. In the end, nearly all the Texans defending the Alamo were killed. However, their brave fight gave spirit to the struggle and helped the Texan forces win the war.

"Remember the Alamo!" became the battle cry of the Texan forces. By April 1836 the Mexican army was defeated. The Mexican general Santa Anna signed a peace treaty. Texas became an independent nation.

The Alamo was a fort in San Antonio, Texas, where a famous battle was fought in 1836.

War with Mexico

In 1845 Texas became the 28th state to join the United States. Many in the Mexican government had not approved of the treaty Santa Anna had signed in 1836. As a result, the declaration of statehood led to war in 1846 between the United States and Mexico.

Mexico lost the war in 1848. The United States and Mexico signed the Treaty of Guadalupe Hidalgo. In the treaty Mexico accepted the Rio Grande as the boundary between Mexico and Texas. Also, in return for $15 million, the United States gained vast new territory that had belonged to Mexico. This included what are now the states of Utah, California, Nevada, and most of Arizona, New Mexico, Wyoming, and Colorado.

Civil War

Like European history, American history is scarred with many wars. Between 1861 and 1865, Americans fought a bloody civil war between the northern and southern states.

Slavery was an important issue between the North and South. However, it was not the immediate cause of the war. After Abraham Lincoln was elected President, the southern states broke away from the United States. They formed a separate nation called the Confederate States of America. Lincoln could not allow the South to break up the Union. He felt he had no choice but to go to war to save the Union.

The North had many more people than the South. The North also had more manufacturing and industry. It was able to produce more guns and cannons. The South was still mainly agricultural. Its main crops were cotton and tobacco. The southern plantations depended on enslaved workers.

Northerners expected the war to be over soon. They were also sure they would be the winners. However, they were in for a surprise. The very first battle of the war, at Bull Run on July 21, 1861, was easily won by the South! Furthermore, the Confederate army went on to win one battle after another. The army was led by brilliant generals such as Robert E. Lee and Stonewall Jackson.

The turning point of the war came at Gettysburg, Pennsylvania. Lee and his forces retreated from the battlefield. Later, in 1863 Lincoln's *Emancipation Proclamation* took effect, outlawing slavery in areas rebelling against the Union. By the end of the war, about 200,000 African Americans had fought for the North.

By 1864, Ulysses S. Grant had won many union victories in the West. In that year, Lincoln appointed Grant commander of all Union forces. By 1865 much of the South lay in ruins. The southern armies had also

The word *Union* (with a capital U) means the Union of all the states. In the Civil War, Union also meant those on the side of the North, such as Union soldiers.

become much weaker. The North had cut off all of the South's supply routes. Lee's army was trapped in Virginia by Grant's army. Lee decided it was hopeless to keep on fighting. He surrendered to Grant on April 9, 1865, at Appomattox Court House in Virginia.

The bloodiest war in American history was over. More than 600,000 people had been killed. Many cities and farms had been destroyed. However, the North had won the war and the Union had been saved. All of the states were now united.

✓ Check Your Understanding

Write your answers in complete sentences.

1. Why did war break out between Britain and the United States in 1812?

2. Why did the United States and Mexico go to war in 1846?

3. What was the main cause of the American Civil War?

Industry in the United States

Many changes occurred in the United States during the early 1800s. The introduction of the steam locomotive led to great improvements in overland transportation. In addition, Samuel Morse's telegraph, first demonstrated in 1837, led to greatly improved communication. In 1834 Cyrus McCormick invented a mechanical **reaper.** This machine allowed farmers to harvest grain much more quickly than before. Beginning in the early 1800s, some businesses began building factories. Inside the factories were machines that enabled workers to produce goods more rapidly.

After the Civil War, changes occurred more quickly. More and more factories were built. Machines began to replace hand labor as the main means of manufacturing.

At this time, a new nationwide network of railroads was being built. In 1869 the transcontinental railroad was completed. It linked up the eastern and western parts of the country. It also helped speed up the settlement of the West.

The railroad system helped businesses to distribute their goods more quickly. In addition, there were more and more goods available. Inventors developed new products. Businesses were able to make the products in large quantities. The United States now had its own industrial revolution.

Many big businesses developed during this period. Some involved the production of coal, petroleum, steel, and industrial machinery. New England, New York, and Pennsylvania became important industrial centers in the North. The United States was on its way to becoming an industrial giant.

Further Expansion: Alaska and Hawaii

"A foolish purchase!" "Who wants a hunk of frozen land?" Many Americans said that about the territory known as Alaska. In 1867 Secretary of State William Seward had persuaded the United States to buy Alaska from Russia. The price was just over $7 million. In 1897, gold was discovered in Alaska. It was only then that Americans began to realize the value of the purchase.

Remember
The United States also made a huge land purchase in 1803, the Louisiana Purchase.

The United States' interest in Hawaii began in 1820. That year a group of Protestant missionaries from New England arrived in Hawaii. In 1835 the first sugar plantation began operating there. It was owned by an American company. Commercial development of the pineapple began in the mid-1800s. Also, around this time, hundreds of U.S. whaling ships began to visit Hawaii regularly. In 1887 the United States signed a treaty with Hawaii. It gave the United States the right to use Pearl Harbor as a naval base. The United States' interests were now well established on the islands.

Queen Liliuokalani of Hawaii

In 1893 the Hawaiians staged a revolution against Liliuokalani, queen of Hawaii. Americans, who by that time owned most of Hawaii's industry, encouraged and led the revolt. Queen Liliuokalani left her throne. In 1900 Hawaii became a territory of the United States.

The United States used the Monroe Doctrine to keep European interests out of the Americas. Meanwhile, the United States gained more and more territory for itself.

The Spanish-American War

A war broke out between the United States and Spain in 1898. As a result of this war, the United States gained still more territory.

The United States wanted Spain out of the Caribbean area. Many Americans felt sympathy for the Cubans who lived under harsh Spanish rule. Some Americans also saw a chance for the United States to gain more power.

Relations between the United States and Spain were tense. Then, in February 1898, the U.S. battleship *Maine* exploded in the harbor at Havana, Cuba. Many Americans blamed Spain. By April, the Spanish-American War had begun.

By August of that same year, the war was over. The United States was the **victor.** In December, Spain and the United States sent representatives to Paris to sign a treaty. The Treaty of Paris gave the United States possession of Puerto Rico, the Philippines, and the Pacific Island of Guam. Spain gave Cuba its freedom.

U.S. Power

By the early 1900s, the United States was the strongest country on the American continents. It held control over lands gained in the Spanish-American War. During that war, the U.S. Navy sent a battleship from

You Decide

Today some experts believe the explosion of the *Maine* was probably an accident. Were Americans right to declare war? Why or why not?

San Francisco to Cuba. It had to sail all the way around the tip of South America. This is a distance of 13,000 miles. If there had been a canal across Central America, the trip would have been only about 5,000 miles.

U.S. President Theodore Roosevelt wanted to build such a canal across Panama. However, Colombia ruled Panama. Furthermore, Colombia would not grant the United States the land it needed for the canal. To get around this problem, the United States encouraged Panama to declare its independence from Colombia.

Panama's rebellion in November 1903 was a success. The United States gained the right to build the canal. Panama ceded the United States a canal zone that was ten miles wide. The Panama Canal and the Canal Zone belonged to the United States. However, in 1977, the United States and Panama signed a treaty. In keeping with the treaty, Panama regained control of the Canal Zone in 1979. Then in 1999, Panama gained control of the canal itself.

With the canal built, the United States grew as an economic, military, and industrial power. It became important in **international** affairs. The United States was becoming a major force in the modern world.

Timeline Study

From the information on the timeline, do you think the United States felt the Monroe Doctrine applied to itself? Why or why not?

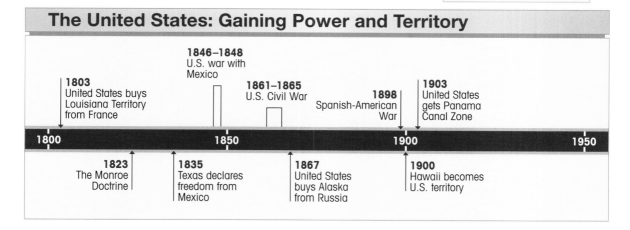

The United States: Gaining Power and Territory

1803
United States buys Louisiana Territory from France

1846–1848
U.S. war with Mexico

1861–1865
U.S. Civil War

1898
Spanish-American War

1903
United States gets Panama Canal Zone

1800   **1850**   **1900**   **1950**

1823
The Monroe Doctrine

1835
Texas declares freedom from Mexico

1867
United States buys Alaska from Russia

1900
Hawaii becomes U.S. territory

Chapter 21 Review

Summary

The Monroe Doctrine said that the United States would not allow Europeans to set up new colonies in the Americas.

The United States expanded by adding the Louisiana Purchase, Alaska, and Hawaii.

War with Mexico established the southern border of the United States.

The United States was torn apart by a bloody civil war from 1861 to 1865. The North won the war, and the Union was preserved.

The United States became an imperialist, expansionist nation. The United States purchased Alaska and attacked Hawaii. In the Spanish-American War, the United States obtained Puerto Rico, the Philippines, and Guam. The United States built the Panama Canal connecting the Atlantic and Pacific oceans.

Vocabulary Review

Write *true* or *false*. If the statement is false, change the underlined term to make it true.

1. A <u>reaper</u> is the winner of a battle.

2. The United States was the <u>victor</u> in the Spanish-American War.

3. Land controlled by a nation or state is its <u>territory</u>.

4. Many nations belong to an <u>international</u> group.

Chapter Quiz

Write your answers in complete sentences.

1. How did the United States gain the Louisiana Territory?

2. How did the United States gain Utah, Nevada, and California?

3. Who won the Battle of Bull Run?

4. **Critical Thinking** What do you think would have happened to the United States if the South had won the Civil War?

5. **Critical Thinking** Why might some countries have objected to the way the United States obtained the Panama Canal Zone?

Using the Timeline

Use the timeline on page 315 to answer the questions.

1. How many years passed between the time Texas declared freedom from Mexico and the U.S. war with Mexico?

2. How long did the Civil War last?

Write About History

Complete the following activities.

1. Suppose you lived in 1867. Write a letter to the editor of your local paper. Explain how you feel about Seward's purchase of Alaska.

2. Suppose you lived in 1897. Gold was just discovered in Alaska. Write a letter to the editor of your local paper. Explain how you feel about Seward's purchase of Alaska.

In 1900, U.S. troops helped to put down the Boxer Rebellion in China.

Learning Objectives

- Describe the Manchus' attitude toward other Chinese people and the world.
- Describe the Open-Door Policy.
- Tell how Sun Yatsen put an end to Manchu rule in China.
- Tell how Commodore Matthew C. Perry opened the doors of trade to Japan.
- List the ways in which Japan modernized after a powerful emperor took over in 1867.
- Explain how Japan's industrialization led to Japanese imperialism.

Words to Know

policy	a rule; a method of action or conduct
addicted	having a strong habit that is hard to give up
smuggle	to move something into or out of a country secretly because it is against the law
interference	meddling in another's affairs without being asked
modern	of the present time, up-to-date

The Manchus Establish the Qing Dynasty in China

Manchuria is a region in the northeastern part of China. At one time, it did not belong to China. In 1644, the Manchus—the people of Manchuria—invaded northern China. They overthrew the Ming dynasty that was then in power. Then they conquered the rest of China. The Manchus set up their own dynasty called the Qing Dynasty. The Manchus would remain in power for more than 250 years. However, the Qing dynasty would be the last of the Chinese dynasties.

The Manchus were a proud people—too proud, perhaps. They thought they were better than the other Chinese people. They passed a law saying that a Manchu could not marry a Chinese. They forced Chinese men to wear a Manchu hairstyle. This was a long braid down the back of the head. The British later called the long braid a *queue*. The word *queu* is from a Latin word meaning "tail."

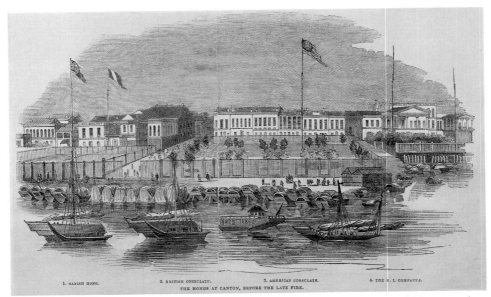

1. DANISH HONG.   2. BRITISH CONSULATE.   3. AMERICAN CONSULATE.   4. THE M. L. COMPANY S.

THE HONGS AT CANTON, BEFORE THE LATE FIRE.

Danish, British, and American ships used harbors to trade with China, such as this one in Canton.

The Manchus not only looked down on other Chinese, they also looked down on the rest of the world. Until the mid-1800s, foreign trade was allowed through only one Chinese city—Guangzhou, or Canton. When European nations and the United States asked for more trade with China, the Manchu rulers always refused.

During the first 150 years of Manchu rule, China enjoyed prosperity. Agriculture increased, and the handicraft industry did, too. The population expanded rapidly. However, by the late 1700s, the times had changed. The population had increased more quickly than the food supply. Life became harder for most people.

China Under the Qing Dynasty

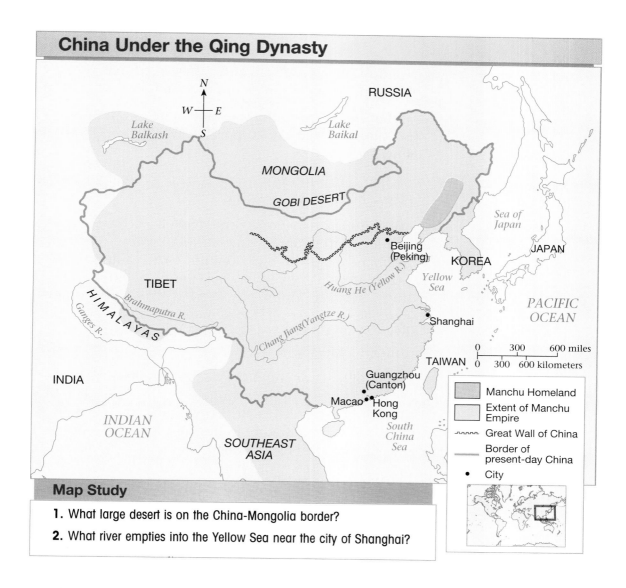

Map Study

1. What large desert is on the China-Mongolia border?

2. What river empties into the Yellow Sea near the city of Shanghai?

China also suffered because of the Manchus' isolationist **policies.** Once China had been a leader in science and medicine. By the 1800s, however, the Chinese had fallen behind the Europeans in all areas of science and invention. From this point on, the Manchus would rule a troubled China.

The Opium War

Europeans wanted tea and silk from China. They also wanted a new source of raw materials.

"But there is nothing we want from you in return," the Manchus told the Europeans. "Why should we allow trade?"

Then the Europeans found something many Chinese did want. They found opium.

Opium is a dangerous drug made from the seeds of poppies. Many poppies grew in India. European merchants began to bring opium to China during the early 1800s. Many Chinese became **addicted** to the drug. Therefore, China passed a law making the opium trade illegal. However, the demand for opium was still there. Now the Europeans **smuggled** the drug into China, making large profits.

In 1839, a Manchu official seized 20,000 chests of opium from British merchants in Guangzhou. He had the opium burned. The British were angry. They said valuable property had been destroyed. Great Britain went to war with China, demanding better trading rights. China had little chance against Britain's armies. In 1842, the Chinese surrendered. They signed the Treaty of Nanjing.

This was the first of what the Chinese called the Unequal Treaties. China not only had to pay for the lost opium but also for the cost of the war. China had to open five ports to British trade. China also had to give the island of Hong Kong to Great Britain. The new treaties totally protected British merchants from Chinese law. No British citizen could be tried for any crime in a Chinese court—even if the crime were committed in China. The Chinese felt helpless.

You Decide

Do you think the major powers today would be more likely to go to war to protect the drug trade or to destroy it? Why?

Chinese Rebellion

The Manchus had trouble with foreigners and trouble with people in China. Chinese farmers were not happy under Manchu rule. They said that the rulers were greedy and unfair. Most Chinese farmers were very poor. Finally, the peasants rebelled. They called their rebellion *Taiping,* meaning *Great Peace.* The Taiping Rebellion lasted from 1850 to 1864. Millions of lives were lost. When it was over, the Manchus still ruled China.

Remember
During the late 1700s, French peasants rose up against their lords.

The peasants might have won their fight. They might have overthrown the Manchu government. Yet foreign **interference** worked against them. Western governments wanted to keep the Manchus in power. Western powers worried that they might lose their trade rights if the Manchus were overthrown. Great Britain, the United States, and other Western nations supported the Manchus. Western governments sent military help, and the peasants were defeated.

War with Japan

Next, the Manchus faced war with Japan. China had had claims on Korea for hundreds of years. When a rebellion broke out in Korea in 1894, the Chinese sent troops in to crush it. Japan had interests in Korea, too. Japan also sent in its troops. The rebellion was put down. Then, neither Japan nor China would withdraw its troops. Instead, the two countries began fighting each other.

By April 1895, the Japanese had defeated the Chinese. China had to give up much of its claim on Korea. China also had to give the island of Taiwan to the Japanese. By 1910, Japan would take complete control of Korea.

The Chinese-Japanese war left China weak. From then on, Manchu rulers commanded little respect. The Manchus feared that European nations might step in and divide China into colonies. The United States suggested an Open-Door Policy. This meant that all countries would have equal rights to trade in China. The Manchus agreed to this policy. The Chinese had once kept everyone out. Now, they opened their ports to the world.

Learn More About It

THE BOXER REBELLION

In 1898, the Manchu empress Cixi ruled the Qing dynasty. She was very old-fashioned. She wanted to stop any change in China. Perhaps, she remembered China's glorious past. If she had her way, she would keep China the way it was.

Then something happened in 1900, during the empress's reign. A group of Chinese rebelled against all foreigners in China. The revolt was called the Boxer Rebellion. The empress Cixi secretly supported the rebels.

The Boxers were members of a secret society. Westerners called them Boxers because they practiced Chinese exercises that resembled shadow-boxing. The Boxers attempted to kill all foreigners in China. They were put down by an international army that included soldiers from the United States.

China was forced to make payments to the foreign countries to make up for the rebellion. However, the United States used much of the money it received to educate Chinese students. Because of this, the United States won China's favor.

✔ Check Your Understanding

Write your answers in complete sentences.

1. What was the Manchu dynasty called?

2. In what ways did Great Britain benefit from the Unequal Treaties?

3. Why did the Chinese peasants rebel against the Manchus from 1850 to 1864?

Sun Yatsen and the Chinese Nationalists

The Qing dynasty would be the last dynasty to rule China. Rebellions had weakened the government. The war with Japan had cost China both land and power. Many foreign countries had interests in China now. In addition, the weak Manchus were unable to protect China against the foreigners. China needed a new government to survive.

In 1911, a Chinese doctor named Sun Yatsen was in Denver, Colorado. He had been traveling throughout Japan, Europe, and the United States. He was trying to raise money to help overthrow the Manchu government. When he heard about sparks of revolution in China, he returned there. He led the

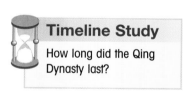

Timeline Study

How long did the Qing Dynasty last?

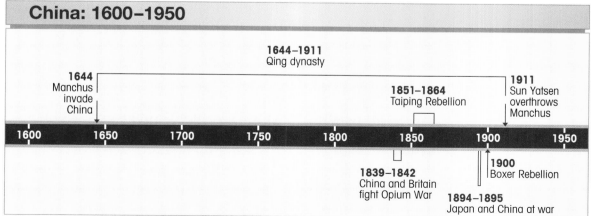

China: 1600–1950

1644–1911
Qing dynasty

1644
Manchus invade China

1851–1864
Taiping Rebellion

1911
Sun Yatsen overthrows Manchus

1600   1650   1700   1750   1800   1850   1900   1950

1900
Boxer Rebellion

1839–1842
China and Britain fight Opium War

1894–1895
Japan and China at war

revolution and overthrew the Manchu empire. On January 1, 1912, he became the first president of China's new republic. The last Manchu emperor, Puyi, gave up the throne on February 12, 1912. He was only six years old at the time.

Sun's term as president was short, less than two months. Then a strong, military officer, Yuan Shikai, took over. Sun and his followers remained. They organized the *Guomindang,* or Nationalist party. Meanwhile, for years the Chinese people suffered under harsh rulers who fought each other for power.

By 1922, the republic had failed and civil war was widespread. With the support of the Soviet Union and of Chinese Communists, Sun and his Nationalist party trained an army. They set out to bring China together under a Nationalist government.

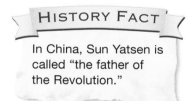

Sun Yatsen died in 1925, but his work was finished by Jiang Jieshi. By 1928 Jiang was able to set up a Nationalist government in China. More days of war and revolution were ahead. However, China had left its great dynasties behind and moved into the **modern** world.

Japan Opens Its Doors

After 1600, Japan had become an isolated nation. The whole country was under the rule of the Tokugawa family. All foreign trade and travel were forbidden. Japan did not allow foreign products to enter its ports. Japan did not send any products to other lands either. Japan would not accept visitors from other countries. In fact, if a foreign sailor were shipwrecked on Japan's shores, he was in for trouble. He could be arrested or even killed.

In 1853, an American naval officer, Commodore Matthew C. Perry, changed all that. Commodore Perry sailed four U.S. warships into Tokyo Bay. He brought a letter from the U.S. President. The letter asked the

Japanese to change their policies. It asked for better treatment of any shipwrecked American sailors. It asked that American whaling ships be allowed to buy supplies at Japanese ports. It asked that Japan agree to trade with the United States.

The Japanese were impressed by Perry and his U.S. ships. They had never seen such large vessels or such mighty guns. Perry was a stern man. He met the Japanese with dignity. He refused to speak to anyone except the highest officials. Perry left his requests for the Japanese to consider.

The next year, Commodore Perry returned to Japan. This time, he brought even more ships. The ruling shogun spoke with Perry. Then the Japanese ruler

Commodore Matthew Perry arrives in Tokyo in 1853 and is greeted by Japanese officials.

signed a treaty with the United States. Japanese ports would be open to U.S. ships. It was the beginning of a new Japan.

A Modern Japan

In 1858, Townsend Harris, a U.S. diplomat, signed a more extensive treaty with Japan. That same year, Japan signed trade treaties with Great Britain, France, the Netherlands, and Russia. Japan was no longer an isolated nation.

Then came years of change. Japan was torn between its old ways and the new. Some Japanese wanted to drive the foreigners out of Japan again. They said the treaties Japan had signed were Unequal Treaties. Others wanted to accept the Western world and learn what they could. They realized that their feudal system of government was outdated. The rule of the shoguns with their samurai warriors had to end.

You Decide

Why do you think some Japanese considered the treaties to be unequal?

In 1867, a young emperor named Mutsuhito came to power. He and his followers began to modernize Japan. Their motto was, "Knowledge shall be sought throughout the world." The emperor adopted *Meiji* as his title, which means *enlightened rule.* He was to rule Japan until 1912. These years are known as the Meiji period. The Japanese traveled to other nations. They wanted to learn what they could about industry, education, transportation, and banking. They built thousands of schools. They also invited foreigners to teach in Japan.

In 1889, Japan's first constitution was written. The Japanese still considered the emperor divine. The emperor still held the power, but he accepted advice from elected representatives.

By the 1890s, Japan was keeping step with the modern world. Japan had done away with the samurai and now had a modern army and navy. Japan had steel mills, shipyards, and electrical power plants. In just over 25 years, Japan had made amazing progress. It had gone from an isolated, feudal nation to become one of the world's industrial powers.

Japanese Imperialism

As industry grew, Japan needed more raw materials. Like many strong nations, Japan decided to set up overseas colonies to supply those raw materials. To Japan, gaining such colonies meant war.

From 1894 to 1895, Japan was at war with China. China and Japan had conflicting claims in Korea. Japan, with its new, modern military, easily defeated China, and took the island of Taiwan.

In 1904, Russia tried to stake claims in Korea. Japan declared war. The Russo-Japanese War was costly to both sides, but the war was over in 1905. Again, the Japanese were the victors. Japan took over some lands in China that had been controlled by Russia. In 1910, Japan took complete control of Korea. Japan's victory over Russia surprised the world. For the first time, an Asian nation had proved to be stronger than a European nation. This was to be only the first chapter in the story of Japanese imperialism.

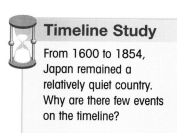

Timeline Study

From 1600 to 1854, Japan remained a relatively quiet country. Why are there few events on the timeline?

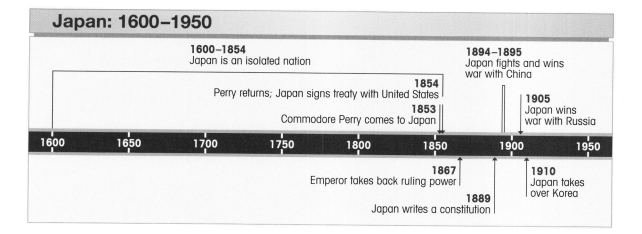

Japan: 1600–1950

1600–1854
Japan is an isolated nation

1894–1895
Japan fights and wins war with China

1854
Perry returns; Japan signs treaty with United States

1853
Commodore Perry comes to Japan

1905
Japan wins war with Russia

1600   1650   1700   1750   1800   1850   1900   1950

1867
Emperor takes back ruling power

1910
Japan takes over Korea

1889
Japan writes a constitution

Summary

The Manchus conquered China in 1644 and established the Qing dynasty. They tried to limit foreign trade in China. China and Britain fought a war after China destroyed an illegal British opium cargo.

Chinese peasants rebelled in the Taiping Rebellion in 1851. The rebellion was put down by the Manchus and Westerners.

The United States persuaded China to have an "open-door policy" toward foreign trade. In 1900, the Boxers tried to drive foreigners out of China but were crushed by foreign armies.

In 1911, Chinese Nationalists overthrew the Manchus and ended dynasty rule in China.

In 1853, Commodore Perry negotiated trade treaties with Japan.

In 1867, a young emperor began to modernize Japan. Japan became a powerful industrial nation in just over 25 years. To gain raw materials, Japan became an imperialist power.

modern
interference
smuggle
addicted
policy

Vocabulary Review

Complete each sentence with a term from the list.

1. Foreign _____ during the Taiping Rebellion in China may have changed the outcome of the uprising.

2. A person who is _____ to something must work hard to break the habit.

3. If you _____ goods out of a country, they are not legal in the new country.

4. Emperor Mutsuhito helped Japan become a _____ nation.

5. A nation's foreign _____ determines the way the nation acts toward other nations.

Chapter Quiz

Write your answers in complete sentences.

1. How did the Manchus feel about other Chinese?

2. Why did the Manchus agree to the Open-Door Policy?

3. How did Emperor Mutsuhito help to change Japan?

4. **Critical Thinking** Why did the dynasties come to an end in China?

5. **Critical Thinking** Why did Japan become imperialistic?

Using the Timelines

Use the timelines on pages 325 and 329 to answer the questions.

1. What is the topic of each timeline?

2. One year after Japan took over Korea, what happened in China?

Write About History

Complete the following activity.

With a partner, create a large timeline that shows events in both China and Japan. Display the timeline on a wall of your classroom.

As Europeans moved into India, they brought western ideas with them. They built railroad stations, such as this one in Agra, Uttar Pradesh, India.

Learning Objectives

- Tell how the British East India Company came to rule India.
- Tell how the Sepoy Rebellion began and how it led to direct British rule.
- List five good things Britain did for India.
- Explain why many Indians were unhappy with British rule.
- Identify Mahatma Gandhi, and tell what was different about his way of revolution.

Chapter 23 Imperialism and India

Words to Know

agent	a person who has the authority to act for some other person or company
impose	to force one's ideas or wishes on another
indirectly	in a roundabout way
superiority	a feeling of being better than others
nonviolent	without using force; without causing injury
resistance	the act of opposing; working against
civil disobedience	the refusal to obey rules, orders, or laws
fast	to go without food

The Fall of the Mogul Empire

Aurangzeb, the last powerful Mogul emperor, died in 1707. The Moguls had ruled India for almost 200 years. Aurangzeb, a Muslim, had been a harsh ruler. He had angered the Hindus by destroying many of their temples. He had tried to force non-Muslims to convert to Islam.

After the death of Aurangzeb, the Mogul Empire began to break up. Once again, India was divided into small kingdoms. The rajas of the different kingdoms quarreled with one another. The Mogul rulers no longer had any real power.

As the Moguls weakened, stronger countries saw their chance. Europeans would take advantage of the unsteady government in India.

The British East India Company

Trading between Europe and India had been going on for a long time. In 1498, the Portuguese explorer Vasco da Gama reached India by sailing around Africa. From that time on, European merchants made regular voyages to India. Dutch, Portuguese, French, and British traders fought each other for control of the Indian trade.

HISTORY FACT

Captains of East India Company ships were called East Indiamen. The company allowed them to use part of the cargo space to keep goods for themselves. As a result, they were able to retire very wealthy men.

In 1600, a private business called the British East India Company was formed. Its purpose was to trade with India. It set up trading posts along India's coastline at Bombay, Calcutta, and Madras. At around this time, the Dutch East India Company was formed. It began operating out of Java, in Indonesia.

The Europeans gained little in India as long as the Mogul Empire was strong. However, by the mid-1700s, there was no longer a strong central government in India. The British East India Company became very involved in what went on in that country. It took sides in Indian civil wars. It also supported Indian rulers who gave it favorable trade rights.

When the French began the French East India Company, the British went to war with the French. In 1757, Robert Clive led the British to victory against the French. Both Clive's army and the French army used Indian soldiers to fight their war. The Indian soldiers were called *sepoys*. The British drove the French out of India. After that, the British East India Company became a powerful force in India.

The East India Company Rules

Soon, **agents** of the East India company became stronger than the local rajas. By 1850, the British agents controlled more than half of the land in India. The British put their own people into all the important positions. The British led sepoy armies. They also became wealthy landholders.

The British **imposed** their own ways on Indian society. They built Christian churches and spoke out against the Hindu caste system. Many of the Indians did not like the English ways. They did not like the East India Company either. For almost 100 years, Britain **indirectly** ruled India through the British East India Company. India was not officially a British colony. However, the British held all the power.

Learn More About It

THE SEPOY REBELLION

To protect their own power, the East India agents from Britain built up armies of sepoys. Most of the British army officers did not try to understand Indian customs and culture. They insisted that the Indians accept British ways.

The sepoys grumbled about this. Then in 1857, the British started using a new kind of bullet in India. To open the cartridge, a soldier had to bite off its end. The new cartridges were greased with the fat from cows and pigs. The Muslim religion forbids its followers to eat pork. Hindus are not allowed to eat the meat of a cow. Therefore, the sepoys refused to bite the bullets. When British officers ordered them to bite open the cartridges, the sepoys rebelled.

The British put down the Sepoy Rebellion in 1858. Many lives were lost in the battle. Britain saw that the British East India Company could no longer be trusted with control of India.

When Britain took over rule of India, Queen Victoria herself came to visit the British colony.

British Rule

In 1858, the British Parliament took over the rule of India. India became a colony of Great Britain. It was now called "British India," or the "British Raj."

A viceroy ran the colony. He was appointed by the British monarch. In 1877, the British held a splendid ceremony in India. On this occasion, Queen Victoria was named empress of India.

The British profited from their Indian colony. They called India the "Jewel of the British Empire." In turn, the British government tried to treat Indians more fairly than the British East India Company had.

The British tried to solve the problems of poverty that had always troubled India. They helped farmers dig irrigation canals. They set up hospitals in cities and in some villages. They built railroads and factories, roads and schools. The British tried to do away with the harsh caste system that kept many people so poor.

Yet many Indians were unhappy. Some were poorer than ever. India's raw materials were all going to British industry. Manufactured goods were being brought in from Britain, killing off India's own industries. Machine-made cloth poured in from Britain. This resulted in Indian spinners and weavers being put out of work. Furthermore, all of India's top jobs went to the British.

It was clear to the Indians that the British looked down on them. The British did not allow Indians in their restaurants or hotels. To the people of India, it seemed as if British imperialism encouraged British feelings of **superiority**.

Remember
In China the Manchus looked down on the rest of the people. In 1912, the Manchus were overthrown.

Ideas of Independence

The British chose some Indian students to send off to school in Great Britain. They planned to give the students "English" ideas and training. However, the plan backfired. Once the students from India learned about English democracy, they wanted independence for their own people.

In 1885 a group called the Indian National Congress was founded. It was made up of educated Indians. They said they were meeting to improve relations with Britain. In truth, they were discussing revolution. In the early 1900s, there were some violent uprisings. The British always crushed them. To improve the situation, the British allowed a few Indians to be included in the government. A few years later, the British increased the number of Indians in the government. However, the protests continued.

Then on April 13, 1919, British troops fired on an unarmed crowd in Amritsar. Nearly 400 Indians were killed, and at least 1,200 were wounded. The Amritsar Massacre marked a turning point in British-Indian relations. From then on, Indians knew what they could expect from the British. They were determined to keep on fighting for independence. However, no real progress toward independence came until leadership went to a man called Gandhi.

✓ Check Your Understanding
Write your answers in complete sentences.

1. What was the purpose of the British East India Company?

2. Why did the sepoys refuse to bite the bullets greased with animal fat?

3. Why did the British Parliament take over rule of India?

Mahatma Gandhi

Mohandas K. Gandhi was born in 1869. He was a Hindu. His family belonged to the merchant caste. Gandhi studied law in London. He worked as a lawyer in South Africa for 21 years. At that time, South Africa was ruled by Great Britain. Gandhi worked for the rights of Indians who were being discriminated against. In 1915 Gandhi returned to India. There, he began to work for independence from Britain. In 1920 he became leader of the Indian National Congress.

Gandhi had new ideas. He said that the way to freedom was not through violence or bloodshed. Gandhi taught **nonviolent resistance** and **civil disobedience.**

Calmly and peacefully, Gandhi led Indians to refuse to obey the British government. "Conquer by love," he taught. His followers called him *Mahatma* Gandhi. *Mahatma* means "Great Soul."

"We cannot win against British guns," Gandhi said. "The British only know how to fight against guns. We will show them a new kind of resistance." Gandhi said that civil disobedience was a weapon stronger than guns. He told Indians to refuse to work in British mines, shops, and factories.

Gandhi led a revolution for independence. It was, for the most part, a revolution of poor people. Although Gandhi was a Hindu, he did not believe in the caste system. He lived among the poorest Indians, the untouchables, for many years. He lived simply, often wearing only a linen loincloth.

You Decide

Do you think nonviolent resistance is a good method for making change today?

Mahatma Gandhi became an important leader in India's fight for independence.

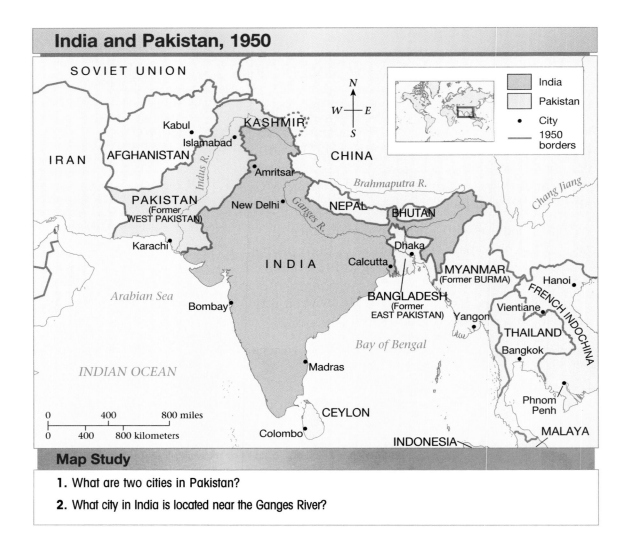

India and Pakistan, 1950

Map Study

1. What are two cities in Pakistan?

2. What city in India is located near the Ganges River?

In one act of resistance, Gandhi led thousands of Indian women to the train tracks. There they lay down, stopping the British trains. When the British put an unfair tax on salt, Gandhi peacefully led a march 200 miles to the sea to get salt from the ocean.

Gandhi was often arrested for his activities. He spent a total of 7 years in jail. However, in time the British began to listen to Gandhi and his followers.

Gandhi Fasts for Peace

The British knew that the Indian people no longer wanted them in their country. The British knew it was just a matter of time before they would be forced to leave. The British offered independence to India. The Muslims however, demanded a separate nation. Their protests led to bloody rioting between Muslims and Hindus. As a result, India was divided into two nations. Pakistan would be a Muslim nation, and India would be Hindu.

Mahatma Gandhi saw his country gain independence in 1947. Unfortunately, more fighting between Hindus and Muslims came with independence. There was terrible loss of life. Entire villages were wiped out. Gandhi insisted that the fighting stop. He went on a **fast**, refusing to eat until the bloodshed ended. He almost starved to death. At last, Hindu and Muslim leaders promised to stop the fighting. They did not want their leader to die.

Gandhi's fast ended on June 30, 1948. Shortly after that, Gandhi was shot down by a Hindu gunman. Both Hindus and Muslims mourned a great leader.

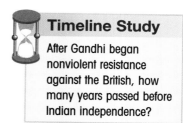

Timeline Study

After Gandhi began nonviolent resistance against the British, how many years passed before Indian independence?

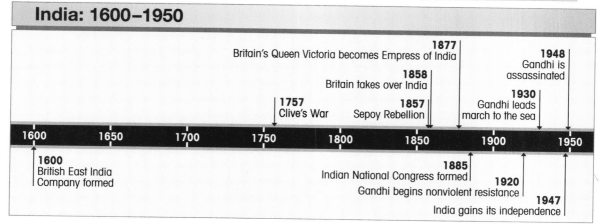

India: 1600–1950

1877
Britain's Queen Victoria becomes Empress of India

1948
Gandhi is assassinated

1858
Britain takes over India

1757
Clive's War

1857
Sepoy Rebellion

1930
Gandhi leads march to the sea

1600 1650 1700 1750 1800 1850 1900 1950

1600
British East India Company formed

1885
Indian National Congress formed

1920
Gandhi begins nonviolent resistance

1947
India gains its independence

Summary

Mogul rule in India weakened in the early 1700s.
The British East India Company, a private trading business, began to rule India.
Indian soldiers, called *sepoys,* rebelled against the British East India Company in 1857.
The British brought some improvements to India. However, the British felt superior to Indians and did not allow them to control their own country.
A group of educated Indians formed the Indian National Congress to talk about independence from Great Britain.
Mahatma Gandhi led India to independence by encouraging nonviolent civil disobedience.
In 1947, India won independence and was divided into India and Pakistan.

civil disobedience

resistance

fast

impose

superiority

Vocabulary Review

Write a term from the list that matches each definition below.

1. To go without eating for a considerable time

2. Refusal to obey bad rules, orders, or laws

3. Working against something

4. To force one's will on another person or group

5. A feeling of being better than somebody else

Chapter Quiz

Write your answers in complete sentences.

1. What gave the Europeans the chance to take advantage of India?

2. Why did Gandhi lead a march to the sea?

3. Why was India divided into two nations?

4. **Critical Thinking** Why do you think the British called India the "Jewel of the British Empire"?

5. **Critical Thinking** Why do you think so many Indian people followed Gandhi?

Using the Timeline

Use the timeline on page 341 to answer the questions.

1. Did the Sepoy Rebellion take place before or after Britain took over India?

2. When did the Indian National Congress form?

Write About History

Complete the following activity.

Form groups of four students. Discuss a problem in your community or in the nation. List some ways to solve the problem. Would nonviolent resistance help to solve it? Why or why not?

The kingdom of Zimbabwe in southern Africa was surrounded by thick stone walls, which were built in the 1300s.

Learning Objectives

- Name the early kingdoms of western Africa.
- Tell how Mali became a wealthy kingdom.
- Explain why Europe had little contact with Africa south of the Sahara before the 1400s.
- List the European nations that took part in the slave trade.
- Explain why Europeans wanted colonies in Africa.

Chapter 24 / Imperialism and Africa

Words to Know

caravan	a group of people traveling together, often through a desert
staff	a pole used for support in walking or to hold a flag
dominance	the act of ruling, controlling, being most powerful
prejudice	dislike of a people just because they are of a different race or religion, or are from another country
racism	the idea that one race is better than another
conference	a meeting of people to discuss something
inferior	not as good as someone or something else

Early Kingdoms

One of the world's earliest civilizations was that of the ancient Egyptians, in Northern Africa. The Egyptian pharaohs built great pyramids and temples. In time, other nations founded colonies in northern Africa. The Phoenicians built the city of Carthage. Then the Romans came and built their own cities. Still later came the Arab conquerors. Their armies swept across northern Africa, bringing Islam with them.

All this happened in Northern Africa. However, there were civilizations in the rest of the continent, south of the Sahara.

Along the Nile River, just south of Egypt, is a country called Sudan. During the time of ancient Egypt, this land was called Nubia. A civilization arose there about 2000 B.C. The people of Nubia, or Kush, as it was also called, were black. In about 1500 B.C., Egypt conquered

Ancient Kingdoms of Africa, 1500

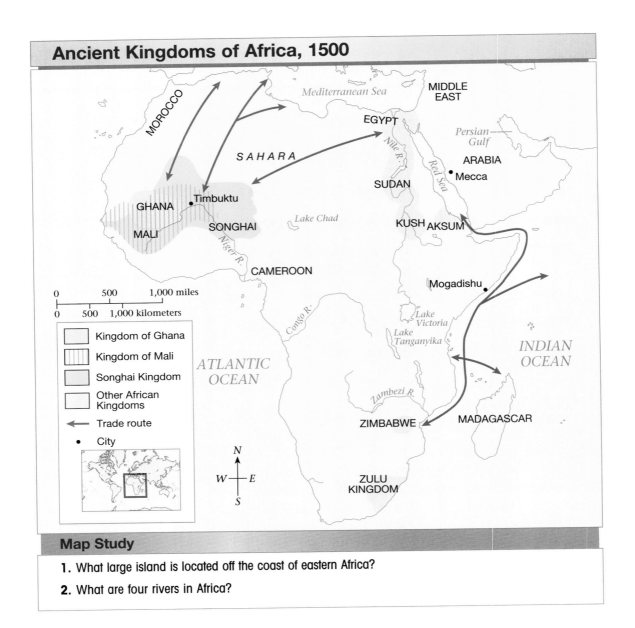

Map Study

1. What large island is located off the coast of eastern Africa?

2. What are four rivers in Africa?

Kush. For the next 500 years, Kush was ruled by the Egyptians. The Kushites were greatly influenced by them. Kush became an important center of art, learning, and trade. However, by about 1000 B.C., the Egyptians had lost much of their power. The Kushites were able to drive out the Egyptians.

At about this time, the Kushites began mining iron. They used the iron to make tools and weapons. The Kushites kept growing stronger. In about 750 B.C., they conquered Egypt and ruled there until about 670 B.C.

The civilization of Kush lasted until about A.D. 350. Kush was then conquered by the neighboring kingdom of Aksum. By then, both Kush and Aksum had come under the influence of the Roman Empire and Christianity. Kush was to remain Christian until the 1300s when Arabs appeared in the region. The Kushites then converted to the Muslim religion.

In western Africa, just on the southern side of the Sahara, is a vast area of grasslands. Great Kingdoms of black Africans grew up there.

By about A.D. 1000, Arab traders from northern Africa began to cross the Sahara in **caravans.** The trade caravans brought goods that the people of western Africa needed. They brought tools and clothing. They also brought the thing that the people needed most— salt. The climate south of the Sahara is very hot and dry. People needed salt to stay healthy. They needed salt to preserve their food. Salt was so important that the people were willing to trade gold for it. Luckily there was plenty of gold available in western Africa.

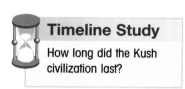

Timeline Study

How long did the Kush civilization last?

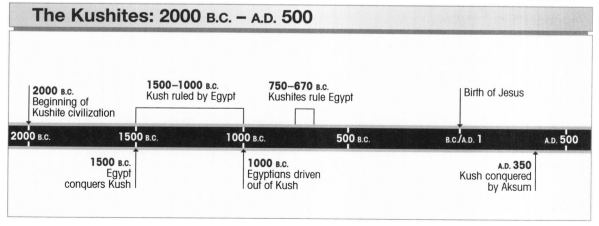

The Kushites: 2000 B.C. – A.D. 500

2000 B.C.
Beginning of Kushite civilization

1500–1000 B.C.
Kush ruled by Egypt

750–670 B.C.
Kushites rule Egypt

Birth of Jesus

2000 B.C.　　　1500 B.C.　　　1000 B.C.　　　500 B.C.　　　B.C./A.D. 1　　　A.D. 500

1500 B.C.
Egypt conquers Kush

1000 B.C.
Egyptians driven out of Kush

A.D. 350
Kush conquered by Aksum

The Kingdom of Ghana

During the A.D. 400s, a kingdom called Ghana grew up in western Africa. The kingdom began to prosper about A.D. 1000. This is when the Arabs from northern Africa became interested in trade with Ghana. They had learned that Ghana was rich in gold. However, trade turned out to be a mixed blessing for Ghana. The Arab trading caravans brought not only goods but religion to Ghana. In time, Ghana's rulers became Muslims. In contrast, most of the people living in Ghana did not convert. They still practiced their own ancient worship of many gods.

Muslim rulers tried to force the people to practice Islam. This weakened the kingdom. The Mandingo people of a kingdom called Mali took over Ghana near the end of the thirteenth century. By 1300 the kingdom of Ghana was gone, replaced by Mali.

Mansa Musa, the Mali King

You Decide

Would Mansa Musa's policies be good for a leader to follow today? Why or why not?

From 1312 to 1337, the Mali kingdom was ruled by a man named Mansa Musa. *Mansa* means "king". Mansa Musa was a good king. He built Mali's wealth by encouraging and then taxing caravan trade. Mansa Musa was a Muslim. He invited Arab scholars to come to Mali to teach. The city of Timbuktu became a center of Muslim learning.

Mansa Musa became famous when he made his pilgrimage to the holy city of Mecca, in Arabia. He decided to show the rest of the world just how wealthy his kingdom was. He took a splendid caravan with him on his pilgrimage to Mecca. Across the grasslands and deserts he went, along with thousands of his people. Mansa Musa took hundreds of enslaved people with him.

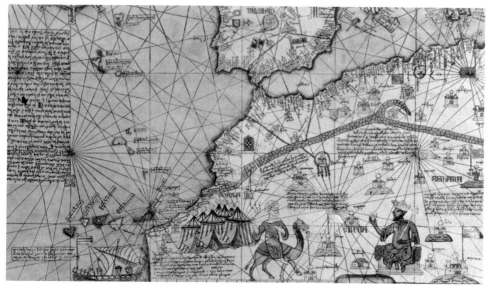

This Spanish map, created in 1375, includes a drawing of Mansa Musa. It gives clues about Musa's power, his wealth, and the extent of his rule.

Each slave carried a solid gold **staff.** He also took at least 80 camels, each loaded with bags of gold dust. Everywhere he went, the Mali ruler gave out gold and other gifts. Stories quickly spread about the fabulous wealth of the kingdom of Mali.

The Kingdom of Songhai

When Mansa Musa died, Mali weakened. A kingdom called Songhai took over control of Mali during the 1400s. One of the Songhai rulers was a king named Askia Mohammed. Askia ruled from 1493 to 1528. This was a time of growth in Songhai power. The city of Timbuktu reached its height as an important center of trade and of learning. Songhai remained strong until the late 1500s. Then the Moroccan king, Mohamed al-Mansur, The Victorious, attacked. The Moroccans had guns. The Songhai warriors fought with spears. Songhai was defeated.

✓**Check Your Understanding**

Write your answers in complete sentences.

1. What goods and ideas did the people of western Africa and the Arabs trade?

2. Which people took over Ghana near the end of the thirteenth century?

3. What religion was the ruler of the Mali kingdom from 1312 to 1337?

Other Peoples of Africa

Early in the first century A.D. a great migration began in Africa. Africans in what is now Nigeria and Cameroon moved southward into the forests of central Africa. The population had been growing, and the people needed more land. Migration continued over the next 1,000 years. These people spoke Bantu languages. They settled in many parts of central, eastern, and southern Africa.

By about A.D. 1100, trading cities dotted the eastern African coast. A city called Mogadishu was one of the largest. The people living in coastal towns had frequent contact with Arab traders. They became Muslims, and they followed many Arabic customs. They spoke Swahili. The language is still used in much of central and southern Africa.

HISTORY FACT

Swahili is a Bantu language that uses many Arabic words.

A number of kingdoms arose in southern Africa. One of these was the kingdom of Zimbabwe. Another was the kingdom of the Zulus. The Zulus moved into southern Africa in the 1600s. They were powerful warriors. During the 1800s, they had a strong military under a ruthless ruler named Shaka.

Shaka led his armies to conquer other kingdoms. Meanwhile, southern Africa was being settled by the Dutch and the British. The Zulus fought against European rule. In 1879, the British conquered the Zulu kingdom.

The Europeans in Africa

Africa was not an easy continent to explore. The Sahara kept many European traders from traveling south by land. During the Renaissance, however, interest in travel grew. Sailors sailed better ships. In the 1400s, the Europeans began to arrive in Africa by sea routes.

The Portuguese were the first to sail the waters along Africa's coast. Prince Henry the Navigator sent ships along the west coast. He was searching for a trade route to India. Portuguese sailors soon learned of the gold in western Africa. They called a section of the African coastline the *Gold Coast.*

In 1497, a Portuguese sea captain, Vasco da Gama, discovered the sea route around Africa. Soon, Portugal set up trading posts along Africa's coasts. In 1571, Angola, in southwestern Africa, became a Portuguese colony.

Then the Portuguese found something in Africa that was a better money-maker than gold. They found that they could get rich by buying and selling human beings.

Slavery

There had been enslaved people in Africa for a long time. When Africans conquered other Africans, they often made slaves of their captives. However, African slavery was very different from the kind of slavery the Europeans practiced. The Africans treated enslaved people like human beings. Children of African slaves were free. The Europeans treated enslaved people like goods to be traded and sold, not like people.

The Portuguese were the first European slave traders. By the early 1500s, the Portuguese were capturing Africans and packing them onto crowded ships. Many Africans died on the terrible voyages. Those who survived had to work as slaves in mines and on plantations in the West Indies. Soon, the Spaniards were also shipping slaves to the Americas.

By the mid-1600s, the French, English, and Dutch had joined in the profitable slave trade. Some Africans helped supply the Europeans with slaves. Sometimes, tribes fought each other to capture people to supply the slave traders. The fighting between tribes weakened Africa.

The slave markets wanted only the healthiest, strongest young Africans. Over time, at least 10 million men and women were taken out of Africa and sold into slavery. The loss of some of its finest people also weakened Africa. Africa was in no position to defend itself against European imperialism.

Fortunately, many people finally recognized that slavery was wrong. By the 1800s many countries made slave trading illegal. In 1834, Britain outlawed slavery in its colonies. Other European countries soon did the same. The United States abolished slavery in 1865. By 1888 slavery was illegal throughout the Americas.

WORDS FROM THE PAST
Songs of Slavery and Freedom

When enslaved Africans arrived in the Americas, they brought rich cultures with them. In the Americas, their cultures were forbidden. However, enslaved Africans created a rich culture of their own, based on their memories of Africa and their life on the plantations of America.

From the 1600s through the mid-1800s, enslaved Africans created songs called *spirituals.* Spirituals are expressive religious songs that use African harmonies and rhythms. The words of spirituals tell of enslavement and struggle.

The music enslaved Africans created served many purposes. As their ancestors had done in Africa, enslaved Africans sang while they worked.

During the mid-1800s, some spirituals helped enslaved people escape to freedom in the North on the Underground Railroad. For example, the song "Swing Low, Sweet Chariot," is about the Underground Railroad.

The spirituals were important to the development of today's gospel music, the blues, and jazz.

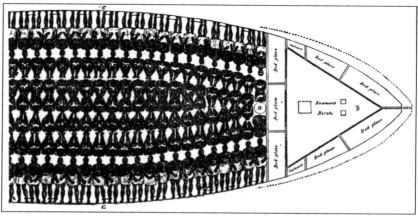

This is a diagram showing the inside of a slave ship.

European Imperialism

American and European slave trade in Africa finally came to an end. However, Africa had not seen the end of European **dominance** and **prejudice**. In the 1800s there had been an Industrial Revolution in Europe. Now Europeans needed raw materials and new markets for finished products. European nations wanted new colonies. These nations saw that the continent of Africa had lots of land.

The Industrial Revolution led to imperialism. However, there was another reason that led the Europeans into Africa. That was **racism**. Some Europeans simply thought they were better than the dark-skinned peoples of the world. Some thought it was their duty to bring their own culture to the black Africans. Therefore, the Europeans took over Africa.

Europe Divides Up Africa

In 1884 European nations held a **conference** in Berlin, Germany. The United States and the Ottoman Empire sent representatives, too. No one invited African representatives. The conference set up rules for forming colonies in Africa. By 1914 Europeans had taken over almost all the land in Africa.

Remember
Religion came along with invaders at many points in history. Sometimes the new religion was welcomed. Often it was resisted.

The Europeans formed some of their colonies very easily. They made agreements with local chiefs. They gave the chiefs presents and promised chances for trade. Some leaders simply gave away their kingdoms.

European missionaries helped set up colonies. They had come to convert the Africans to Christianity. Often they were very unwelcome. Yet again, the Europeans felt it was their duty to show the Africans the missionaries' idea of a better way.

Soon there were only two independent countries left in all of Africa. Ethiopia, in the northeast, was the larger one. Liberia, on the west coast, was the other. Founded in 1822 by freed American slaves, Liberia had declared its independence in 1847.

Life in Colonial Africa

It is easy to see the injustices of European imperialism in Africa. African culture was damaged. The Europeans did not understand tribal differences and tribal customs. Most did not even try to understand.

The Europeans forced the Africans to learn new ways. They tried to make the Africans feel **inferior.** They forced the Africans to accept European government, religion, and languages. They drew up colonial boundaries without giving any thought to splitting up tribes.

Some of the things the Europeans did in Africa helped the Africans. However, most of those things helped the Europeans. Railway systems, roads, and schools were built, and the continent of Africa was opened up to the rest of the world.

In the years ahead, new ideas would come to Africa. These would be ideas of freedom, of self-government— and, in some cases, of revolution.

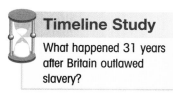

Timeline Study

What happened 31 years after Britain outlawed slavery?

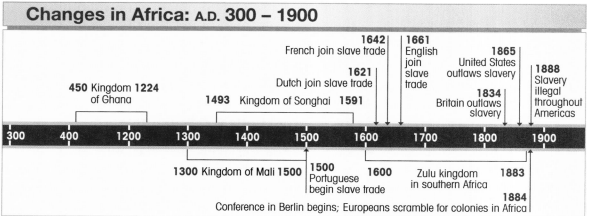

Changes in Africa: A.D. 300 – 1900

1642 French join slave trade

1661 English join slave trade

1865 United States outlaws slavery

1888 Slavery illegal throughout Americas

450 Kingdom 1224 of Ghana

1621 Dutch join slave trade

1493 Kingdom of Songhai 1591

1834 Britain outlaws slavery

300 400 1200 1300 1400 1500 1600 1700 1800 1900

1300 Kingdom of Mali 1500

1500 Portuguese begin slave trade

1600

Zulu kingdom in southern Africa 1883

1884 Conference in Berlin begins; Europeans scramble for colonies in Africa

Chapter

24 Review

Summary

The ancient African civilization of Kush was greatly influenced by the Egyptians.
There were rich kingdoms called Ghana, Mali, and Songhai in western Africa.
Europeans began arriving in Africa by sea in the 1400s.
The Portuguese found that they could make money by taking Africans abroad and selling them as slaves.
The British, French, and Dutch soon joined the slave trade.
The Industrial Revolution and racial prejudices played a part in European colonization of Africa.
In 1884 a conference in Berlin laid down ground rules for colonizing Africa.
By 1914 almost the entire continent of Africa had fallen under European imperialism.

Vocabulary Review

Write *true* or *false*. If the statement is false, change the underlined term to make it true.

1. When people show <u>dominance</u> toward others, they rule over them or use their power on them.

2. In colonial Africa, Europeans tried to make Africans feel <u>inferior</u>, or not as good as Europeans.

3. About 1000 A.D., trade <u>conferences</u> were crossing the desert to bring goods to Africa.

4. <u>Racism</u> is the mistaken idea that one race is better than another.

5. A <u>caravan</u> is a meeting to discuss something.

Chapter Quiz

Write your answers in complete sentences.

1. Where was the Kush civilization?

2. During Songhai rule, what happened to Timbuktu?

3. Which European countries were involved in slave trade in Africa?

4. **Critical Thinking** How can salt be as valuable as gold?

5. **Critical Thinking** How did the colonial powers show that they thought Africans were inferior?

Using the Timelines

Use the timelines on pages 347 and 355 to answer the questions.

1. How long did the Kushite civilization last?

2. Were the Kushites in power a longer time before or after the birth of Jesus?

3. How many years after the Dutch did the English join the slave trade?

Write About History

Complete the following activity.

Form groups of four students. Make a booklet of the early kingdoms of Africa. Describe the way of life and the accomplishments of each kingdom.

Unit 8 **Review**

Comprehension Check

Write your answers in complete sentences.

1. What are five inventions that changed industry in the late 1600s and in the 1700s?

2. What kind of leaders governed Latin American nations after independence?

3. How did the United States gain Alaska and Hawaii?

4. How did the United States gain Puerto Rico, the Philippines, and Guam?

5. What are five positive things the British did in India?

6. Why did Europeans have little contact with Africa south of the Sahara before 1400?

7. How did the Kingdom of Mali become rich?

8. What European nations took part in the slave trade in Africa during the 1600s?

Writing an Essay

Answer one of the following essay topics.

1. Explain how European and Japanese industrialization led to imperialism and the desire for colonies.

2. Explain the importance of the Panama Canal to the United States.

3. Describe foreign interference in China during the 1800s.

4. Discuss the reasons the people of India wanted to overthrow British rule.

5. Compare slavery in Africa with the European practice of slavery.

Group Activity

Work with a partner to make an illustrated timeline of the 12 most important events in Unit 8. Share your timeline with the class. Explain why you chose each event.

History in Your Life
How can you apply Gandhi's methods of creating change to your own life?

Nationalism and the Spread of War and Revolution

Napoleon invaded the Italian peninsula in 1796 and did away with old boundary lines.

Learning Objectives

- Define nationalism and explain why it develops.
- Tell how the spirit of nationalism led to the unification of Italy.
- Name three men who helped unify Italy.
- Tell how Bismarck united Germany under a Prussian kaiser.
- Describe two main features of the new German nation.

Chapter 25 — The Unifications of Italy and Germany

Words to Know

anthem	the official song of a country
unification	bringing together into one whole
society	a group of people joined together for a common purpose
prime minister	the chief official of the government in some countries
diplomat	a person in government whose job is dealing with other countries
confederation	a group of independent states joined together for a purpose
legislature	a group of people who make the laws of a nation or state
chancellor	the head of government, or prime minister, in some European countries
militarism	a national policy of maintaining a powerful army and constant readiness for war

Nationalism is a feeling of strong loyalty to one's country and culture. Such a feeling often develops among people who speak the same language and follow similar customs. Nationalism leads people to honor their flag and to sing a national **anthem**. It leads people to risk their lives to support their nation.

The spirit of nationalism helped the French fight off countries that were against their revolution. It gave the colonies in the Americas the strength to break away from the European imperialists.

In the nineteenth century, the spirit of nationalism led to the **unification** of Italy and of Germany. In each place, people were feeling the bonds of language, customs, and culture. In each place, people decided it was time to unite as a single nation.

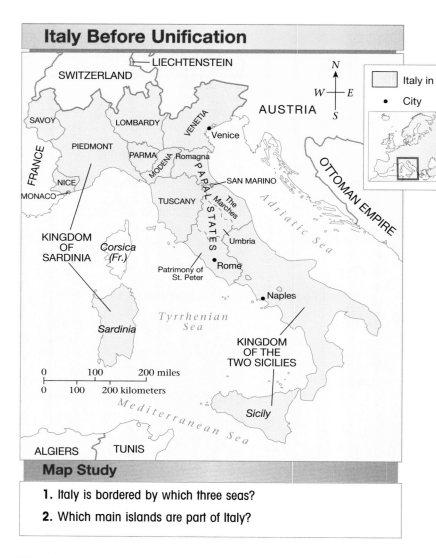

Italy Before Unification

LIECHTENSTEIN

SWITZERLAND

SAVOY

LOMBARDY

VENETIA

AUSTRIA

Venice

PIEDMONT

PARMA

Romagna

MODENA

PAPAL STATES

SAN MARINO

NICE

MONACO

TUSCANY

The Marches

Adriatic Sea

OTTOMAN EMPIRE

KINGDOM OF SARDINIA

Corsica (Fr.)

Umbria

Patrimony of St. Peter

Rome

Naples

Sardinia

Tyrrhenian Sea

KINGDOM OF THE TWO SICILIES

0   100   200 miles

0   100   200 kilometers

Mediterranean Sea

Sicily

ALGIERS   TUNIS

N

W   E

S

Italy in

• City

Map Study

1. Italy is bordered by which three seas?

2. Which main islands are part of Italy?

Nationalism in Italy

During the early Roman times, Italy had been a united country. It was the center of the Roman Empire. However, late in the fifth century A.D., the Roman Empire fell. Italy was divided into many small kingdoms. For more than a thousand years, different nations and monarchs fought for control of the Italian territories. French troops, Spanish troops, German troops—all

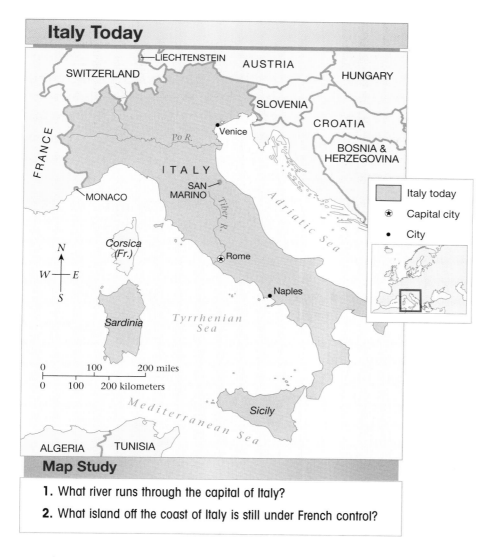

Italy Today

FRANCE

SWITZERLAND · LIECHTENSTEIN · AUSTRIA · HUNGARY

SLOVENIA

CROATIA

Venice

Po R.

ITALY

SAN MARINO

Tiber R.

Adriatic Sea

BOSNIA & HERZEGOVINA

MONACO

Corsica (Fr.)

Rome

Naples

N W E S

Sardinia

Tyrrhenian Sea

0   100   200 miles
0   100   200 kilometers

Mediterranean Sea

Sicily

ALGERIA   TUNISIA

Legend:
- Italy today
- ⊛ Capital city
- • City

Map Study

1. What river runs through the capital of Italy?

2. What island off the coast of Italy is still under French control?

marched through Italy. Then in 1796, Napoleon Bonaparte invaded the Italian peninsula and took power.

Napoleon granted Venetia to Austria. Venetia was the kingdom that included the city of Venice. Napoleon put the rest of the small kingdoms under his own rule. In 1804, he crowned himself ruler of the new kingdom. The crown he wore bore these words: "God gave it [the Italian peninsula] to me; woe to him who dares touch it."

Napoleon's actions gave rise to the spirit of nationalism. This spirit would one day carry Italy to independence. Napoleon did away with old boundary lines and joined the little kingdoms together. By doing this, he gave Italians a chance to look at themselves as members of one group. The idea that all of them were Italians began to grow.

Secret Societies

As feelings of nationalism grew, Italians began to think about unity. They dreamed about one independent Italy. However, by 1815, Italy was once again divided into many kingdoms and states. Most of them were either ruled by Austria or by the pope. The Italians who wanted to unify Italy had some barriers to overcome.

Austria tried to crush any ideas of unity. Austria wanted Italy to remain weak and divided. The pope also tried to crush any ideas of unity. He feared nationalism as a threat to his own power.

The people, however, wanted to be free. They wanted to join together as one nation. Secret revolutionary **societies** sprang up. During the mid-1800s, three men became leaders of the movement toward a unified Italy. Italians called these men "The Soul," "The Brain," and "The Sword."

The Soul

The Soul of Italy was a man named Giuseppe Mazzini. In 1830 he joined a group that was working to unify Italy. That same year, he was exiled because of his political activities. He would remain in exile for 18 years. In 1832 Mazzini organized a secret society known as "Young Italy." The society's goal was to free the Italian peninsula from Austrian rule. Young Italy wanted to join the country together under one government.

In 1848, revolutions broke out in many European countries. Mazzini returned to Italy to stir up a revolution there. The ruler of the kingdom of Sardinia favored the revolutionaries. He tried to help their cause by declaring war on Austria. However, Austrian and French armies helped put down the Italian revolt. Not only did the revolution fail, but Sardinia was also defeated. Mazzini had to go into exile once again.

The Austrians forced the Sardinian king from his throne. His son, Victor Emmanuel II, became king of Sardinia in 1849.

The Brain

The new king of Sardinia was also in favor of Italian unity. He named Camillo Benso, Conte di Cavour, as his **prime minister.** This act moved Italy closer to freedom. Camillo di Cavour would soon be known as "The Brain," the leader of the unification movement.

Cavour was a **diplomat,** a master of foreign affairs. He recognized Austria as an enemy to unification. In 1858, he arranged a defense agreement between Sardinia and France. The next year, Austria declared war on Sardinia. However, French and Italian soldiers pushed the Austrians almost as far east as Venice. Sardinia gained the nearby regions of Lombardy. Then in 1860, Romagna, Modena, Parma, and Tuscany showed their respect for Sardinia's accomplishments. They united with Sardinia and turned against Austria.

The Sword

Giuseppe Garibaldi was a revolutionary most of his life. When he was 26, he joined the secret society, Young Italy. Garibaldi was a soldier in the battle for freedom. His attempts to lead Italy to independence won him the nickname of "The Sword."

Giuseppi Garibaldi fought for Italian independence.

Failed rebellions forced Garibaldi to flee Italy or face death. He returned in 1848 to fight under Mazzini. When this revolution failed, he went into exile again.

In 1859 Garibaldi was back in Italy. He joined the fight for freedom led by King Victor Emmanuel of Sardinia. Garibaldi led an army of 1,000 volunteers to Sicily. His men were called "Red Shirts" because they wore red shirts as uniforms.

When Garibaldi and his army reached Sicily, many Sicilians joined them. Sicily was soon free. Then Garibaldi, "The Sword," led his army north on the Italian mainland. He headed for Naples. Cavour, "The Brain," sent an army south. By the end of 1860, the two armies had freed most of Italy. In 1861 Victor Emmanuel II became ruler of an almost completely united Italy.

Unification, at Last

Only Rome and the northern kingdom of Venetia were still not free. The pope ruled Rome, and Austria ruled Venetia. In 1866, the Italians helped Prussia defeat Austria in war. In return for its support, Italy was given Venetia.

Then came Rome. Garibaldi tried to take Rome twice, but failed. He was defeated by French troops who came to aid the pope. In 1870, Italy got another chance at Rome. France was fighting a war against Prussia. France took its troops out of Rome to help fight the Prussians. It was Italy's time to move! The pope's own small army could not fight off the Italian troops. Rome finally became part of the united nation of Italy. In 1870, Rome became the capital of Italy.

You Decide

The United States has a volunteer army today. Do you think this is a good idea? Why or why not?

✓Check Your Understanding

Write your answers in complete sentences.

1. What is nationalism?

2. What three men helped unify Italy?

3. In what year did Rome become the capital of a unified Italy?

Nationalism in Germany

Just as he did in Italy, Napoleon lit the first flames of nationalism in Germany. Napoleon took over large parts of Germany in 1806. These lands were made up of many small kingdoms. Napoleon decided to join them together to rule them more easily. He called the group of kingdoms the **Confederation** of the Rhine. People living within the confederation began to have a sense of loyalty toward one another.

When Napoleon was defeated in 1815, a new German Confederation was formed. Thirty-nine states, including Austria and Prussia, were joined together. Since Austria was large, it considered itself the leader. However, Prussia had a well-organized government and real strength—military strength.

Many Germans thought about unifying the states under a central government. Only Austria was against German unity. Austrians thought they could remain more powerful with the German states divided. It was not until 1862 that Germany moved toward becoming one nation.

> **HISTORY FACT**
>
> The 39 states agreed to be members of the German Confederation, but each one remained an independent state.

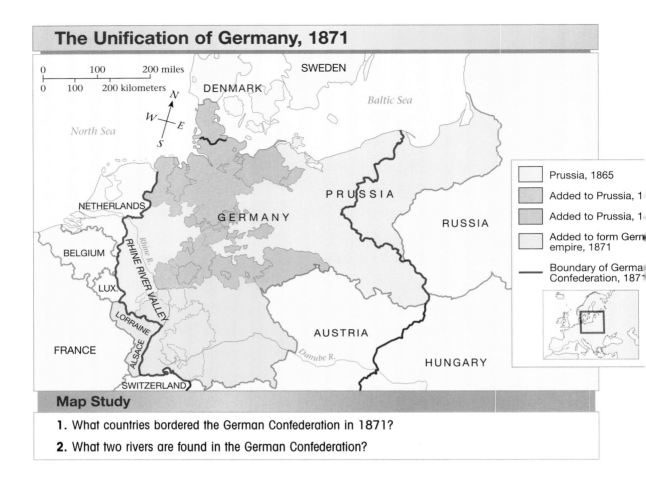

The Unification of Germany, 1871

0   100   200 miles
0   100   200 kilometers

SWEDEN
DENMARK
Baltic Sea
North Sea
NETHERLANDS
GERMANY
PRUSSIA
RUSSIA
BELGIUM
RHINE RIVER VALLEY
Rhine R.
LUX.
LORRAINE
ALSACE
FRANCE
AUSTRIA
Danube R.
HUNGARY
SWITZERLAND

Legend:
- Prussia, 1865
- Added to Prussia, 1
- Added to Prussia, 1
- Added to form Germ empire, 1871
- Boundary of Germa Confederation, 1871

Map Study

1. What countries bordered the German Confederation in 1871?

2. What two rivers are found in the German Confederation?

Otto von Bismarck

The king of Prussia, Wilhelm I, was having problems with his **legislature**. King Wilhelm wanted to add to his already mighty army. However, the legislature would not give them the money that he needed. King Wilhelm turned to a Prussian landowner and soldier to help him. His name was Otto von Bismarck. In 1862, Wilhelm appointed Bismarck prime minister.

Otto von Bismarck had a strong sense of Prussian loyalty. Bismarck was not interested in democracy or individual rights. He believed that duty to one's country was most important.

WORDS FROM THE PAST
Bismarck's Policy of "Blood and Iron"

Bismarck thought the goals of the individual and the state were the same. He promised the Prussian king a firm hand over the legislature and the people. The new prime minister thought that could be accomplished with a strong army. "The importance of a state," Bismarck said, "is measured by the number of soliders it can put into the field of battle. . . . "

Bismarck followed a policy of "blood and iron." In other words, it was a policy of war. "The great questions of our day," he said, "cannot be settled by speeches and majority votes, but by blood and iron."

Bismarck encouraged King Wilhelm to unite the German states under one rule—Prussian rule. "My highest ambition is to make the Germans a nation," Bismarck said.

How was this to be done? Bismarck's answer was war.

Otto von Bismarck expanded and unified Germany.

You Decide

Bismarck was called the "Iron Chancellor." Why do you think he was given this name?

The Unification of Germany

In 1864, Bismarck began a war with Denmark. After just seven months of fighting, Prussia seized two provinces from Denmark. In 1866, Prussia and Italy defeated Austria in the Seven Weeks' War. The German Confederation was dissolved.

Then Prussia formed the North German Confederation in 1867, without Austria. Most of the German states joined. The Confederation's seat of power was Prussia, and at its head was Wilhelm I.

Kaiser Wilhelm I

Bismarck would not be satisfied until all the German states were united under Wilhelm's rule. He decided on the best way to join the states. He would rally them together against one common enemy. For that purpose, in 1870, Bismarck started a war with France. Prussia's mighty armies won easily. They took the provinces of Alsace and Lorraine as their prize.

At the end of the war, all German states joined with Prussia. They formed a united German Empire. On January 18, 1871, the new German Empire was officially declared. It was also called the *Second Reich*. King Wilhelm I of Prussia was crowned its emperor, or *kaiser*.

The German Nation

There were two main features of the new Germany. First, Germany was not a democratic nation. Germans accepted rule by a single person. Bismarck became the **chancellor** of Germany. He was responsible only to Kaiser Wilhelm I. Neither the kaiser nor the chancellor had to answer to any legislature or to any elected representatives. These two men alone had complete power in Germany.

Second, Germany had a strong tradition of **militarism.** Bismarck's "blood and iron" policy had become the German way. German nationalism meant pride in a mighty military force.

The Krupp armament factory supported the German military.

Germans gave their soliders respect and honor. It was a German's privilege to belong to a great army. It was an honor to fight for the glory of the empire.

Much of Germany was geared toward a strong military. Large businesses supported the army. Major industrialists, like Friedrich Krupp of the Krupp Iron and Steel Works, devoted factories to making war machines. Krupp built guns and cannons. The whole nation stood behind the military effort. Germany was ready for war!

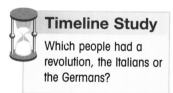

Timeline Study

Which people had a revolution, the Italians or the Germans?

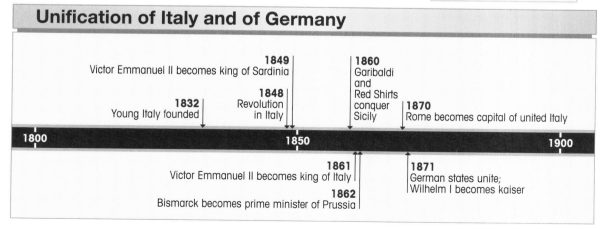

Unification of Italy and of Germany

1849 Victor Emmanuel II becomes king of Sardinia

1860 Garibaldi and Red Shirts conquer Sicily

1832 Young Italy founded

1848 Revolution in Italy

1870 Rome becomes capital of united Italy

1800 — 1850 — 1900

1861 Victor Emmanuel II becomes king of Italy

1871 German states unite; Wilhelm I becomes kaiser

1862 Bismarck becomes prime minister of Prussia

Chapter

25 Review

Summary

The spirit of nationalism led the people of Italy to seek to unite under a central government. During the nineteenth century, the Italians worked toward independence and unification.

In 1870, Italy was totally united. Sardinia's king Victor Emmanuel II became the king of Italy.

During the nineteenth century, many Germans wanted to see a unified Germany. Austria opposed the unification of Germany. The prime minister of Prussia, Otto von Bismarck, waged war in a movement toward unification.

Bismarck won his wars, and in 1871 Germany was united. Prussia's Wilhelm I became the kaiser of the German Empire.

Germany developed a strong tradition of loyalty to strong leaders and of militarism.

militarism
anthem
unification
diplomat
prime minister

Vocabulary Review

Complete each sentence with a term from the list.

1. The _____ is the most important official in some countries, such as Britain.

2. Nationalism and _____ are two ideas that sometimes go together.

3. Italians were interested in _____ to bring together people with a common language and common customs and culture.

4. A national _____ is a national song.

5. A _____ is a person who deals with other countries for his or her own country.

Chapter Quiz

Write your answers in complete sentences.

1. What was the purpose of Young Italy?

2. What was the Second Reich?

3. How did German industry help the nation get ready for war?

4. **Critical Thinking** How did Napoleon help to develop a spirit of nationalism among Italians?

5. **Critical Thinking** What are some positive ways to unite a country?

Using the Timeline

Use the timeline on page 371 to answer the questions.

1. When did Victor Emmanuel II become king of Italy?

2. When did Wilhelm I become kaiser of Germany?

Write About History

Complete the following activity.

Write a paragraph that compares and contrasts the way Italy and Germany became nations. Exchange your paragraph with a partner. Discuss the ideas in your paragraphs. Revise your paragraphs to make your ideas clearer.

During World War I, soldiers dug trenches six to eight feet deep to hide and defend themselves.

Learning Objectives

- Explain what is meant by a "balance of power."
- Name the two alliances made by 1914.
- Tell what event directly triggered World War I.
- Tell how the presence of U.S. soldiers and supplies affected the outcome of the war.
- Describe the terms of peace at the end of the war.

Chapter 26 / World War I

Words to Know

alliance	a group of nations joined together for some purpose
sniper	a person who shoots from a hidden spot
neutral	joining neither side in a war
trench	a long ditch dug in the ground to protect soldiers in battle
front	a place where the actual fighting is going on during a war
submarine	a warship that travels under the water
torpedo	to attack or destroy with a large, exploding, underwater missile
armistice	an agreement to stop fighting; a truce before a formal peace treaty
casualty	a soldier who has been killed, wounded, captured, or is missing

World War I began on July 28, 1914. No one nation wanted a war. However, all the major powers in Europe had been gathering military strength for many years.

The nationalism of the 1800s led to stronger armies. People who were loyal to their own nations felt that military strength showed pride and power.

The imperialism of the 1800s also created a need for strong armies. Nations had their colonies to protect. Each nation feared that it might lose what it had without a strong military.

The Balance of Power

Relations between countries were strained in the early 1900s. By 1914, Europe had divided itself into two sides. Nations formed **alliances**. They promised to protect each other and to help each other in case of war.

Europe, 1914

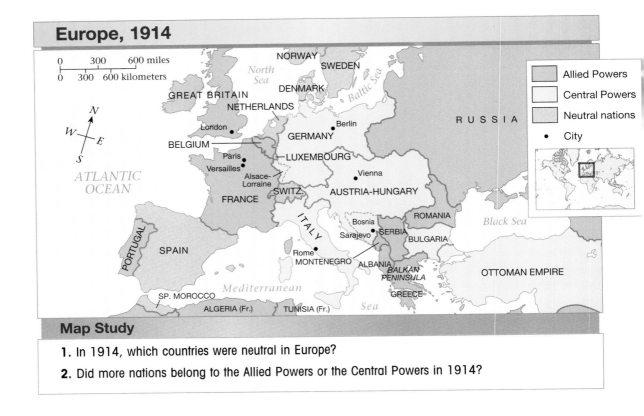

Map Study

1. In 1914, which countries were neutral in Europe?

2. Did more nations belong to the Allied Powers or the Central Powers in 1914?

One group of nations was called the *Central Powers*. The nations of the Central Powers included Germany, Austria-Hungary, the Ottoman Empire (Turkey), and, for a short time, Italy. The other group of nations was called the *Allies*. On that side were Britain, France, Russia, and many smaller nations.

Each alliance tried to keep the other from getting too strong. The two alliances wanted to keep a "balance of power" in Europe.

Rising Tensions

As the year 1914 began, there was tension throughout Europe. France and Germany had been bitter enemies for years. France had lost a war against

Bismarck's armies in 1871. Ever since then, France wanted to get back the provinces of Alsace and Lorraine.

Remember
In 1871, Bismarck had attacked France to help unite Germany against a common enemy.

Russia and Austria-Hungary had an ongoing quarrel. They disagreed about the territorial borders and control of areas, including Bosnia, in the Balkans. The Balkans is a southern peninsula of Europe.

Nations watched each other as each one built up its military forces. Airplanes, bigger warships, and machine guns made armies more capable of destruction. One country would build new arms. Then another would panic and race to keep up. No one wanted war, but everyone was getting ready.

The War Begins

It took a single incident in July 1914 to explode the already tense situation in Europe. The Austrian archduke Francis Ferdinand was assassinated. This is named as the incident that began the First World War.

Archduke Ferdinand was the next in line to the throne of Austria-Hungary. He and his wife, Sophie, were visiting Sarajevo, a city in the Austrian province of Bosnia. Many Serbs also lived in Bosnia. Some of them believed Bosnia should belong to Serbia.

Archduke Ferdinand and his wife were traveling by motor car on a road in Sarajevo. They were a fine-looking pair. The archduke wore a white uniform, and his wife wore a matching white gown. Riding in an open car, they were clear targets. As the royal procession drove through the streets, two shots rang out. Archduke Ferdinand and his wife were both killed by a **sniper.**

The assassin, Gavrilo Princip, was a Serb. He was a member of a Serbian revolutionary group called the "Black Hand."

Austria-Hungary blamed the Serbian government for the assassination. On July 28, 1914, it declared war on

The assassination of Archduke Francis Ferdinand led to the start of World War I.

Serbia. Now the alliances came into play. Germany stood behind Austria-Hungary. Russia came to the aid of Serbia. France came to Russia's aid. Soon, Britain joined in to help its allies. World War I had begun.

The Great War

World War I is sometimes called "The Great War." It was not really a worldwide war. Most of the fighting took place in Europe. Furthermore, not every country in the world was fighting. However, more than 30 countries, including all of the major powers, were involved. The Great War's effects were certainly felt worldwide.

At first, the Central Powers seemed to be winning. Germany and Austria-Hungary and their allies made gains. Italy had been allied with the Central Powers. However, Italy remained **neutral** in the early part of the war. Then in 1915, Italy changed its alliance. It joined forces with the Allies.

HISTORY FACT

Switzerland was one of the few European nations to remain neutral throughout the war. It would also stay neutral during World War II.

Trench Warfare

The Central Powers wanted to take France. They came within 25 miles of Paris. However, the French and British held them off in a major battle, the Battle of the Marne. Then both sides dug in. The soldiers dug long **trenches.** Armies could hide in the trenches and shoot at each other. Some trenches were more than a mile long.

The **fronts** were lined with networks of trenches. There were three fronts in Europe. The Western Front ran from Belgium to Switzerland. The Eastern Front ran from the Baltic Sea to the Black Sea. The Italian, or Southern, Front ran between Italy and Austria-Hungary.

The battle trenches along the fronts became home for the soldiers. They ate in the trenches and slept in the trenches. Many soldiers died in the trenches.

Most of the battles of World War I were fought in Europe. However, there was also some fighting in Africa and in the Middle East. The powerful British navy kept control of most of the seas.

The United States Enters the War

Despite Britain's great navy, German **submarines** were terrorizing the oceans. They attacked enemy merchant ships without warning. Then in 1915, Germany attacked a British luxury liner. The *Lusitania* was **torpedoed** and sunk. The death list of 1,198 persons included 128 Americans. In 1917, German submarines began attacking ships of neutral nations. Several American merchant ships were sunk.

In April 1917, the U.S. President, Woodrow Wilson, made an announcement. He said that it was time to "make the world safe for democracy." The United

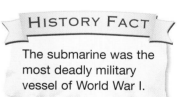

HISTORY FACT

The submarine was the most deadly military vessel of World War I.

The sinking of the Lusitania *increased tensions between Germany and the United States.*

States declared war on Germany and joined the Allies. The United States entered the battlefields just in time. The Allies needed help. The United States sent fresh soldiers and supplies of arms to Europe. The scale in the balance of power was now tipped in favor of the Allies.

Then in November 1917, a revolution took place in Russia. The new government signed a peace treaty with Germany and pulled out of the war.

✓ Check Your Understanding

Write your answers in complete sentences.

1. What is meant by a "balance of power"?

2. The assassination of Archduke Ferdinand was the spark that set off World War I. What were three other reasons for the tense situation in Europe?

3. Why did the United States enter the war?

Learn More About It

WARTIME INVENTIONS

The war brought many changes in the world. New inventions were perfected in a hurry to meet war needs. The Germans developed submarines to travel under the water like sharks. The submarines were also called "U-boats" (underwater boats). They moved unseen, seeking their prey.

Allied countries could not find a defense against the submarines for the first 3 years of the war. Eventually, depth charges were used to destroy the submarines. Fast British ships known as subchasers carried the depth charges. These ships also used zigzag courses to avoid German submarines.

The submarines were very successful. Only 203 German submarines were destroyed during the whole war. On the other hand, the German submarines sank 6,604 Allied ships.

For the first time, airplanes were used for war. At first they were just used for scouting, watching the enemy, and taking pictures. They were not used for fighting until later in the war.

Planes were improved rapidly. In 1914, an airplane could go 90 miles an hour. By 1917, they were flying at 175 miles an hour. They carried bombs and machine guns. Some pilots became famous as war aces for shooting down five or more enemy airplanes.

Germany used zeppelins in the air. Zeppelins were huge, cigar-shaped crafts that were 600 feet long. They were inflated with hydrogen gas and used in bombing raids over Britain and France.

British engineers invented the tank, an armored vehicle with caterpillar tracks. The big tanks rumbled their way across the battlefields of Europe. There were other new weapons, like poison gas and flame throwers. Each side tried to outdo the other with more powerful weaponry.

The End of the War

With new American soldiers and supplies, the Allies began to push back the Germans. The other Central Powers had given up. Germany stood alone, and German armies were losing ground.

Germany asked for an end to the war. On November 11, 1918, an **armistice** was declared. All fighting was to stop at 11:00 A.M. that day.

The Treaty of Versailles

After the war, leaders of the Allied nations and Germany met in Versailles, France. Their purpose was to write a peace treaty. The treaty, which was signed in 1919, made many demands on Germany.

Germany lost all of its colonies and had to return Alsace and Lorraine to France. Germany took all blame for the war, so it had to pay for many of the war's costs. Furthermore, Germany promised to disarm. The nation was not supposed to rebuild its navy or air force. It was allowed to maintain only a small army. This was quite a blow to a nation that had taken such pride in a powerful military.

Turkey was another big loser in the war. In 1919, most of the Middle East and North Africa was still ruled by the Ottoman Empire, or Turkey. However, the end of the war brought about the end of the Ottoman Empire. Most of the Arab lands that had been ruled by the Turks now fell under British control.

Europe After World War I

New nations

Map Study

1. What were the new nations in Europe after World War I?
2. What countries now bordered Germany to the east?

The League of Nations: A Peacekeeper

The Great War ended four years after it had begun. Those four years meant the loss of almost eight million soldiers. Millions of others died, too. They died of disease and of starvation, side effects of the war. Russia suffered the most **casualties** in World War I.

The total cost of the war to all countries involved was more than $337,000,000,000. All of Europe was weakened.

When the war ended, leaders of the world's nations looked at the results. They decided there must be a better way to solve conflicts between nations. President Wilson proposed setting up a League of Nations. European leaders welcomed the idea. They knew that their people would support such a league. Wilson was confident that the American people would support it as well.

You Decide

Do you think the United States was right not to join the League of Nations? Why or why not?

In 1920, the League of Nations was set up. Its headquarters were in Geneva, Switzerland—a neutral, peaceful country. Representatives of member nations could meet there to discuss their problems. It was the first organization designed to keep the peace of the entire world.

Many nations joined the League. Some, including the United States, did not. Wilson was greatly disappointed. Many people in the United States did not

Some Casualties of World War I

Allies		Central Powers	
Russia	9,150,000	Germany	7,142,558
British Empire	3,190,235	Austria-Hungary	7,020,000
France	6,160,800	Turkey	975,000
Italy	2,197,000	Bulgaria	266,919
United States	323,018		

like the idea of Wilson's League. A certain part of Wilson's plan caused major problems. That was Article Ten. It mentioned threats to any member nation of the League. It said that if any threats were made, the other members would aid the threatened nation.

Americans felt they had seen too much of war. They did not want to have anything to do with Europe and its problems anymore. They thought Article Ten seemed to invite trouble.

President Wilson put up a strong fight. He made speeches all around the country. He did everything he could to try to convince Americans to join the League. However, the Senate voted against it in March 1920. Wilson died in 1924, a defeated man. He had warned that another world war was not far off. He had said that only the League of Nations could prevent it. Yet all his talk was in vain. Many Americans did not want to hear him.

The League of Nations had no army to enforce its decisions. The League was based on good will and the idea that nations wanted peace. The war years, 1914 to 1918, had left everyone fearful of war. Now the whole world was anxious to avoid war. People everywhere were hopeful that a war would never be fought again.

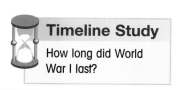

Timeline Study

How long did World War I last?

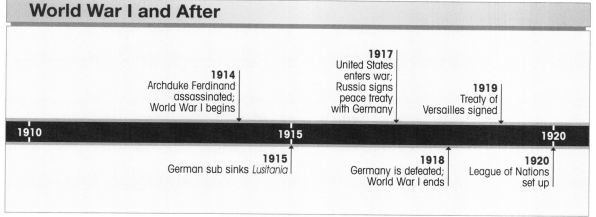

World War I and After

1917
United States enters war; Russia signs peace treaty with Germany

1914
Archduke Ferdinand assassinated; World War I begins

1919
Treaty of Versailles signed

1910   1915   1920

1915
German sub sinks *Lusitania*

1918
Germany is defeated; World War I ends

1920
League of Nations set up

Chapter

26 Review

Summary

World War I began in 1914. The assassination of the Austrian archduke, Francis Ferdinand, triggered World War I.

The war was fought between the Central Powers and the Allies. The Central Powers included Germany, Austria-Hungary, and before the war, Italy. The Allies included Britain, France, and Russia. The United States entered the war on the side of the Allies in 1917.

Wartime developments and inventions included the submarine, improved airplanes, and more powerful weapons.

World War I ended in 1918. The Treaty of Versailles, signed in 1919, set up terms for peace.

The League of Nations was founded after the war in hopes of maintaining world peace.

alliance
neutral
trench
fronts
submarine
casualty

Vocabulary Review

Complete each sentence with a term from the list.

1. A soldier lived, fought, and often died in the long ____ he dug.

2. Three places where fighting went on, called ____, extended across much of Europe.

3. Nations could form an ____ to protect and help each other in time of war.

4. A German underwater ship called a ____ attacked enemy ships without warning.

5. Russia suffered the most ____ in World War I.

6. Some nations did not take sides in the war. They were ____.

Chapter Quiz

Write your answers in complete sentences.

1. What two alliances were formed in Europe before World War I?

2. Why was World War I called the Great War?

3. How did the United States help the Allies beginning in 1917?

4. **Critical Thinking** Do you think the Treaty of Versailles made too many demands on Germany? Why or why not?

5. **Critical Thinking** Do you think the League of Nations was a weak organization? Why or why not?

Using the Timeline

Use the timeline on page 385 to answer the questions.

1. After the Germans sank the *Lusitania,* how long did it take for the United States to enter the war?

2. What happened in 1919?

Write About History

Complete one of the following activities.

1. With a partner, prepare an illustrated talk about two ships, planes, or weapons of World War I. Prepare two drawings, with parts labeled. Have one person explain how the ship, plane, or weapon was used in war. Have the other person explain the drawing. Then exchange roles if you wish.

2. Suppose you and your partner lived in 1919. You know President Wilson is pushing the idea of the League of Nations. You are against it, but your friend is for it. Write and perform a discussion you might have.

In 1905, protests by Russian workers led to violence in the streets.

Learning Objectives

- List the main events in Russia's early history.
- Explain why Peter the Great wanted to open a "window to the West."
- Explain how Bloody Sunday touched off a revolution in 1905.
- Describe how the common people of Russia felt about their country's involvement in World War I.
- Identify Czar Nicholas II, Karl Marx, the Bolsheviks, Lenin, and Stalin.

Chapter 27 ▷ Revolution in Russia: The Birth of the Soviet Union

Words to Know

geography	the natural surface features of Earth, or any part of it
dialect	a form of a language used only in a certain place or among a certain group
communism	a political system based on an absence of social class, on common ownership of industries and farms, and on a sharing of work and of goods produced
collective	run by a group; for example, a collective farm
censor	to examine communications before they are released and to remove any parts that are objected to

The **geography** of Russia is varied. The country takes in frozen wastelands, thick forests, and wide plains known as *steppes*. There are also sandy deserts and huge snow-capped mountains. In addition, some of the longest rivers in the world are in Russia.

The people of Russia are just as varied as the geography. Some are tall and blond-haired, others are olive skinned and dark-haired. Some have European backgrounds, while others have Asian backgrounds. Altogether, Russian people speak dozens of different languages and **dialects.**

In area, Russia is the largest country on Earth. However, the country was not always so large, and it was not always strong.

The Early History of Russia

In earlier chapters, you read about the Byzantine Empire that emerged after the fall of Rome. You read how that Empire fell to the Ottoman Turks in 1453. However, much of Byzantine civilization survived in a new nation in eastern Europe. That nation was Russia.

As far back as A.D. 400 a people known as Slavs lived in forests north of the Byzantine Empire. The Slavs became traders. Along their trade route a town called Novgorod was established.

The Slavs of Novgorod were threatened by a roving people of Turkish descent. The Vikings, a tribe of Northmen from Scandinavia, came to help the Slavs defend Novgorod. The Vikings were also called the Rus. In 862, Rurik the Viking became the ruler of Novgorod, and the land of the Rus and the Slavs soon became known as Russia.

Rurik the Viking

Around 882, the Vikings captured the town of Kiev to the south of Novgorod. Kiev and Novgorod united under the rule of Viking Prince Oleg. Oleg set up the first Russian state and ruled from its capital at Kiev. The state was called Kievan Russia.

In 980, Vladimir I, great-grandson of Rurik, became the ruler of Kievan Russia. Vladimir wanted to unite Kievan Russia under one religion. He admired the Eastern Orthodox church and made sure that it was established as the official religion of Kiev.

In 1019, the son of Vladimir I became the very able ruler of Kievan Russia. He was known as Yaroslav the Wise because he made Kiev a center of learning.

Then, around 1237, a huge army of Asian warriors invaded Russia. Their leader was Batu Khan, a grandson of Genghis Khan. Batu Khan destroyed one town after another, including Kiev. Russia became part of the Mongol empire.

The Russian Czars

The Mongols ruled for over 200 years. Then they grew weaker because of fighting among their leaders. Finally, in 1480, a group of Russian princes defeated the Mongols. Ivan III and his son, Basil III, led those princes. In 1547, Basil's son became the ruler, the first czar of all Russia. The first czar's name was Ivan IV. He became known as *Ivan the Terrible.*

Ivan IV changed Russian government. Earlier rulers, called Grand Dukes, had accepted advice and criticism from other nobles. Not Ivan IV—as czar, he moved the head of the government to Moscow and made himself all-powerful. It is said that one noble who dared to disagree with Ivan IV was tossed to the hounds, and he was torn to shreds!

Ivan ruled by terror. With threats of cruel punishment, he frightened the Russian people into doing his bidding. Hundreds of people were murdered by Ivan and his special police force. Ivan even killed his oldest son with his own two hands.

Ivan the Terrible

Ivan fought many wars. He increased Russia's territory. However, he made the daily lives of his people worse. Under Ivan the Terrible, the peasants were dreadfully poor. There was lots of land, but there were not enough people to keep the economy strong.

Ivan did grant the right to trade in Russia. This brought in money for the upper classes. Yet it did little to improve the lives of the common people. After Ivan, Russian rulers would seem kindly in comparison.

During the 1600s, Russia added to its territory. It took more of the Ukraine. It also extended its control of Siberia eastward to the Pacific Ocean. Slowly, Russia increased its contact with the rest of the world. Czar Michael Romanov took the throne in 1613.

He encouraged trade with the Netherlands and England. He brought foreign engineers and doctors to Russia. Michael's son Alexis followed him. He, too, was open to European customs and cultures.

Peter the Great: A "Window to the West"

Toward the end of the seventeenth century, a czar named Peter ruled in Russia. Peter had big plans. He wanted to make Russia more powerful. His goal was to make Russia equal to the nations of western Europe. Peter brought more Europeans into Russia. He brought

Peter the Great wanted to make Russia like the nations of Western Europe. He wanted Russian men to cut off their beards to look more European.

engineers, artists, soldiers, and scientists to teach Russians the ways of western Europe.

Still, Peter did not learn all he wanted to know. To learn more, he went on a journey. He traveled to the Netherlands to study shipbuilding. He also continued his studies in England, where he visited factories, schools, and museums. He also visited France, Germany, and Austria.

When Czar Peter returned, he had many new ideas. He wanted to "westernize" his people. He ordered his subjects to wear European-style clothing instead of long, Asian-styled robes. He demanded that all Russian men cut off their beards to look more European. To set an example, Peter called his nobles together and cut off their beards himself. When people rebelled against Peter's no-beard orders, he demanded a tax from any man wearing a beard.

Peter changed the old Russian calendar to make it match the European calendar. He gave women more freedom. He put the Russian church under complete control of his government.

Peter's desire to westernize Russia led him to his quest for a "window to the West." Peter wanted to open a Russian port on the ice-free Baltic Sea. Sweden stood in his way, so in 1700 he attacked Sweden. The war lasted until 1721. A peace treaty gave Russia land along the eastern Baltic coast.

Meanwhile, in 1703 Peter began building the city of St. Petersburg. It would be Peter's European "window." It was built along the Neva River, where the river flows into the Gulf of Finland. In 1712, Peter moved the nation's capital from Moscow to St. Petersburg.

This is a view from the Fontanka Canal in St. Petersburg.

Peter brought new ideas, industrialization, and strength to Russia. That is why he was given the name *Peter the Great.* However, he did little for the common people. Russian peasants were still poor and completely at the mercy of their czar.

In 1762, Empress Catherine II became ruler of Russia. Catherine continued many of Peter's policies. She kept the "window to the West" open. She brought French culture to the nobles of Russia and improved their education. She was called *Catherine the Great.* However, she, too, did little for the peasants. In 1773, Catherine's armies had to put down a peasant revolt. Catherine ruled Russia for 34 years. She joined forces with the rulers of Austria and Prussia. Together they conquered Poland, and they divided up the land. Russia's territory was greatly increased during the reign of Catherine II.

In 1812, Russia's relations with the West took a turn for the worse. That year, France's Napoleon Bonaparte invaded Russia. In Chapter 18, you read how this turned out to be Napoleon's big mistake. After taking Moscow, Napoleon's army began to run out of supplies as the weather turned bitter cold. Napoleon had to order a retreat. Only about one out of six of the men in his army lived to reach France.

HISTORY FACT

The great Russian author Tolstoy wrote about Napoleon's invasion of Russia in his famous novel, *War and Peace.*

"Bloody Sunday" and the 1905 Revolution

Russian peasants had lived under a feudal type of system for hundreds of years. Wealthy nobles owned all the farmlands. In 1861, the peasants were freed, but their lives were scarcely better. As industrialization came to Russia, factories sprang up in the cities. Thousands of peasants left the farms. They moved to the cities to work in the factories. Often, the peasants found the factory owners as unfair and uncaring as the land-owning nobles had been. In 1905, many of the peasants protested to demand changes. On January 22, 1905, workers and their families marched in the streets of St. Petersburg. Workers wanted higher wages and a voice in government. In response, the czar's soldiers killed or wounded hundreds of men, women, and children that day. January 22, 1905, became known as Russia's "Bloody Sunday."

Bloody Sunday was the end of any peaceful demand for change. Strikes, riots, and revolutionary battles broke out. In order to put a stop to the revolt, Nicholas II agreed to set up an elected Duma, or parliament. The Duma would have the power to rule on any proposals for new laws. Some people were satisfied with this change. Others felt that the Duma was not enough. The Duma lasted until 1917.

Many of the revolutionaries in Russia had read the works of Karl Marx. Marx was a German thinker of the 1800s. Marx pictured a perfect world in which there would be no classes and in which government would be unnecessary. Marx's ideas were known as **communism.** Some of the revolutionaries in Russia wanted to see Marx's ideas become a reality in their country.

You Decide
Czar Nicholas II did not trust his people. In fact, he feared them. Do you think a ruler who fears the people can rule well? Why or why not?

WORDS FROM THE PAST
Karl Marx and the *Communist Manifesto*

In 1848, Karl Marx and his friend Friedrich Engel wrote a pamphlet called the *Communist Manifesto.* "A spectre [spirit or ghost] is haunting Europe—the spectre of communism," the Manifesto began. "Workingmen of all countries, unite," the *Manifesto* ended.

The *Manifesto* said that all history is the history of class struggles. It said that just as the serfs had gained their freedom from the nobles, workers in industry would revolt against the factory owners. The *Manifesto* described the first steps toward communism. One step was that children would not be allowed to inherit their parents' money when their parents died.

Karl Marx

Marx was born in Prussia (Germany) in 1818. His parents were middle class. Although they were Jewish, Marx's father converted to Christianity. Karl Marx was raised as a Christian. Later in life, he was famous for saying, "Religion is the opium [drug] of the people."

As a young man, Marx studied philosophy at university. After graduation he became a writer and an editor. He got involved with organizations of working people, and he turned to the study of economics.

Das Kapital was Marx's most famous book. It was published in 1867. Part of the book described the poor conditions of the working class. Marx said that eventually capitalism would die and another better, classless, or Communist, society would take its place.

For most of Marx's adult life, he and his family lived in London, England. He researched his pamphlets and books at the British Museum. After Marx died in 1883, he was buried in Highgate Cemetery, in London. His ideas continued to have influence. They were important to the development of the U.S.S.R., a Communist state.

✓**Check Your Understanding**

Write your answers in complete sentences.

1. Why do you think Czar Ivan IV became known as Ivan the Terrible?

2. Why did Czar Peter want to open a "window to the West"?

3. Why was January 22, 1905 called Bloody Sunday?

World War I and the Overthrow of Czar Nicholas II

Russia entered World War I shortly after it began in 1914. The war brought severe food shortages to Russia. The poor people became even poorer. The common people of Russia were not interested in fighting Germany. However, Czar Nicholas II had already plunged Russia into the war.

In March 1917, the people of Russia demanded more food. The starving workers and peasants revolted. Czar Nicholas II was overthrown, and a new government took over. The czar and his family gave up the throne. The government promised democracy in Russia. It did not, however, end Russia's involvement in World War I. The people were against the war. It was draining supplies, killing the men, and taking the food.

HISTORY FACT

In 1918, Czar Nicholas and his family were executed by the Bolsheviks. The remains of the royal family were recently discovered.

Lenin and the Bolshevik Revolution

Later that year, a man named Vladimir Ilyich Lenin returned to Russia from exile in Switzerland. Lenin had always hated the government of the czar. Lenin's brother had been hanged as a revolutionary. Lenin himself had been exiled.

Lenin read Karl Marx. He became a Communist revolutionary who believed in rebellion and in a classless society. On his return to Russia, Lenin became the leader of a Communist group called the Bolsheviks. *Bolshevik* means "member of the majority." Lenin and the Bolsheviks promised to give the people what they wanted: "Peace, land, and bread."

In November 1917, the Bolsheviks overthrew the government. Karl Marx had pictured a society that would someday have no need for government. However, Lenin felt that a strict Communist party should be in charge in Russia. The country would need a planned economy. Furthermore, the Communist Party would draw up the plans. The country would be governed by councils called *soviets*. The soviets would be headed by Bolsheviks.

The Union of Soviet Socialist Republics (U.S.S.R.)

In 1918, Moscow became the nation's capital once again. That year, Russia was torn apart by a civil war. The Communists had taken power in the large cities of central Russia. However, resistance developed in many other parts of the country. The "Whites," or anti-Communists, had moved quickly to organize armies to fight the "Reds," or Communists. By 1921 most of the fighting was over. The Whites had been defeated.

In 1922, Russia became the Union of Soviet Socialist Republics (U.S.S.R). By then, Lenin had put the Communists firmly in charge. He had organized a strong police force. Every day, the police arrested, jailed, and even killed enemies of communism. The police force often made its arrests secretly at night. Many members of the clergy were arrested. Communists believed that religion was in the way. Religion misguided people, the Communists said.

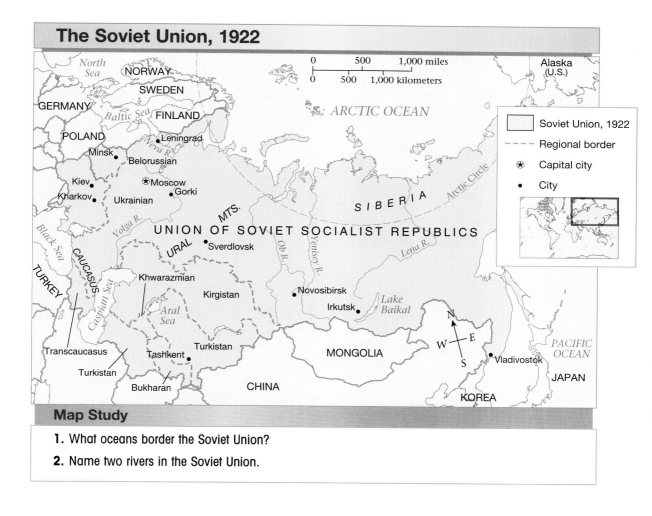

The Soviet Union, 1922

0 500 1,000 miles
0 500 1,000 kilometers

North Sea

NORWAY

SWEDEN

GERMANY

Baltic Sea FINLAND

POLAND

Leningrad

Minsk

Neva R.

Belorussian

Kiev

Kharkov

Moscow

Gorki

Ukrainian

Black Sea

Volga R.

CAUCASUS

TURKEY

Caspian Sea

URAL MTS.

Sverdlovsk

ARCTIC OCEAN

Arctic Circle

SIBERIA

UNION OF SOVIET SOCIALIST REPUBLICS

Ob R.

Yenisey R.

Lena R.

Khwarazmian

Kirgistan

Aral Sea

Novosibirsk

Irkutsk

Lake Baikal

Transcaucasus

Tashkent

Turkistan

Turkistan

Bukharan

CHINA

MONGOLIA

KOREA

Vladivostok

JAPAN

PACIFIC OCEAN

Alaska (U.S.)

N
W E
S

	Soviet Union, 1922
- - -	Regional border
✱	Capital city
•	City

Map Study

1. What oceans border the Soviet Union?

2. Name two rivers in the Soviet Union.

Some members of the nobility and of the middle class were labeled enemies of the state. They were arrested, jailed, and executed. The government took their businesses.

The Bolshevik Revolution was supposed to help the peasants. Now, Lenin ordered farmers to turn their crops over to the government. Some farmers rebelled. There was more fighting. Throughout the early 1920s, the Communists struggled to maintain power. For a brief period, the Communists let up on their hold over factories and farms in order to win support.

The Red Army marches in a parade. The Red Army was created by the Communist government after the Bolshevik Revolution of 1917.

Then, in 1924, Lenin became ill and died. He is remembered as the "Father of the Revolution." After his death, Joseph Stalin, a well-known Communist Party member, took control.

Joseph Stalin

Joseph Stalin was born in 1879 in the country of Georgia. He was educated in a religious school. His mother wanted him to become a priest. Then Joseph Stalin read the works of Karl Marx. "There is no God!" he announced at age 13. When he grew up, he became a revolutionary and then a leader in the Communist Party.

Stalin's real name was Dzhugashvili. In 1913, he adopted the name *Stalin,* which means *man of steel* in Russian. Stalin took power after Lenin's death. He ruled the Soviet Union from 1924 until his death in 1953.

Joseph Stalin controlled the Soviet Union through fear and terror.

Stalin built up Russia's economy and industry. He saw to the building of new factories and more heavy machinery. The peasants were forced to work on **collective** farms. He insisted that farmers use the new government machines. However, he did not show the farmers how to operate them. Farm production went down. There were food shortages again.

Stalin made himself strong by destroying anyone who opposed him. Suspected enemies were shot or exiled to Siberia. People learned to be loyal to the Communist Party and to Stalin.

Many people were unhappy living under such a tyrant. Stalin made life especially hard for Soviet Jews. Yet throughout the country, there were food shortages for everyone. In addition, certain goods, like clothing, were also hard to come by.

Soviet newspapers and radio programs told nothing of the country's problems. Sources of news said only what Stalin wanted them to say. Furthermore, Stalin would **censor** any news that came in from the rest of the world. Stalin did not allow the Soviet people to travel outside the Soviet Union. This was one reason that the Soviet Union was said to be surrounded by an Iron Curtain.

British prime minister Winston Churchill made the term *Iron Curtain* popular. He used it in a speech in the United States in 1946.

Stalin had statues of himself put up all over the Soviet Union. He insisted that the statues be built to make him look taller and more handsome than he really was. Stalin actually rewrote Soviet history. He tried to make it sound as if the Soviet people had actually chosen him to be their leader.

Russia has a long history of being ruled by tyrants. Ivan the Terrible, Peter the Great, and many other czars were ruthless dictators. However, many people think that Stalin was the most destructive and tyrannical dictator of all.

Timeline Study

How long was Russia involved in World War I?

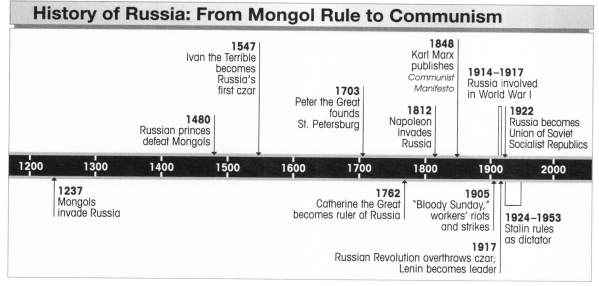

History of Russia: From Mongol Rule to Communism

1547 Ivan the Terrible becomes Russia's first czar

1848 Karl Marx publishes *Communist Manifesto*

1914–1917 Russia involved in World War I

1703 Peter the Great founds St. Petersburg

1812 Napoleon invades Russia

1480 Russian princes defeat Mongols

1922 Russia becomes Union of Soviet Socialist Republics

1200 1300 1400 1500 1600 1700 1800 1900 2000

1237 Mongols invade Russia

1762 Catherine the Great becomes ruler of Russia

1905 "Bloody Sunday," workers' riots and strikes

1924–1953 Stalin rules as dictator

1917 Russian Revolution overthrows czar; Lenin becomes leader

Summary

Russia takes in a huge area. It is home to many types of people.
Russian czars came to power after 200 years of Mongol rule. Ivan the Terrible, who ruled by terror, was the first czar. Peter the Great westernized Russia. Catherine the Great continued Peter's policies.
Bloody Sunday, in 1905, began a revolt of the Russian workers.
Czar Nicholas II led Russia into World War I in 1914. The war was unpopular. In 1917, Nicholas II was overthrown.
Later in 1917 the Bolsheviks seized control of the government. The Bolsheviks, who followed Communist ideas, supported Lenin as head of Russia's government.
In 1922, Russia became the Union of Soviet Socialist Republics. Joseph Stalin followed Lenin as leader of the Communist Party and the nation.

Vocabulary Review

Write *true* or *false*. If the statement is false, change the underlined term to make it true.

1. Communism is a political system based on common ownership of industries and farms.

2. You can study geography to learn about the natural features of the earth.

3. A collective is a form of a language used in a certain place or by a certain group.

4. Stalin decided to censor news so that Soviets would not know about events around the world.

5. Under communism, farm production in the Soviet Union went down.

6. People in Russia speak many languages and dialects.

Chapter Quiz

Write your answers in complete sentences.

1. Where did Russia get its name?

2. What kind of government did Lenin think the Russians needed?

3. Why did Russian peasants revolt in 1917?

4. **Critical Thinking** Was life ever easy for Russian peasants? Why or why not?

5. **Critical Thinking** What kind of person was Stalin? Give examples to support your answer.

Using the Timeline

Use the timeline on page 403 to answer the questions.

1. When did Peter the Great found St. Petersburg?

2. What happened in 1922?

Write About History

Complete the following activity.

Suppose you could interview one of the leaders in this chapter. What would you ask him or her? Write five interview questions. Have a partner play the role of the leader and answer the questions.

On August 6, 1945, an atomic bomb fell on Hiroshima, Japan. In seconds, more than 60,000 people were killed.

Learning Objectives

- Name three dictators who came to power before World War II.
- Explain how Germany helped to bring about World War II.
- Identify the Allied powers and the Axis powers.
- Explain how the United States became involved in the war.
- Describe how the war finally ended in Europe and in Japan.

Chapter 28 World War II

Words to Know

depression	a period of low business activity and high unemployment
fascist	a dictator and his or her followers who takes away the rights of the people and glorifies war
anti-Semitism	prejudice against Jews
scapegoat	a person or group blamed for the mistakes and problems of others
concentration camp	a prison camp for people thought to be dangerous to a ruling group
genocide	an attempt to kill all the people of a certain race or religious group
Holocaust	the killing of Jews and other peoples by the Nazis
pact	an agreement

After World War I, the League of Nations hoped to keep the peace. World War I had been costly in lives and in money. No one was anxious for another war. Yet only 20 years after World War I ended, another war began.

The 20 years between World War I and World War II were troubled years. In the early 1930s, nations struggled through **depressions**. Businesses went broke. Millions of workers were out of jobs. Farmers could not sell their crops to unemployed people. Banks closed. Poverty spread throughout the world. Historians would call the 1930s the "Great Depression."

There were other troubles, too. In India, people were fighting for freedom from British rule. Civil wars were raging in China and Spain. In addition, Japan, Italy, and Germany began building empires.

The Rise of Dictators

The years between World War I and World War II brought new govenments to several nations. They were governments ruled by dictators. The Great Depression created a perfect climate for the rise of dictators. Hungry, hopeless people wanted to see changes. They were ready to turn to a strong leader who promised a better future. Most of the dictators, however, were men with evil ideas and purposes. They wanted power and control.

A man named Benito Mussolini took control of Italy in 1922. He and his followers were called **fascists.** Mussolini won favor with his people by building roads and factories. He improved his country's economy and industry, but he insisted on absolute rule. Anyone who refused to obey Mussolini was jailed or killed.

Benito Mussolini, a fascist, took control of Italy in 1922.

Mussolini wanted Italy to become a great empire. He wanted to win colonies, to make war, and to take new lands by force. In 1935 Mussolini sent troops into Ethiopia, a free African country. The League of Nations protested. However, it could not stop Mussolini's drive into Africa.

In Japan, General Hideki Tojo arose as a dictator. He wanted to build an empire in Asia. Under the leadership of Tojo and other generals, Japanese forces invaded the Chinese province of Manchuria in 1931. When the League of Nations protested, Japan left the League. By 1932, Japan had claimed Manchuria. Japan invaded China again in 1937, taking over miles of coastal lands. By 1938, Japan controlled all of China's major ports and industrial centers.

During the 1930s, Japanese military officers began taking over their own government. Anyone who got in their way or protested was either jailed or assassinated. By 1940, Tojo had become minister of war. Finally, in 1941, he became premier. Japan still had an emperor, but the emperor had no real power.

Hitler

The country most willing to accept a dictator and to follow him without question was Germany. Germany had suffered greatly after World War I. German pride had been crushed. A country whose nationalistic spirit was based on military greatness had been beaten in war. German armies had been reduced to almost nothing. In addition, the Treaty of Versailles had forbidden rebuilding the German military.

The depression hit hard, and Germany still had war debts to pay. Germans were out of work and hungry. Many were angry and ready for revenge.

This situation in Germany led people to accept Adolf Hitler as their leader in 1933. Hitler was the head of the National Socialist, or *Nazi,* party. Hitler and the Nazis seemed to have an answer to Germany's problems. Hitler appealed to the Germans' wounded pride. He told them that they were a "super race" who should rule the world. He promised to return Germany to a position of power and glory.

Hitler spoke of winning back Germany's lost lands. He promised a new German empire, the Third Reich. In 1935 he began rebuilding Germany's armed forces. This had been forbidden by the Treaty of Versailles. However, nothing was done to stop the Nazis from arming themselves.

As Hitler gave Germany new hope and national pride, he built his own strength. Few people dared speak out against Adolf Hitler!

The three dictators—Hitler, Mussolini, and Tojo— each wanted an empire. In 1936 Hitler and Mussolini joined forces. They called their alliance the Rome-Berlin axis. They chose the name "axis" to suggest that all of Europe revolved around Germany and Italy. In 1940 Japan joined the Axis. Germany, Italy, and Japan planned to conquer the world and divide it up!

Adolf Hitler promised to return Germany to a time of power and glory.

Hitler's Weapon: Hate

Hitler strove to bind his people together with the feeling of hatred. He aimed that hate at all people who were not white and Germanic. Hitler believed that the German race was stronger, better, and smarter than any other. He gave fiery speeches that stirred German emotions. He told the people that Germans should be "masters of the world."

Hitler directed his fiercest hatred at the Jewish people. He encouraged **anti-Semitism**, a mindless hatred of Jews. He told the German people that the Jews were the cause of all their troubles. Hitler's lies gave the unhappy Germans a **scapegoat**. Now they had a simple way to explain away their troubles: They blamed them all on the Jews.

Hitler united Germany under a banner of hatred and fear. He made people afraid to disobey him. Hitler's secret police backed his rule. They arrested anyone who spoke against him. **Concentration camps** were built to imprison Hitler's enemies.

Remember
Long before Hitler, Alexander the Great wanted to conquer the world. Later, so did Napoleon.

Hitler won Germany's loyalty. Then he turned to the rest of Europe. "Today Europe," Hitler declared, "tomorrow the world!"

World War II Begins

In 1938 Hitler set forth on his conquest of Europe. His troops marched into Austria and took over the country. Austria was now a part of Germany.

"This is wrong," said Great Britain and France. "Hitler has broken the Treaty of Versailles." However, they did not act to stop him.

Next, Hitler turned to Czechoslovakia. Hitler claimed that Germans living there were treated poorly. He asked for a border region in Czechoslovakia. He said that this would be his last request for territory. Great Britain and France had sworn to protect Czechoslovakia. To keep peace, however, they signed a treaty with Hitler. They gave him 11,000 square miles of Czech lands. This area was known as the Sudetenland. Six months later, Hitler took over the rest of Czechoslovakia. The British and French policy of trying to satisfy Hitler by giving in had not worked.

On September 1, 1939, German armies invaded Poland. This time, Great Britain and France acted. On September 3, 1939, they declared war on Germany. World War II had begun.

Hitler's *Blitzkrieg*

The German army took Poland in less than a month. Then Hitler pushed west. Norway and Denmark fell to Germany, too.

Hitler's style of warfare was called a *blitzkrieg,* which means "lightning war." His armies moved fast, using quick attacks with planes, tanks, and troops. The people of Europe would remember the German planes bombing railroads, highways, and cities. They would remember the armored cars moving in next, followed by the Nazi foot soldiers.

The German *blitzkrieg* then fell upon the Netherlands, Luxembourg, and Belgium. Next came France.

When the Germans attacked France, they had some help from Italy. France's armies were unable to stop Hitler. With Germans at the gates of Paris and with planes overhead, the French surrendered. In June 1940, the French admitted their defeat. It was said that Hitler received the news of France's surrender with great joy. A story went around that he danced a little "victory jig."

Remember
France had been Germany's bitter enemy since losing a war to Bismarck in 1871.

WORDS FROM THE PAST
Winston Churchill, June 4, 1940

Winston Churchill had become prime minister of Great Britain on May 10, 1940. That was the same day that Germany invaded Belgium, Luxembourg, and the Netherlands. Soon after that, Belgium surrendered to Germany. It looked as if it would only be a matter of days until France fell to the Nazis. People in Britain began to worry about what would happen to their own country.

Winston Churchill

On June 4, Churchill gave a speech to the British House of Commons. He wanted to raise the spirits of the British people. He said that even though all of Europe might fall, ". . . we shall not flag or fail. We shall go on to the end . . . we shall fight in the seas and oceans . . . we shall fight on the beaches, we shall fight on the landing-grounds, we shall fight in the fields and in the streets, we shall fight in the hills; we shall never surrender . . ."

The Battle of Britain

With the fall of France, only Britain remained in Hitler's way. Hitler decided not to attack the island of Great Britain by sea. Britain's navy was too powerful. Hitler would launch an air attack instead.

The Battle of Britain was the first major air war in history. Beginning in July 1940, thousands of German planes attacked Britain. They bombed cities and airfields. However, the British would not be defeated.

British civilians worked out air raid plans to protect their neighborhoods. Citizens even strung piano wire from balloons to catch Nazi planes. The skilled young pilots of the British Royal Air Force (RAF) fought hard. With speedy Spitfire planes and with newly developed radar, they fought off the German planes.

You Decide

Britain's spirit remained strong in spite of the constant bombing. Do you think the United States would be as strong in this situation? Explain.

Readers chose books in a London library damaged by bombs.

From September 1940 until May 1941, German planes bombed London almost every night. These attacks became known as the *London Blitz*. By May 1941, it was clear that the German bombing attacks had failed. Germany had lost more than 2,600 planes. It was Germany's first defeat in World War II.

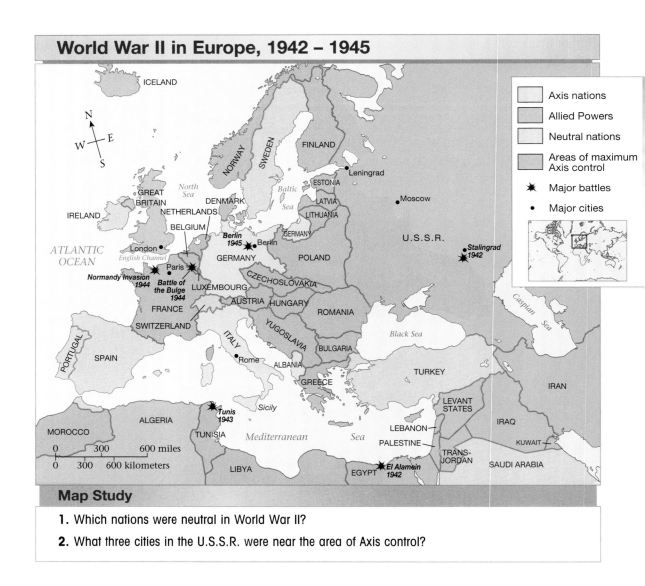

World War II in Europe, 1942 – 1945

Map Study

1. Which nations were neutral in World War II?

2. What three cities in the U.S.S.R. were near the area of Axis control?

Hitler Moves East

Unable to take Britain, Hitler's armies moved eastward. The Germans took Romania and its oil fields. Then Italy invaded Greece. Greece's armies fought bravely against the Italians. However, when Hitler joined the Italians, Greece had to surrender.

Next, the Axis nations invaded Yugoslavia. Most of Europe had now fallen under Hitler. His next goal would be the conquest of the Soviet Union.

Hitler Turns on the Soviet Union

Like Napoleon Bonaparte, Hitler chose June 22 as the day to attack Russia. Napoleon had attacked on June 22, 1812. Now Hitler attacked on June 22, 1941, with three million German soldiers. He expected Russia to fall in a matter of weeks.

The Russians surprised the world by fighting back with amazing strength and determination. Soldiers and civilians alike stood up against the Germans. However, the Germans advanced toward Moscow. Just as in the fight against Napoleon, Russians burned whatever they could not move. They destroyed food supplies, machinery, and factories so the Germans could not use them. The Germans approached Moscow, but they were unable to take the city. People from all over Russia poured in to defend it.

Like Napoleon, Hitler did not count on the fierce Russian weather. Hitler's soldiers did not even have winter clothing. Furthermore, the winter of 1941–1942 turned out to be the worst in years. Nazi soldiers froze on the icy Russian plains. It was beginning to look as if Hitler might have made a mistake by invading Russia. Indeed, by 1944 the Soviets had pushed the Germans out of the Soviet Union.

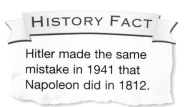

HISTORY FACT

Hitler made the same mistake in 1941 that Napoleon did in 1812.

✓Check Your Understanding

Write your answers in complete sentences.

1. What were the three Axis powers and the dictators who ruled them?

2. What action by Germany started World War II?

3. What is the meaning of *blitzkrieg*?

The Holocaust

Hitler forced his own ideas on the people he conquered. They were evil ideas of a "super race." People who did not fit Hitler's ideal of the super race were considered inferior. They were used as slave laborers or thrown into concentration camps.

Some Europeans fought the Nazi ideas. They formed resistance groups and waged secret, undercover wars. They wrecked telephone and telegraph lines to stop German communication. They blew up bridges and derailed trains. They killed Nazi officers. They helped Allied prisoners escape.

The Nazis answered the resistance by murdering hundreds of innocent men, women, and children. Nazi terror was aimed most directly at Europe's Jews. First, Hitler forced Jews out of their jobs. He took away their businesses and their property. Then Jews were made to live in special areas.

In 1941, Hitler's plans reached their evil peak. He announced his "final solution" to what he called the "Jewish problem." That solution was **genocide.**

Jewish people over the age of six were forced to wear a yellow star that said "Jude," or Jew.

Hitler sent millions of people to concentration camps. Worse than any prison, these camps were slave-labor camps. In the camps, millions of men, women, and children were executed. Many people were spared execution only to be worked or starved to death.

Over six million Jews died in Nazi concentration camps. Hitler's efforts to destroy all Jews is called the **Holocaust.** The Nazis also murdered millions of others—Russians, Poles, Gypsies, Slavs—all "inferior" enemies of Hitler.

The Nazi death camps are one of history's greatest horrors. "How could the world have let this happen?" question the ghosts of Hitler's victims. Survivors of the Holocaust tell of wishing for death in a world too evil to bear.

HISTORY FACT

Healthy prisoners were sometimes hired out as slaves for private businesses. Often, they were worked and starved to death in factories and other businesses.

The United States Declares War

You Decide

Why do you think the United States remained neutral until December 1941?

The United States was a neutral nation from 1939 until 1941. It was not directly involved in the war.

The United States did, however, send aid to Germany's enemies. The United States sent food, arms, and raw materials to Great Britain and Russia. However, it took a direct blow from Japan to bring the United States into World War II.

Japan was trying to create its empire in Asia. Japan felt that the United States stood in the way of its control of the Pacific Ocean. On December 7, 1941, Japanese planes bombed the Pearl Harbor naval base in Hawaii. The attack took the United States by surprise. Japan sank or damaged 13 ships and about 170 planes. Nearly 2,500 U.S. soldiers, sailors, and civilians died in the surprise attack.

In Japan, Emperor Hirohito declared war on the United States. In the United States, President Franklin D. Roosevelt asked Congress to declare war on Japan. After a vote in Congress, Roosevelt addressed the nation. "We are now in this war," he declared. "We are in it all the way."

Four days later, Germany and Italy honored their **pact** with Japan. They declared war on the United States.

By the end of 1941, the war really had become a world war. The Axis countries stood on one side. The Allied countries, which now included the United States, stood on the other.

The Tide of War Turns Toward the Allies

In 1942, Soviet and German armies were locked in battle. The battlefront stretched about 2,000 miles through the Soviet Union, from the Arctic Ocean to the Black Sea. In the north, Leningrad (formerly St. Petersburg) was under siege by the Nazis. The siege began in August 1941 and would last until January 1944. About a million Soviets died during the siege, most of them from starvation.

In September 1942, the German Sixth Army attacked Stalingrad (now called Volgograd). For five months, Soviet soldiers fought the Germans. The battle raged back and forth from one block to the next. Finally, on January 31, 1943, the German Sixth Army surrendered. Only 90,000 of the original force of 350,000 German soldiers were still alive.

The Battle of Stalingrad marked a major turning point in the war. Now the Soviet army went on the offensive. The Soviets began to take back cities that had been captured by the Germans.

Meanwhile, fighting had been going on in northern Africa. Hitler had taken over most of Europe. Now he could be attacked only from Britain, the Soviet Union, or from North Africa. North Africa became important.

General Erwin Rommel, known as the clever "Desert Fox," led the Germans in Africa. Early in 1943, U.S. General Dwight D. Eisenhower set a trap for the Desert Fox and defeated the Germans. In May 1943, German and Italian forces in Africa surrendered.

The Allies invaded Italy next. It was, according to President Roosevelt, the "beginning of the end" for the Axis countries. The Allies accepted the Italian surrender in 1943. However, German forces continued to fight in Italy. Rome was finally freed on June 4, 1944.

> **HISTORY FACT**
>
> The name *Leningrad* was changed back to St. Petersburg in 1991.

Allied soldiers landed in Normandy, France, for the longest land and sea attack in history.

The Invasion of Europe

Hitler still felt sure of his strength in Europe. But the Allies were preparing an invasion. By 1944 they were ready to free France. German forces protected the Normandy coast facing Great Britain. The Allies planned to invade Normandy. The day of the invasion was called "D-day."

D-day came at 2 A.M. on June 6, 1944. General Eisenhower was in charge of the attack. The first wave of troops crossed the English Channel. By 6:30 A.M., more than 150,000 Allied soldiers waded ashore on the beaches of Normandy. Within five days the Allies had fought many miles inland.

The Allies began their sweep through France. In August, they freed Paris. By October the Nazis were driven from all of France, as well as from Belgium and Luxembourg.

Germany Surrenders

The Germans were soundly defeated in December 1944 in the Battle of the Bulge. According to Winston Churchill, it was the greatest U.S. victory of the war.

At last, early in 1945, the Allies invaded Germany. Germany's capital, Berlin, fell on May 2. On May 7, 1945, Germany surrendered. The war in Europe was over.

Deaths of Two Dictators

The leaders of Germany and Italy had created terrible death and destruction. What became of the leaders of these fallen powers?

In Italy, fascist leader Benito Mussolini met an ugly end. Mussolini tried to escape from Italy, to run from the antifascists. When captured, he begged for his life.

Despite his pleas, Mussolini was executed—shot without a trial. His body was hung upside down outside a gas station in Milan, Italy. Italians shouted at the body, kicking it and throwing stones at it. A man who had lived by cruelty and terror met a cruel end.

Germany's Hitler died two days later. On April 30, 1945, reports came that the dictator had killed himself. He had been hiding in a bomb shelter beneath the flaming, shattered city of Berlin. Unable to face defeat, Hitler and his wife Eva Braun both committed suicide.

The War with Japan

The war had ended in Europe, but not in the Pacific. After Pearl Harbor, the Japanese had taken the Philippines, most of Southeast Asia, and islands in the Pacific.

General Douglas MacArthur led the U.S. forces against the Japanese in the Pacific. Although his campaigns were successful, the Japanese would not give up. Most of Japan's navy and air force had been destroyed by August 1945. However, there was no surrender. The Japanese felt it was their duty and their honor to fight to the very end.

The Japanese turned to desperate measures. *Kamikaze* pilots became human bombs. They did this by strapping themselves into planes filled with explosives. Then they flew their planes into U.S. warships.

It seemed time for the terrors of war to end. However, the greatest terror was still to come.

The Atom Bomb

The atomic bomb explodes over Nagasaki.

Scientists had discovered how to split the atom to create great energy. This energy could be used as a weapon. By 1940, German scientists were working to develop an atomic bomb. In 1942, the Manhattan Project began to develop the bomb in the United States. Working on the project in the United States were scientists such as Enrico Fermi and J. Robert Oppenheimer. They, with the help of many others, finally built the powerful weapon.

U.S. President Harry S Truman made the difficult decision. The atomic bomb would be the quickest way to end the war.

Japan was warned, but the Japanese refused to surrender. Therefore, on August 6, 1945, an American plane dropped the atomic bomb on Hiroshima, Japan. In seconds, more than 60,000 people were killed, and Hiroshima was gone.

Still, Japan did not surrender, and three days later, a second A-bomb was dropped. This bomb fell on Nagasaki's 250,000 people.

At last, on September 2, 1945, the Japanese surrendered. It was their first military defeat in 2,000 years. General Tojo was arrested and convicted as a war criminal. He was hanged on December 23, 1948.

The Costs of War

World War II was over at last. It was the most expensive war in history. The figures were shocking.

- Over a trillion dollars had been spent for arms and war machinery.
- About fifty-five million lives were lost. (This includes civilian and military losses.)
- Germany lost almost three million soldiers.
- Japan lost more than two million soldiers.
- Italy lost about 160,000 soldiers.
- The U.S.S.R. lost about 7,500,000 soldiers.
- Britain lost about 270,000 soldiers.
- The United States lost more than 400,000 soldiers.
- France lost about 200,000 soldiers.

Many millions of civilians had died. Millions of others were homeless. The world was left with questions to answer. How could people have so easily accepted the horrors of the Nazi concentration camps? What about the atom bomb? What was to become of a world that possessed such a terrible and powerful weapon?

The United Nations

The League of Nations had tried to keep the peace after World War I. However, the League had failed. How could future wars be prevented? Since the beginning of World War II, U.S. President Franklin Roosevelt and other national leaders were thinking about it. In June of 1941, representatives of nine countries met in London to talk about it.

There those officials signed a pledge to work for a free world. This pledge was called the *Inter-Allied Declaration*.

By early 1942, the idea of a "United Nations" gained wide support. In January, representatives from 26 nations met in Washington, D.C. There they signed a pact calling for world peace and freedom for all people. The agreement also called for eventual disarmament and economic cooperation. The pact they signed was called the *Declaration by United Nations*.

At that time, of course, there was still a world war going on. By 1944, however, it was clear that the Allies would win the war. Allied representatives began planning the new organization. In February 1945, a date was set for a United Nations meeting in San Francisco. As scheduled, the meeting was held on April 25.

At that first meeting of the United Nations, a constitution was established. Representatives from 50 nations signed the United Nations Charter. The delegates also set up a Security Council with permanent members from five countries. They were

The United Nations building is in New York City.

the United States, the Soviet Union, Great Britain, France, and China. Each member had veto power over any decision the Security Council made. Just one veto would keep a decision from going into effect.

On October 24, 1945, the United Nations became official. The new organization had a big job ahead of it. Its aim was to protect world peace and to safeguard human rights throughout the world. In 1949, the cornerstone was laid for U.N. headquarters in New York City.

Whenever a world problem comes up, the United Nations meets to work for a peaceful settlement. Delegates from every member nation attend meetings of the United Nations' General Assembly. They try to solve problems without war. Other branches of the United Nations work on problems of education, trade, labor, health, and economics.

The weapons of the world have grown to unbelievable destructive power. The purpose of the United Nations has become more and more important. The United Nations has one victory as its major goal—the victory over war.

Timeline Study

What event happened the same year that France fell to Germany?

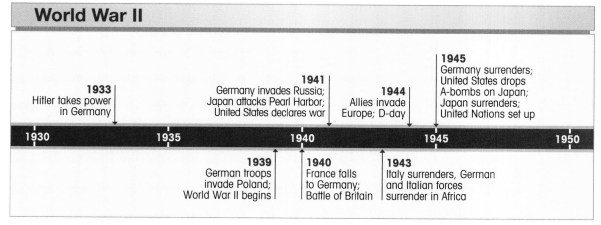

World War II

1933
Hitler takes power in Germany

1941
Germany invades Russia; Japan attacks Pearl Harbor; United States declares war

1944
Allies invade Europe; D-day

1945
Germany surrenders; United States drops A-bombs on Japan; Japan surrenders; United Nations set up

1930 — 1935 — 1940 — 1945 — 1950

1939
German troops invade Poland; World War II begins

1940
France falls to Germany; Battle of Britain

1943
Italy surrenders, German and Italian forces surrender in Africa

Summary

Hitler of Germany, Mussolini of Italy, and Tojo of Japan were three strong dictators that came to power between World War I and World War II.
Two alliances fought each other in World War II. The Axis powers were Germany, Italy, Japan, and many smaller nations. The Allied nations were Britain, France, Russia, the United States, and many smaller nations. The United States joined the war in 1941, after Japan attacked Pearl Harbor.
Hitler had evil ideas of a "super race" that was meant to rule the world. He especially hated the Jews and tried to destroy them. In the Holocaust, he imprisoned and murdered millions of Jews. He also murdered millions of other people who did not fit his idea of the super race.
World War II began in 1939, after Germany invaded Poland. The war was fought in Europe, Asia, and Africa. D-day began the Allied sweep to regain Europe. Terrible weapons, including two atomic bombs dropped by the United States on Japan, were used in the war.
World War II ended after Germany surrendered in December 1944 and Japan surrendered in September 1945.

genocide

depression

pact

scapegoat

fascist

Vocabulary Review

Complete each sentence with a term from the list.

1. Hitler made the Jews into a _____ by blaming them for all the troubles in Germany.

2. Business activity goes down and unemployment goes up during a _____.

3. Germany, Italy, and Japan signed a _____ to support each other in World War II.

4. A follower of the dictator Mussolini was a _____.

5. The killing of people of a certain race or religion is _____.

Chapter Quiz

Write your answers in complete sentences.

1. How did the Great Depression help the rise of dictators?

2. How did Hitler use hate as a weapon?

3. Which country lost the most soldiers in the war?

4. **Critical Thinking** Do you think the Holocaust could happen again? Why or why not?

5. **Critical Thinking** How did the dropping of the atom bombs on Japan change the world?

Using the Timeline

Use the timeline on page 425 to answer the questions.

1. When the United States entered the war, how long had it been going on?

2. When was D-day?

Write About History

Complete the following activity.

Form a group of four. Make a large wall chart about World War II. Use the information in this chapter and in encyclopedias and other books. Suggested headings are Battles, Weapons, Leaders, Nations and Their Flags, Famous Speeches, the Holocaust, the Atom Bomb, Costs of the War, the United Nations, Winners and Losers.

Unit 9 Review

Comprehension Check

Write your answers in complete sentences.

1. How did the Italians take control of Rome?

2. Why was Prussia the strongest state in unified Germany?

3. How did Bismarck manage to form a united Germany?

4. What event is usually named as starting World War I?

5. What international organization was set up after World War I ended?

6. Why were the workers and peasants of Russia against Russia's involvement in World War I?

7. When Lenin put Communists in charge in the Soviet Union, what was their attitude toward religion?

8. How did Germany help cause World War II?

Writing an Essay

Answer one of the following essay topics.

1. Discuss the way Napoleon unknowingly encouraged Italian and German nationalism.

2. Explain why World War I was called the Great War.

3. Compare the life of the peasants under the czars and under communism.

4. Explain how Hitler put his ideas of a "super race" into practice.

Group Activity

In your group, list the wars mentioned in Unit 9. Then discuss if each war might have been avoided, and if so, how it could have been avoided. Make a list of ideas for peace in the future. Share the list with the rest of the class.

History in Your Life
Millions of U.S. soldiers fought in World War II. How can you show your appreciation?

The Berlin Wall was built by the East German Communists to separate East and West Germany in 1961. The wall kept East Germans from leaving.

Learning Objectives

- Describe how Germany was divided after World War II.
- Explain why the cold war began.
- Describe life in the Soviet Union under Nikita Khrushchev.
- Identify major crisis periods in Soviet–U.S. relations.

Chapter 29 — Changes in Europe

Words to Know

satellite	a country that depends on and is controlled by a more powerful country
isolationism	a policy of staying out of the affairs of other countries
capitalist	having business and industry privately owned and operated for profit
detente	an easing of tensions between countries
ratify	to formally approve

Europe After World War II

Europe was weakened by World War II. European countries were no longer the powerful nations they had been. It was time for these nations to rebuild. Many nations, including Italy and France, set up democratic governments. Charles de Gaulle served as the first president of postwar France.

U.S. President Harry S Truman called for a plan to help put Europe back on its feet. The Marshall Plan, named for U.S. Secretary of State George C. Marshall, provided money for European recovery. From 1947 until 1951, the United States gave thirteen billion dollars' worth of food, raw materials for industry, and machinery to European nations.

War-torn nations welcomed the aid. However, the Soviet Union and its Communist **satellites** refused to accept the Marshall Plan. This refusal was just one act that would divide the world into two camps.

The Eastern European countries did not turn to democracy. They became Communist satellites of the

Soviet Union. They had been freed from the Germans by the Soviet Union at the end of the war. However, they remained under Soviet control.

Germany in Ruins

What of the defeated empire? Germany was a shambles after World War II. Cities and farms had been bombed. The economy was ruined.

The winning nations divided Germany into four sections. Great Britain, France, the United States, and the Soviet Union each took control of a section. Each country put troops inside its zone to keep order.

After a few years the United States, France, and Britain tried to bring Germany together as one republic. However, the Soviet Union refused. As a result, the democratic nations combined their regions to form West Germany, or the Federal Republic of Germany. The Soviet-controlled zone became known as East Germany, or the German Democratic Republic.

The city of Berlin is located in the eastern part of Germany. It was divided into East Berlin, a Communist section, and West Berlin, under democratic West German control. In 1961, the Communists built the Berlin Wall to separate the city's two sections. They also wanted to keep East Berliners from leaving to live permanently in the West.

The United States and the World After World War II

The United States, unlike Europe, was not shattered by World War II. No battles tore apart U.S. lands. Wide oceans kept the United States separate and safe. The United States also had the power of the atomic bomb. At the end of World War II, the United States was the strongest nation in the world.

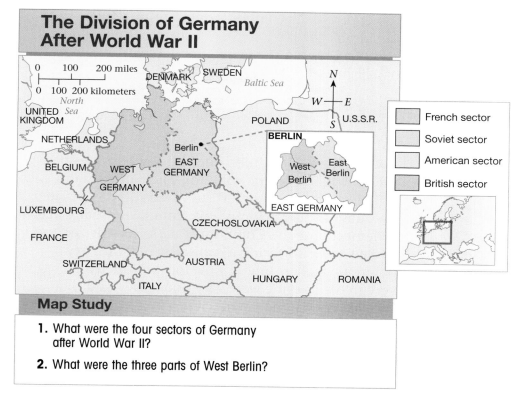

The Division of Germany After World War II

0   100   200 miles

0   100   200 kilometers

North

Sea

Baltic Sea

N
W — E
S

DENMARK   SWEDEN

UNITED KINGDOM

NETHERLANDS

BELGIUM   WEST GERMANY

LUXEMBOURG

FRANCE

SWITZERLAND   AUSTRIA

ITALY

POLAND   U.S.S.R.

Berlin

EAST GERMANY

CZECHOSLOVAKIA

HUNGARY   ROMANIA

BERLIN

West Berlin   East Berlin

EAST GERMANY

- French sector
- Soviet sector
- American sector
- British sector

Map Study

1. What were the four sectors of Germany after World War II?

2. What were the three parts of West Berlin?

Except for its involvement in World War I, the United States had mostly kept to its own business. It followed a policy of **isolationism.** World War II connected the United States with the rest of the world. In 1945, the United States became one of the first countries to join the United Nations. The world was changing. Countries were becoming more and more dependent on each other. The United States could no longer stand alone, minding its own business.

The Cold War

During World War II, the United States and the Soviet Union were allies. After World War II, the two countries became the most powerful nations on Earth. In fact, they were known as *superpowers.* Each had different ideas about what an ideal society should be like.

Soviet peoples lived under communism, while Americans lived in a free democracy. Disputes and tensions between the two nations grew. The cold war had begun.

The cold war was not an outright conflict. It did not involve actual battles or bombings. The cold war was a war of ideas.

Both the Soviet Union and the United States had their own allies in the cold war. The United States and its allies thought communism was bad. They pointed out that people in Communist countries usually had little freedom. The Communist nations criticized the United States for being a **capitalist** nation. They pointed out that some people in the United States were very rich and some were very poor. They said that because of this, the United States was an unfair society.

You Decide

Do you think the Communist criticism of the United States was fair? Why or why not?

Americans worried about a Communist takeover of the whole world. President Truman announced that the United States would give aid to any country fighting communism. He made a plan for military and economic support. This plan became known as the Truman Doctrine. Both Greece and Turkey were given aid under this plan.

Communism often grew strong in poor countries. Financial aid under the Marshall Plan helped to keep European nations strong enough to resist Communist ideas.

NATO

In 1949, sides were clearly drawn in the cold war. The United States led the setting up of the North Atlantic Treaty Organization (NATO). Members of NATO included the United States, Britain, France, Italy, Canada, and several smaller nations. In 1954 West Germany became a member.

NATO began as a defense against communism. Member nations promised to help each other. They said that an attack against any one of them would be taken as an attack against all.

In 1955, the Soviet Union created its own alliance to balance the NATO alliance. It was called the Warsaw Pact. It included the Soviet Union and its Communist allies in Eastern Europe.

Economic Alliances

NATO and the Warsaw Pact were military alliances. The cold war also prompted European nations to form economic alliances. The Soviet Union developed ties with its European allies. These ties gave the Soviet Union a market for its manufactured products. The economic allies, in turn, supplied the Soviets with raw materials.

Remember
The world was also divided into alliances before and during the two world wars.

Many Western European countries joined together to promote trade and common interests. The organization that these countries formed was known as the European Union by the late 1990s. The European Union consisted of 15 full member nations—Austria, Belgium, Denmark, Finland, France, Germany, Greece, Ireland, Italy, Luxembourg, the Netherlands, Portugal, Spain, Sweden, and the United Kingdom. It was best known as an advocate for a single currency, the euro, and a lowering of trade barriers between the member countries. The euro has now been introduced in some member countries.

The Nuclear Arms Race

The Soviet Union and the United States tried to stay in step with each other. Each superpower feared that the other would become more powerful.

One measure of power is the buildup of weapons. When the United States exploded the atom bomb in

1945, it made America fearsome and powerful. Other nations wanted that power, too. In 1949, the Soviet Union exploded its first atomic bomb. By 1952, Great Britain also had the atomic secret. Then the United States pulled ahead again in the race for destructive power. In 1954, the United States tested a hydrogen bomb. It was thousands of times more powerful than the atomic bomb that had fallen on Hiroshima. Soon Great Britain, France, and the Soviet Union had hydrogen bombs, too.

Now the People's Republic of China has the bomb. So do India, Israel, and Pakistan. The world has given itself something to fear. As nations struggled to keep pace in the cold war, the stakes became higher. There are now enough nuclear weapons in existence to destroy the world many times over.

You Decide

Did the nuclear arms race make Americans safer? Why or why not?

The Soviet Union After World War II

After World War II, Joseph Stalin worked to rebuild Soviet industry. He set up labor camps, forcing workers to build, build, and build some more. Between 1945 and 1965, Soviet industry boomed. Yet life was not easy for the Russian worker. Stalin had caused shortages of food and clothing with his emphasis on heavy industry.

After Stalin's death in 1953, there was a struggle for power. Then a new leader, Nikita Khrushchev, rose to the top of the Communist Party.

Khrushchev accused Stalin of the arrests and death of many citizens. Khrushchev promised that now the country would be led by the party rather than by a single dictator.

Soviet premier Nikita Khrushchev

Under the rule of Khrushchev, life became better for the people of the Soviet Union. Khrushchev halted some of the activities of the secret police. The government allowed somewhat greater freedom of speech. The workweek was shortened to 40 hours.

In addition, Khrushchev tried to raise the standard of living for ordinary people. His economic plan included a greater production of consumer goods. However, progress was very slow.

The Spread of Communism

The Soviet Union helped spread communism to other parts of the world. China, Mongolia, North Korea, as well as some nations in Southeast Asia and in Africa, turned to communism. In addition, Cuba, only 90 miles from the United States, became a Communist dictatorship under Fidel Castro.

In 1962, the Soviets tried to build missile bases in Cuba. To stop Soviet ships, U.S. President John F. Kennedy set up a blockade around Cuba. The cold war nearly turned hot at that point. The Cuban missile crisis brought the world to the edge of another big war. However, Khrushchev agreed to take the missiles out of Cuba, and the situation cooled.

> **HISTORY FACT**
>
> Kennedy promised not to invade Cuba. He also said the United States would remove missiles from Turkey.

In 1963, Khrushchev's farm program collapsed. Russia had to buy a huge quantity of grain from the West. That year Soviet industrialization slowed down. Then Khrushchev came under heavy criticism for the way he had handled the Cuban situation. In 1964 he was forced to retire. Leonid Brezhnev and Alexei Kosygin replaced him as leaders of the Communist Party. Now life became worse for the people of the Soviet Union. Once again, people had to be very careful about what they said.

✓**Check Your Understanding**

Write your answers in complete sentences.

1. What was the Marshall Plan?

2. How was Germany divided after World War II?

3. What was the cold war?

Soviets and Americans Talk of Peace

Both the United States and the Soviet Union realized that another world war would bring disaster. Between the quarrels and the peaks of tension, they met to try to solve their problems. The two countries even set up a "hot line" to prevent the cold war from turning into a "hot" war. The hot line was a telephone line between the leaders of the United States and the Soviet Union.

Soviet and American officials began to talk about more cooperation between their countries. The new relationship was called **detente**. The nations began to share ideas in science and in space exploration. Trade relations improved.

U.S. President Richard M. Nixon and Leonid Brezhnev, general secretary of the Soviet Communist Party, signed the SALT agreement on May 26, 1972.

In 1972, the two powers held Strategic Arms Limitation Talks (SALT). They agreed to set some limits on nuclear arms. A second SALT agreement was later proposed. SALT II, however, was never **ratified,** or approved, by the U.S. Senate.

Increased Tensions

In 1979, the Communists took over the government of Afghanistan. The Muslim people of Afghanistan rebelled. Soviet troops went in to put down the rebellion. The United States, and many other nations were angered by the Soviet invasion of Afghanistan. The U.S. Congress even refused to approve the SALT II agreement.

During the early 1980s, tensions between the United States and the Soviet Union continued to increase. The United States sent more missiles to Europe. Then, in 1983, a Korean Air Lines passenger jet was shot down over Soviet territory. More than 200 people were killed, many of them Americans. The Soviets said the jet was spying. The United States was angry. Detente was over, and Soviet–U.S. relations grew even colder.

Timeline Study

In what year was a wall built to separate East and West Berlin?

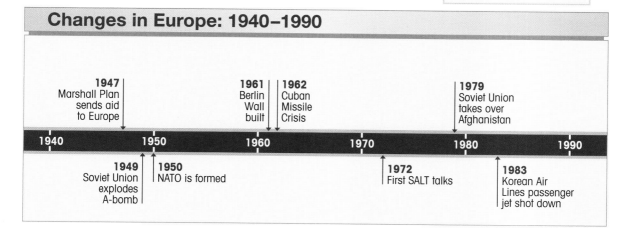

Changes in Europe: 1940–1990

1947 Marshall Plan sends aid to Europe

1961 Berlin Wall built

1962 Cuban Missile Crisis

1979 Soviet Union takes over Afghanistan

1940 — 1950 — 1960 — 1970 — 1980 — 1990

1949 Soviet Union explodes A-bomb

1950 NATO is formed

1972 First SALT talks

1983 Korean Air Lines passenger jet shot down

Summary

The Marshall Plan gave aid to war-torn Europe.

After World War II, Germany was divided into a democratic West Germany and a Communist-controlled East Germany.

The United States and the Soviet Union were allies during World War II. However, after the war, a cold war began between them.

The Soviet Union had Communist satellites in Eastern Europe, and it encouraged the spread of communism throughout the world.

The two superpowers held peace talks to try to limit the buildup of nuclear arms.

capitalist
satellite
detente
ratified
isolationism

Vocabulary Review

Write a term from the list that matches each definition below.

1. Officially approved

2. Running business and industry for profit

3. The relaxing of tensions between countries

4. The idea of staying out of international affairs

5. A country that is controlled by a more powerful country

Chapter Quiz

Write your answers in complete sentences.

1. What was the Marshall Plan?

2. How did the Communists decide to keep people from leaving East Berlin?

3. What is NATO?

4. **Critical Thinking** Why do you think progress was slow when Khrushchev tried to improve the standard of living in the Soviet Union?

5. **Critical Thinking** Suppose you lived in 1962. How do you think you would feel about the Cuban missile crisis?

Using the Timeline

Use the timeline on page 439 to answer the questions.

1. In what year was the Berlin Wall created?

2. In what year did the Soviets invade Afghanistan?

Write About History

Complete the following activity.

Form a group of three or four. Discuss whether you think the Olympics should be canceled or boycotted for political reasons. Write up your conclusion to share with the rest of the class.

Nelson Mandela, leader of the African National Congress (ANC), celebrates after his release from prison in 1990.

Learning Objectives

- Describe India's problems of civil war, religious differences, and widespread poverty.
- Tell how Mao Zedong and the Communists took over China.
- Describe Japan's role in the world economic community since World War II.
- Explain U.S. involvement in Vietnam.
- Explain the effects of apartheid inside South Africa.
- Describe the development of former colonies in Africa after World War II.

Chapter 30 / Changes in Asia and Africa

Words to Know

corrupt	dishonest, evil, selfish
commune	a group of people working or living closely together
guerrilla	one of a group of fighters who are not part of a regular army, and who usually make surprise raids behind enemy lines
refugee	a person who flees his or her country or home
minority	a smaller number, less than half
sanction	action taken by a nation against another for breaking international law
majority	a greater number, more than half
apartheid	the separation of races based mainly on skin color
curfew	a time after which certain people cannot be on the streets
repeal	to cancel; put an end to

India After World War II

In Chapter 23, you read about India winning its independence from Britain in 1947. At that time, Indian leaders agreed to divide India into two separate nations, India and Pakistan. India fell under the control of the Hindus. The Muslims controlled Pakistan. A further complication was the division of Pakistan into East and West Pakistan.

India held its first general election in 1951. Jawaharlal Nehru was elected as the first prime minister of the Republic of India. Nehru led India until he died in 1964. In 1966, his daughter Indira Gandhi was elected prime minister.

There were food shortages and labor strikes in India during Mrs. Gandhi's years as leader. For a time, she lost her position, but she returned to power in 1980. Then, in 1984, Indira Gandhi was assassinated by members of her own security force. The assassins were members of the Sikh religion. Sikh rebels were seeking a separate state in Punjab, their region of India. After Gandhi's assassination, her son Rajiv became prime minister. Rajiv resigned in 1989.

The late 1980s and early 1990s brought violence to several parts of India. A decision to bring the state of Punjab under the control of the central government led to fighting between Hindus and Sikhs. Muslim and Hindu Indians clashed over possession of a holy temple. In 1991, Rajiv Gandhi made another bid for the office of prime minister. He was assassinated during that election campaign.

Over the years, India has had border disputes with its neighbors. This led to fighting between India and China in 1959 and in 1962. In 1965, India and Pakistan fought a three-week-long war. Both countries claimed the same area called Kashmir, in northern India.

In 1971, civil war broke out in Pakistan. The people of East Pakistan complained because the center of government was based in West Pakistan. The war led to East Pakistan becoming a separate nation called Bangladesh. In 1998, India and Pakistan continued their rivalry. Both nations tested nuclear weapons to prove they could launch a nuclear attack on each other.

India's Problems

India has always had to deal with poverty and food shortages. The country has a huge population. It must struggle to provide enough food for all its people. India is a major producer of farm products. However, there is never enough food to go around.

Poverty and food shortages affect many people in India.

It is said that almost two-thirds of India's people go to bed hungry every night.

The government has tried to teach farmers new methods to increase production. It has allowed Western businesses to come in and build chemical factories. There was hope that the chemicals would increase crops. In general, India benefited from the chemicals. However, in 1984, an accident at one U.S. chemical plant caused the worst industrial disaster in history. There was an explosion at a factory in Bhopal, India. A cloud of highly toxic gas spread into the heavily populated area surrounding the plant. Several thousand people who breathed the poisonous fumes died.

India is trying to combat its poverty with programs for economic growth. Indian leaders try to build industry. They want to make better use of their country's resources, such as coal and iron ore. India also spends billions of dollars building dams to provide power.

Age-old customs contribute to the food shortages. While India has tried to industrialize, most of its people still cling to old ideas. In 1950, the government

You Decide

Millions of poor people live on the streets of India's cities. How do you think rich countries can help homeless people?

tried to improve life by outlawing the "untouchable" category in the Hindu caste system. Until then, people called untouchables had been forced to live in the dirtiest, poorest parts of villages. Their children were not allowed to go into schools. They had to sit on the steps outside and listen. When untouchables walked through village streets, they were supposed to brush away their footsteps with a broom. India has had to move beyond some old ideas to make life better for its people. In 1997, Indias first lowest caste president, K. R. Narayan, took office.

China After World War II

In the years after World War II, a power struggle was going on in China between two political parties. They were the Nationalists and the Communists.

Back in 1928, Jiang Jieshi and his Nationalist party had come to power. Some members of the Nationalist party believed in communism. The Communists felt that Jiang favored rich landowners and business people. Therefore, the Communists broke away from the Nationalists. In 1927, the Communists took over the city of Shanghai.

Jiang expelled the Communists from the Nationalist party. A struggle began between Chinese Nationalists and Chinese Communists. Stalin and the Soviet Union supported the Communists. Stalin encouraged them to win the support of China's factory workers.

China's strength however, did not lie in the city workers. It lay in the farm peasants. A man named Mao Zedong, who had been born a peasant, turned to the peasants for Communist strength.

During World War II, the Communists helped defend the peasants of northern China against the Japanese. Mao and the Communists won the peasants' loyalty.

After the war, the Communists and Nationalists continued their struggle for China. There were four years of civil war. The Nationalists had better supplies and a larger army. However, they no longer had the support of the people. Many Nationalist leaders were **corrupt.** They wanted to become rich themselves while the Chinese people went hungry. The Communists divided land and food fairly among the people. In this way, they received the peasants' support.

By 1948, the war had turned in favor of the Communists. Jiang Jieshi and the Nationalists decided it was time to get out. They left mainland China to live in Taiwan. In 1949, mainland China was taken over by Mao Zedong and the Communists. They called their nation the People's Republic of China.

This is a statue of Mao Zedong who set up a Communist government in mainland China.

The Soviet Union was quick to recognize the new government. So too were many other nations. Yet the United States refused to recognize the Communist government.

The United States recognized the Nationalist government in Taiwan and supported it. Taiwan, calling itself the Republic of China, kept China's seat in the United Nations. In 1971, mainland China replaced Taiwan in the U.N. In 1972, U.S. President Richard Nixon made an eight-day visit to the People's Republic. In 1979, the United States finally recognized the People's Republic of China or mainland China, as the only legal government of China. However, the United States continued many unofficial contacts with Taiwan.

You Decide

Why do you think it took so long for the United States to recognize the People's Republic of China?

Communism in China

More than one-fifth of the population of the world lives in China! Producing enough food to feed more than one and a quarter billion people is no simple matter. The Communists knew they had to solve that problem. They took land away from rich farmers.

They set up huge farm **communes.** The peasants had to work on these communes. Sometimes, as many as 10,000 people worked on a single commune. The government also took over industries, built new factories, and trained workers.

The Communists insisted on the support and loyalty of all the people. Workers had to attend meetings at which they read aloud from Mao Zedong's writings. They talked about how Mao's ideas could make them better citizens of a better China.

The Cultural Revolution

Mao and the Communists worried that people might prefer the Old China to the New China. They held their Communist meetings to teach people to think the Communist way. Enemies of communism were punished. They were brainwashed, or forced to accept the Communist way of thought.

For a while, Mao's harsh policies worked. However, from 1965 to 1968, there was a decline in China's economy. During this period, Mao called his policies a "Cultural Revolution." The Cultural Revolution was supposed to build loyalty for the Communists. Young students, called "Red Guards," became soldiers for communism. They helped Mao enforce his policies.

Farm production fell. China closed its doors to visitors from the rest of the world. The Chinese leaders wanted to make sure that no anti-Communist ideas could filter in.

After Mao's death in 1976, trade relations between China and the rest of the world improved. Under Deng Xiaoping and other leaders, China underwent a period of modernization.

Although Deng was willing to give the Chinese more economic freedom, he was not willing to grant political freedom. In the spring of 1989, hundreds of

HISTORY FACT

Today, Jiang Zemin is president of China. Zhu Rongji is premier. A group of leaders run China. They are committed to reforming industry in their country.

thousands of students gathered in Tiananmen Square in Beijing to demand more democracy. The demonstration was crushed by the army, as tanks rolled through the square. Since then, China and the West have disagreed over China's treatment of the protesters and others in the country. China had a fast-growing economy in the 1990s. China has allowed people to own businesses and trade with the West. In 2000, the U.S. Congress voted to give China permanent normal trade relations. Many people in the United States still worried about the lack of freedom and human rights in China.

Conflict in Korea

Korea, with its northern border on China, became a hot spot in the world in 1950. Korea had been controlled by the Japanese from 1910 to 1945. In 1945, the country was divided into two parts. North Korea had the support of Soviet Communists. South Korea had U.S. support.

In 1950, North Korea suddenly attacked South Korea. The Communists threatened to take over the whole country.

South Korea turned to the United Nations for help. A U.N. army made up mostly of U.S. soldiers came to South Korea's aid. The U.N. troops and South Koreans pushed the Communists back, almost to the Chinese border. The Chinese sent 780,000 soldiers to help North Korea.

The U.S.-South Korean troops fought the Chinese-North Korean troops for three years. In 1953, a truce was finally declared. The division between North and South Korea remained. Today the United States supports efforts to reunify Korea. In 2000, North Korea and South Korea held a summit. Later, some family members that had been separated held reunions in the capitals of South Korea and North Korea.

Japan After World War II

The explosion of the atomic bomb left Japan reeling. Japan surrendered, and World War II was over. Then the Allied forces occupied Japan. U.S. general Douglas MacArthur was the Supreme Commander. His job was to build a democracy in Japan.

A new democratic constitution, written in 1946, gave power to an elected prime minister. It also gave women the right to vote. Japan would be allowed to keep its emperor, but he would have no power. In 1951, the government was put back into the hands of the Japanese. The Allied occupation had ended.

The new Japanese constitution stated that Japan would not maintain a strong military. As a result, the Japanese turned from a policy of war to one of industrial and economic growth.

Today Japan has become a world leader in industry. Japan is one of the world's largest steel producers. It is the second largest manufacturer of automobiles and electronics equipment. It also is a leading shipbuilder. This is quite an accomplishment since Japan has few natural resources of its own. The country's industrial success depends on trade, the import of raw materials, and the export of finished products.

Japan is a small, crowded country. There is little room to grow food. Again Japan depends on imports, bringing in at least 30 percent of its food. Japan has also had to combat problems caused by overcrowding, such as pollution and housing shortages. However, Japan has made amazing progress.

Japan's economic success has brought criticism from other nations. The Japanese have been able to invest heavily in industry because they have a very low defense budget.

During the 1980s, some countries began to complain that competition from Japanese exports was hurting

You Decide

Japan is now one of the richest countries in the world. Why do you think Japan was able to become a great industrialized country after defeat in World War II?

their own industry. They also said that Japan was discouraging the import of foreign products. In 1981, Japan agreed to limit its exports of automobiles to Canada, the United States, and West Germany. It also began to remove some restrictions on imports. In 1990, Japan and the United States signed a trade agreement making it easier for foreign companies to do business in Japan. By the late 1990s, Japan, like other world powers over the years, had trade and economic difficulties.

Southeast Asia After World War II

Japan took over much of Southeast Asia during World War II. Before the war, all of the area, except Thailand, was colonized by European nations. After the war, anticolonial feelings were strong. The nations of Southeast Asia wanted to be free.

Some countries gained independence easily. Others had to struggle. When nations such as the Philippines, Burma, Indonesia, Malaysia, and Singapore became independent, they all faced problems. In many of them there were bitter civil wars.

Conflict in Vietnam

In the 1800s, France took over an area of Southeast Asia called Indochina. Indochina was made up of the countries of Vietnam, Laos, and Cambodia. During World War II, Japan took Southeast Asia from the French. Then France regained Southeast Asia after the war.

However, Southeast Asia was not anxious to return to French rule. Nationalists and Communists had gained a foothold there. In 1946, the fighting began. The Vietnamese Communists wanted to force the French out of Vietnam. The French set up a government in the South. The Communists, under their leader, Ho Chi Minh, set up a government in the North. The Communists defeated the French in 1954.

Then a conference was held in Geneva, Switzerland, to decide what would happen next. Vietnamese Communists and representatives from France, Cambodia, Laos, China, Britain, the United States, and the Soviet Union all came to that conference. They made their decision. Vietnam was divided into two zones. Ho Chi Minh and the Communists would continue to rule the North. South Vietnam was supposed to hold an election to choose its own form of government.

However, a free election never took place. Ngo Dinh Diem took leadership and refused to hold elections. Meanwhile, North Vietnam grew stronger with the support of Communist China and the Soviet Union. The political situation in South Vietnam remained unsettled.

The Vietcong, Communist **guerrilla** fighters, began an attempt to take over South Vietnam in 1957. In 1963, South Vietnam's leader, Diem, was assassinated. The country's problems increased. The government changed hands nine times in three years.

The United States Gets Involved

The Soviet Union and China continued to give aid to North Vietnam. In the 1960s, the U.S. government sent aid to South Vietnam because it believed in the domino theory. If dominoes are stood in a line together, the fall of one domino will knock down the others. The domino theory was the idea that if one country became Communist, neighbors would fall to the Communists, too.

At first, the United States sent money and supplies. Then in 1965, U.S. President Lyndon B. Johnson sent more than 3,500 U.S. marines to Da Nang, South Vietnam. They were the first U.S. combat troops to join the fight. Thousands more would follow. By 1969, there were more than 543,000 U.S. troops in Vietnam.

Americans Protest U.S. Involvement

Many Americans did not want the United States to get into the war in Southeast Asia. When American soldiers began dying in Vietnamese jungles, the protests grew stronger. Hundreds of thousands of people marched against the war, in cities all across America. "Bring home our troops!" they shouted.

However, the war went on. More and more Americans were killed or wounded. The Vietcong remained strong. There did not seem to be any end in sight.

By the end of the decade, the United States was a nation in turmoil. The growing antiwar movement had helped to touch off a general youth protest movement. The middle-class youth of America were questioning and protesting all the values of their parents.

Also during the 1960s, there had been a series of assassinations that had shocked the nation. President John F. Kennedy, in 1963, and his brother Robert F. Kennedy, in 1968, had been shot to death. So had

You Decide
Antiwar protesters felt that the war in Vietnam was a matter that should be fought and decided by the Vietnamese themselves. Do you think they were right to protest against the war? Why or why not?

Antiwar demonstrators protested American involvement in Vietnam.

African American leaders Malcolm X, in 1965, and Martin Luther King, Jr. in 1968. This was the last straw for many African Americans. They were becoming angry and frustrated at not being able to share in the prosperity of white America. Now feeling that they had nothing to lose, they took their cause to the streets. Rioting occurred in many U.S. cities.

In 1973, the United States decided to take its troops out of Vietnam. About 58,000 Americans had been killed. About 365,000 had been wounded. Furthermore, the war had not been won.

In general, the 1970s in the United States was a quieter time than the 1960s. However, one more great shock was in store for Americans. In 1972, a team of burglars broke into Democratic headquarters in a building called the Watergate. They were caught. There was a long investigation. The burglars proved to have been working for people in the White House. The White House attempted a cover-up. When the cover-up failed, President Richard Nixon had to resign from office in August 1974.

People everywhere mourned when Dr. Martin Luther King, Jr. was assassinated on April 4, 1968.

Refugees from Communism:
The Boat People

In 1975, Saigon, the capital of South Vietnam, fell to the Vietcong. The name of the city was changed to Ho Chi Minh City. Vietnam was united as a Communist country in 1976. Then the "dominoes" fell. Communists took power in Laos and Cambodia.

The Communist rulers of Cambodia, called the *Khmer Rouge,* murdered millions of Cambodians. The situation in Cambodia became very unstable. In 1978, Vietnam invaded Cambodia. For the next ten years, Vietnam had control of the country. In 1989, Vietnam withdrew from Cambodia, giving in to pressure from the Soviet Union. Since then, the Khmer Rouge has lost its power. National elections were held in 1998.

Many people in Vietnam, Laos, and Cambodia did not want to live under Communist rule. They fled their homelands. Many **refugees** escaped by boat.

Vietnamese refugees sought freedom from communism.

They became known as "boat people"—people who no longer had a home. A large number came to the United States. Some died making their escapes. All suffered hardships along their way. Today many boat people have made successful lives in the United States.

Africa After World War II

Remember
The European colonial powers had carved up Africa without considering traditional boundaries.

During the nineteenth century, Africa was divided into European-ruled colonies. In 1945, at the end of World War II, most of Africa remained under European rule. Exceptions were the countries of South Africa, Ethiopia, Liberia, and Egypt. Many Africans joined the armies of their European colonizers during the war. When they returned to Africa, they wanted independence.

The years after 1945 saw European colonies in Africa gain freedom, one by one. Some won their independence peacefully. For other nations such as Algeria, freedom came only through struggle and revolt.

Several colonies ruled by the British gained independence during the 1950s. Sudan, the largest nation in Africa, won freedom from Britain in 1956. Some of the free nations changed their names. When the Gold Coast won its freedom in 1957, it became Ghana.

Kenya was an African nation that had to struggle for independence from Britain. A rebellion by a group known as the *Mau Mau* lasted from 1952 until 1956. Jomo Kenyatta was their leader. He was thrown in jail in 1953. Britain granted independence to Kenya in 1963. Then Kenyatta became the leader of the new, free nation. In the 1990s, Kenya suffered unemployment and conflict within the country. In 1998, the U.S. embassy in Nairobi was bombed. The United States blamed bin Laden, a terrorist.

Freedom Brings New Problems

Freedom did not always mean an end to problems and unrest. The new nations had troubles of their own. In 1966, the eastern part of Nigeria separated and became a country called Biafra. This led to civil war. With the war came starvation, disease, and death. Biafra was defeated by the Nigerian government in 1970. As a separate country, Biafra no longer existed.

Problems plagued Uganda when General Idi Amin took over the independent government in 1971. Amin arrested and executed anyone he thought was against him. Finally, the people revolted. In 1979, they forced Amin from power. Civil wars and military strife have also taken place in Angola, Ethiopia, Rwanda, Sudan, and other countries. In Ethiopia, this strife contributed to a famine that killed about one million people in the 1980s. Again, in 2000, Ethiopia was threatened with famine after a 3-year drought.

Rhodesia Wins Black Majority Rule

Independence did not bring an end to racial prejudice in some new African nations. Sometimes, those nations had more problems with the new governments than with the European rulers. When Rhodesia gained independence from Britain in 1965, black Africans had no voice in government. A white **minority** ruled for 15 years.

Britain wanted black Rhodesians to have rights. However, the new white rulers said no. Britain asked the United Nations to place **sanctions** on Rhodesia. Black revolutionaries began a guerrilla war.

In 1980, Rhodesia's first black **majority** government finally came to power through a general election. The new government officially changed the nation's name. Rhodesia became Zimbabwe, an ancient African name for that part of the continent.

> **HISTORY FACT**
>
> In April 2000, Ethiopia's president Robert Mugabe introduced a new distribution of land. Violence against white farmers resulted. White people hold 70 percent of the land in Ethiopia, although they make up only 1 percent of the population.

South Africans celebrate together in Capetown, South Africa.

A Changing South Africa

Of all the independent countries in Africa, South Africa was ruled by a white minority for the longest period of time. It was ruled by *Afrikaners* for many years. They were descendants of Dutch colonists who began settling in South Africa as early as 1652. The Afrikaners felt that the country belonged to them. They helped win South Africa's independence from Britain in 1910.

The Afrikaners wanted to keep white people in control. In 1948, they set up a policy of **apartheid**, or separation of races. They passed laws to separate people according to race. By law, people of certain races could live, own property, or run businesses only in certain zones.

Curfews regulated the time black people had to be off the streets of South Africa. Separate trains, beaches, schools, and other facilities were provided for blacks and whites. Laws did nothing to stop whites from getting the best facilities and blacks the worst.

You Decide

What do you think were the worst aspects of apartheid?

Many people in South Africa and around the world were strongly against apartheid. However, many South Africans who protested were arrested, and apartheid continued nevertheless.

During the 1980s, the United States and other countries placed sanctions on South Africa. The white South African government now came under growing pressure to do something about ending apartheid.

In 1990, South African president F. W. de Klerk decided to "unban" the African National Congress (ANC). This meant that the ANC, a black anti-apartheid political party, would now be legal. De Klerk also released the jailed leader of the ANC, Nelson Mandela. Both leaders began working together on a difficult task. They had to find a way to end apartheid that would be acceptable to both blacks and whites.

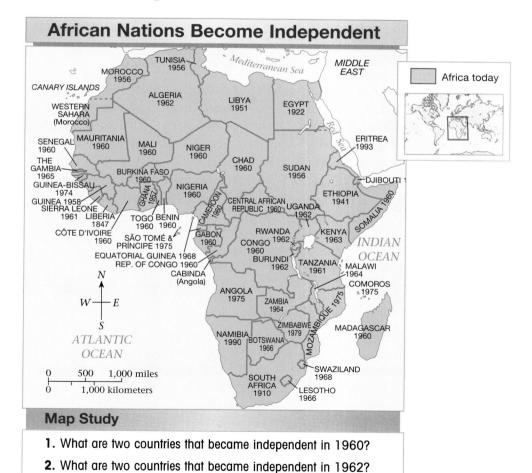

African Nations Become Independent

Africa today

Map Study

1. What are two countries that became independent in 1960?

2. What are two countries that became independent in 1962?

In 1990 and 1991, the South African government **repealed** its apartheid laws. No longer was segregation of hotels, restaurants, and public places required by law. No longer could laws determine where a person could live. Nelson Mandela, as well as other anti-apartheid leaders, looked forward to the day when the black majority would be heard in government. A constitution giving nonwhites full voting rights was completed in 1994. After the repeal of the apartheid laws, countries around the world lifted their sanctions against South Africa.

Change does not often come easily. There are many South Africans who resisted the end of apartheid. However, change did come. A new constitution protected the rights of all South Africans. In 1994, Nelson Mandela became the president of South Africa. He served until 1999, when he chose not to run for reelection.

There have been other political changes in South Africa in recent years. A conflict dating back to 1915 came to an end. In that year, South Africa took control of its neighbor, Namibia, away from Germany. For the next 75 years, South Africa ruled Namibia. The United Nations declared South Africa's rule of Namibia to be illegal. Black nationalists fought to rule their own country. In 1990, Namibia became independent.

Africa Today

At one time, Africa was mistakenly called the "Dark Continent." To outsiders, it was an unexplored land of mystery. Later, it became a land to be owned, and it was divided up among strong European countries. Then World War II ended the days of European-ruled colonies in Africa. The new nations of Africa, however, continue to face serious problems such as poverty, disease, and food shortages. Many areas lack schools, hospitals, and medical equipment.

Severe droughts have added to Africa's food shortages. During the 1980s, many Africans starved to death in the worst drought in the continent's history. The death toll was especially high in Ethiopia.

In recent years, drought and civil war left over one million Africans starving in the nation of Somalia. Since 1960, various Somali warlords had battled for control of parts of the country. Their armies blocked attempts to get food to starving people. In December 1992, the United States and the United Nations approved a plan to aid the Somalis. U.S. troops led an international force to Somalia. Soon after, UN forces left because of the fighting.

Africa is the second largest continent on Earth. It has been slow to develop. Today, however, free African nations are growing stronger. More Africans are attending school. They are developing the skills needed to improve their standard of living. African nations are learning to work together. The Organization of African Unity (OAU) is an association of African nations that tries to find peaceful solutions to quarrels between African countries. They hope that unity will lead to economic and political progress. As the nations grow stronger, Africa takes a place of greater importance in the world.

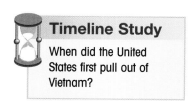

Timeline Study

When did the United States first pull out of Vietnam?

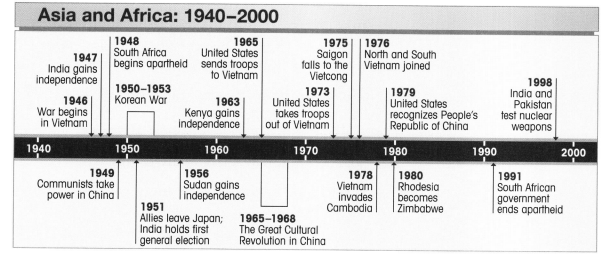

Asia and Africa: 1940–2000

1947 India gains independence

1948 South Africa begins apartheid

1965 United States sends troops to Vietnam

1975 Saigon falls to the Vietcong

1976 North and South Vietnam joined

1946 War begins in Vietnam

1950–1953 Korean War

1963 Kenya gains independence

1973 United States takes troops out of Vietnam

1979 United States recognizes People's Republic of China

1998 India and Pakistan test nuclear weapons

1940 — 1950 — 1960 — 1970 — 1980 — 1990 — 2000

1949 Communists take power in China

1956 Sudan gains independence

1978 Vietnam invades Cambodia

1980 Rhodesia becomes Zimbabwe

1991 South African government ends apartheid

1951 Allies leave Japan; India holds first general election

1965–1968 The Great Cultural Revolution in China

Summary

India is the world's largest democracy. Border disputes, religious conflicts, and food shortages are among the problems of India and its neighbors Pakistan and Bangladesh.
In 1949, the Communists gained power in mainland China. The Nationalists left the mainland for Taiwan. Communist China has not granted its people political freedom, but it has allowed more private ownership and trade with the West.
The United States fought wars in Korea and Vietnam on the anti-Communist side. Many Americans protested against U.S. involvement in the Vietnam War.
Many European colonies in Africa gained independence after 1945.
In South Africa, apartheid officially began in 1948 and ended in 1991. In 1990, Nelson Mandela, head of the African National Congress, was released from jail. He eventually became president of the country.
African nations struggle to solve problems of poverty, disease, and food shortages. Many are growing stronger, despite their history of colonial rule.

Vocabulary Review

Write *true* or *false*. If the statement is false, change the underlined term to make it true.

1. A <u>refugee</u> is a fighter who makes surprise raids from behind enemy lines.

2. A blockade is one form of <u>sanction</u> by one nation against another.

3. In a <u>commune,</u> a group of people live closely together and may share many things.

4. A <u>sanction</u> is a time when certain people must be off the streets.

5. A <u>minority</u> is more than half.

Chapter Quiz

Write your answers in complete sentences.

1. What was outlawed in India in 1950?

2. How did Mao and the Communists win the support of Chinese peasants?

3. What major change happened in Africa after World War II?

4. **Critical Thinking** How did the limits on the Japanese military help the Japanese economy after World War II? Give two examples.

5. **Critical Thinking** Do you think you would have liked being a young person in the 1960s? Tell about Vietnam and other important events in your answer.

Using the Timeline

Use the timeline on page 461 to answer the questions.

1. After World War II ended, how long did the Allies stay in Japan?

2. When did apartheid end in South Africa?

Write About History

Complete the following activity.

Work with a partner. Find a recent news story about one of the countries in this chapter. Write three questions that can be answered by the news story. Then read the story to your class, or tell about it in your own words. After you finish the story, ask your classmates the questions.

President Bill Clinton looks on as Israeli Prime Minister Yitzhak Rabin, left, and Palestine Liberation Organization (PLO) Chairman Yasser Arafat shake hands after signing a peace accord.

Learning Objectives

- Tell why Jews considered Palestine their homeland.
- Tell why Arabs thought that Palestine should be theirs.
- Explain why many Palestinians ended up in refugee camps.
- Describe the results of Anwar Sadat's visit to Israel in 1977.
- List the conflicts that continue in the Middle East today.
- Discuss the importance of oil to the Middle East and the world.

Chapter 31 The Middle East

Words to Know

Zionism	the movement to set up a Jewish nation in Palestine
hostile	unfriendly, showing hate or dislike
traitor	one who betrays a cause, a friend, or a nation
terrorist	a fighter who hopes to achieve certain goals by using force and random violence to frighten people
hostage	a person held prisoner by an enemy until certain demands are met

Nationalism in the Middle East

People of the Middle East were often ruled by other lands. For hundreds of years, the Middle East was part of the Ottoman Empire. After World War I, most of the Middle East fell under British control. Egypt, however, gained its independence from Britain in 1922. Meanwhile, France took control of Syria and Lebanon.

World War II weakened the European countries. This left the door open for Arab nationalists to gain independence for their countries. Most important, Arabs took control of their own oil fields. Oil deposits had been discovered in Iraq in 1927 and in Saudi Arabia in 1938. More huge oil fields were later found along the Persian Gulf. European and U.S. oil companies had moved in to control the oil fields. The Middle Eastern nations saw little of their own oil wealth. However, after World War II, many Arab nations gained tremendous riches and power because of their oil.

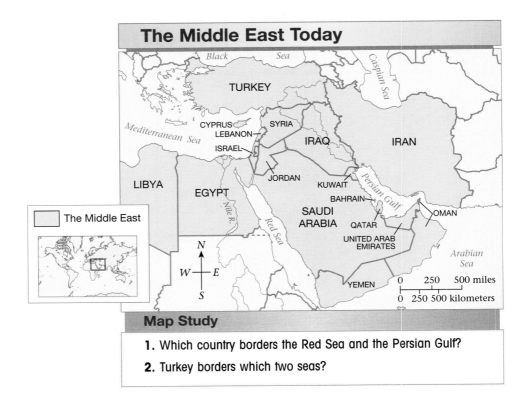

The Middle East Today

The Middle East

Map Study

1. Which country borders the Red Sea and the Persian Gulf?
2. Turkey borders which two seas?

A Jewish Homeland in Palestine

In ancient days, the Jews considered Palestine their homeland. They called it a land promised to them by God. They built a temple in Jerusalem, the holy city.

Almost 2,000 years ago, the Romans drove the Jews out of Palestine. Some Jews settled in an area of Palestine called Galilee. However, most of the Jews fled from Palestine. They scattered around the world.

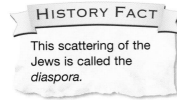

HISTORY FACT

This scattering of the Jews is called the *diaspora.*

Many Jews never gave up their dream of the promised homeland. In the late 1800s, Jews in Eastern Europe were persecuted. Some Jews started a movement called **Zionism.** Their goal was to make Palestine an independent Jewish nation. Jews from Europe began to settle in Palestine, which at that time was ruled by the Ottoman Turks.

By 1914, about 85,000 Jews were living there. After World War I, Britain promised to create a Jewish homeland in Palestine. Meanwhile, the Arab population of Palestine had been increasing, too. There was a problem. The Arabs living there did not like that Jews were moving into Palestine.

After World War II, Zionism became more popular. Jews who had felt Hitler's persecution were ready for a homeland of their own. Many came to Palestine.

The State of Israel

In 1947, the United Nations voted to end British rule over Palestine. The U.N. knew there was a conflict between Arabs and Jews in Palestine. Arabs said the land had been theirs for 2,000 years. Jews said it had been theirs before the Arabs. Therefore, the United Nations divided Palestine into two parts. One part was for Jews and the other for Arabs. The Jews agreed to the U.N. plan. However, the Arabs were angry. They wanted all of Palestine to be an Arab state.

On May 14, 1948, David Ben-Gurion, the Zionist leader in Palestine, read a declaration of independence. He declared that the Jewish part of Palestine was the new state of Israel.

Israel was recognized immediately by the United States and then by the Soviet Union. The Arab nations declared war on Israel. On May 15, 1948, Israel was invaded by armies from the Arab nations of Syria, Egypt, Lebanon, Iraq, and Jordan.

Refugees of War

The Israelis were greatly outnumbered. They also had a shortage of weapons. However, Israel won the war against many odds. An agreement between Israel and Arab states was signed in 1949. The state of Israel was firmly established. The lands left to the Arabs became part of Jordan.

You Decide

Do you think the U.N. was wise to divide Palestine into two parts?

About 700,000 Arabs fled Israel, becoming refugees. The homeless Palestinian Arabs lived in crowded refugee camps outside of Israel. Many still live there. These Palestinian refugees believed that their homes were stolen. Some of them formed a group of fighters called the Palestine Liberation Organization (PLO). Their goal is to win back their land.

After the war in 1948, about 700,000 Jews living in Arab nations were forced to leave. Jews left Iraq, Yemen, Libya, and other countries. Most went to live in Israel.

Israel had won the 1948 war. However, the problems of the Middle East were far from settled.

Middle East Tensions

Soon the superpowers became involved in the Israeli-Arab conflict. In 1955, the Soviets offered to sell arms to Egypt. This was followed by a conflict over the Suez Canal.

In 1956, Egypt took over the canal from Britain and France. Britain, France, and Israel then attacked Egypt. The United Nations arranged a cease-fire. The Suez Canal was held by Egypt. The Arabs, however, became even more **hostile** toward Israel.

In June 1967, another war began. Israel fought the Arab nations of Egypt, Jordan, and Syria. In the first few minutes of the war, Israeli planes attacked the Arab airfields. Almost all of the Arab airplanes were destroyed on the ground. Then the Israeli army pushed through the Sinai Peninsula all the way to the Suez Canal. The war was over in six days! Israel occupied all of the Sinai Peninsula, the Gaza Strip, and the West Bank. The West Bank was the section of Palestine that had become part of Jordan. Israel also took control of East Jerusalem.

Arab nations grew angrier. In 1973, Egypt, Syria, Jordan, and Iraq launched a surprise attack on Israel. It was called the *Yom Kippur War* because the Arabs attacked on the Jewish holy day called *Yom Kippur*. This time, the Arabs almost won. Israel managed to defend itself. However, it paid a high price in the number of lives lost.

You Decide

What do you think would have happened to Israel if it had lost any of its wars?

✓ **Check Your Understanding**

Write your answers in complete sentences.

1. Why did the Jews consider Palestine their homeland?

2. Why did the Arabs think Palestine belonged to them?

3. Why was the war in 1973 called the Yom Kippur War?

Families in the disputed city of Palestine live in sometimes hostile surroundings.

Learn More About It

ANWAR SADAT

In 1977, Egypt's president Anwar el-Sadat visited Israel. His visit surprised the world. It was the first move toward peace with Israel that any Arab leader had ever made. Then U.S. President Jimmy Carter invited Sadat and Israel's prime minister, Menachem Begin, to the United States. There the three leaders held discussions on how to end the Israeli-Arab conflict. These meetings led to the signing of the Camp David Accords in 1979. Israel promised to return all of the Sinai Peninsula to Egypt in exchange for peace. Israel also promised to allow the Palestinians in Gaza and on the West Bank to govern themselves.

Much of the world praised Sadat. In 1978, Sadat and Begin shared the Nobel Peace Prize. However, many Arab nationalists were angry. They said that Sadat was a **traitor** to the Arab cause. In 1981, Sadat was assassinated by extremists.

Middle East Conflicts Today

The fighting in the Middle East was not over. The Palestine Liberation Organization (PLO) still wanted a home for Palestinians. In 1970, the PLO was forced out of Jordan. In 1975, it became involved in a civil war in Lebanon.

From bases in Lebanon, the PLO carried out **terrorist** attacks into Israel. Palestinian terrorists were also active in other parts of the world.

In 1982, Israel invaded Lebanon in order to destroy PLO bases. The PLO was forced to leave Lebanon. However, once the Israeli army withdrew from Lebanon, the PLO came back.

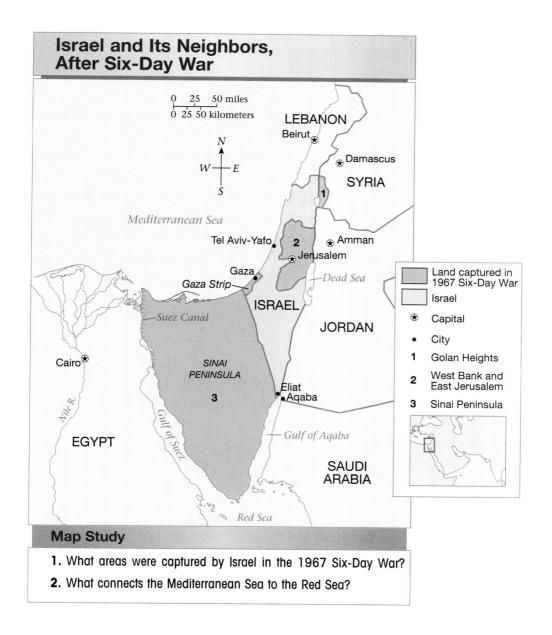

Israel and Its Neighbors, After Six-Day War

Land captured in 1967 Six-Day War
Israel
⊛ Capital
• City
1 Golan Heights
2 West Bank and East Jerusalem
3 Sinai Peninsula

Map Study

1. What areas were captured by Israel in the 1967 Six-Day War?

2. What connects the Mediterranean Sea to the Red Sea?

In December 1987, violent protests by Palestinians broke out in the West Bank and Gaza. The uprising, known as the *intifada,* continued until the 1990s. The Palestinians want an independent state. They are especially angry that Israel allows Jewish settlers to take away some of their land. However, the Israelis have given control of some of the Gaza Strip and the West Bank back to the Palestinians.

The PLO has agreed to stop acts of terrorism, and it began negotiating with Israel. Israelis have a difficult choice to make. They can give up the occupied lands and hope that this will bring about a lasting peace. This is the question they face as they negotiate with the Palestinians and Arabs.

In January 2001, hopes for peace seemed stalemated again. Despite a great deal of involvement by U.S. President Bill Clinton, sticking points, such as the future of Jerusalem, remained unresolved.

Lebanon's civil war began in 1975 and lasted until 1990. Muslims battled Christians for power. Different Muslim groups also battled each other. In 1983, the United States became involved in the war. U.S. troops entered Lebanon as peace-keepers. The troops were taken out of Lebanon only after many U.S. Marines were killed by Muslim terrorists. Syria also sent troops into Lebanon, who used force to end the civil war in 1990.

The civil war all but destroyed Lebanon, leaving its cities in shambles. Beirut, the capital of Lebanon, had been known as the "Paris" of the Middle East. Much of it was left in ruins.

The country of Iran has seen conflict, too. Iranians were unhappy with their leader, the Shah. The Shah had a vicious secret police who ensured he kept power.

In 1979, a 76-year-old Muslim leader, the Ayatollah Khomeini, returned to Iran from exile in France. Khomeini led a successful revolution against the Shah.

He then set up a Muslim republic following strict Islamic rules. Khomeini's followers wanted the Shah to stand trial for crimes they said he had committed. However, the Shah had fled to the United States. Then in November 1979, Iranians captured the U.S. embassy in Teheran, Iran's capital. They took American **hostages,** and they demanded the Shah's return.

Much of the world was angered by the Iranian action. However, Iran would not give up the hostages. The Shah died in Egypt in July 1980. Finally, in January 1981, the American hostages were freed.

Meanwhile, in 1980, Iran was attacked by its neighbor, Iraq. There had been bitter disputes over territory. Iraq hoped to win a quick victory over Iran. Saddam Hussein, leader of Iraq, thought that Iran had been weakened by the Islamic revolution. However, neither nation could beat the other. The war dragged on for many years.

American hostages arrive at Andrews Air Force Base *in the United States after their release.*

There were huge land battles. Then both sides began firing missiles at each other's cities. In addition, each country began to attack oil tankers in the Persian Gulf. In 1987, the U.S. sent its navy to the Gulf to protect the flow of oil.

Finally, in 1988, the United Nations was able to arrange a cease-fire between Iran and Iraq. Both countries had suffered such huge losses that they were willing to begin talking about ending the war.

Remember
The United Nations has been very involved in Middle East relations. In 1947, the U.N. voted to end British rule over Palestine and divided Palestine into two parts.

The Persian Gulf War

In August 1990, Iraq invaded the small neighboring nation of Kuwait. Iraqi leader Saddam Hussein wanted to make Kuwait and its rich oil fields a part of his country. Kuwait fell only hours after the Iraqi attack.

Saddam Hussein continues to threaten world peace.

The United Nations protested Iraq's capture of Kuwait. When Iraq threatened the border of Saudi Arabia, the United States and other nations sent their own military forces to the Persian Gulf. They were ready to defend Saudi Arabia against a possible Iraqi invasion and to liberate Kuwait.

On November 29, 1990, the United Nations sent Hussein a warning. It would use "all necessary means" if Iraq did not withdraw from Kuwait by January 15, 1991. Hussein did not respond to the warning, and, on the evening of January 16, bombs and missiles began to rain down on Iraq. A ground war began on February 23. By February 28, Kuwait was free, and a cease-fire had begun.

The Gulf War ended when Kuwait was freed. The war did not, however, destroy Saddam Hussein's control over Iraq or his threats of aggression. Saddam Hussein refused to cooperate with U.N. inspections to see that he was not building weapons of mass destruction. In the year 2001, Saddam Hussein was still a threat to world peace.

Peace Talks Bring Progress

In the 1990s, the United States and Russia sponsored peace conferences between Israel and the Arab nations of the Middle East. Israeli, Palestinian, and Arab leaders agreed to meet to try to cool heated conflicts. They wanted to make the Middle East more stable. Progress is slow. Israel has given the Palestinians control over some of the occupied lands. Israel and Jordan have also signed a peace treaty. In early 2000, the United States helped move Syria and Israel toward peace. However, by early 2001, the peace talks had broken down because Israel refused to give up the Golan Heights.

Oil pipelines run through Saudi Arabian oil fields. Saudi Arabia has the richest known oil reserves of any country in the world.

Oil Power

You Decide

Do you think it is good for the United States to be so dependent on Middle East oil?

Much of the Middle East has oil. All nations need oil, and world supplies are limited. The Middle East's oil fields give the Arab countries power.

An organization called OPEC (Organization of Petroleum Exporting Countries) manages that power. OPEC members include the oil-producing nations of the Middle East, Asia, and Africa, as well as the South American country of Venezuela.

OPEC sets the price of oil. OPEC can force up oil prices or withhold oil from certain countries. This gives OPEC tremendous power. During the Israeli-Arab wars of 1967 and 1973, the Arabs used their oil as a weapon. They cut off the flow of oil to the West. In 1973, this resulted in a severe oil shortage in the United States. Drivers were forced to wait in long lines at the gas pumps. They also had to pay a much higher price for each gallon they bought. Through the 1990s and into the twenty-first century, OPEC used its power to control other countries.

Some people in the Middle East are very, very wealthy because of oil. However, much of the oil wealth remains in the hands of a few. Most profits from oil sales go toward building a strong Arab military.

Most Middle East oil comes from Saudi Arabia. Another important oil producer is Libya. In 1969, Muammar al-Qaddafi came to power after he and his followers overthrew the king of Libya. Qaddafi has shown great interest in expanding his country's borders. He tried to seize territory from Chad, the country that borders Libya on the south.

In April of 1986, a disco in West Berlin that was popular with American service people was bombed. Two people were killed and 200 were injured. The United States learned that Libya was responsible for this act. In retaliation, U.S. warplanes struck targets in Libya.

Qaddafi spent much of Libya's oil profits on new weapons and a stronger army. He also supported terrorist actions against Americans and Israelis. However, in 2001, a top official in Libya said his country was prepared to restore its ties with the United States.

Life in the Middle East

The Middle East is, without a doubt, a land of war and conflict. It faces serious problems that will have to be dealt with. Still, the Middle East has fine, modern cities, well-educated people, fertile farmlands, and productive industries.

Israel is one of the most industrialized and advanced nations of the Middle East. About 85 percent of Israel's people live and work in modern cities. Israel's farms are a source of pride. Most of Israel's land is poor. Some of the land is too rocky or steep for farming. Other areas get little rainfall. Only through hard work and agricultural know-how could those lands be productive. Still, Israel produces most of its own food.

Land in Israel along the Sea of Galilee is fertile due to irrigation and the hard work of the Israeli people.

Huge irrigation systems pump in water through underground pipelines. Scientists experiment with turning saltwater from the Mediterranean and Red seas into fresh water to soak their fields.

The Israelis have not won the perfect land. However, they have worked hard to build their nation.

Long before the first century A.D. the first civilizations were forming along the Tigris and Euphrates rivers and along the Nile River. Those early peoples concerned themselves with producing food and irrigating dry lands. They battled invaders who would take their lands. They argued over how they would worship their gods. In some ways, those people had much in common with today's Middle Eastern people.

Timeline Study

During which year did militant Iranians capture the U.S. embassy in Teheran?

The Middle East: 1940–2001

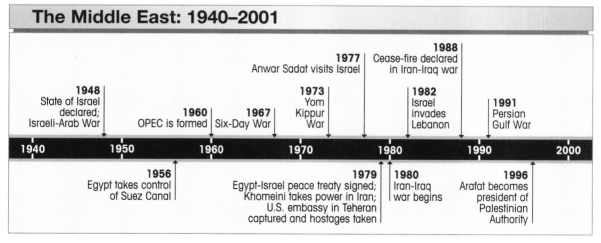

Chapter

31 Review

Summary

Most Middle Eastern nations gained Independence from Britain and France after World War II.
Zionists wanted to set up a Jewish state in Palestine. The United Nations divided Palestine between Arabs and Jews.
In 1948, the Jews set up the state of Israel. The remaining lands of Palestine became part of the Arab state of Jordan. Since 1948, Arabs and Israelis have fought wars for control of those lands. Conflict or the threat of conflict continues.
Many Palestinians who had fled from Israel were forced to live in crowded refugee camps. They formed the PLO and demanded their lands back.
In 1990, Iraq invaded its neighbor, Kuwait. In the Persian Gulf War, the United States and other nations used military force to free Kuwait.
Many Arab nations have wealth and power because of the world's dependence on their oil.

Zionism
hostile
traitor
terrorist
hostage

Vocabulary Review

Complete each sentence with a term from the list.

1. A _____ may not be freed until certain demands are met.

2. A person who betrays his or her country by giving its secrets away is a _____.

3. An unfriendly nation is _____.

4. The movement to create a Jewish state in Palestine is _____.

5. A _____ tries to bring about change by frightening people with random violence.

Chapter Quiz

Write your answers in complete sentences.

1. Why did many Palestinians end up in refugee camps in the late 1940s?

2. Why was Anwar Sadat's visit to Israel important?

3. Why did the United States and other nations fight against Iraq in the Gulf War?

4. **Critical Thinking** Do you think the United States should try to help bring peace to the Middle East? Why or why not?

5. **Critical Thinking** How do you think the United States and other countries could become less dependent on Middle Eastern oil?

Using the Timeline

Use the timeline on page 479 to answer the questions.

1. When did the oil-rich nations of the Middle East form their own organization?

2. Which came first, the Six-Day War or the Yom Kippur War?

Write About History

Complete the following activity.

Write a poem about your hopes for peace in the Middle East. Revise the poem as needed. Practice reading your poem, and present it to the rest of the class.

Boris Yeltsin led Russia to democracy and freedom after the Soviet Union collapsed.

Learning Objectives

- List three changes in the Soviet Union for which Mikhail Gorbachev was responsible.

- Explain how the Soviet Union disbanded and became an alliance of independent republics.

- Discuss the importance of Boris Yeltsin as leader of an independent Russia.

- Recognize the freedom movement that swept Eastern Europe in the late 1980s.

- Identify leaders and events in Russia since the collapse of the Soviet Union.

The Death of the Soviet Union

Chapter 32

Words to Know

hostility	feelings of hate or acts of war
coup	a bold, sudden move to bring about change in a government
reunification	the act of joining together again

Some of the most dramatic changes in recent history occurred within the Soviet Union and its Eastern European satellites during the late 1980s and early 1990s. Soviet policy turned from militarism and aggression to a freer and more open society. After years of cold war, the Soviet Union and the United States, the world's two superpowers, began to make peace.

Changes in the Soviet Union began in 1985 when a man named Mikhail Gorbachev came to power. Gorbachev introduced new policies within the Soviet Union and improved Soviet relations with other nations.

Mikhail Gorbachev Works to Improve Relations

Friendly relations with western countries were important to Gorbachev's plans for the Soviet Union. Good relations, he hoped, would lead to trade agreements and economic improvements. They might also lead to a more secure and peaceful world. In 1987, Gorbachev and U.S. President Ronald Reagan signed the INF Treaty (Intermediate-Range Nuclear Force Treaty). For the first time, both sides agreed to get rid of an entire class of nuclear weapons. In 1991, the Strategic Arms Reduction Treaty (START) was signed in Moscow.

Gorbachev and U.S. President George Bush agreed to the treaty. It would reduce nuclear weapons on both sides by 30 percent.

Gorbachev took other steps to show that his country had changed its attitude toward the West. In 1989, he brought Soviet troops home from Afghanistan. He agreed to stop supplying military aid to the Communist Sandinista government in Nicaragua (see Chapter 33). He pressured Cuba's Communist leader, Fidel Castro, to bring home the Cuban troops from Angola in Africa. They had been involved in a civil war there. Gorbachev also persuaded Vietnam to withdraw its forces from Cambodia.

Gorbachev and *Glasnost*

Although Mikhail Gorbachev was a Communist, he encouraged his nation to be more open to information and ideas from the democratic West. He put into action a policy of *glasnost,* or "openness." Suddenly, Soviet citizens had more freedom of speech and basic human rights than ever before.

A new branch of the Soviet government was set up. Its members were directly elected by the people. Soviet citizens could choose people they wanted to represent them in the government. The newly elected people did not even have to be members of the Communist Party. For the first time, the Communist leaders had to listen to the opinions and complaints of the Soviet people.

The policy of *glasnost* led many of the republics within the Soviet Union to demand the right to manage their own affairs. The Baltic states of Estonia, Latvia, and Lithuania even went so far as to seek outright independence from Moscow.

You Decide

How would you feel if you were a Soviet citizen and were able to vote for the first time?

One unfortunate result of *glasnost* was an increase in **hostilities** between different national groups within the Soviet Union. In many places, longstanding disagreements boiled over into outbreaks of violence. For example, violence broke out between Armenians and Azerbaijanis as to who owned a particular territory in the Caucasus Mountains. Many people were killed as a result.

Gorbachev knew that by the late 1980s, the Soviet economy was in serious trouble. He also knew that he would have to make major changes in order to see any improvement. Therefore, he proposed a policy of *perestroika,* or "restructuring." Factories and businesses around the country would no longer be controlled by Moscow. Each would be responsible for running its own operations. In addition, individual Soviet citizens would be allowed to engage in small-scale private business.

Mikhail Gorbachev

Gorbachev also welcomed U.S. corporations to set up joint operations in the Soviet Union. A number of U.S. companies signed agreements with the Soviets. In Moscow, the largest fast-food restaurant of a major U.S. chain of restaurants opened for business.

Many people in both the Soviet Union and the United States were declaring that the cold war was finally over. Yet in spite of all the changes taking place, Soviet citizens had questions. Would Gorbachev's plans be successful? What would happen if Gorbachev were to fall from power?

An Attempted Coup

Hard-line Soviet Communists criticized Gorbachev's new policies. During 1990, the Soviet Union was faced with a widespread economic crisis. Food shops in many cities were empty. Conflicts continued in some of the republics. Some Soviets believed that Gorbachev was changing things too quickly.

In August 1991, a group of hard-line Communist leaders made a move to take over power in the Soviet Union. They announced that Gorbachev had been "taken ill" and had left Moscow for a "rest." However, the **coup** failed. Since Gorbachev had begun reform in 1985, Soviet citizens had been introduced to new freedoms. Despite hard times, they were not ready to give up their rights.

Following the failure of the coup, change came even more rapidly. Citizens toppled statues of Communist heroes that had long stood in city squares. The city of Leningrad took back the name it held before the coming of communism. It became St. Petersburg again. The country also became known as the Union of Sovereign States. The attempted coup only hastened the death of communism inside the Soviet Union.

The Commonwealth of Independent States

In December 1991, the Soviet Union disbanded. It was replaced by 15 independent nations. Gorbachev had returned to power, but he was unable to hold the union together. Three of the 15 republics that made up the Soviet Union—Latvia, Estonia, and Lithuania—had declared their independence earlier that year. On December 21, leaders of 11 of the 12 remaining republics signed agreements creating the Commonwealth of Independent States. This was a loose alliance of fully independent states. The Communist Party was no longer in charge. Mikhail Gorbachev stepped down. Boris Yeltsin, president of the republic of Russia, became a leader and spokesperson for the new Commonwealth. Yeltsin had long been calling for an end to Communist rule.

On February 1, 1992, Boris Yeltsin met with U.S. President George Bush. The leaders declared an end to "cold war hostility." The United States and other nations of the free world pledged to send aid to help in rebuilding the economy of the new nations.

The Soviet Union died, and 15 new nations were born with many problems. The people still faced economic woes. Food and medicine continued to be in short supply. In some of the new nations, lives continued to be lost as different factions battled for control.

Russia, or the Russian Federation, is the largest and most powerful of the new nations. It took the seat at the U.N. that had been held by the Soviet Union. Russia has been fighting rebels in the Republic of Chechnya off and on since 1994. The rebels want to separate from Russia.

✓ **Check Your Understanding**
Write your answers in complete sentences.

1. What is the meaning of *glasnost?*

2. What is the meaning of *perestroika?*

3. Who became the leader and major spokesperson for the Commonwealth of Independent States?

A Wave of Freedom Sweeps Soviet Satellites

The Soviet Union was not the only country going through changes during the late 1980s and early 1990s. As a result of Gorbachev's policy of *glasnost,* the Soviets loosened their control over their satellite countries in Eastern Europe.

Independent Republics

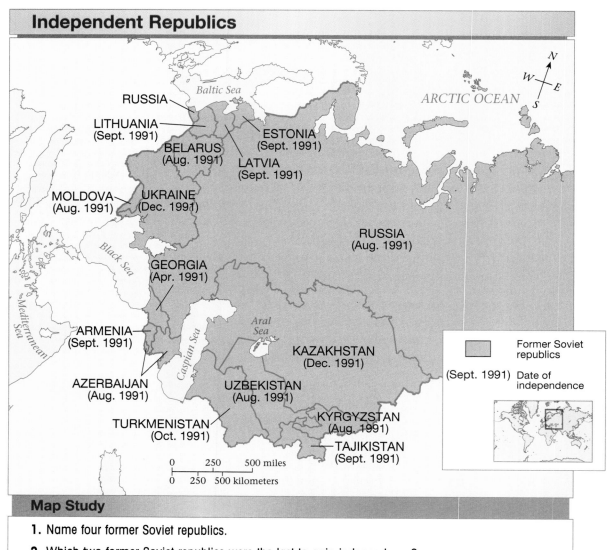

Map Study

1. Name four former Soviet republics.

2. Which two former Soviet republics were the last to gain independence?

Back in 1956, Hungary had tried to cut its ties with the Soviets. It wanted to set up its own government, one free of Soviet influence. However, Soviet troops marched into Hungary, crushing the movement for independence.

Then in 1968, there was trouble in Czechoslovakia. The Soviet government felt that the Czechoslovakian Communist Party was losing control of the country. The Russians were afraid that too much freedom of speech would turn the people away from communism. In August 1968, Soviet tanks rumbled through Czechoslovakia. Soon, new people were running the Czech government—people chosen by Moscow.

Lech Walesa

During the 1970s, many workers rioted in Poland. They were demanding higher pay and better working conditions. They wanted a union, something unheard of under Communist rule. In 1980, the Polish government allowed the workers to form the union. The new worker's union was called Solidarity. Its leader was a man named Lech Walesa.

In 1982, the government began to fear that many of Solidarity's demands went against Communist ideals. That year, the Communists arrested Solidarity's leaders and declared the union illegal. Many people inside Poland and in the West insisted that the Soviet Union had forced the Polish government to outlaw Solidarity.

Throughout the 1980s, economic conditions in Poland continued to worsen. By 1989, the Polish leaders were ready to try a different approach. Encouraged by the radical changes taking place inside the Soviet Union, they made Solidarity legal again. Solidarity then formed a political party. When the first free elections in Poland were held, the union's leaders were voted into office to run the government. Lech Walesa became president. However, in 1995, after Poland experienced economic troubles, Walesa lost the presidency. A former Communist was elected president.

In 1990, free elections in East Germany led to a non-Communist government. East Germany and West Germany then began the process of **reunification**, which was accomplished later that year.

In Hungary and in Czechoslovakia, the Communist leaders decided to set up multiparty political systems through free elections. The Communist leaders of Bulgaria gave in to the wishes of their people and resigned. In Romania, a bloody revolt in 1989 ended in the arrest and execution of the Communist dictator, Nicolae Ceausescu, and his wife Elena. Eastern European countries wanted to establish closer ties with the West. It now seemed to people all over the world that the Iron Curtain had finally lifted.

In Germany, people celebrated the fall of the Berlin Wall.

Learn More About It

THE FALL OF THE BERLIN WALL AND THE REUNIFICATION OF GERMANY

For 28 years a 26-mile-long wall had divided East Berlin from West Berlin. Ever since it had been built, East Berliners had been risking their lives to cross the wall to freedom. The Berlin Wall symbolized the split between a free, democratic West and an oppressed, nondemocratic East.

Then, in late 1989, democratic movements swept the Soviet Union and much of Eastern Europe. In September 1989, thousands of East Germans crossed the newly opened border from Hungary to Austria. From there they made their way to West Germany. The East German government recognized one simple fact: It could no longer keep its citizens prisoners behind a wall. After the East Germans agreed to open the gates to the Wall, people took matters into their own hands. They began to tear down the Berlin Wall.

In 1990, East Germany held its first free elections since World War II. The Communists were voted out of office. The new leaders of East Germany worked out a plan with West Germany to join into a single, reunified country. Helmut Kohl was elected the first chancellor of the reunified Germany. Once combined, the two Germanys had over 80 million people, more than any other nation in Europe. It had a powerful economy and a strong military. A united Germany was a mighty force in the European community.

Ethnic Groups Clash as Yugoslavia Breaks Up

Remember
During the fifteenth century, Bosnia and Serbia were conquered by the Turks. For 400 years they were part of Turkey's Ottoman Empire.

New freedoms did not necessarily mean peace in Eastern Europe. As communism released its hold on Yugoslavia, separate republics began declaring their independence. Yugoslavia was made up of six republics: Serbia, Croatia, Slovenia, Bosnia-Herzegovina, Macedonia, and Montenegro. Though it covered an area the size of Wyoming, it was home to 30 nationalities. The largest groups of people were Serbs and Croats. In Yugoslavia 41 percent of the people were Eastern Orthodox Christians, 32 percent were Roman Catholics, 12 percent were Muslims.

In June 1991, the republics of Croatia and Slovenia formally declared themselves independent. Civil war began in Croatia as Croats and ethnic Serbs fought for control. By the end of 1991, at least 6,000 people had been killed and 15,000 wounded in the Serbian-Croatian conflict.

The republic of Bosnia-Herzegovina declared itself independent in February 1992. Independence was supported by the Bosnian Muslims. They made up about 44 percent of the republic's population. The Eastern Orthodox Serbs (about 34 percent of the population) opposed the declaration. Violence broke out between Serbs and Bosnians. Thousands of Bosnians were killed. Fierce fighting continued until 1995 when a peace plan called the Dayton Accords was signed. The plan was sponsored by the United States. NATO troops, including American troops, were sent to Bosnia to keep the peace.

Trouble in the area that was once Yugoslavia has continued. Soon after Bosnia left Yugoslavia, another republic, Macedonia, declared its independence. Yugoslavia still appears on many maps, but now it only consists of two republics—Serbia and Montenegro. Ethnic Albanians living inside Serbia began to push for freedom. In Serbia, the Serbs terrorized and killed many ethnic Albanians in Kosovo. Kosovo had been a self-ruling province in Serbia. Serbia's president, Slobodan Milosevic, started ruling Kosovo and forcing many ethnic Albanians to leave. In response, NATO bombed Serbia in 1999. More ethnic Albanians, or Kosovars, fled to nearby countries. After the bombing, NATO peacekeeping troops, including U.S. troops, went to Kosovo to protect the people. Many ethnic Albanians who had been forced from their homes returned to Kosovo.

A U.N. court charged Serbia's president, Slobodan Milosevic, with war crimes. In the year 2000, Serbs rejected him when he ran for president. When Milosevic would not accept election results, the Serbs protested. Milosevic finally accepted defeat in October 2000.

Timeline Study

Did the Soviet Union disband before or after reform swept Eastern Europe?

The Fall of Communism in the Soviet Union and Eastern Europe

1985 Mikhail Gorbachev becomes leader of Soviet Union

1987 INF treaty signed

1991 Soviet Union disbands; republics form Comonwealth of Independent States

1995 Dayton Accords signed; negotiate peace between Serbs, Bosnians, and Croats

1999 NATO troops bomb Serbia

1980 — 1990 — 2000

1989 Soviet troops leave Afghanistan; Solidarity wins control in Poland; Berlin Wall opens; democratic reform sweeps Eastern Europe

1990 Germany reunified

1992 Bosnia-Herzegovina declares independence; war begins between Serbs and Bosnians

2000 Milosovic forced from office as president of Serbia

Chapter

32 Review

Summary

After he came to power in 1985, Mikhail Gorbachev introduced new policies that gave Soviet citizens more freedoms and improved Soviet relations with Western nations.

New treaties between the Soviet Union and the United States promised to drastically reduce nuclear arms.

The Soviet citizens faced extreme economic problems and shortages of food and medicine.

In 1991, the Soviet Union disbanded. Eventually nations formed a loose alliance called the Commonwealth of Independent States. Boris Yeltsin became leader of independent Russia and the Commonwealth of Independent States.

During the late 1980s, democratic reform swept Eastern Europe, spurred by changes in the Soviet Union. A climax in the wave of freedom came when the Berlin Wall fell in late 1989.

Parts of Eastern Europe have been very unstable as nations and ethnic groups struggle to move forward.

| reunification |
| hostility |
| coup |

Vocabulary Review

Write a term from the list that matches each definition below.

1. A sudden takeover

2. When countries join together again

3. Feelings of hate

Chapter Quiz

Write your answers in complete sentences.

1. How did Gorbachev change the Soviet economy?

2. What alliance did most of the former Soviet republics form?

3. What happened to Germany after the fall of the Berlin Wall?

4. **Critical Thinking** In your opinion, why did the Soviet Union die?

5. **Critical Thinking** Should the United States send troops to try to resolve conflicts in Eastern Europe?

Using the Timeline

Use the timeline on page 493 to answer the questions.

1. When did Solidarity win control in Poland?

2. What happened during the same year Bosnia-Herzogovina declared independence?

Write About History

Complete the following activity.

Form a group of four or five. Create a television newscast about the death of the Soviet Union and the fall of communism in eastern Europe. One classmate is the anchor. The three other classmates report from three different areas in Eastern Europe. Be sure to make notes to use during the newscast.

Fidel Castro has been in power as the dictator of Cuba since 1959.

Learning Objectives

- Describe the effect of Fidel Castro's takeover of Cuba on U.S.-Cuban relations.

- Explain why the United States aided Nicaraguan rebels in their fight against the Sandinistas.

- Describe why the United States helped the government of El Salvador stay in power.

- Explain Mexico's political and economic situation.

- Explain how rapid population growth has affected Latin America.

- Discuss the reasons the United States invaded Panama in 1989.

Chapter 33 — Latin America After World War II

Words to Know

stronghold	a place dominated by a certain group which they have made safe and secure
moderate	not extreme
humane	kind, showing care for other human beings
refuge	shelter or protection from danger

Before World War II, representatives from the nations of the Americas met in a Pan-American conference. They pledged themselves to a Good Neighbor Policy. They promised that no nation would interfere with the affairs of another nation. Then came World War II. During the war all Latin American nations supported the Allies. Brazil and Mexico even provided troops.

When World War II ended, the United States took a renewed interest in Latin America. The U.S. government hoped to keep communism out of the Western Hemisphere and to encourage good relations between the nations of the Americas. In 1948, the Organization of American States (OAS) was founded. Among its members were the United States and all of the independent countries of Latin America. OAS countries pledged to join together in defending the Americas and in peacefully settling any quarrels.

Since the 1950s, the United States has sent billions of dollars to help Latin American countries solve their social and economic problems. Technical experts from the United States have helped improve Latin American agriculture, industry, education, and health care.

In more recent years, U.S. aid was sometimes unwelcome. Some Latin Americans said the United States was not really interested in helping them but was sending aid to protect its own interests. They said the United States should stay out of the affairs of other nations.

Revolution in Cuba

The first half of the twentieth century was a time of change and instability in Latin America. Revolutions overthrew a number of dictators. However, the end of dictatorship did not always bring about stability. New governments did not always grant rights to the people.

A 1959 revolution led to major changes on the island nation of Cuba. A former lawyer named Fidel Castro and his army of guerrilla fighters overthrew the military dictatorship of Fulgencio Batista. Castro set up a Communist dictatorship. Under communism, Cuba became closely allied with the Soviet Union. Castro pledged to help Communist rebels gain control in other Latin American countries. The United States refused to recognize the Castro government in Cuba. Friendly relations ended between the United States and the small country only 90 miles from its shores.

Political Unrest in Central America

After the Castro revolution, Communist activity increased in Latin America. In 1979, Cuban Communists supported a revolution in Nicaragua. A Communist group called the Sandinista National Liberation Front overthrew Nicaragua's dictator, Anastasio Somoza. The Sandinistas took control of the government. Although Somoza had done little to improve life for his people, he had supported U.S. policies throughout Central America. The United States criticized Somoza's use of violence. The United States also feared that a new Sandinista government would provide a Communist **stronghold** in Central America. The United States accused the Nicaraguan Sandinistas of helping Communist rebels in neighboring El Salvador and relying on Soviet aid and support.

A group called the Contras (*contra* means "against" in Spanish) rebelled against the Sandinistas. U.S. President Ronald Reagan announced that the United States would provide military and economic aid to the Contras. Many Latin Americans criticized the United States for interfering in the politics of another nation. Some U.S. citizens also questioned their country's involvement. In 1985, the U.S. House of Representatives voted to ban aid to the Contras. However, it was later discovered that illegal aid continued for several years.

Remember
Ronald Reagan feared that the domino theory, one nation after another falling to communism, could apply to Latin America.

A civil war went on in Nicaragua until 1989. Then President Daniel Ortega signed a treaty with Contra rebels. The Contras agreed to lay down their arms and refuse outside aid. Ortega promised that Nicaragua would hold democratic elections in 1990. That year, in a surprise victory, Violeta Barrios de Chamorro defeated Ortega and became the new president of Nicaragua.

Civil War in El Salvador

Nicaragua was not the only Central American country engaged in a civil war during the 1980s. Unrest had rocked El Salvador for many years. In 1979, the military took control of the government. Anti-government rebels were backed by Cuba and by the Communists in Nicaragua. The United States sent aid to El Salvador's military government. President Reagan said the United States had to defend itself against communism. Again, some U.S. citizens protested the aid. They said that the military government was not worthy of support because it promoted violence that had killed thousands of Salvadoran civilians.

In 1984, El Salvadoran voters elected Jose Napoleon Duarte to the presidency. He promised a more **moderate** and **humane** government. Rebel guerrilla attacks, however, continued. The civil war finally ended in 1992. A peace treaty between the government and rebel forces promised military and political reform. The war in El Salvador lasted about 13 years and took the lives of nearly 75,000 people.

Learn More About It

THE IRAN-CONTRA AFFAIR

The United States Congress banned military aid to the Nicaraguan Contras in 1985. However, in 1986, the American people learned of a secret arms deal that funneled money to Nicaragua. The affair was a two-part scandal.

Part One: It was discovered that U.S. officials secretly sold missiles and missile parts to the Middle Eastern nation of Iran. This was at a time when the United States was publicly speaking out against Iran, calling it a terrorist nation. As a result of the weapons sales, Iranians persuaded terrorists in Lebanon to release some U.S. hostages. U.S. policy, however, strictly forbade trading arms for political hostages.

Part Two: The U.S. Congress had specifically forbidden military aid to the Contras. However, profits from the Iranian arms sales were illegally used to aid the Contras in Nicaragua.

Soldiers fought a civil war in El Salvador for over 12 years.

The United States Invades Panama

As civil war raged in El Salvador, a storm was brewing in the Central American nation of Panama. In 1987, General Manuel Noriega was commander of the Panamanian defense forces. Although Panama's president was Eric Arturo Delvalle, all the real power lay in the hands of General Noriega.

Noriega was corrupt. He was an accused drug smuggler. He was known to tamper with election votes so that his candidates would win. When a national election was held in May 1989, Guillermo Endara, a Noriega opponent, won the most votes. Noriega ignored the election results. He claimed victory.

The U.S. government wanted to see General Noriega removed from power. On December 23, 1989, U.S. President George Bush sent 24,000 U.S. troops to Panama to drive Noriega from power. At a U.S. military base, Guillermo Endara was sworn in as president.

> **You Decide**
>
> Do you think the United States had the right to send troops to Panama to drive Noriega from power? Why or why not?

General Noriega spent 10 days in hiding before he surrendered to American military forces. He was brought back to the United States to stand trial on drug charges. In 1992, a U.S. District Court in Miami, Florida, convicted Noriega of drug trafficking.

Throughout the 1980s, protests against military governments grew in several Latin American countries. In many cases, these protests brought free elections. By the early 1990s, civilian leaders elected by the people had replaced military governments in such places as Guatemala, Argentina, Brazil, Chile, and Paraguay.

✓ **Check Your Understanding**
Write answers in complete sentences.

1. Under Fidel Castro, Cuba allied itself with what superpower?

2. What were three of the Latin American nations in which civilian governments replaced military governments by the early 1990s?

3. Why did U.S. President Reagan believe it was important to support anti-Communist forces in Latin America?

Learn More About It

WAR IN THE FALKLANDS

In April 1982, Argentina launched an attack on a British colony in South America. The Falklands, a group of islands off the Argentinian coast, have been a British colony since 1833. Most of the people living there are British. When Argentina tried to seize control of the Falklands, Britain's Prime Minister Margaret Thatcher sent forces to protect the colony. It was a short but bloody war. On June 14, Argentina surrendered. The Falklands remained under British control.

Today the Falkland Islands are a territory of the United Kingdom. The islands are also claimed by Argentina.

Changes in Mexico

Political corruption and a growing population put Mexico into an economic crisis during the 1980s. During the 1970s, the discovery of vast oil fields in southern Mexico had promised new riches. The government increased spending on public works and on industry and expected to pay for new development with income from oil. In the early 1980s, however, the price of oil fell, and so did Mexico's hopes for prosperity. The country was left in serious debt.

Mexico's economic crisis caused rising unemployment. The population kept growing rapidly, adding to the number of unemployed. A growing population, high foreign debt, and falling oil income meant economic troubles for Mexico.

Many Mexicans turned their anger and disappointment toward the government. Political unrest increased. During the oil boom, Mexico's

This cathedral in Mexico City was built on top of the ruins of an Aztec temple.

peasants and its urban poor saw hope for their future. Now that hope was gone. They became more aware than ever of the great gap that existed between the few rich people and the many poor ones. As Mexico's economy weakened, the number of Mexicans illegally entering the United States grew. They crossed the border in search of work and a better standard of living.

In 1992, the United States, Canada, and Mexico announced plans for the North American Free Trade Agreement (NAFTA). The agreement offered a chance for economic growth for all three nations. Among the terms of the agreement were proposals to eventually end tariffs on all farm products and many other goods. The treaty also aimed to ease immigration laws for business executives and professionals, and to allow trucks free access to border routes between the three countries. The agreement was approved by the governments of the three nations. It promised a boost to Mexico's economy. After some difficult years, the Mexican economy grew from 1997 to 2000.

In the mid-1990s, rebels in the state of Chiapas demanded more land for the people. The Mexican government is in control of the state today. However, some fighting between armed civilians over land claims still happens.

Unrest in Haiti

Civil unrest has plagued the Caribbean island nation of Haiti in recent years. Revolutions and government takeovers have been spurred by poverty, drought, hurricanes, and famine. Between early 1986 and mid-1990, Haiti had five different governments. In the 1990s, the United States led a multi-national force to restore Haiti's elected leader to office.

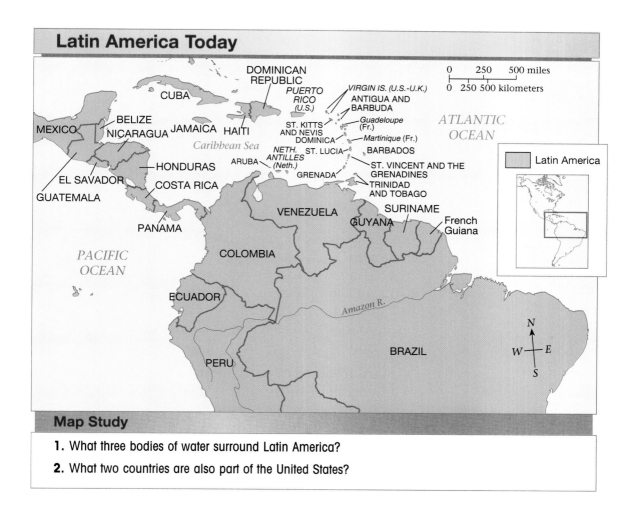

Latin America Today

DOMINICAN
REPUBLIC

CUBA

PUERTO
RICO
(U.S.)

VIRGIN IS. (U.S.-U.K.)

ANTIGUA AND
BARBUDA

0   250   500 miles
0   250 500 kilometers

MEXICO

BELIZE

NICARAGUA

JAMAICA

HAITI

Caribbean Sea

ST. KITTS
AND NEVIS
DOMINICA

Guadeloupe
(Fr.)

Martinique (Fr.)

ATLANTIC
OCEAN

Latin America

HONDURAS

EL SAVADOR

GUATEMALA

COSTA RICA

ARUBA

NETH.
ANTILLES
(Neth.)

ST. LUCIA

GRENADA

BARBADOS

ST. VINCENT AND THE
GRENADINES

TRINIDAD
AND TOBAGO

PANAMA

VENEZUELA

GUYANA

SURINAME

French
Guiana

PACIFIC
OCEAN

COLOMBIA

ECUADOR

Amazon R.

PERU

BRAZIL

N

W   E

S

Map Study

1. What three bodies of water surround Latin America?

2. What two countries are also part of the United States?

Violence against civilians has led many Haitians to
flee their country. In 1991 and 1992, some 35,000
Haitian refugees were stopped by the U.S. Coast Guard
as they tried to enter the United States illegally. Most
of them were returned to Haiti, although many in the
United States felt they should be allowed to seek **refuge**
in the United States.

Latin America Today

Latin America's economy grew during the 1960s and early 1970s. By the late 1970s, however, economic growth declined. Latin American industry depended upon certain imports. It needed refined goods and machinery. This became a problem when prices on these imports rose sharply. At the same time, the prices on Latin America's raw agricultural and mineral exports dropped.

During this period, the Latin American nations were spending more and making less. Many had to borrow huge sums of money. Some of these nations have had trouble raising the money they need to repay their loans. By 2000, many positive changes had taken place in Latin America. In most countries, the economy had been improving. Democracy was growing. Women were gaining rights. Education had become a priority.

Brazil has the largest economy in South America. In fact, Brazil has the ninth largest economy in the world. Although the Brazilian government had to devalue its money in 1999, the economy still grew.

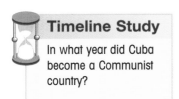

Timeline Study

In what year did Cuba become a Communist country?

Latin America: 1948–2000

1948
OAS founded

1959
Castro sets up
Communist government
in Cuba

1979
Sandinistas take power in Nicaragua

1982
Falklands War

1983
U.S. troops go to Grenada;
Democratic rule returns to Argentina

1988
Democratic elections end military rule in Chile

1989
U.S. troops
go to
Panama

1990
Nicaragua holds democratic elections

1992
War ends in
El Salvador

1994
North American
Free Trade
Agreement
takes effect

2000
Opposition
candidate wins
presidency
in Mexico

1950   1960   1970   1980   1990   2000

Learn More About It

BRAZIL PLEDGES TO PROTECT ITS RAIN FOREST

The rain forests of South and Central America are a resource that is important to the whole world. The forests are not only beautiful. They have a direct effect on the world's climate. Yet in many regions, vast areas of the rain forests have been burned or cut down to make way for cattle ranches and farms. In 1987 and 1988, satellite pictures showed the tremendous damage being done to Brazilian forest lands.

The world will pay a price for the destruction of its rain forests. Trees remove carbon dioxide (CO_2) from the air. Many scientists believe that a buildup of CO_2 will result in a global warming. This global warming is sometimes called the "greenhouse effect." In addition, Brazilian fires set to burn the rain forests add CO_2 to the atmosphere. This increases the greenhouse effect.

In 1988, Brazil's president promised an end to the mass burning of the Amazon forests. In 1989, Brazil initiated an environmental program aimed at protecting its rain forests. Brazil demonstrated its concern for the environment by hosting representatives from 178 countries at an Earth Day Summit in June 1992. Today, Brazil has adopted an environmental plan. It has also adopted the Environmental Crimes Law with strong penalties.

Summary

After World War II, the United States tried to keep communism out of Latin America.
In a 1959 revolution, Fidel Castro set up a Communist dictatorship in Cuba.
The United States invaded Panama to remove General Manuel Noriega from power.
Many Latin Americans and U.S. citizens criticized the United States government for interfering in the affairs of other nations and for aiding harsh governments.
Mexico faced an economic and political crisis in the 1980s and 1990s.
Latin America has had many problems. However, in recent years the region has become more democratic and more financially stable.

Vocabulary Review

Write *true* or *false.* If the statement is false, change the underlined term to make it true.

1. Cuba is a Communist <u>moderate</u> in the Western Hemisphere.

2. A <u>humane</u> government would care about poor people.

3. A <u>refuge</u> is a safe place for people who are in trouble.

4. A <u>stronghold</u> government is not extreme in its policies or actions.

Chapter Quiz

Write your answers in complete sentences.

1. What happened to Cuba-U.S. relations after Castro took power in Cuba?

2. Why did the United States fight on the side of the rebels in Nicaragua?

3. Why did the United States fight on the side of the government in El Salvador?

4. **Critical Thinking** Why do events in Mexico affect the United States?

5. **Critical Thinking** How could the destruction of rain forests in Brazil affect your life?

Using the Timeline

Use the timeline on page 506 to answer the questions.

1. Which came first, the Falklands War or the U.S. invasion of Panama?

2. When was the Organization of American States founded?

Write About History

Complete one of the following activities.

1. With a group of three or four students, discuss U.S. relations with Cuba. Do you think the United States should have friendly relations with Cuba even if it is a Communist country? List the reasons your group says yes or no.

2. Interview a person who has lived in a Latin American country. Prepare questions in advance. Share the answers with the rest of the class.

New York City is considered a center of world trade and finance.

Learning Objectives

- Name two uses of nuclear power.
- Explain why the present era is sometimes called the Space Age.
- Explain how advances in communication and transportation make the world seem smaller.
- Tell what is meant by a "developing" nation.
- Tell what is meant by a "developed" nation.

Chapter 34 / The World Today

Words to Know

nonrenewable	not replaceable once it is used up
satellite	an object put into orbit around Earth
cosmonaut	Russian word meaning astronaut
astronaut	a person trained to make space flights
technology	science put to use in practical work

People call these times the "Nuclear Age," the "Space Age," or the "Computer Age." Today's world is full of brand new inventions and discoveries. There are things now that Alexander the Great, Julius Caesar, Napoleon Bonaparte, or even dreamers like Leonardo da Vinci could never imagine. Yet in spite of all the progress, people today still have much in common with their ancestors.

The Nuclear Age

The last half of the twentieth century has sometimes been called the Nuclear Age. Actually, the idea of nuclear power began about 1905, with Albert Einstein. Einstein suggested that energy was contained in every atom. The first actual use of that energy came in 1945 when the United States exploded two atomic bombs over Japan. Those explosions ended World War II and began an age of development for atomic energy.

The explosion of the first atomic bomb started the powerful nations of the world on a race. It was a deadly race to build bigger weapons. Countries tried to outdo each other in the number and size of the bombs they built.

Now many nations have a weapon so destructive that the results of another world war are impossible to imagine. Therefore, nations try to avoid that war. They meet and talk about peace. They discuss ways to limit the buildup of nuclear arms. The United States and the Soviet Union held talks and signed treaties.

You Decide

Do you think the world is a safer or a more dangerous place since the breakup of the Soviet Union? Explain why or why not.

In 1991, the Soviet Union broke up. Its separate republics became 15 new nations. The nuclear weapons of the old Soviet Union are no longer under control of a single government. The cold war is over, and old enemies have friendlier relations. However, there is concern whether these new nations will handle their nuclear arms responsibly. Nuclear weapons in the hands of unstable governments or of terrorists threaten the safety of the whole world. It is a reality that today's people must live with.

Peaceful Uses of Nuclear Energy

Although it was first used in a bomb, nuclear power has peacetime uses, too. The most important use is as a source of energy.

All nations use oil, coal, and natural gas for energy. These are all **nonrenewable** energy sources. Once they are used up, they are gone. As the population grows, the demand for energy also grows. People worry that we will run out of those traditional sources of energy.

The energy created in the nucleus of the atom can be used to run factories, to heat homes, and to light cities. Today this energy is produced in nuclear power plants around the world. Nuclear power is expensive. However, it can provide unlimited energy for thousands of years. The question is: Is it safe?

Nuclear power plants have strict safety regulations. Accidents, however, can happen. In 1979 at the

A serious accident occurred in 1979 at Three-Mile Island nuclear power plant in Harrisburg, Pennsylvania.

Three-Mile Island nuclear power plant in Pennsylvania, failing equipment and human mistakes caused a near meltdown. There were no tragic results, but the public was frightened. People became aware that a disaster could happen. Stricter safety rules were set up. Yet, some people still wondered about the future of nuclear power. They worried that the risk was too great.

In 1986, a nuclear disaster occurred in the Soviet Union. There was a meltdown and explosion at the Chernobyl nuclear power plant. Twenty-three people died, and many nearby towns were evacuated. One thousand square miles of soil in the area was badly contaminated by radiation. The explosion sent a cloud of radiation across Ukraine and other parts of the Soviet Union, and across several other European nations. Thousands of Soviet citizens—men, women, and children—were exposed to radioactive fallout. In time, many of these people died of cancer or other

> ### HISTORY FACT
>
> In a meltdown, the cooling system fails and the core of the nuclear reactor actually melts.

diseases. Traces of radiation were also found in animals, in milk, and in plant life far from the actual accident site. No one is sure just what the long-range effects of such radiation might be.

Many people protest the building of nuclear power plants. They say that no amount of energy is worth the risk of nuclear disaster. Others maintain that nuclear power is a safe answer to the world's energy crisis. They point out that many people have died in coal mining accidents over the years. Compared to this, only a few have died in accidents related to nuclear power plants.

Those in favor of nuclear power also point out that it is clean. It causes much less pollution than coal or oil. However, those against nuclear power have one very solid argument for their point of view. No safe method has yet been discovered for disposing of nuclear waste.

✓ **Check Your Understanding**
Write your answers in complete sentences.

1. Why is the last half of the twentieth century sometimes called the "Nuclear Age"?

2. What are three nonrenewable energy sources?

3. Why do some people think that nuclear energy is very dangerous?

The Space Age

Sometimes the present era has been called the "Space Age." The Space Age began in 1957. That is when the Soviet Union launched the first **satellite** made by humans into orbit around Earth. The satellite was called *Sputnik I*. Soon after, the United States launched its first satellite, *Explorer I.* The space race had begun.

The space shuttle program provides a way for astronauts to learn more about our universe.

In 1961, the Russians put the first human being into space. He was **cosmonaut** Yuri Gagarin. Then in 1969, U.S. **astronaut** Neil Armstrong became the first person to walk on the moon. Six hundred million people around the world watched this event on TV.

The first woman went into space in 1963. She was the Soviet cosmonaut Valentina V. Tereshkova. In 1983 the United States sent its first woman astronaut, Sally Ride, into space aboard the shuttle *Challenger*.

The exploration of space is exciting. It is also difficult, expensive, and dangerous. In January 1986, the space shuttle *Challenger* exploded shortly after takeoff. All the people on board were killed. There have also been other accidents in which people have died.

However, many people feel that the rewards from space exploration are worth the risks.

Space was an area in which the United States and the Soviet Union raced to be the best. Space, however, can also be an arena for peace. In July 1975, three American astronauts and two Soviet cosmonauts met in space. As planned, their two spaceships hooked up. U.S. space shuttles regularly delivered supplies and people to the Russian space station *Mir*. American and Russian astronauts lived and worked together in space. They conduct joint scientific experiments and both nations shared the results.

In early 2001, an American and two Russians were living on the International Space Station (ISS). The ISS is an orbiting science laboratory. The ISS will be completed in space.

The Space Age has only begun. Many people expect that before too long, we will have colonies on the moon. People from Earth may someday live on Mars and on

Learn More About It

THE COMPUTER AGE

Computers are electronic machines. They solve problems and answer questions. They store information. Computers are used around the world to help people do their work, find information, communicate with others, and play games.

Computers have been improved steadily since World War II. At first they were very large, very expensive, and difficult to run. Now they are much smaller and are used by millions of people. A computer that once filled an entire room now fits into a package the size of a notebook!

At first people worried that computers would replace humans in many jobs. In some cases, this has happened. However, computers have created many more new jobs. Computers give people the time and freedom to get more work done. They also provide recreation for millions of people.

With computers, people all over the world can communicate almost instantly.

other planets. Spaceships that do not include humans to operate them have already landed on Mars and Venus and sent back pictures. Other ships have flown close to Jupiter, Saturn, Uranus, and Neptune. Perhaps someday, we may even go to other solar systems!

The Shrinking World

Developments in transportation and communication have made the world seem smaller. People in one part of the world now know what is happening elsewhere.

Television changed twentieth-century life as much as any other one invention. The power of TV seems likely to continue into the twenty-first century. Many Americans protested involvement in the Vietnam War because television cameras brought the action to them. They saw for themselves the suffering of American soldiers and Vietnamese villagers.

You Decide
The present era is often called the "Information Age." Do you think the name fits? Why or why not?

Television news takes the Israeli-Arab conflict into millions of homes. People of the world have seen the end of apartheid in South Africa as well as hunger in Ethiopia and Somalia with their own eyes.

Also, hundreds of communications satellites circle the Earth. They beam radio, television, telephone, and computer signals around the world. On the computer, people form friendships throughout the world, using e-mail. They keep up-to-date on world events by Internet. Satellites in space can take weather pictures to make forecasts anywhere in the world.

New methods of travel have also made the world smaller. A trip across an ocean takes only hours.

A Global Economy

As the world seems to grow smaller, nations have a greater influence on each other. Trade has long affected cultures and civilizations. Ideas have always mingled as trade increased. Now it is routine for nations to trade their goods and ideas worldwide. They depend on each other for an exchange of raw materials and manufactured goods.

The Pacific Rim is a term used to describe lands bordering the Pacific Ocean. During the 1980s, the Pacific Rim became the world's fastest-growing trading area. Electronic equipment, cars, and other products left Japan, Taiwan, and South Korea bound for foreign markets.

The popularity of foreign products weakened the economy of the United States. Since the 1970s, the United States has imported more goods from other nations than it has exported. Hundreds of U.S. factories have closed or laid off workers because products being made abroad are being purchased in large quantities by U.S. consumers.

At first the United States tried to solve its economic problems by setting up trade restrictions. Congress set limits on the number of imports that could enter the country. Foreign companies found ways to get around the restrictions. Japanese automakers built factories in the United States. By 1989, many "American-made" cars were manufactured in U.S. plants owned by Japanese companies.

This was not a new strategy. The United States had been setting up factories all over the world for years. In fact, during the 1980s, many U.S. companies built factories in foreign lands to take advantage of inexpensive labor. Today many companies are multinational. Japanese companies own some entertainment and food businesses in the United States. U.S. auto companies have interests in auto companies in other countries.

The health of one nation's economy depends greatly on that of other nations. All countries need places to export the goods they make. All countries also need to import some. Countries made trade alliances and free-trade agreements to tear down barriers and encourage fair trade. In 1988, the United States and Canada signed a free-trade pact. It ended restrictions and tariffs on almost all products. In 1994, the United States, Canada, and Mexico began free trade between all three nations.

Remember
Trade developed among early civilizations. Many things you own are imports.

European nations have joined together in the European Union (EU). The goal of the EU is to ensure completely free trade and free movement of money and people between member nations. The World Trade Organization (WTO) has 135 member nations. In 2000, some people in the United States protested against the WTO. In Seattle, protesters included workers who were afraid their jobs would go to other countries. Environmentalists who wanted stronger protection for the environment were there, too.

Developed Nations and Developing Nations

Some nations in the world are called "developed" nations. They have many industries. They import and export products. Most people who live in developed nations have a fairly high standard of living. Most people there can read and write. They benefit from the advances of modern science and **technology**. The United States, Russia, Canada, France, Great Britain, Japan, the Scandinavian countries and Germany are just some of the developed nations.

Many countries are less developed. They are sometimes called "developing" nations. Many people in developing nations are poor. Many people farm the land, but their methods of agriculture are often outdated. There are fewer industries in developing nations. Their standard of living is lower, and many people cannot read or write.

In developing countries, many people live in traditional ways. It is important to preserve aspects of traditional life while making economic gains.

HISTORY FACT

Developing countries include about 120 countries and more than half of the world's people.

Haiti, Afghanistan, and Mexico are examples of developing countries. Many South American and African nations are developing countries. Some of these nations, like Nigeria and Venezuela, have rich oil deposits.

The developing countries are more dependent on other nations. Their economies can be easily upset by weather, by a year of bad farm crops, or by a war. Sometimes the more developed countries help the developing nations by lending them money or sending supplies. The United States has sent thousands of Peace Corps volunteers to developing countries all over the world. There the volunteers teach modern farming methods, health care, and engineering.

Learn More About It

AIDS—A DEADLY CHALLENGE

During the 1980s, a new disease swept across the world. Scientists identified the disease in 1981. They named it acquired immune deficiency syndrome (AIDS). They discovered it was caused by a virus—the human immunodeficiency virus (HIV). This virus destroys the body's defenses against infection. They also found that the virus that causes AIDS spreads from person to person. Because of this, scientists and doctors feared there would be a worldwide epidemic.

Since 1981, AIDS has shown up in countries around the world. It exploded into the most widespread epidemic in central Africa. High numbers were also found in the small Caribbean nation of Haiti. By the end of the 1990s, there were very few countries in which this killer disease had not struck.

The AIDS virus can only be spread two ways: through direct blood-to-blood contact or through an exchange of body fluids. No cure has been discovered although several promising treatments have been developed. The best chance of controlling the disease is through education. If people understand the nature of the disease, they are less likely to contract the virus.

The number of AIDS cases is growing worldwide. The medical community searches for a way to halt the AIDS epidemic and to save those already stricken with the virus. It is one of the most urgent challenges of the new century.

What Does the Future Hold?

Picture the days of ancient Greece. Think about a Greek athlete running an Olympic race. It is 700 B.C. The young man pulls ahead of the other racers on a dusty road. He gasps the warm air. His lungs ache with the effort. As he crosses the finish line, he closes his eyes and raises his arms over his head in victory.

When he opens his eyes again, he expects to find himself surrounded by cheering Greeks. He can almost feel the crown of olive leaves about to be placed on his head.

Instead . . . the racer finds himself in a crowded, modern stadium. It is A.D. 2004, Athens, Greece, the 28th Summer Olympics. People are cheering, but they are not all Greeks. They are people from around the whole world. Furthermore, no olive leaves await the racer. Instead he is awarded a shiny, gold medal. Somehow our racer has been jolted forward in time more than 2,000 years.

What will the racer find? What undreamed-of wonders will our racer discover?

He will find a whole new world of medicine. Doctors can actually replace worn-out or diseased body parts. Sometimes those replacements come from people who have died. Other times the parts are manufactured. The young Greek time-traveler can hardly believe it. These modern doctors can even replace a person's heart!

People treat each other in a different way now. The Greek racer is surprised to find himself surrounded by women athletes. Women, he will discover, have a whole new role in society. In many places they are treated as equals with men. They work side by side with men in all kinds of jobs. Women have become leaders in science, in medicine, and in business.

Spaceships to the moon, automobiles that speed people to their destinations, airplanes, television, telephones . . . the list of new wonders is endless.

These are medals from the 2000 Olympics, which were held in Sydney, Australia.

Has anything remained the same? Most people still live in family groups, although many of those groups are smaller. People still have the same basic needs for food and shelter. In addition, people still have trouble getting along. There are still those who want to be conquerors and who seek power at all costs. There are still those who must struggle to hold on to their cultures and their homes. People from different backgrounds still do not know and understand each other well enough. Sadly, people still fear what they do not understand.

Human beings are still curious, too. They still need to learn, to explore, and to discover. There will always be some questions to answer: What lies beyond the sun? Are there worlds and peoples other than our own? Can the inhabitants of this world ever live together completely at peace?

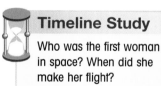

Timeline Study

Who was the first woman in space? When did she make her flight?

The World: 1940–2000

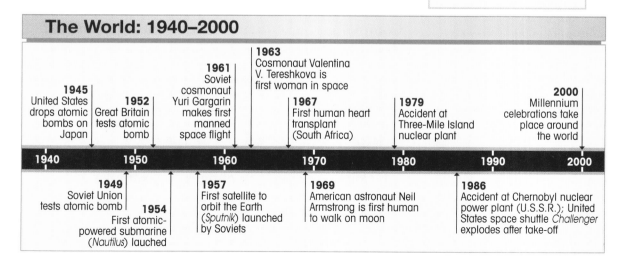

1945 United States drops atomic bombs on Japan

1952 Great Britain tests atomic bomb

1961 Soviet cosmonaut Yuri Gargarin makes first manned space flight

1963 Cosmonaut Valentina V. Tereshkova is first woman in space

1967 First human heart transplant (South Africa)

1979 Accident at Three-Mile Island nuclear plant

2000 Millennium celebrations take place around the world

1940 — 1950 — 1960 — 1970 — 1980 — 1990 — 2000

1949 Soviet Union tests atomic bomb

1954 First atomic-powered submarine (*Nautilus*) lauched

1957 First satellite to orbit the Earth (*Sputnik*) launched by Soviets

1969 American astronaut Neil Armstrong is first human to walk on moon

1986 Accident at Chernobyl nuclear power plant (U.S.S.R.); United States space shuttle *Challenger* explodes after take-off

Chapter

34 Review

Summary

Nuclear power is used for weapons and as a source of energy in peacetime. People worry about the dangers of an accident in a nuclear power plant and about the safe disposal of nuclear waste.

Television and the Internet sometimes make people more aware and concerned about what is going on around the world.

Nations have become economically interdependent. Many are forming free-trade alliances that remove barriers to international trade.

Developed nations have advanced technology, a higher standard of living, and strong trade programs. Developing nations are less developed, poorer, and more dependent on other countries.

Many breakthroughs in energy, space, communications, and social mobility have occurred in the present age. However, people still have to deal with problems of ignorance, prejudice, persecution, and war.

satellite
technology
astronaut
nonrenewable
cosmonaut

Vocabulary Review

Complete each sentence with a term from the list.

1. An _____ travels into space for the United States.

2. A _____ from the Soviet Union was the first person in space.

3. A _____ resource cannot be replaced once people use it up.

4. Computers and cell phones are examples of _____.

5. The United States has put a _____ into space, which orbits around Earth.

Chapter Quiz

Write your answers in complete sentences.

1. What are two uses of nuclear power?

2. When did the Space Age begin?

3. Why does the world seem to be shrinking?

4. **Critical Thinking** What are some dangers of a global economy?

5. **Critical Thinking** What is the major difference between a developed nation and a developing nation?

Using the Timeline

Use the timeline on page 523 to answer the questions.

1. When was the first human heart transplant?

2. Who made the first manned space flight?

Write About History

Complete the following activity.

Suppose you are the Olympic racer from 700 B.C. Your partner is an Olympic athlete at the 2004 Olympics. Write a conversation the two of you would have about changes in the world. Practice the conversation and share it with some of your classmates.

Unit 10 **Review**

Comprehension Check

Write your answers in complete sentences.

1. What nations were the superpowers after World War II?

2. What were the SALT treaties?

3. Why did the United States fight in Vietnam?

4. How did apartheid affect the people of South Africa?

5. What are the main causes of conflict in the Middle East?

6. What happened in Eastern Europe in the late 1980s and early 1990s?

7. Why did the United States invade Panama in 1989?

8. What are two challenges the world faces today?

Writing an Essay

Answer one of the following essay topics.

1. Describe relations between the Soviet Union and the United States during the cold war.

2. Explain how the 1960s were a time of turmoil in the United States.

3. List some of the problems new countries in Africa had to face after independence.

4. Explain the importance of Middle East peace to the rest of the world.

5. Describe recent positive changes in Latin America.

Group Activity

In your group, list nicknames such as the "Computer Age" for the present time. Then create some other nicknames and add them to the list. Vote on the best nickname for the present time. Make an illustrated banner with the nickname.

History in Your Life

How do you think the global economy will affect you and your family? Could it affect where members of your family live and work, or what kinds of products you will buy?

Appendix

Glossary

A.D. (Anno Domini)   dating from the time Jesus was born

acupuncture   treating pain or illness by putting needles into certain parts of the body

addicted   having a strong habit that is hard to give up

agent   a person who has authority to act for some other person or company

agriculture   the use of land for growing crops and raising animals; farming

alliance   a group of nations joined together for some purpose

ambition   the drive to become powerful, successful, or famous

ancestor   a person from whom one is descended

annul   to cancel; to make something no longer binding under law

anthem   the official song of a country

anti-Semitism   prejudice against Jews

apartheid   the separation of races based mainly on skin color

apprentice   a person who learns a trade under a master

aqueduct   a channel that carries flowing water over a long distance

archaeologist   a scientist who studies cultures of the past by digging up and examining the remains of ancient towns and cities

armistice   an agreement to stop fighting; a truce before a formal peace treaty

arsenal   a place where guns and ammunition are stored

artifact   a handmade object, such as a tool or weapon

assassinate   to murder a leader or other important person

astronaut   a person trained to make space flights

astronomy   the study of stars, planets, and other heavenly bodies

athlete   a person trained to take part in competitive sports. The ancient Greek word athlete means "one who tries to win a prize in a contest."

B.C. (Before Christ)   dating from before the time Jesus Christ was born

barbarians   uncivilized primitive people; people living outside Greece or Rome in the days of the Roman Empire

barter   to trade goods or services without using money

betray   to give help to the enemy; to be unfaithful to

bishop   a high-ranking church official; from the Latin word that means "overseer"

burro   a small donkey, usually used as a pack animal

campaign   a series of battles all aimed at one military end

canal   a manufactured waterway

capital   a city or town where the government of a nation or state is located

capitalist   having business and industry privately owned and operated for profit

caravan   a group of people traveling together, often through a desert

cartridge   a small metal or cardboard tube that holds gunpowder and a bullet

caste   a social class in India

casualty   a soldier who has been killed, wounded, captured, or is missing

censor   to examine communications before they are released and to remove any parts that are objected to

chancellor   the head of government, or prime minister, in some European countries

chariot   an open two-wheeled cart, pulled by horses

citizen   a person who has certain rights and duties because he or she lives in a particular city or town

city-state   an independent city and the surrounding land it controls

civil disobedience   the refusal to obey rules, orders, or laws

civil war   a war between people who live in the same country

civilization   the society and culture of a particular people, place, or period

class   a group of people according to social rank

clergy   people trained or ordained for religious work

collective   run by a group; for example, a *collective* farm

colonial   having settlements in far-off lands

colony   a group of people who settle in a far-off land but are still under the rule of the land they came from

commandment   a law or order, most often a religious law, as in the Ten *Commandments* in the Bible

commonwealth   a nation in which the people hold the ruling power; a republic or democracy

commune   a group of people working or living closely together, often sharing property and tasks

communism   a political system based on an absence of social class, on common ownership of industries and farms, and on a sharing of work and of goods produced

concentration camp   a prison camp for people thought to be dangerous to a ruling group

confederation   a group of independent states joined together for a purpose

conference   a meeting of people to discuss something

conquer   to get control by using force, as in a war

conqueror a person who gains control by winning a war

conquistador a Spanish conqueror

constitution the basic laws and rules of a government

contract a legal written agreement between two or more people

convert change from one religion to another

corrupt dishonest, evil, selfish

cosmonaut Russian word meaning astronaut

coup a bold, sudden move to bring about change in a government

craft a trade or art that takes special skill with the hands

crescent something shaped like a quarter moon

crucifixion the putting to death of someone by nailing or tying that person to a cross

culture the way of life—religion, ideas, arts, tools—of a certain people in a certain time

cuneiform a wedge-shaped form of writing used in ancient Sumer

curfew a time after which certain people cannot be on the streets

declaration a public statement

decline a period of increasing weakness

democracy a government that gives the people the ruling power

depressions period of low business activity and high unemployment

descendant a person who comes from certain ancestors

desert dry, sandy land with little or no plant life

detente an easing of tensions between countries

dialect a form of a language used only in a certain place or among a certain group

dictator a ruler who has total power

dike a wall built along a river or sea to hold back the water from low land

diplomat a person in government whose job is dealing with other countries

discrimination treating a person or people unfairly because of his or her race or religion

divine of or having to do with God or a god; like a god

divine right the idea that a monarch's right to rule comes directly from God

dominance the act of ruling, controlling, being most powerful

dominate to be most important, most powerful, strongest

domino a small, rectangular piece of wood or plastic used in a game; one side of the piece is either blank or marked with dots

dungeon a dark underground room used as a prison

dynasty a series of rulers who belong to the same family

elect to choose someone for an office by voting

emperor a person who rules a group of different countries, lands, or peoples

empire a group of lands all ruled by the same government or ruler

enlightened knowing the truth

estate a large piece of land with a large home on it

exiled forced to live away from home in a foreign land

factory a building where goods are made by machinery

fallow land not used for farming during a season

fascists dictators and their followers who take away rights of the people and glorify war

fast to go without food

fertile able to produce large crops, as in rich soil

feudalism the political and military system of much of Western Europe during the Middle Ages

fleet a group of warships under one command

forge to work into shape by heating and hammering

fortress a building with strong walls for defense against an enemy

forum a public square in an ancient Roman city; lawmakers met there

fraternity brotherhood

front a place where the actual fighting is going on during a war

frontier land just beyond the border of a country

galleon a large Spanish sailing ship of long ago, having many decks

general a high-ranking military officer

genocide an attempt to kill all the people of a certain race or religious group

geography the natural surface features of Earth, or any part of it

glacier large, slow-moving mass of ice and snow

governor a person chosen to run a province or territory

guerilla one of a group of fighters who are not part of a regular army, and who usually make surprise raids behind enemy lines

guild an organization formed to protect the interest of workers in one craft or trade

guillotine an instrument used for cutting off a person's head; it has two posts crossed by a heavy blade

hacienda a large Spanish-style ranch or country home

harness leather straps that fasten a horse to a plow, cart, or wagon

heretic a person who is against the teachings of a church

hermit one who lives alone, away from others

hieroglyphics a system of writing using pictures or symbols to represent objects, ideas, or sounds

historian someone who writes about the past; an expert in history

Holocaust the killing of Jews and other peoples by the Nazis

homage a pledge of loyalty; a promise to serve, made to kings and lords during the Middle Ages

hostages people held prisoner by an enemy until certain demands are met

hostile unfriendly, showing hate or dislike

hostility feelings of hate or acts of war

humane kind; showing care for other human beings

humanism a concern with the needs and interests of human beings rather than religious ideas

idol an image of a god that is used as an object of worship

imperialism the practice of conquering other lands, forming colonies in other lands, or controlling the government and wealth of weaker lands

import to bring into one country from another

impose to force one's ideas or wishes on another

impressed affected thoughts and feelings

independence freedom from control by others

indirectly in a roundabout way

industry business and manufacturing

inferior not as good as someone or something else

influence the power to affect other people or things

insurance a guarantee that a person or company will be paid money to cover losses

interest money paid for the use of other people's money

interference meddling in another's affairs without being asked

international having to do with many nations

investment money lent to businesses in order to get even more money back

investor a person who expects to make a profit by lending money to a business

irrigate to bring water to dry land by means of canals

isolate to set apart from others

isolationism a policy of staying out of the affairs of other countries

journeyman a worker who has finished his apprenticeship and receives wages, but who is not yet a master

junks flat-bottomed Chinese sailing ships

jury a group of people who listen to the facts and decide if a person on trial is guilty or not guilty

knight   a high-ranking soldier of the Middle Ages who received his title from a noble

labor union   a group of workers who join together to protect their wages, working conditions, and job benefits

legislature   a group of people who make the laws of a nation or state

liberator   one who frees a group of people

loincloth   a small cloth worn about the hips and lower part of the stomach

loom   a machine for weaving thread or yarn into cloth

loyal   faithful and true to one's country or to a person

maize   Indian corn

majority   a grater number, more than half

manor   the lands belonging to a medieval lord, including farmland, a village, and the home of the owner

medieval   belonging to the Middle Ages

merchant   a person who buys and sells goods for a profit; a trader

Middle Ages   the period of European history extending from the Fall of Rome in A.D. 476 to about A.D. 1450

migrate   to move away from one country or region to settle in another

militarism   a national policy of maintaining a powerful army and constant readiness for war

minority   a smaller number, less than half

missionary   a person sent by a church to other countries to spread a religion

moderate   not extreme

modern   of the present time, up-to-date

monarch   a ruler, like a king, queen, or emperor

mosaic   a design made by putting together small pieces of colored stone, glass, or other material

motto   a word or phrase that expresses goals, ideas, or ideals

mummy   a dead body kept from rotting by being treated with chemicals and wrapped in cloth

mural   a large picture painted on a wall

myth   a story often about gods or goddesses, that is handed down through the years and is sometimes used to explain natural events

nationalism   love of one's nation; patriotism

natural resource   material that is provided by nature, such as forests, minerals, and water

navigate   to plan the course of a ship; to sail or steer

neutral   joining neither side in a war

nomad   a person who moves from place to place looking for food for his or her animal herds

nonrenewable   not replaceable once it's used up

nonviolent   without using force; without causing injury

oath   a serious promise, often pledged in the name of God

pact   an agreement

papyrus   a writing paper the Egyptians made from water plants of the same name

paradise   a place or condition of perfect happiness; heaven

Parliament   England's body of lawmakers

patriot   a person who is loyal to his or her own country and shows a great love for that country

patron   a wealthy person who supports artists

pendulum   a weight hung so that it swings freely back and forth; often used to control a clock's movement

peninsula   a long piece of land almost completely surrounded by water (from the Latin word meaning "almost an island"

persecute   to treat in a cruel way, to hurt or injure

petition   a written request, often with many signatures, to a person or group in authority

pharaoh   a king of ancient Egypt

philosopher   a person who studies and tries to explain the meaning of life and death, the difference between right and wrong, and the purpose and principles of art and beauty

pilgrimage   a visit to a holy place

piracy   the robbing of ships on the ocean

plague   a deadly disease that spreads quickly

policy   a rule, a method of action or conduct

pollution   waste materials in the air or water

pope   the head of the Roman Catholic Church

population   people living in a place, or the total number of those people

prejudice   dislike of a people just because they are of a different race or religion, or are from another country

prime minister   the chief official of the government in some countries

prophet   a religious leader who claims to speak for God; one who tells what will happen in the future

protest   to speak out against or act against something

province   a part of a country, with its own local government, much like a state in the United States

Puritan   a member of a sixteenth- or seventeenth-century English group of Protestants; Puritans wanted to make the Church of England simpler and stricter

pyramid   a huge stone structure with a square base and four triangular sides that meet in a point at the top. Egyptian rulers were buried in the pyramids

racism   the idea that one race is better than another

ratify   to formally approve

raw material   matter in its natural condition, not changed by some human process

reaper   a machine for cutting down and gathering grain crops

recognize   to accept the government of a country and deal with it in business and trade

reform   to change for the better

refuge   shelter or protection from danger

refugee   a person who flees his or her country or home

reign   the rule of a monarch; or to rule as a king, queen, or emperor

reincarnation   a belief that living souls are reborn in a new body

Renaissance   the revival of art, literature, and learning in Europe in the fourteenth through sixteenth centuries

repeal   to cancel; put an end to

representation   sending one or more people to speak for the rights of others before a body of the government

representative   a person who is chosen to act or speak for others

republic   a government in which the citizens have the right to elect their representatives to make laws

resistance   the act of opposing, working against

reunification   the act of joining together again

revolt   to rise up against a government; to refuse to obey the people in charge

revolution   a complete change, especially in a way of life or a government

riot   a violent disturbance created by a crowd of people

saga   a long story of brave deeds

samurai   a class of warriors in the Japanese feudal system

sanction   an action taken by one nation against another for breaking international law; for example, a shipping blockade

satellite   a country that depends on and is controlled by a more powerful country; an object put into orbit around Earth

scapegoat   a person or group blamed for the mistakes and problems of others

scholar   a person who has learned much through study

scribe   a person whose job it was to write out copies of contracts and other manuscripts. People worked as *scribes* before the invention of printing.

sculptor   a person who makes statues out of wood, stone, marble, or other material

senate   a governing or lawmaking body

serf   a person legally tied to the land

settlement   a small group of homes in an area that has not been populated

shareholder   a person who owns one or more parts (shares) of a business

shogun   a great general governing Japan

shrine   a place of worship believed to be sacred or holy

shuttle   a device in weaving that carries thread back and forth between threads stretched up and down

siege   the surrounding of a city by soldiers who are trying to capture it so that food, water, and other supplies cannot get in or out

smuggle   to move something into or out of a country secretly because it is against the law

sniper   a person who shoots from a hidden spot

society   a group of people joined together for a common purpose

sought   looked for, searched for

specialize   to work in, and know a lot about, one job or field

staff   a pole used for support in walking or to hold a flag

stock   shares in a business

stronghold   a place dominated by a certain group which they have made safe and secure

submarine   a warship that travels under the water

superiority   a feeling of being better than others

surplus   more than what is needed

swamp   an area of low, wet land

symbol   an object that stands for an idea

sympathy   feeling sorry for another's suffering

tablet   a small, flat piece of clay used for writing

tax   money paid to support a government

technology   science put to use in practical work

temple   a building for the worship of a god or gods

territory   the land ruled by a nation or state

terrorist   a fighter who hopes to achieve certain goals by using force and random violence to frighten people

textile cloth or fabric made by weaving

theory an explanation of how and why something happens, usually based on scientific study

tomb a grave, usually one that is enclosed in stone or cement

torpedo to attack or destroy with a large, exploding, underwater missile

traitor one who betrays a cause, a friend, or a nation

transportation the act of carrying from one place to another

trapper a person who traps wild animals for their furs

treaty an agreement, usually having to do with peace or trade

trench a long ditch dug in the ground to protect soldiers in battle

tribe a group of people living together under a leader

tribute a payment or gift demanded by rulers of ancient kingdoms

truce a time when enemies agree to stop fighting

turmoil a condition of great confusion

tyrant a ruler who has complete power

uncivilized primitive; without training in arts, science, government

unification bringing together into one whole

upstream in the direction against the flow of the river; at the upper part of a river

Vandal a member of a Germanic tribe that invaded the Roman Empire

vassal a noble who received land from a king in return for loyalty and service

viceroy the governor of a country or province, who rules as the representative of the monarch

victor the winner of a battle, war, struggle, or contest

vision something seen in the mind or in a dream

ziggurat a huge, towerlike temple

Zionism the movement to set up a Jewish nation in Palestine

Index

Industrial Revolution, 281–291
  effects on lives of workers, 287–290
  in Great Britain, 282–290
  and imperialism, 354
  results of, 287–291
  in United States, 312–313
Inquisition, 196, 202
Intermediate Nuclear Force Treaty, 483
Intifada, 472
Inuit, 229
Inventions (*see also* Industrial Revolution)
  Assyrian, 65
  Egyptian, 47–48
  and Industrial Revolution, 282
  Olmec, 80
  Phoenician, 55–56
  of Renaissance, 188–189, 190–191
  Sumerian, 33, 34, 35
  wartime, 381
Iran, 20, 473, 474
Iraq, 20, 469, 474, 475
Ireland, 140, 255
Iron and iron working (*see* metal-working
  and metals)
Irrigation, 30, 42, 478–479
Isabella, Queen, 202, 237
Islam, 158–163 (*see also* Muslims)
Israel, 58–59, 467–469, 477
  conflict with Arabs, 467–472
Israelites, 56–58
Istanbul (Constantinople), 127, 167
Italy, 112, 370, 376, 378, 408
  ancient, 362
  in Middle Ages, 140
  nationalism in, 362–364
  secret societies in, 364, 365
  unification of, 361, 366
  in World War II, 408, 409, 411, 415, 419
Ivan the Terrible, 391

J
Jackson, Thomas "Stonewall," 311
Jahan, Shah, 226
James II, king of England, 256–257

Japan, 221–225, 407, 410, 518–519
  end of feudal system, 328
  first constitution, 328
  imperialism of, 329
  industrialization of, 450
  Meiji period, 328
  modernization of, 328–329
  trade with United States, 327–328
  war with China, 323–324, 329
  in World War II, 421–423
  after World War II, 450–451
Jefferson, Thomas, 258–259, 307
Jericho, 21
Jerusalem, 59, 158, 164, 166, 466, 468
Jesuits (Society of Jesus), 196–197
Jesus, 124, 125
Jews, 53, 58, 161, 166, 202 (*see also*
  Holocaust; Israel)
  and Israel, 467
  in Palestine, 466–467
Jiang Jieshi, 326
John I, king of England, 176–177, 252
Johnson, Lyndon B., 452
Jordan, 20, 467, 468, 469
Judah, 59
Julius II, Pope, 187
Jutes, 138

K
Kay, John, 283
Kennedy, John F., 437, 453
Kennedy, Robert F., 453
Kenya, 456
Khomeini, Ayatollah, 472–473
Khrushchev, Nikita, 436, 437
King, Martin Luther, Jr., 454
Knights, 150–151
Koran, 162, 163
Korea, 323, 449
Kosygin, Alexei, 437
Krupp, Friedrich, 371
Kublai Khan, 219, 220, 223
Kushites, 345–347
Kuwait, 474–475

Acknowledgments

Grateful acknowledgment is made to the following for illustrations, photographs, and reproductions on the pages indicated.

Cover: African Waist Pendant: © 2000, Waist pendant representing Idia, mother of Oba Esigie, part of ceremonial costume, Benin, 16th century/The Bridgeman Art Library; Astronaut: Tony Stone; Sphinx: Tony Stone; Astrolabe: The Granger Collection; Decorative Box from Russia: Dorling Kindersley; Fan: Dorling Kindersley; Aztec Calendar: National Museum of Anthropology, Mexico City/Michael Zabe/Art Resource NY.

Unit 1: p. 2: Erich Lessing/Art Resource; p. 4: Bettmann/Corbis; p. 7: North Wind Picture Archives; p. 14: Art Resource; p. 18: Nik Wheeler/Corbis; p. 19: George Simpson/Black Star/Picture Quest; p. 21: James Jacques Joseph, The Jewish Museum, NYC/Art Resource.

Unit 2: p. 28: The Art Archive; p. 32, The Granger Collection; p. 33: Gianni Tortolli/Photo Researchers, Inc.; p. 36: Tom Lovell/National Geographic Image Collection; p. 40: Roger Wood/Corbis; p. 46: Gianni Dagli Orti/The Art Archive; p. 49: Archivo Iconografico/Corbis; p. 52: Leonard de Selva/Corbis; p. 57: Topham/The Image Works; p. 60: Francoise de Mulder/Corbis; p. 64: The Art Archive; p. 68: Keren Su/Corbis; p. 72: Dagli Orti/Art Archive; p. 80: Charles & Josette Lenars/Corbis.

Unit 3: p. 86: Kevin Schafer/Corbis; p. 91: Michele Burgess/Index Stock Imagery/Picture Quest; p. 97: Jamie Squire/Allsport; p. 100: Archivo Iconografico/Corbis; p. 102: The Art Archive; p. 110: Andrew Brown, Ecoscene/Corbis; p. 114: Araldo de Luca/Corbis; p. 116: Alinari/Art Resource; p. 123: John Neubauer/PhotoEdit; p. 125: Scala/Art Resource; p. 127: The Art Archive.

Unit 4: p. 134: Hulton Getty/The Liaison Agency; p. 137: Erich Lessing/Art Resource; p. 140: Giraudon/Art Resource; p. 142: Ted Spiegel/Corbis; p. 146: Victoria & Albert Museum/The Bridgeman Art Library; p. 150: The Art Archive; p. 152: North Wind Picture Archive; p. 156: The Granger Collection; p. 159: Keren Su/Corbis; p. 163: Robert Harding/Corbis; p. 167: Giraudon/Art Resource; p. 171: Gianni Dagli Orti/Corbis; p. 177: Bettmann/Corbis.

Unit 5: p. 182: Bettmann/Corbis; p. 186: Scala/Art Resource; p. 193: Private Collection/The Bridgeman Art Library; p. 194: Gianni Dagli Orti/Corbis; p. 200: AP/Wide World Photos; p. 205: The Art Archive; p. 207: The Bridgeman Art Library; p. 208: ArchivoIconografico, SA/Corbis; p. 210: Scala/Art Resource.

Unit 6: p. 216: Alvaro de Leiva/The Liaison Agency; p. 220: Hulton Getty/The Liaison Agency; p. 222: Hulton Getty/The Liaison Agency; p. 224: Explorer Archives, photographed by Gisele Namur/Mary Evans Picture Library; p. 232: Roman Soumar/Corbis; p. 236: Burstein Collection/Corbis; p. 240: Michel Zabe/Art Resource.

Unit 7: p. 250: Archive Photos/The Liaison Agency; p. 255: Nancy Carter/North Wind Picture Archives; p. 256: The Granger Collection; p. 259: The Burstein Collection/Corbis; p. 262: Hulton Getty/The Liaison Agency; p. 264: Erich Lessing/Art Resource; p. 265: Peter Willi/The Bridgeman Art Library; p. 269: Gianni Dagli Orti/The Art Archive; p. 270: Réunion des Musées Nationaux/Art Resource; p. 272: Bettmann/Corbis.

Unit 8: p. 280: Private Collection/The Bridgeman Art Library; p. 284: The Granger Collection; p. 286: The Granger Collection; p. 288: Corbis; p. 290: The Stapleton Collection/The Bridgeman Art Library; p. 294: Galen Rowell/Corbis; p. 297: Réunion des Musées Nationaux/Art Resource; p. 303: Hubert Stadler/Corbis; p. 306: Kevin Schafer/Corbis; p. 310: Paul S. Howell/The Liaison Agency; p. 314: The Granger Collection; p. 318: Corbis; p. 320: The Granger Collection; p. 327: Bettmann/Corbis; p. 332: Jeremy Horner/Corbis; p. 336: David Cumming; Eye Ubiquitous/Corbis; p. 339: Hulton Deutsch Collection/Corbis; p. 344: Christine Osborne/Corbis; p. 349: The Granger Collection; p. 353: Hulton Getty/The Liaison Agency.

Unit 9: p. 360: Gianni Dagli Orti/The Art Archive; p. 365: The Art Archive; p. 369: Corbis; p. 370: Hulton Getty/The Liaison Agency; p. 371: Topham/The Image Works; p. 374: Hulton Getty/The Liaison Agency; p. 378: Leonard de Selva/Corbis; p. 380: Topham/The Image Works; p. 388: Archivo Iconografico, SA/Corbis; p. 390: The Granger Collection; p. 391: Bettmann/Corbis; p. 392 AKG London; p. 393: Steve Raymer/Corbis; p. 396: Corbis; p. 400: Scala/Art Resource; p. 401: AKG London; p. 406: Hulton Getty/The Liaison Agency; p. 408: Topham/The Image Works; p. 409: The Art Archive; p. 412: Archive/Picture Quest; p. 413: Fox Photos/Hulton Getty/The Liaison Agency; p. 417: Corbis; p. 417 (Jude Star): Bettmann/Corbis; p. 420: Archive Photos/Hulton Getty/The Liaison Agency; p. 422: Corbis; p. 424: Joseph Sohm, ChromoSohm/Corbis.

Unit 10: p. 430: Corbis/Bettman; p. 436: Express Newspapers/Archive Photos/The Liaison Agency; p. 438: Wally McNamee/Corbis; p. 442: Pete Turnley/Corbis; p. 445: Jeremy Horner/Corbis; p. 447: Michael Yamashita/Corbis; p. 453: Dennis Brack/Black Star/

Picture Quest; p. 454: Michael Mauney/Black Star; p. 455: Pete Turnley/Corbis; p. 458: Pete Turnley/Corbis; p. 464: Dennis Brack/Black Star/Picture Quest; p. 469: Peter Turnley/Corbis; p. 473: Alon Reininger/Contact Press Images/Picture Quest; p. 469: Peter Turnley/Corbis; p. 474: Claude Salhmi/The Liaison Agency; p. 476: John Moore/The Image Works; p. 478: Hanan Isachar/Corbis; p. 482: Peter Turnley/Corbis; p. 485: The Liaison Agency; p. 489: Peter Turnley/Corbis; p. 490: AP Photo/Lionel Cironneau/Wide World Photos; p. 496: AFP/Corbis; p. 501: The Liaison Agency; p. 503w: Nik Wheeler/Corbis; p. 510: B. Yarvin/The Image Works; p. 513: George Lepp/Corbis; p. 515: Digital Image ©1996, Corbis/Original image courtesy of NASA/Corbis; p. 517: Steve Chenn/Corbis; p. 522: AFP/Corbis.